The Rebel Prince

Wedding picture of Prince Louis Ferdinand and Princess Kira
at Cecilienhof (Potsdam) May 2, 1938.

THE
REBEL PRINCE

MEMOIRS OF

Prince Louis Ferdinand

OF PRUSSIA

INTRODUCTION BY LOUIS P. LOCHNER

Chicago • HENRY REGNERY COMPANY • 1952

Copyright 1952
HENRY REGNERY COMPANY
Chicago, Illinois

To my dear
KIRA
and our seven children
FRIEDRICH WILHELM, MICHAEL, MARIE CECILÌE, KIRA,
LOUIS FERDINAND, CHRISTIAN SIGISMUND, and XENIA
these memoirs are affectionately
dedicated.

Acknowledgments

IN WRITING my memoirs I was fortunate enough to have the helpful advice and friendly collaboration of a number of persons whose assistance is herewith acknowledged with heartfelt thanks.

Merle A. Potter, former American Military Governor of Bad Kissingen, where my family and I had sought refuge from the advancing Bolshevik troops, is the spiritual progenitor of this effort of mine. It was he who first urged me with persuasive enthusiasm to tell the story of my life.

Louis P. Lochner, my friend of several decades, heartily endorsed the plan and, though an ocean separated us, seemed to be sitting constantly at my side as I wrote, helping me over rough places and offering friendly suggestions in the flow of letters exchanged between us as this book took shape.

Erik Reger, one of Germany's most distinguished representatives of the Fourth Estate, generously let me draw upon his vast knowledge and journalistic experience to assure accuracy of historic and political detail.

Fred L. Black, a member of the Ford organization during the period of my service there, painstakingly checked and re-checked the chapters dealing with Henry Ford and his automobile empire.

Ben Donaldson, in charge of public relations for the Ford Motor Company, was tireless in his efforts to supply illustrations for this volume.

Last but by no means least, my beloved wife Kira has rendered me an inestimable service in that she has kept a diary without the aid of which many a detail narrated in this book would have escaped my memory. Self-effacingly, as is the custom of devoted spouses, she placed her diary notes at my disposal.

LOUIS FERDINAND
Prince of Prussia

Bremen-Borgfeld, Germany
Autumn, 1952

CONTENTS

LIST OF ILLUSTRATIONS

Introduction

T IME AND AGAIN since the memoirs of Prince Louis Ferdinand of Prussia were accepted for publication I have been asked by many who know about my long friendship with the Hohenzollern scion, "Who did the translation?"

They are quite surprised when I tell them that the prince, who knows at least six languages, wrote two books—one the American version of *The Rebel Prince* in English, the other a German version of it in his native tongue.

More accurately, the book of memoirs which is herewith offered was written in Midwestern American. True, he had learned English in his childhood from a London governess, but English was as much taboo in Germany during World War I as was German in our country. Accordingly, he had almost forgotten the language of Shakespeare when he ventured on his first journey to the United States in 1929 at the age of almost twenty-two. Instead, he had so completely mastered Spanish as his favorite language that he might just as easily have written the story of his life in that beautiful tongue.

His grasp of the American language resulted partly from intensive reading, partly, of course, from his association with scholarly men like Poultney Bigelow and the late President Roosevelt, but above all from his apprenticeship as a mechanic and subsequent salesman in the Ford organization.

I am reminded of an episode on the SS *Bremen,* when the wife of a famous artist with a penchant for tactless criticism reproached my friend with the words: "Prince Louis Ferdinand, there's one thing I don't like about you—you always talk that horrible Midwestern slang. Why don't you talk like your father, the crown prince?"

The prince's instant repartee was, "You see, madame, my father speaks with an Oxford accent; I prefer the Ford accent."

The Rebel Prince is, first of all, a completely honest book. Louis Ferdinand does not attempt to make himself any better than he is. He does not try to hide anything. He exposes his indiscretions, his mistakes, his errors of judgment, even his deplorable conflict with his older brother with the same passion for truth that causes him to reveal certain side lights concerning such controversial figures as Kaiser Wilhelm II or King Alfonso XIII—side lights calculated to make the reader wonder whether the hitherto accepted estimates of these two men may not be prejudiced.

These memoirs further indicate that the man who now heads the Hohenzollern dynasty rebelled from early childhood against snobbishness, rigid court etiquette, aloofness from the common people, narrowness of outlook, blatant militarism, exaggerated Prussianism, and every form of bigotry.

Among the most fascinating chapters are those which deal with his education under the ever watchful eye of an unrelenting tutor.

One of the most ingratiating traits of the author of *The Rebel Prince* is his humanness, his interest in and sympathy for people. Throughout the years of my service as chief of the Berlin bureau of The Associated Press my friend Louis Ferdinand never entered my inner editorial sanctum without first having shaken hands outside with every American and German employee. It was his way with everybody with whom he came in contact. If he visited our home, the maid and the *portier* were always greeted with an inquiry into their health and well-being. If we lunched together, he always evinced warm interest in the personal problems of the waiters. In short, Prince Louis Ferdinand loves people. Many episodes in this book bear testimony to this fact. As a corollary, he detested Nazism with its total disregard of human values.

The experiences of World War II, which were quite as terrible for the prince, his unusually intelligent and attractive wife, and his lovable children as they were for millions of other Europeans, have further deepened his concern for his fellow men and his understanding of their problems.

Friendship to him is a two-way street. He demonstrated this to our family during the anxious days immediately preceding Hitler's declaration of war on the United States in December 1941. An order had been issued that no member of the armed forces might have any social relations with Americans. Prince Louis Ferdinand defied the order. He kept on visiting us. Once Pearl Harbor had occurred and the breach with our country was imminent, we took it for granted that his visits had come to an end. Even then, however, our friend insisted upon paying us a final farewell call, though his tall figure made him unusually conspicuous and our apartment house, like all others, had its Nazi agent.

We shall never forget this act of true friendship and courage.

LOUIS P. LOCHNER

The Rebel Prince

Chapter One

The "Chinese" Baby

(1907–11)

THE TROUBLE started when my parents wanted to give a name to their second son, who looked like a Chinese baby at his birth on November 9, 1907, in the Marble Palace at Potsdam. The fact is I had a yellow skin—no doubt a mild case of jaundice—hence the "Chinese baby."

My parents had chosen the name of Michael, my older brother having as first-born received the traditional names of our family for the senior male child, Friedrich Wilhelm. It was especially my mother who wanted to call me after her Russian grandfather, Grand Duke Michael, whom she deeply respected and revered. Moreover, the Angel Michael is the patron saint of the German people and my mother always had a great fondness for him.

But my grandfather the Kaiser, as chief of the family, felt differently about this matter. To him, I believe, this name sounded too Russian for a Prussian Prince. He refused his consent. His wishes had to be complied with, and my distressed parents had to think of some other name for their Chinese baby.

Thus, at the very threshold of my life I lived up to the later dictum of my mother: "There was always something the matter with Lulu." I seem to have continued to prove the correctness of my mother's appraisal through many years that followed.

It was my father who suggested the name of Louis Ferdinand. Nobody could argue that it did not accord with the traditions of our house. My grandfather gave his consent, albeit rather reluctantly. Apparently he never really liked this name. For, when Kira and I wanted to give it to my first-born he flatly refused after a long and friendly argument. It had again to be Friedrich Wilhelm.

Now, why all this fuss about that name?

My parents showed considerable boldness in calling their second-born after an ancestor known as the Hero of Saalfeld. The older Louis Ferdinand was a highly controversial figure. Born November 18, 1772, the third son of Frederick the Great's youngest brother Ferdinand, my namesake was killed in the Battle of Saalfeld in 1806 while fighting against the troops of Napoleon, who regarded him as one of his strongest and most dangerous opponents.

Many people consider Louis Ferdinand the Hohenzollern of greatest genius after Frederick the Great. He is a romantic figure in the history of our house. Endowed by nature with the best physical and mental gifts, he not only was a good soldier but was also an accomplished pianist and a composer of note.

The great tragedy of his life was that he was not allowed to develop these gifts in a big way. King Friedrich Wilhelm III kept his brilliant young uncle at arm's length and assigned him to small garrisons, afraid of his popularity and of his friendship for his beautiful wife Queen Louise.

My ancestor tried to drown his disappointment and boredom by living a life which was not a model for conventionalists. He had several affairs with women, which were talked about all over Europe. Since his father was extremely stingy and he, himself, had a good heart for everybody, Louis Ferdinand became the prey of usurers and embezzlers and frequently ran into debt. At Saalfeld, it seems, he exposed himself to such a degree that his death could be called voluntary. Many books have been written, mostly by women, and numerous historical arguments have ensued about this Prussian Prince, both favorable and derogatory. My parents certainly belonged to his admirers, whereas my grandfather considered him a black sheep.

The name Louis Ferdinand somehow has implied a program of life for me. It has meant full approval and enjoyment of everything beautiful and good that life has to offer. It has also meant a disregard for conventions and uncompromising opposition to any kind of tyranny.

I am very grateful to my parents for giving me this name of which I am proud. Though I shall never dare to compare myself to my great ancestor, I may nevertheless say that this name has had a certain bearing on my own life. I, too, have been looked upon as the black sheep of the family, who did not fit into the general picture of Hohenzollern traditions and conventions. My life, too, took a course different from what it was expected to take.

Besides my name, there is my birthday which seems to have had at least a symbolic influence on my life.

November 9 was the *Dixhuit Brumaire,* on which day the French Directorate was abolished and Napoleon's domination began. It was also the day of the German revolution in 1918.

The Marble Palace in which I was born is a rather odd building. It was constructed by Friedrich Wilhelm IV in the middle of the nineteenth century on the shores of the *Heilige See* (Holy Lake), surrounded by a beautiful park designed in the English style and known as the New Garden. It consists of a two-story red brick main building surmounted by a cupola, which makes it resemble a Roman chapel. It has two low, one-story wings which stretch out into the garden rectangularly. These two wings on the inner side each had an open arcade built of white marble— hence the name of the palace.

I was born in one of the rooms of the left wing. Though my mother had her bedroom and sitting room on the second floor of the main building, she bore her first three babies in this room. Later on it became our playroom.

I understand that my birthplace at present is used as a restaurant by the Soviet occupation troops of Potsdam. The gardens in which I used to play as a little boy have been transformed into an amusement park.

The first four years of my life were spent mostly in this palace. Though we lived for the greater part of the winter season in our Berlin abode, the so-called Crown Prince's Palace Unter den Linden, and although my parents also took us to other places in Germany, there is nothing I remember of these years outside of Potsdam.

Our Marble Palace was anything but comfortable from a modern point of view, yet we felt perfectly at home. We could play in the park— the grounds in the neighborhood of the palace were closed to the public

—to our hearts' desire. In this part of the park we could move quite freely and even evade the watchful eyes of our nurses.

Two sentries were placed in front of our home. They were changed
every two hours. Others were placed at the entrance gates to the park.
They usually stood in a little sentry box which protected them from bad
weather. In recent years I met several people who mounted guard at the
Marble Palace in those early days. One of them told me that I made quite
a nuisance of myself by walking back and forth in front of the sentry box.
For, each time I turned up, the sentry, according to the rules, had to
emerge and stand at attention. Finally, when the poor man was almost
at his wits' end and was burning with fury, my father appeared on the
scene. I was given a good spanking and had to apologize to my victim,
who got twenty marks into the bargain and a day off. My father used
this incident to impress his second son with the fact that these sentries
were doing their duty and had not been stationed there to be made fun of.

From the beginning of our childhood days we were taught by both our
parents to consider all who were in a serving capacity not as our inferiors
but as our friends who deserved our full respect. My father adopted this
principle in military life. He was thoroughly opposed to any kind of drill
which might turn into annoying and pestering the subordinates. This
democratic attitude endeared him to all soldiers he came in contact with.
It proceeded from the very depth of his respect for the human being as
such.

We used to play another trick on the sentries. Knowing that they were
strictly forbidden to speak to anybody when on duty, we would walk up
to them, asking them questions to tempt their sense of duty. Usually, to
our great disappointment, we succeeded only in producing something
resembling a smile on the sentries' faces.

During the first four years of my life I was entrusted to the care of
women, just as my older and younger brothers also were. The first
woman to handle me was my mother's midwife. She was an energetic
person, born in Berlin and endowed with a great sense of humor. She
was called whenever a new little member was about to enlarge our
family.

Another personality who regularly put in an appearance at such occasions was Professor Walter Bumm, head of the women's clinic of the

University of Berlin and at that time Germany's most renowned gyne-
cologist.

During my first year I got my food supply from a *Spreewälderin* (liter-
ally, woman from the Spreewald, a region south of Berlin where people
still speak a Slav dialect). These women were famous for their healthy
constitutions and were hired as wet nurses by the wealthier classes.

There was only one thing the matter with the buxom Spreewälderin
assigned to me as my "filling station"—she was an unwed mother! When
my highly moral grandmother the Kaiserin learned of this she insisted
upon the immediate substitution of another Spreewald wet nurse armed
with proper nuptial certificates.

After I had graduated into a more substantial class of nourishment the
Spreewald woman was released and a Swiss nurse, Fräulein von Ernst,
was hired. She was an educated and undoubtedly competent governess
for children who had outgrown their diapers. But I was still a diaper
addict. Also, I seem to have indulged in veritable marathons of crying
which even Fräulein von Ernst's attempts to hypnotize me could not stop.
In despair she asked to be relieved from her heavy duties. Selma Zoske, a
German girl from Berlin, was hired. We used to call her "Selmi-Selmi"
and took a great liking to her.

Besides Selmi-Selmi there were two *Prinzen-Lakaien,* or men servants,
Paul Schmidt and Johann Rüge, picked from the First Regiment of
the Guards. They were tall, splendid-looking men of Pomeranian peasant stock, as loyal and trustworthy as anybody in the whole of Germany.

It was their duty to serve us at table. The food had to be carried almost
half a mile from the main kitchen through a subterranean corridor. In
the days when the Marble Palace was built it was the custom to have the
kitchens in a separate building in order to avoid any kind of kitchen
odors. At the *Neue Palais,* or New Palace, where my grandparents the
Kaiser and Kaiserin used to live at Potsdam, the kitchen was even at a
greater distance than ours.

These men servants always accompanied us when we drove out in our
horse-drawn carriage. They then sat next to the coachman. Had the
monarchy continued, these men, once we had outgrown their services,
would have been given some job in the civil administration like most of

their colleagues who had served in the army more than twelve years.

When my parents had to slash their household budget after the revolution in 1918, our male help was taken over by the Prussian State. In their spare time they were often engaged by the foreign embassies in Berlin to serve formal dinners. I loved to observe the shocked faces of some of my hosts or table companions when during some official diplomatic dinner I suddenly discovered some old servant of ours whom I promptly engaged in a conversation, thus somewhat spoiling the atmosphere of staid etiquette and formality.

One of my earliest recollections is a Christmas Eve spent at my grandfather's palace at Potsdam. Both my parents had gone on a trip of several months to India. My older brother Wilhelm, my younger brother Hubertus, and I—Friedrich and my two sisters not having been born as yet —were left in the care of our grandparents. So we moved over with our whole nursery to the New Palace, which lies in beautiful Sans Souci Park about three miles from the Marble Palace. Wilhelm was four at this time, Hubertus one, and I three.

The New Palace was a much larger building, built by Frederick the Great after the Seven Years' War to show the world that he was not "broke" after that long war. It slightly resembles Versailles, though I like it even better than the famous French palace. In its center is a huge cupola, on the top of which three nude women hold up the Prussian crown. It is generally believed that by this allegory my ancestor, who was famous for his sarcastic wit, wished to make fun of his three great female opponents who had not been able to crush him: Empress Maria Theresa of Austria, Empress Catherine of Russia, and Madame Pompadour of France.

We children occupied rooms on the third floor, which had also been used by my father and his brothers during their childhood. These rooms were really in the attic, but they were very large and comfortably furnished. Each one had only one window opening out on the garden. These windows were round and therefore referred to as Bull's Eyes.

My grandparents' rooms were on the second floor. The ground floor was taken up by several enormous halls, one of which, the *Muschelsaal* (Shell Hall), had walls covered with shells and precious stones.

All of my uncles with their wives joined their parents and Wilhelm and me on that Christmas Eve. We all assembled in my grandmother's sitting room. At six o'clock sharp a court chamberlain announced that everything was ready. We formed a long procession and marched down the main staircase through several flights of rooms until we reached the Shell Hall. A huge Christmas tree was standing in the center. Along the walls smaller Christmas trees were placed next to a number of tables, one tree for each of us. The reflection of the hundreds of candles against the multicolored shells on the walls made a deep impression on my childish mind.

My grandfather first showed my grandmother to her table, then he accompanied his sons and daughters-in-law to their tables. Finally our turn came, which we awaited with great impatience.

Our tables were covered with beautiful toys. I was particularly attracted by a miniature railway with all sorts of gadgets spread out on the floor. My grandfather, who had gone back to look at his own presents, noticed that my brother and I were trying hard but ineffectively to get the trains started. After all, we were only three and four years old! So grandfather got down on his knees and helped us get everything going. Most of the evening he sat on the floor playing with his two grandchildren until finally dinnertime came and both of us had to be brought to our quarters.

This was the only Christmas, as far as I can remember, which we spent with my grandparents in Germany. Many years later we celebrated another Christmas with them. But this was during their exile at Amerongen, Holland, in 1920.

With the exception of this Christmas party I unfortunately remember virtually nothing of those months in the New Palace, except that my grandparents definitely made us feel at home. In later years we visited them there regularly but never again lived with them for a longer period.

Many times when my grandfather was absent or busy with affairs of state we went to have tea with our grandmother. We loved these invitations, not only because of the delicious cakes served, but principally because we sincerely adored our *Grossmama*. Though we saw much less of our grandfather than we did of our grandmother, we also had a warm affection for him and were by no means ill at ease in his presence as his own children were to a certain extent.

Chapter Two

Happy Boyhood in Danzig

(1911–13)

WHEN my father returned from his trip to India in 1911 he was given command of the Death's Head Hussars Regiment at Danzig.

I believe that these years in Danzig have had a decisive influence in the molding of my character. It is often said that a person's soul is really formed during the period from three to six years of age. I am unable to judge if that theory is correct, but as I observe my own seven children I believe it likely to be true in many ways.

There is hardly any city (it was totally destroyed by the Soviets in March 1945) in the whole of Germany which I liked better than Danzig both for its architecture and for its location. It stretched out for several miles along the Bay of Danzig, a part of the Baltic Sea, and was surrounded by sloping hills covered with beautiful woods. The city fitted completely into this frame which the Supreme Architect Himself had created for her. It was the abiding presence of nature—the combination of the blue sea and the green woods—which gave Danzig its unique character.

Danzig in those years was an important international seaport. The near-by bathing resort of Zoppot was equally popular with Germans and foreigners. The latter came chiefly from Poland, then a part of Imperial Russia. This distinctive atmosphere—the *genius loci*—has left a lasting impression on my mind and soul. My mother, who like my grandfather had a great love for everything connected with the sea, succeeded in inculcating this same penchant in her children. I believe that my urge to visit places and see things in distant lands, which finally took me to the Americas and later around the world, dates back to those years.

Though my parents could have had a much larger place at their disposal in a pleasant location, as I was told by some Danzig friends many
years later, they decided for reasons of economy to move into a small
town house in the main street of Langfuhr, a suburb of Danzig. It had
an ugly façade of yellow bricks, was two stories high, and contained
about twelve rooms. Our children's rooms, as well as my parents' bedroom and dressing room were located on the second floor. Wilhelm and
I had a bedroom with a balcony for ourselves. It connected with a room
for our governess. Then came the *Kinderstube,* where we used to have
our meals and where we did our playing.

Old timers from Danzig like to relate today how at times, just as dawn
came, a certain young Hohenzollern was wont to appear on the balcony
of his and his brother Wilhelm's room to communicate with the outside
world in a costume otherwise worn only in the Garden of Eden.

A staircase led down into a hall which served as my mother's sitting
room. One of our main sports consisted in sliding down these stairs,
using a wooden tablet as a toboggan. Many a time when my mother had
guests for tea we demonstrated our vehicle and invited the guests to participate in our fun. My parents enjoyed the embarrassed looks of their
older guests, such as dignified old generals or the mayor of the town with
their wives, when they came to make an official call. My parents, far
from minding the interruptions, seemed to welcome them as a means of
putting their parties on a more informal basis. On occasion they even
patronized our toboggan themselves. Their suffering guests then could
not but follow the example of their hosts and throw dignity and poise
overboard.

My mother and father each had a writing room on this first floor. Next
to the main entrance was our schoolroom and a small workshop in which
my father in his spare time did wood carving. This was the trade my
father had taken up to carry out a wish of his father, who requested each
of his sons to learn some handicraft in accordance with the two-hundred-
year-old Hohenzollern tradition.

Since neither of my parents believed in the rigid formality of court
life, our household resembled that of any well-to-do German citizen. Our
style of life was much more democratic than that of many a less prominent family in Germany. The atmosphere was *gemütlich.* There was

none of that cold splendor of palaces for which I never could develop any liking.

My father devoted most of his time to his regiment. It was composed almost exclusively of men who served voluntarily and were for the most part farmers' sons from East and West Prussia.

My father liked to play practical jokes on us, which we thoroughly enjoyed. Once, when we came into the dining room by way of the terrace, my parents were having lunch. I went to say good morning to my father, for I had not yet seen him that day. After he had kissed me, he took a handful of mashed potatoes and smeared them all over my head and face. I did not mind this at all. But our governess decidedly did.

Another practical joke was frequently played in the evenings. My brother and I were always put to bed by our English governess after a sound scrubbing. Time and again my father would put in an unexpected appearance when everything was set for a quiet night. He would grasp the nearest jug of water and pour the contents into our beds. The ill-disguised disapproval on the face of our governess and a silver coin of three marks which followed the deluge each time aroused our youthful applause and expectancy.

The name of our governess was Miss Brimble. My parents, who both spoke English fluently, wanted us to acquire that most useful language in childhood.

I clearly remember the day when we were confronted with our new governess for the first time. My brother and I had been deeply attached to our German nurse Fräulein Bergner, who had taken the place of Selmi-Selmi. When we were told that Fräulein Bergner was going to leave us and that a complete stranger was to replace her, I was deeply distressed and very resentful. I greeted the new arrival from Albion with the words: "I do not want you to stay here with us, and if you do, I shall call in a forester and have you shot on the spot."

Miss Brimble has described this welcoming speech of mine in a book entitled *In the Aerie of the Hohenzollern Eagle,* which she wrote after she had left us shortly before the outbreak of World War I.

It did not take her very long to break down our resistance and to win our sincere affection in spite of the fact that she had rather strange methods of punishing us if we did not obey her. One was to make us eat soap, another, to have us sit up late at night. I believe she did all she could to develop an international spirit in her pupils. We both learned to speak English as naturally as we spoke our native language. We frequently conversed in English with our parents.

The war abruptly ended our progress with the English language. Public opinion would not tolerate the use of the language of the arch-enemy by the children of the ruling family. The natural consequence was that we forgot all we had learned as children. We had to begin all over again at high school, but this time with German teachers and with much greater difficulty.

During the war and the years after, I lost track of Miss Brimble. It was not until the summer of 1933, when I visited England, that I discovered her with the help of the British press.

In London I made the acquaintance of Bruce Lockhart, author of *British Agent, Retreat from Glory,* and other books. He was then work-ing for Lord Beaverbrook, writing the "Londoner's Diary" for the *Evening Standard*. I told Bruce about my old governess and asked him whether he could help me find out where she lived.

"Nothing simpler than that," he replied. He used his daily column to ask his readers to help a young Hohenzollern find his British governess. Bruce got heaps of answers and suggestions. After three days the where-abouts of Miss Brimble had been traced.

The *Evening Standard* invited her to London. She was living in some small country town. We met at Lockhart's office. Our *Wiedersehen* was very touching. Pictures were taken. Later the two of us had lunch at Coaglino's, a smart Italian restaurant. The happy days of Danzig and Potsdam passed in review. Miss Brimble asserted that her one-time pupil had not changed a bit but was just as naughty as in her time. We drove to the station together. The parting of ways came only too soon. There was a hearty kiss and tears on both sides.

According to my mother, I am the most Russian of her children. Half Russian herself, she was very happy about this and tried to strengthen my Russian tendencies, even though this was not in keeping with Prus-sian traditions. Here, perhaps, are the roots of my internationalism which became more and more pronounced as I grew older. Miss Brimble mentions in her book that on one occasion, when asked by my grand-mother the Empress if I liked being a German, I had given the shocking answer that I'd rather be a Russian! My mother also claims that as a very small child I pronounced the German words with a Russian accent although I had never actually heard any Russian spoken in those days.

This foreign influence was also emphasized by my Russian grand-mother, the Grand Duchess Anastasia of Mecklenburg. Unfortunately, because of the First World War I saw much too little of her. We used to visit her at her lovely hunting lodge, *Gelbensande,* on the Baltic Sea, where my parents had become engaged. I adored my "Granny," and ap-parently my feelings were reciprocated. Mama says that I was the favorite grandchild of the Grand Duchess. Although I always pestered her with all sorts of small wishes, she invariably fulfilled them and never lost pa-tience with me.

Doubtlessly Miss Brimble also had a lot to do with shaping my inter-national outlook. She may even have gone too far with her influence.

Our elementary education in Danzig was in the hands of a teacher named Wilms. He was a tall, fine-looking man with a big black beard and a warm, kind heart. He had considerable trouble teaching me how to read and write. I am sorry to say that I have never succeeded in writ-ing properly. My handwriting was so bad that during one of the last years at high school I had to take lessons in penmanship because my des-perate teachers were unable to decipher what I had written. After leaving high school I resorted to a typewriter. I am helpless without that useful instrument. Nobody, myself included, is able to read my scrawl. When I had to leave my typewriter behind during my flight from Cadinen early in 1945 to avoid being caught by the Soviets, I felt like an illiterate.

I may note in passing that my children do not seem to have inherited their father's inability to write properly. Apparently they are taking after their mother who writes a beautiful hand and is very clever at doing all sorts of things with her hands, including painting and sculpturing.

Both my parents were great lovers of outdoor life and sports. They in-sisted that their children spend as much time in the open air as weather permitted. Danzig-Langfuhr was ideal for open-air life.

During our first year there we drove into the environs of Langfuhr twice a day in our *Landauer* (open carriage). Miss Brimble usually oc-

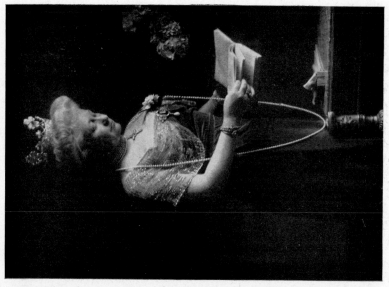

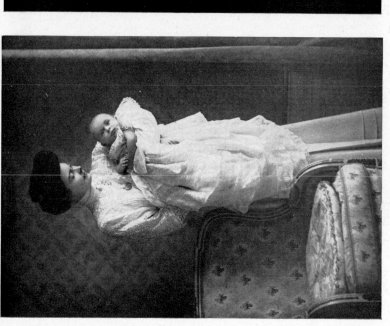

Left: The infant Prince with his mother, the Crown Princess Cecilie. *Right*: The Prince's grandmother, Kaiserin Auguste Victoria.

Above: The Crown Prince, with his sons, Prince Louis Ferdinand and Prince Wilhelm. *Below:* The Kaiser with his grandsons, Louis Ferdinand at the left.

cupied the rear seat with Wilhelm who, as the oldest, sat on her right,
according to the requirements of court etiquette. I was put on the middle
seat with my brother Hubertus because I frequently got into an argument followed by a fight if I sat with Wilhelm. Miss Brimble thought it
undesirable to have the public as eyewitness to the family squabbles of
the young generation of Hohenzollerns.

The carriage was driven by Coachman Schulz, "Schulsik" to us children. Next to him sat one of our footmen. Whenever I could, I climbed
onto the coachman's seat and installed myself on Schulsik's lap. He willingly let me take the reins.

Depending upon the weather, we drove either to the beach or into the
woods. The little fishing village of Broesen, forty-five minutes away by
Landauer, was the nearest point at the shore from our house. To get to
Broesen we had to cross the *Exerzierplatz* (parade grounds), a rather
deserted space with only a poor farmhouse on it. It had become a tradition with us to stop at this lonely shack and talk to the poverty-stricken
tenants. Wilhelm and I always raced each other to be the first to dis-
tribute a little money we had been saving for the occasion.

We preferred the beach at Broesen because, with the exception of a
few fishermen who were mending their nets, there were no other people
around to stare at us. The fishermen took the small intruders for granted.
If Miss Brimble felt in a good mood we were allowed to buy some fresh
fish, which we were very proud to bring home and to show to our parents. We spent many hours daily on the beach or paddling around in the
water.

On rainy days, or when the air was too cool for us to run around in
our birthday suits at the beach, we drove into the woods. Or, we passed
through the little town of Oliva, another suburb of Danzig, famous for
its old convent and beautiful gardens, en route to the wooded hills
thirty minutes away.

To get some physical exercise we usually had to get out of the carriage
and walk part of the way. The carriage was supposed to follow us slowly
or just wait until we got back. I loathed walking then, and I still do. I
always tried to find some excuse to sneak back to the carriage and sit
with my friend Schulsik who let me drive the horses. My good governess
soon realized her pupil's reluctance to use his legs and shut her eyes to

my dodging those hikes. All my life I have tried to learn to manipulate the latest mechanical means of locomotion, including the piloting of an airplane. After the collapse of Hitler's "Thousand Year Empire" in 1945 I was forced for many months to use my legs with not even a bicycle upon which to fall back. Kira claimed this was good for me. But still I didn't like it!

My father was an excellent horseman, and horseback riding was one of his favorite sports. It was but natural that he should want to see his boys on mounts almost from the cradle.

As riding teacher we were given one of my father's equerries, a former sergeant of the Garde du Corps Regiment. His name was Arndt. We kept him right up to the day of the 1918 revolution.

Our first horses were two Shetland ponies—Wilhelm's a stallion called Puck, mine a mare named Molly. I kept Molly throughout the years we lived in Danzig. My brother, who was considerably taller than I, outgrew his pony and was given a polo pony called Zobel.

As soon as we were able to stick to the backs of our horses we rode out instead of using the carriage. At first I was more on the ground than on Molly's back. Often I had to maneuver her alongside some elevation in the ground or a fallen tree to enable me to get back in the saddle.

Father's ambition was to make us look like real horsemen; so he had his English tailor and bootmaker come over from London to make us some riding breeches and riding boots. We both felt very proud and important wearing these foreign creations.

My father, who in many respects had adopted the English style of life, also liked English clothes. He was criticized by some of his narrow-minded countrymen for indulging in habits which contrasted sharply with the stiff Continental way. He had also adopted the English manner of horseback riding; that is, he let the reins fall very loose and stretched out his legs. This was a sacrilege in the eyes of our riding teacher who strictly followed the Continental riding school. Only my father could dare commit that breach of German cavalry regulations.

Many a time we would meet him at the city limits of Langfuhr as he returned with his regiment from the day's exercises just before lunch. He would invariably hoist Wilhelm or me up on his horse, while the other brother was taken over by his A.D.C. It was always a great moment for us to ride into town with our father, the band playing some fetching cavalry march. As boys do, we copied our father's style which differed from everybody else's and was much more comfortable besides. My riding instructor Arndt would protest, saying: "Now, Prince Lulu, for Heaven's sake please don't stick out your legs a couple of miles and remember to pull back your reins."

I would retort: "That's the way Papa does it, so why shouldn't I do it also?"

If poor Arndt had known any Latin he would probably have answered: *"Quod licet Jovi non licet bovi."* Instead, he merely got red in the face and looked in another direction.

World War I put an abrupt stop to my equestrian career. Although I adored this sport, I was not able to resume it until twenty-two years later when my young family and I moved to Cadinen. There we had a small but very fine horse-breeding station. East Prussia has always been the cradle of Germany's best warm-blooded horses. In addition, we bought two Shetland stallions and a mare for our children. I began to apply the same methods of physical education to my children that I had received from my parents. Germany's collapse and the necessity of our fleeing from the Soviets ended all this early in 1945. But Kira and I have resumed physical exercises with our children since taking up our abode near Bremen, though for the present still without horses!

But back to the days in Danzig:

My general attitude and development into a sort of "rebel" of the family may to a great extent have had its roots in my relationship to my older brother Wilhelm. Some scientists say that there is such a thing as a mentality or complex of a second-born. This phenomenon did not become evident in the case of my granduncle, Prince Heinrich of Prussia, in his relation to my grandfather the Kaiser, nor in the case of my uncle, Prince Eitel Friedrich, in his relation to my father. In these two cases the ranking position of the older brother was accepted as a fact by the younger, mainly because the mental superiority of the first-born was evident. In the case of Frederick the Great and his younger brother Heinrich this could not be said. A great rivalry existed between the two, which led to a profound mutual dislike. Some experts believe that, as a military leader and strategist, Heinrich was superior to his older brother to whom all the glory went. I am unable to judge the merits of this argument.

From early childhood it was impressed upon me that my older brother was to play first fiddle. I do not hesitate to say that I felt jealous of his position. It was logical for my parents to groom their first-born from the very beginning for the tremendous responsibility which he would one day have to assume. My mother tells me that my father, also, was brought up by his parents in a manner that never let him forget that he was destined to become emperor. They even encouraged him to assert a certain authority over his younger brothers and only sister. This situation apparently was accepted without question by the younger children. In my case it was not. Although my brother had a rather mild temperament and did not take advantage of his position, the antipathy was there and even increased the older we both grew.

I deeply regret that this was so. In retrospect I believe that we could have become a fine team, each using his particular inclinations and gifts for the good of our country! I cannot completely absolve those responsible for our education for the unhappy situation that developed. They not only failed even to attempt to bridge that rift but sought to deepen it by encouraging our antagonism. I remember quite clearly rows with my brother which invariably ended in fist fights and bleeding noses. The grownups who witnessed these conflicts made no attempts to pacify us. On the contrary, they frequently incited us to even harder combat, evidently having the time of their lives watching the two little cocks fight it out. To them it appeared to be a harmless thing. Actually it severed the ties between two small souls. I rather suspect that our differences were in later years encouraged by certain factions at court which tried to play us off one against the other.

Our two characters were completely different. According to my mother, my older brother was very docile and orderly. I had a profound dislike for any kind of authority and discipline. My brother had an inborn passion for everything connected with soldiery; in fact, he was a born soldier. This is not at all surprising. The Hohenzollerns have been a family of soldiers for many centuries, though not soldiers only, a fact that is often overlooked. Thus the military tradition of my family came to my brother naturally. He had inherited it. I had not.

It was also quite natural for my parents to be glad to see Wilhelm follow the traditional pattern. It would have been extremely embarrassing and annoying if the heir apparent to the throne of Prussia and Germany had not shown any liking for, nor ability in, the profession of arms. In my case things were different. It really did not matter much whether I fitted into the picture or not, although second sons also have been called upon to rule in my family. Witness the case of Emperor Wilhelm I.

My rebel attitude, then, can to a great extent be traced to my opposition to my elder brother. I disliked things military because he liked them. But the second-born complex does not explain everything. From what my mother tells me, a strong individualistic streak was discernible in my character from early youth. I was critical and suspicious and did not easily accept things or teachings just because they had been handed down as traditions or historical dogmas. In court circles it was bruited about that the oldest son of the German Crown Prince lived up to the requirements of his position almost to the letter, whereas unfortunately his second son seemed to exhibit rather dangerous tendencies which, if not closely watched and curbed, might easily turn him into a liberal or even something worse! I cannot but smile when I picture to myself the conservative advisers of the dynasty shaking their heads in grave concern about that unruly bud on the family tree. They continued to worry about me even after the Hohenzollerns were no longer on the throne.

That I disliked military science and lacked ability for it was of course soon discovered by my older brother. During World War I, he organized a small army consisting of his brothers and a few other friends. Our drill grounds were in Bellevue Park in Berlin. Wilhelm was the commander in chief. His aide was Nico von Stumm, whose mother was a lady in waiting to my mother. Besides Nico there were his two sisters and the children of Prince Hohenlohe, the Austrian Ambassador to Germany, two girls and one boy. All these children were our age.

As time went on everybody received a promotion with the exception of myself. My brother judged me to be unfit for anything higher than a simple private. For a while I was more or less reconciled to my fate. But one day the only "G.I." of the "Imperial Army" seceded and started his own army which was run more on the lines of a Chicago rum gang than of a Prussian Army.

This secession had very disagreeable consequences for my brother's organization. I was joined by the feminine members of his company with the exception of Cissy Stumm, who remained loyal to Wilhelm. Fritzi Hohenlohe also joined my ranks.

We retired to a wooded hill where a deep hole was dug. This served as a dungeon for friend and enemy alike. My brother's forces occupied a miniature fortress built many years ago for my father and his brothers. Our main task was to spy on the "enemy" who had worked out an elaborate system of passes that had to be shown on entering a certain radius around the "fortress."

To Kira's and my great satisfaction there is not a vestige of antagonism between my two oldest boys, Friedrich and Michael, now thirteen and twelve years old, respectively. They squabble, heckle, and frequently fight, but they are inseparable. Though Friedrich is much taller and stronger than his younger brother Michael, nicknamed Mikie, he never tries to impose his authority as a first-born on his brother or his sisters. Neither Kira nor I would stand for such a thing.

With the exception of one brief period, Wilhelm and I were educated together up to the day we graduated from high school in 1925. The only period of separation lasted hardly a year. It was customary in our family for every male member to be taken out of the nursery at the age of seven and entrusted to a tutor, or *Gouverneur*. The Gouverneur was in charge of the general welfare and education of his pupil and was assisted by professional teachers in his task of developing mind and body as perfectly and universally as possible. My parents had decided to keep us at home under the guidance of a Gouverneur until we were twelve years old and then send us to the Cadets' School at Plön in the province of Holstein. Wilhelm reached the age of seven in July 1914. Lieutenant von Kühne was assigned to him as his first Gouverneur. He was a nice chap who had served in my father's regiment at Langfuhr. Wilhelm left the nursery and became a "man." It hurt my pride considerably to be left behind in the hands of women—hence still a "baby."

One thing I remember vividly about Herr von Kühne is the first and only spanking I received from anyone outside the family. It required boldness on his part to administer it, for my parents had given strict orders that none of their children must be chastised by members of the household. Kühne certainly had good reason for disregarding the order.

My brother, under the guidance of his tutor, had decorated a small private wharf of ours at Zoppot Beach with flags, flowers, and garlands. What the special occasion was I can't remember. In an unguarded moment I tore down all the flags and decorations. In the midst of my act of vandalism I suddenly felt someone firmly gripping me by the collar, turning me over with my backside up, and vigorously paddling me. My astonishment and shame were much greater than the pain. Nobody had ever dared to touch me, not even Miss Brimble whose authority with me was supreme. And now this blasted Gouverneur had the cheek to give me an ordinary spanking though I was not under his jurisdiction! Had there been a Security Council of the United Nations in existence at the time I should have brought the case before it.

After a lot of yelling and howling on my part Herr von Kühne was able to convince me of the uselessness of my behavior. To my utter astonishment he even invited me to help him and my brother to adorn the landing bridge. The spanking was immediately forgotten. Kühne had won my heart. He had rightly diagnosed my nihilistic activities as stemming from my hurt pride and jealousy, because as a "baby" I had been left out of the enterprise. After that we got along splendidly.

Chapter Three

In a Gilded Cage

(1913–14)

M Y FATHER's assignment at Langfuhr came to an end in 1913 and with it our happy household in the ugly yellow brick villa. My father was recalled to Berlin where he worked in several ministries to become better acquainted with the affairs of state. We took up residence again in the Crown Prince's Palace in Berlin and in the Marble Palace in Potsdam.

Fortunately we did not have to take permanent leave of the lovely region on the Baltic Sea. The city of Zoppot had put a villa at the disposal of my parents, to be used as a summer home. It was considerably smaller than our house in Langfuhr, but there was enough room in it for all of us even though we had to crowd together more. It was a relatively new house, with big windows which let in a lot of sun and fresh air. My parents named it House by the Sea. It stood about two hundred feet above sea level on the edge of hills which sloped abruptly down to the beach and afforded a view of the whole of the Bay of Danzig, the Peninsula of Hela, and a considerable stretch of the Baltic. Back of the house was a patch of farm land which led up to beautiful woods covering thousands of acres. My parents gratefully accepted the offer of the amiable town council of Zoppot. The House by the Sea enabled us to spend every summer throughout World War I at Zoppot. All of us preferred its atmosphere to that of Berlin.

For my parents Zoppot meant independence and lack of ceremony. For us children it meant outdoor life spent mostly on horseback, at the beach, or in and on the water. In short, here was freedom.

Berlin on the other hand was the golden cage. In the capital we could not help but notice that we were in a different position from the rest of the people. If we wanted to play in the Princesses' Garden situated behind the Princesses' Palace only twenty yards from our home, we had to use an archway connecting the two buildings. We were not supposed to cross the street.

I still remember the day when I secretly crossed the street all by myself but did not tell anybody, as I hoped to repeat what to me was a real adventure. When we wanted to get to Bellevue Park, about two and a half miles distant from our palace, we always drove there in an open carriage, weather permitting. As we left the palace the sentinels at the front entrance would present arms. The guards would be called out automatically at the New Guard House directly opposite the Crown Prince's Palace, as would the guards at the Brandenburg Gate and at Bellevue Palace. Many people along Unter den Linden or in the Tiergarten would stop and take off their hats, wave, or even shout a greeting. We were trained to take off our hats, wave back, and smile. I cannot claim that I felt bashful or embarrassed by all this public attention, but after a while both Wilhelm and I felt a great urge to mingle with the crowd and walk along the streets just like other people. This wish of ours was gratified only after the war had started.

But before I discuss this period, I must mention the wedding, in 1913, of my grandfather's only daughter Victoria Luise, known to us as our Aunt Cissy. Hers was a love match with Prince Ernst August of Cumberland. At the same time, however, it had certain political overtones. Ernst August was the grandson of the King of Hannover, whose realm had been incorporated into Prussia after the War of 1866. The Hannoverian royalty had been living in Austria ever since and naturally entertained no particularly cordial feelings towards our family. Everybody hoped that this union would alleviate the tension between the two families. The Prince of Cumberland was to become the ruling Duke of Braunschweig-Lüneburg after the marriage and at the same time to be compensated for his claims to the throne of Hannover.

Both partners to the marriage were very charming and deeply in love with each other. My aunt, as the Kaiser's only daughter, enjoyed great popularity everywhere. She had a vivid and original temperament. She was the darling of her parents and brothers. Ernst August was an exceedingly good-looking young man, intelligent, wise, and tactful but rather quiet as compared with his vivacious wife. He was upright and kindhearted.

In short, this young couple, enveloped in the myth of romance and glamor, in every way lived up to the requirements of a fairy tale.

For all these reasons my grandparents decided to make the wedding an exceptional occasion; it turned out to be the last such spectacle during their reign. Tsar Nicholas II of Russia and King George V of England, my grandfather's cousins "Nicky" and "Georgy," were the outstanding guests among much royalty and many potentates.

Thus, the rulers of the three most powerful countries of those days, all closely related and even resembling each other physically, were actually getting together. They seemed to demonstrate to the world that "blood is thicker than water." Though I was only five years old, the presence of these two granduncles, whom I was to meet for the first and only time, impressed me more than anything else connected with the wedding. Perhaps I felt instinctively that our ruling families formed an international clan and that only by sticking together would they be able to remain in power for the benefit of their countries and for themselves.

In the early afternoon hours of May 24, 1913, my parents, Wilhelm, and I crowded into a gala carriage to drive over to the royal palace in Berlin. I remember that my father said it was a nuisance to use this old-fashioned, terribly uncomfortable vehicle. He would have preferred his new motor car. But court etiquette could not be disregarded. My mother did not feel at ease either. Her long train bothered her. It did not take us long to get to the palace, only a little more than half a mile distant from our home.

I was almost overwhelmed by the great crowd that filled the halls of the palace. In one of the smaller rooms all the relatives had assembled. There were my grandparents, the bride and the bridegroom, and also the Emperor of Russia and the King of England, both wearing German uniforms. They looked almost alike. The Tsar and the King both bent down and gave me a hearty embrace. I shall never forget the eyes of the Tsar. They had a melancholy, almost haunted look. He gave me the impression of being very nervous, as if he expected something unforeseen to happen at any moment. After a while the chief master of ceremonies announced that everything was ready in the court chapel. A long procession was formed.

Wilhelm and I followed our own court chamberlain. My mother was immediately behind us, escorted by the King of England. I became quite annoyed at the chamberlain because he walked much too slowly for my taste. I tried several times to push him from behind. My older brother, aware of the dignity required, tried desperately to restrain me. Those next in line were highly amused at the struggle going on near the head of the procession.

During the wedding service we stood near the altar. The venerable chief court preacher, Dr. Ernst von Dryander, was a man of splendid presence. I remember his reading from a large black book.

No sooner had the ceremony ended than Wilhelm and I were hustled through a side door and driven home. We had not yet reached the age to take part in the wedding banquet.

Once back in our nursery, my brother and I went through the whole ceremony, which we proudly demonstrated to our younger brothers. I was still angry with the "stupid court chamberlain," who had refused to put "pep" into the procession.

Chapter Four

Routine Life During World War I

(1914–18)

WORLD WAR I caught us children at Zoppot. I was then almost seven years old. We were warned to pull down the curtains at night so no enemy ship could discover the lights and aim at the House by the Sea. The term "black-out" for the first time entered my consciousness. Nobody was worrying about airplanes in those days.

We joined our parents at Berlin. I clearly remember the tremendous enthusiasm of the crowds in front of our palace. Although our children's rooms were in the rear of the building, we could hear the crowds shout all through the nights of these first days, calling for my parents and the "little Princes." To satisfy their demands my father got us out of bed once or twice and brought us out on the balcony in our nightshirts.

I believe that during these first days of the war the people of Germany felt closely united with their ruling families and were devoted to our dynasty. It was in those days that my grandfather, addressing the cheering multitudes from the balcony of the *Schloss,* spoke the much-quoted words: *"Ich kenne keine Parteien mehr, ich kenne nur noch Deutsche"* ("I no longer know any parties, I know only Germans"). They were accepted by the majority of the population as completely sincere.

As far as I am able to judge, my family as a whole was definitely popular. This was particularly true of my grandmother Kaiserin Auguste Victoria. My grandmother at the time of her death in April 1921 was venerated almost like a saint. She was a mother and wife who bore the tragedy of her country on her shoulders like a martyr and finally died of a broken heart in exile. Her funeral at Potsdam, attended by two hundred thousand persons from all over Germany, was a vivid proof of her tremendous popularity.

It is also a fact that my father enjoyed a greater popularity than did my grandfather. The Kaiser, contrary to appearances, had an extremely sensitive and shy character and did not have the easygoing, jovial temperament of his first-born. My father was taller than his sire and extremely well built. Women's hearts beat faster when they saw him riding through the streets. Aware of the impression he was creating, he never failed to exhibit the "Prince Charming" side of his character in public. My grandfather was further handicapped by his crippled left arm, although with determined perseverance he had learned to handle a horse solely with his right arm. These and other reasons produced a certain tension between my father and my grandfather.

The fact that my parents had four healthy boys further contributed to their popularity. The line of succession was thus secured. My parents had obviously fulfilled their duty towards the country in that respect! Moreover, a large family always creates more sympathy and interest than a small one, especially with the poorer classes, who rightly accuse the wealthy of being too lazy, selfish, and even cowardly to have more than one, two, or at most three children. My grandparents had set an example with six boys and one daughter; my parents almost matched them with four boys and two girls.

Looking back, I believe that the popularity of our dynasty could have been much greater had we had someone like the modern American public relations expert. We had practically no direct contact with the populace. Our fellow Germans generally saw us only at a distance. True, there were many souvenir post cards with photographs of our family in circulation. Also, the newspapers occasionally published a picture or even an article about us. On the whole, however, we were almost unknown to the broad masses of the people. In this connection Lord Beaverbrook later told me that the Duke of Windsor, when still Prince of Wales, had once complained to him about "those d——d news photographers who never give me a moment's peace."

"I think, Your Royal Highness," the newspaper king replied gravely, "you're lucky it isn't the other way around. After all, that's what you are getting paid for."

Whenever I discussed this question with the old advisers of my parents, they would stiffly remark: "The imperial family does not need any

publicity; it is far above such things." To these people a newspaperman
was just short of being a blackmailer or a gangster. As they saw it, the
Hohenzollerns had to live on a high pedestal in splendid isolation.

Strangely enough, the official representatives of the Weimar Republic
for the most part shared the dislike of publicity with their imperial
predecessors. It remained for the Nazi dictatorship to indulge in an orgy
of high-pressure promotion and deification of Adolf Hitler.

The routine of our lives was at first not affected much by the war.
Winter was spent in Berlin, spring and fall at Potsdam, and the summer
at Zoppot. As in most other German families, however, the head of the
family was missing. I did not see my father more than three or four times
during the entire war. The whole responsibility for our upbringing fell
upon my mother. The job was by no means an easy one. Besides, innumerable public duties devolved upon her. Nevertheless, she bore up
nobly.

The war was only a few weeks old when father sent Lieutenant Max
Fischinger to relieve Herr von Kühne as tutor. I had meanwhile proudly
reached the seven-year milestone, caught up with Wilhelm, and been
emancipated from the nursery. Fischinger, though badly wounded, had
climbed out of the window of a field hospital to lead his troops in a successful attack. Many stories and even verses were written about him as
a national hero.

Fischinger was not of the nobility nor was he a Prussian. He was a
southerner from Württemberg, renowned for the courage of its soldiers
but also for the democratic spirit of its inhabitants. He had a great liking
for the United States, especially for its original inhabitants the Red Indians. His main instruction consisted in reading James Fenimore Cooper's "Leather Stocking Tales" to us. Our imaginations were tremendously inspired by these stories. Secret red-skin expeditions were planned and
carried out, especially on the roofs of our palace and the surrounding
buildings. Bows and arrows were provided by our new Gouverneur, and
harmless civilians, mainly members of our household, were attacked in
the dusk by screaming little figures emitting strange war whoops.

Lieutenant Fischinger also took us out for long walks in the Berlin
streets and the Tiergarten. Our admiration for our new teacher was
boundless. He was opening a new world to us. We had the time of our
lives mingling with the crowd and were highly pleased if nobody rec-

ognized us. Our golden cage had suddenly been thrown wide open.

To our great regret Lieutenant Fischinger, whose health was very poor, left us after a few months. He was followed by Lieutenant Moitzi-schewitz, an Alsatian of Jewish extraction—there was no anti-semitism in our family!—also picked by my father. "Moitzi," as we called him for short, was a very talented young man. He spoke French perfectly, a fact that in part had determined my father's choice. The attitude of the German people in those days was much more bitter towards England than towards France. The French language was *à la mode* whereas English was *verboten*.

Moitzi was very impulsive and perhaps a little impatient for boys of our age. But after a while Wilhelm and I liked him very much. He was by no means as romantic as his predecessor, but he followed the same democratic line of thought and education. Our friendship lasted until his sudden death during the thirties when, according to rumor, he committed suicide to end the ceaseless persecution by the Nazis.

After tutoring us for about a year, Moitzi asked to be relieved. He was determined to return to the front. It was rather hard on an ambitious young officer to play around with two small boys while the biggest war in human history was on. My father fully understood and accepted the resignation.

Moitzi was succeeded by Captain Wilhelm Dietrich von Ditfurth, scion of an old Westfalian noble family. He had gone through the aristocratic Cadets' School at Plön with my Uncle Oskar, my grandfather's fifth son. Later on he had been personal A.D.C. to my Uncle Joachim, my grandfather's youngest son. He had thus started his career at court as a young boy.

Now he was taken out of the general staff and sent to supervise the education of the German heir apparent and his second brother. With respect to military glory this was undoubtedly a setback. I believe Ditfurth at first felt rather badly about it. On the other hand he fully grasped the importance of his assignment and the opportunities which went with it. He had only to read history to realize that men in similar positions often had accompanied their pupils throughout their lives. Once their pupils had ascended the throne, they had risen to top positions. Be that as it may, Ditfurth, nicknamed "Dico," stuck to his job.

Wilhelm had a strong liking for him. Had the monarchy continued and had Wilhelm later occupied the throne for the duties of which Ditfurth was to prepare him, this Gouverneur could have had any position he might desire. But Fate would not have it that way.

Dico was with our family throughout its darkest hours and remained to tutor even my youngest brother, Friedrich, but was killed in 1939 during the first days of the Polish campaign.

It would be extremely ungrateful of me were I not to admit that I owe an enormous lot to this man. But he and I just did not click. Ditfurth was a very serious person with strong principles, puritanical, exasperatingly prosaic, and a disbeliever in the fine arts. He frequently asserted that the "Prussian Infantry Regulations" and the "Time Table for the German State Railways" were the most perfect creations of the human spirit. He spoke forever of *"verdammte Pflicht und Schuldigkeit"* ("d——d duty and responsibility"), by which he meant that the only purpose in life was the acquisition of the highest sense of duty. To him it was almost more meritorious to fulfill a duty which one loathed than one whose performance gave one joy. My grandfather's tutor, Georg Hinzpeter, had belonged to this same strange, ascetic school of thought, and Frederick the Great's youth was a living example of this sort of pedagogy.

Ditfurth tried honestly to fit us for practical life. He made me, for instance, keep track of my monthly allowance of ten marks ($2.10) in the hope that I would learn to appreciate the value of money. In this respect, I am sorry to say, I was a complete failure. Even today Kira manages the family budget!

Nevertheless, Ditfurth has played an important part in my life. As I grow older I realize that my viewpoint was just as one-sided as was Ditfurth's.

The various Gouverneurs who came and went looked after our general welfare and merely supervised our education. The actual school lessons were given by professional teachers. Outstanding among them was Professor Carl Kappus. I have seldom admired and loved any teacher as I did this unusual man. He was half French, but besides speaking French like a native he had command of Spanish, Polish, Russian, and half a dozen Oriental languages. He told me later that he had learned most of these languages when globe-trotting with a wealthy Polish Jew who had been like a father to him. Kappus was very small, almost dwarfish, bald-headed, and endowed with an unusually large nose and might almost have appeared ridiculous except for a pair of eyes which sparkled with intelligence and humor.

I often wondered why Professor Kappus did not teach at a university. He seemed to me too great a scholar to be wasted on schoolboys. Years later I discussed this subject with him. He listened graciously but could not agree. "The best is none too good for the development of a young soul and a young mind," he said. "Later on, once a person has become hardened, it's not so important any more." I know that my beloved tutor was dead right.

Professor and Mrs. Kappus years later often visited us in our little house in Berlin-Grunewald, where my wife and I had settled down in late 1938 after our honeymoon trip around the world. The four of us agreed perfectly concerning the intolerable situation created by the Nazi regime. Kappus told us how much his own profession had been affected by the method of the Nazis.

Kappus was a pedagogue who could make everything he taught interesting. Even mathematics, a subject I always have loathed—he, too, as he once confessed—was presented in such a way that I easily understood what was going on. This was something no other teacher had been able to achieve. The secret of Professor Kappus's pedagogical success was his ability to stimulate his pupil's ambition. He never scolded. But with one or two short, quiet remarks he would make us feel abjectly ashamed of ourselves.

In his spare time Kappus told us many stories about his visits to other countries and about their customs. He stimulated our imagination and broadened our outlook on life. He was politically a liberal and an internationalist. He was a pacifist at heart but could not press that point too openly, since he would then have collided with the military-minded Ditfurth, who nevertheless respected the little professor's mental superiority. Kappus definitely believed in discipline and demanded a wholehearted mental effort, yet he built his authority around the fact that his pupils worked because they did not wish to disappoint their teacher.

Though the routine of our daily lives was not disturbed appreciably by the war, we nevertheless felt its effects with respect to the food situation. Despite our ownership of vast estates, the family lived strictly up to wartime food regulations. During the last year of the war we hardly ever had eggs, very little butter, and less meat.

My mother was very active in visiting hospitals and running relief organizations. Occasionally she took us along on these errands. I always left the hospitals in a very depressed mood because of all the suffering I had seen.

Ditfurth kept us vaguely posted on the military situation. Though I did not grasp much of what he said, I did understand that after the great advances at the beginning a stalemate had ensued. But he did everything possible to hide from us the fact that the war gradually was taking a disastrous turn for Germany.

In the summer of 1917 we had a practical demonstration that the situation was anything but favorable. We were spending the summer in Zoppot. Hitherto, whenever we went to near-by Danzig by train, we were given a reserved compartment. On a certain Sunday, Ditfurth took us to Danzig to visit a submarine. When we boarded the train to return to Zoppot we could not find an empty compartment. Ditfurth called the stationmaster, who was very embarrassed and apologized. He said that if Ditfurth so desired he would have a compartment cleared. But he intimated that the public was in a rather nervous state of mind and there might be trouble. Ditfurth understood. We crowded into a third-class compartment and had the time of our young lives. The other passengers recognized us and were very interested and courteous to us. After this incident we never again asked for a special compartment. Ditfurth felt quite relieved that everything had gone so smoothly.

Chapter Five

Prussia's Two Youngest Lieutenants

(1916–17)

WILHELM and I both reached the age of ten during the war. The tenth birthday was a very important day in the life of a Prussian Prince. On this day he was inducted into the army, donned his first uniform, and was given the rank of a lieutenant. This was a family tradition dating back to Friedrich Wilhelm I. The underlying idea was that from this date on the youthful lieutenant would get enough military training to enable him to command at least a company when he became of age, which in the case of princes was at eighteen and not at twenty-one.

Up to World War I such a day had always been celebrated in grand style. My father and all my uncles except Uncle Adalbert, who joined the navy, had become officers of the First Infantry Regiment of the Guards at Potsdam. The induction ceremonial prescribed that the candidate had first to report to my grandfather, who bestowed the Order of the Black Eagle on him. Afterwards the newly commissioned lieutenant had to join the parade, goose-stepping past the Kaiser. This was a very difficult task for a boy of ten, as all the soldiers of the guards regiment had to be at least six feet tall. The little boy officer had to jump to keep in step with his men, who seemed like giants beside their new superior.

Wilhelm's tenth birthday on July 4, 1916, would undoubtedly have been celebrated in the traditional manner had there been no war. It would have been a great day, not only for the birthday child and his family, but for the whole nation.

But with the war on, neither my grandfather nor my father, who both were at their respective military headquarters, was able to come home for the celebration. A plan to have the ceremony take place at my grand-father's G.H.Q. was quickly discarded because it would have looked like a travesty amid such grim surroundings. Thus poor Wilhelm had to forego an experience which had thrilled his forebears for many genera-tions.

The day was spent quietly at Zoppot, where Wilhelm was heartily congratulated by everybody from mother downward. He had put on his new field-gray uniform. On the left side of his jacket he wore the Star of the Black Eagle which my mother handed him in the name of the head of the family, the Kaiser.

Wilhelm was very unassuming and modest and took his disappoint-ment philosophically. He was very happy to wear the new uniform and to become the youngest officer of the German Army. At a family lunch-eon my mother made a little speech, and then we all drank his health. Afterwards pictures of the new lieutenant were taken on the terrace. It was a perfect summer day.

Instead of participating in the general happiness I had been rather moody all morning, I am ashamed to say. The fact that Wilhelm was having his picture taken in his new uniform did the rest. I was suddenly seized by an attack of acute jealousy. I had the feeling that my brother was about to climb on the throne and was looking at me in contempt. With a sneer I jumped at him. I tried to snatch the silver star on his jacket. My brother, who rightfully judged this moment undignified for a fist fight, tried to evade my assault. He retreated slowly and finally climbed over a high fence into our neighbor's yard. Finally, I calmed down. It had been a very disagreeable scene. I had made a perfect fool of myself and become the laughing stock of all the grownups who wit-nessed my fit.

My own induction took place in Potsdam fifteen months later, on Oc-tober 22, 1917. Though I still had eighteen days to go before celebrating my tenth birthday on November 9, my grandfather decided to make an exception in my case. He was about to return to his headquarters at the front. This was his last day at home and at the same time my grand-mother's birthday. It proved to be the only time in my life that I ever had any official contact with my grandfather as the Supreme Commander of the Army.

My turn had come to put on the brand new uniform. At home, with Ditfurth posing as my grandfather, I had time and again rehearsed the few words with which I was to report for "duty." Though I usually haven't the slightest trouble learning something by heart, I drove poor Ditfurth almost mad as he tried to get that short formula fixed in my cranium. While reporting, I had to stand at attention and keep my whole body rigid. Each time during our interminable rehearsals something would go wrong. I would mix up the words or add some "civilian" gesture which would spoil the whole military effect. Shortly before the great day arrived, and after rehearsing the act for at least the twentieth time, the poor man exclaimed in complete desperation: "Lulu, what can I do with you to make you look and act like a soldier! You are just unmilitary by nature."

At 9:30 that morning my mother, Wilhelm, who had also donned his uniform for the occasion, and I drove from our new home, Cecilienhof, to the New Palace. First we went to congratulate our grandmother on her birthday. All my other relatives, uncles, aunts, and cousins who happened to be in Potsdam had assembled to celebrate the happy occasion and to see my grandfather on one of his rare wartime visits with his family.

I was given a last checkup by Wilhelm, who thoroughly inspected my uniform, especially the buttons. I took one more look at my *Meldung,* which I had scribbled on a piece of paper. Then I marched to the room where the Meldung was to take place, trying hard to look brave. The doors were thrown open by two flunkies and closed automatically behind us.

My grandfather was standing in the middle of the room, flanked by several high-ranking officers. Following Ditfurth's instructions I walked up towards my grandfather and parked myself at the prescribed distance of about three yards exactly opposite him. Thus facing my supreme commander, I began with my "speech." At first things went off smoothly. But the presence of all the other people in the room so embarrassed me that I got hopelessly stuck right in the middle. My grandfather saved the situation by acting as a prompter. When I finally finished—like an eternity it seemed to me—the Kaiser, outwardly grave but with eyes smiling, remarked: "Well, my dear boy, this was not any too brilliant. But I am quite confident that you will have learned this speech by the time you get to be a general, without your grandfather having to be your prompter." After that he welcomed me as the youngest officer of his army, wishing me lots of luck for my future career.

It was only when I had left the room with a great sigh of relief that I became really aware of the fact that my grandfather with his human gesture had saved the situation and restored my self-respect, which otherwise would have been hopelessly lost. In later years I had frequent opportunity to observe this human quality in him.

Here, in the New Palace, I saw him for the last time as the ruler of our country. When I met him again he was an exile in Holland.

We spent the summer months of the year 1918 at Soden an der Werra, a watering place not far from Kassel. Our doctor had advised my mother to send us there instead of our beloved Zoppot. One day my brothers and I were playing a card game called Quartet. Our deck carried pictures of the rulers at war with Germany which were veritable caricatures. My mother happened to walk into our room. When she discovered the derogatory cartoons of the Tsar of Russia and the kings of England, Italy, and Serbia, she exclaimed: "Now, give me all these cards. I don't want you to use them any more when you play Quartet. True, these monarchs are our enemies. But we must not make fun of them. They all are doing their duty, just as *Grosspapa* and Papa are doing theirs." We were a bit surprised and unable to understand my mother's irritation. Only in later years did I realize how right she had been.

Throughout the war we were never once subject to any adverse propaganda about the enemy countries or their leaders; nor did we hear much about the gruesome stories circulated abroad about our own family.

The news that the Russian Emperor, his wife, and his children had been murdered by the Bolsheviks reached us at Soden. I sat for a whole afternoon on a little hill all by myself, musing about the horrible end of these relatives of ours. I recalled how I was struck by the sad look in the Tsar's eyes on the only occasion I had ever met him—the wedding of Aunt Cissy.

Before returning to Potsdam, Wilhelm and I spent two weeks with our grandmother at Wilhelmshöhe, near Kassel. Her health was none too good. Her heart was already badly affected, but her doctor could not restrain her from spending most of her time visiting hospitals. During a Sunday morning service at the court chapel she fainted and had to be carried to her bedroom. She was ordered to use a wheel chair as much as possible. Wilhelm and I were very proud when permitted to push her around in the garden.

Chapter Six

Came the Revolution

(1918)

IN THE autumn of 1918 we were back in Potsdam, blissfully unaware that a revolution was brewing. My birthday was approaching. My ardent wish was for a bicycle. I knew that it was extremely difficult to get such an object at that stage of the war and was, in fact, resigned to go without gifts that year. I was therefore quite happy to find a rough sketch of a bicycle, drawn by my mother, on my birthday table. Mama explained, apologetically, that the bicycle was not quite ready, but that I would certainly be getting it the next few days. I was overjoyed. I could not help but notice, however, that Mama looked rather sad. Our whole entourage seemed worried and nervous.

In the course of the forenoon Wilhelm and I went to the stables to have a look at the horses and carriages which my father had sent back from headquarters along with a large part of the personnel. I met several of the old grooms I had known from prewar and childhood days, and whom I had not seen in years. Mingled among them, however, were also strange, adventuresome-looking characters whom I had never seen before. Their military attire was not in keeping with army regulations. Their demeanor was rather insolent. I did not realize as yet that we were in the midst of general dissolution of military discipline.

When Wilhelm and I returned to Cecilienhof, Mama told us that grandmother had telephoned from the New Palace, urging her to come over with her six children as soon as possible. We asked what that message meant.

"Grossmama believes we shall be safer over there," Mama replied. "But I really don't see the slightest danger for any of us if we stay here." Soon there was another call. Grossmama earnestly implored my mother to come. My mother, who adored my grandmother, could not refuse.

Shortly after luncheon we all drove over to the New Palace. The streets were ominously quiet, almost deserted. Nobody detained us. At the entrance gates to the New Palace the guards presented arms as usual.

My grandmother met us outside the palace on the top of several flights of stairs leading out of a terrace which surrounded the whole edifice. This was unusual. Grandmother otherwise always received us in her drawing room on the second floor. She gave me a hearty embrace and congratulated me on my birthday. But I noticed that she had tears in her eyes.

"Go up to your rooms and have a nap first," she said to us. "Afterwards we shall all have a little birthday party. I am afraid, though, that I haven't much of a present for you, my poor boy, *mais c'est la guerre.*"

We were shown up to the same rooms we had occupied seven years ago during my parents' trip to India. Wilhelm and I again shared the same room. We went to bed but were too excited to shut an eye. By now we had discovered that something was decidedly wrong, though we had not had a chance to talk to my mother who had followed my grandmother into her boudoir. At four o'clock—shortly before teatime—Mama entered our room. In a low voice thick with tears she said: *"Die Revolution ist ausgebrochen. Grosspapa hat heute abgedankt. Der Krieg ist verloren"* ("The revolution has broken out. Grandfather has abdicated today. The war is lost").

My first reaction to this historic announcement was extremely egocentric. I felt tremendously relieved. And why? Because I concluded that I would not have to attend the military school at Plön! Wilhelm and I were to have gone there the following spring. My brother in joyful anticipation had been counting the days until our scheduled enrollment, whereas I had a feeling of utter dread at the very thought of Plön. Little did I know at what a price my delivery from the nightmare had been bought! With the exception of Wilhelm, none of us children realized what a tragic turn events had taken.

The dejected mood of the grownups impressed me strongly. People who up to that day had been vested with every possible authority were unable to conceal their helplessness and despair. From our window I could see my uncles and aunts, all in a long row, walking for hours up and down in front of the palace.

The day after our arrival Ditfurth told us that the guards company had formed a soldiers' council against their own wishes. Very reluctantly they wore red ribbons on their tunics. They continued, nevertheless, to give us the usual salute.

During the first three or four days we did not hear anything from our teachers. With the exception of Professor Kappus, who had been honorably discharged from the navy, they had all been wearing uniforms, as they were only on temporary leave while assigned to our household. Now one after another showed up again in the strangest attires, half civilian, half military. Our mathematics teacher was greeted with a hearty laugh. He who always had been very smartly dressed now wore an old civilian jacket borrowed from a friend, together with gray military trousers. He felt a bit hurt at the hilarity of his pupils and tried to impress upon us that he had had lots of trouble to get through to us.

Slowly we began to realize that the old order had collapsed. With the exception of a few rumors about a trainload of rebellious marines who were allegedly heading for the New Palace to storm it, we had not noticed anything of the revolution. We did not see a single revolutionary soldier. We heard about some disturbances in Berlin. In Potsdam, however, not a single shot was fired. The whole upheaval had taken place with practically no bloodshed. As far as we and our family were concerned, the revolutionaries did not seem to have any ill designs whatsoever upon us.

We spent about ten days at the New Palace. After things had generally quieted down my mother insisted on our returning to Cecilienhof. By that time we knew that my grandfather had gone to Holland. My grandmother had decided to follow the Kaiser into exile and seriously advised my mother to do likewise. Closest friends tried to convince Mama that she and her children would be exposed to all sorts of danger if she remained in Germany. But my mother staunchly refuted all these arguments.

"If they want to kill us, they can do that right here in my own house," she said after our return to Cecilienhof. "But I do not want my children to grow up as exiles if I can help it."

We all are deeply indebted to my mother for her wise decision. She assumed full responsibility in the face of all warning voices. In the light of the horrible events in Russia only a short time previously, her action required great strength of character and supreme personal courage. I am certain that Mama would have measured up to a responsibility of even greater import.

Fifteen years later, in 1933, shortly after Hitler's seizure of power, I had a long conversation on this very point with David Lloyd George. The only other person present when we had our private talk was Field Marshal Jan Smuts.

After tea Lloyd George suggested that he and I walk out on a small terrace of his country home to enjoy the beautiful view. The other guests had remained inside. After a while Smuts joined us. The three of us sat down on a wooden bench, the two great statesmen taking me between them.

Our host began to talk about the latest developments in my own country. Then the conversation drifted back to World War I and the way it had affected my own life and fate.

"You know, Prince Louis," Lloyd George remarked, "we over here never expected nor intended the fall of your dynasty. In the face of public opinion in Britain at that time it would have been impossible for me as Prime Minister to conclude a peace with either your grandfather or your father. But we all thought that a regency for your brother Wilhelm would be set up under your mother and one of your uncles. If your family had remained in power in Germany, I am certain that Mr. Hitler would not be giving us any headaches right now."

"And what surprises is he going to have in store for all of us?" gravely added South Africa's Prime Minister.

It has been proven historically that not even the socialists in Germany wanted our dynasty abolished and that the solution mentioned by Lloyd George would have been acceptable to them. In view of the record of the former British Prime Minister, the surprising thing to me was that Lloyd George made the statement he did. I could not help but wonder whether this was not a case of self-serving hindsight!

My mother has assured me that she would have been willing to assume the responsibility. Unfortunately, there was at that time a lack of far-sighted and determined advisers. Thus, a unique opportunity was missed which would have afforded greater stability to a beaten country in the postwar period.

Chapter Seven

My Bourgeois Life Begins

(1918–20)

W HEN we returned to Cecilienhof from the New Palace our servants told us of an incident which was perhaps typical for the whole spirit of the revolution of 1918. Shortly after we had left our home on November 9 a truck had arrived with about thirty soldiers armed to the teeth. Our people with sinking hearts thought they would be stood up against the wall and shot. But nothing of the sort happened. Quite the contrary. A civilian got out first. He was a well-known Potsdam tobacco merchant, now president of the new Workers' and Soldiers' Council of Potsdam. He had driven out to Cecilienhof to assure himself that we were all right and unmolested. He had brought with him these men who would be very happy to protect the Crown Princess and her children!

From this incident which had many parallels all over Germany, I believe two facts can be deducted:

First, the German people as a whole were not very keen about this revolution; second, the German people in general, unlike the French, English, or Americans, have no talent for revolutions.

Judging from personal experience I believe the revolution of November 9, 1918, was neither a social upheaval nor was it directed primarily against our dynasty or against any other ruling family in Germany. It was a revolution of hunger, caused by the desperate desire of the people for peace at any price, especially after President Wilson had proclaimed his Fourteen Points. The great majority of the people had no particular grudge against the German dynasties. If they had, they would not have restored to their former ruling houses so large a portion of their properties after a nationwide plebiscite. In those war years there was no resistance movement to speak of, such as developed twenty years later under the Hitler regime. If federalization is to be a constructive element in the future development of Europe and not merely a disguised method for keeping Germany as disunited as possible, the historical development of the country should not be overlooked and sacrificed to arbitrary measures conceived as the result of momentary emergencies and tendencies.

My second point—that the German people lack revolutionary talent—is no new discovery. In our day this lack of talent for revolutions is considered a great deficiency. Those who so regard it perhaps do not appreciate the main reason for it—the innate sense and love of order which is deeply rooted in the German character. Both in the United States and in South America, I have been told again and again that the German immigrants and the nationals of German extraction are order-loving. Such a characteristic, I learned during my studies of immigration, is considered very favorably in countries with heterogeneous populations. People with revolutionary inclinations are not particularly welcome in such countries and are rather summarily dealt with as anarchists, nihilists, and so forth. But why should antirevolutionary qualities be welcomed on one side of the ocean but condemned on the other?

We soon settled down to an astonishingly normal though greatly changed life, considering the fact that the war and our throne had been lost. My mother faced the new situation boldly. She was aware that she might have to make every decision all by herself for many years to come. Nobody could foretell when, if ever, my father would be permitted to return to Germany. Our whole standard of living had to be adapted to conditions which were anything but clear or cheerful.

My father as Crown Prince of Prussia had received a sizable annual grant from the Prussian people, besides a subvention or *apanage* paid out of the family fortune. With the abolition of the monarchy my father automatically lost the Prussian grant. In addition, our family estates were sequestered by the New Prussian Government, subject to determination as to what constituted private family property and what belonged to the state. This condition of affairs lasted until the year 1926, when a national referendum restored about half of our landed estates—some 150,000 acres—and several million marks to our family. Meanwhile, we received an allowance from the government which barely sufficed to take care of our most urgent needs. Consequently, my parents were compelled to borrow money from several banks. Among others, the Jewish financier Herbert Guttmann, who lived near us in Potsdam, proved to be of great help.

We had to cut our household expenses drastically. That, alas, meant the discharge of many old employees who had served us faithfully through several generations. We kept them on our payroll just as long as possible. Many, as already indicated, were given jobs in government offices at Berlin and Potsdam.

Our teaching staff, too, had to be dismissed. These men were government employees and had only been loaned to us. Had they chosen to stay with us they would not only have lost their state jobs but also all accrued benefits such as pensions and insurance. My family was in no condition to offer them an equivalent. Our private education had therefore to be given up and the public school substituted. It was decided that we should attend the *Realgymnasium* at Potsdam. Cecilienhof had remained in our possession. Potsdam was our native town and the traditional residence of our family. If there was any sympathy left for us among the population it could be expected with a high degree of probability in Potsdam. This reasoning proved correct. Many Potsdamers owed their thriving trades or government jobs almost entirely to the presence of the Prussian court in their town for more than two centuries. This they gratefully remembered.

My mother contacted the Potsdam school authorities. Dr. Albert Wüllenweber, the headmaster of the Realgymnasium, and *Studienrat* Hartmann, the teacher of the class we were to join, were invited out to Cecilienhof. Both proved to be very kind and accessible. Both assured my mother that despite the revolution there was not the slightest objection to accepting the two sons of the Crown Prince as pupils. On the contrary, their school would be glad to have us. Despite the new revolutionary theories of class equality, the Realgymnasium faculty did not mind having it known that two princes of royal blood were in attendance! The only condition modestly imposed by the school management was that Wilhelm and I would not insist on being addressed by our former titles, as these had been abolished by a special provision of the Weimar Constitution. We were merely to be called Prince Wilhelm and Prince Louis Ferdinand, our legal names.

Before we could enter, there were several subjects on which we had to catch up with the aid of private lessons. They included Latin, history, and —of all things—English! We had spoken it fluently before World War I had opened the floodgates of chauvinism and produced such silly slogans as *"Gott strafe England"* ("God punish England"). Chauvinism had led to a campaign to purge the German language of all words of foreign origin and to use Gothic characters exclusively in German script. Pressure had even been brought to bear on my father to change my name to Ludwig Ferdinand—a pressure which he angrily resisted. Wilhelm and I had almost completely forgotten what Miss Brimble taught us, and we had to make virtually a new start with English.

It was mainly my mother's diplomatic tact and her popularity that made our educational change-over possible. Nobody in those first months after the revolution knew for certain in what direction the new German Republic was likely to drift—whether it would remain more or less in the middle of the road or go definitely to the left. In the latter case, anybody who had had dealings with the former ruling house after the abolition of the monarchy risked at least his career.

In the summer of 1920, after a year and a half of additional private tutoring, we were considered ready to submit to an entrance examination conducted by Dr. Wüllenweber and an official from the Ministry of Education. Our only weak spot was Latin. In every other subject we passed the test satisfactorily. We excelled in French and demonstrated the grammatical skill acquired under the tutelage of our beloved Professor Kappus.

At one point during the history test I caused the dignified educators to laugh heartily.

"Why did Emperor Henry IV go to Canossa?" was the question.

"To get himself out of the mess," was my answer.

"Your answer sounds rather realistic, Prince Louis," said the examiner, "and does not pay exaggerated tribute to that historic event. But why, after all, shouldn't you call things by their proper names? Let me warn you, though: if you always follow that method you may shock a lot of people who resent having history reduced to simple motives."

The verdict on our examination: we were considered fit to enter the Realgymnasium.

Chapter Eight

The Kapp Rebellion

(1920)

OUR EDUCATIONAL program was interrupted by political events. In the spring of 1920 the newly created German Republic was almost overthrown by the so-called Kapp Rebellion. The Spartakists, forerunners of the German Communists, were trying to set up a regime of terror in several parts of the country. Certain rightist groups felt that the republican government headed by President Friedrich Ebert was not energetic enough in suppressing these terroristic movements. Under the leadership of a former Imperial Government official, Wolfgang Kapp, a *coup d'état* was launched with some initial success. The Kapp people occupied Berlin and the main government offices. The Federal Government fled to Stuttgart. Due to lack of financial and political support the Kapp movement had to fold up after a few days. Kapp fled to Sweden, and President Ebert returned to Berlin. Ebert acted with great dignity and skill throughout this crucial situation.

In view of the critical political situation my mother was seriously advised to take us to southern Germany until things had calmed down. This time my mother yielded. The Spartakists did not hesitate to murder in cold blood. A few months spent in the Bavarian mountains near Berchtesgaden might prove wholesome for all of us.

It is indicative of the abnormal conditions then prevailing that we needed special passports to travel from Prussia to Bavaria. The Federal Railway Administration, which even later during the Hitler regime remained loyal to my family, placed at our disposal for this trip the old private car used by my parents during the days of the monarchy.

For more than four months we lived in the beautiful mountain region

King Edward VII of England with the Kaiser on a tour in Germany.

Left: Prince Louis Ferdinand, seated, and his mother, grandmother, and brothers. *Right:* With the Kaiser at Doorn in 1926. Prince Wilhelm and Prince Louis Ferdinand (at the right).

which fifteen years later was to become a part of Hitler's citadel. Our quarters were in an inexpensive boardinghouse managed by some Baltic baroness. It took us some time to overcome the traditional anti-Prussian prejudices of the local population. We tried quickly to adapt ourselves. Mama ordered native *Gamslederne*—short leather trousers made of the hides of mountain goats—for her four boys. We learned to understand and even speak the difficult Bavarian mountain dialect. In addition we took great pains to learn to dance the famous *Schuhplattler* and the more complicated *Watschentanz,* both of which one can see in many American cities with Bavarian restaurants. Wilhelm and I loved to show off our proficiency in these typical peasant dances whenever our mother had guests.

We spent much time on the beautiful *Königsee* and also did some serious mountain climbing under the guidance of a native forester. And yet, notwithstanding the glory and majesty of the mountains, I still prefer the immensity of the ocean, which gives me the feeling of limitless space, yes, of eternity, more even than does an Alpine setting. As a native of the Prussian plains, I always feel hemmed in by mountains after a while.

Our sojourn in the Bavarian Alps came to an end in July 1920. I was now almost thirteen years old. Life in Prussia had returned to normal. Besides, my mother had planned a trip to Holland for August and had arranged for us four boys to accompany her. A year previously she had gone to Holland for the first time but had then taken only Hubertus and Fritzi with her.

In view of my youth and the fact that this was the first journey outside of Germany, I may perhaps be pardoned if the strange new surroundings, the contact with a foreign country, and the good food—hunger was then stalking in Germany—made a deeper impression upon me than the emotional strain of the Wiedersehen with my father and grandparents under such tragic circumstances. At that age I was unable to grasp in its full significance the misfortune which had then befallen us, just as my oldest son, now also thirteen years old, cannot fully grasp what we went through in 1945 and later.

We traveled first to Wieringen, the island in the Zuider Sea which the Dutch Government had assigned to my father as his lonely residence.

My father lived in the Protestant parsonage of a tiny village called Os-
terland. It was a small house, devoid of all modern comfort such as water flowing from a hydrant, or gas or electric light. A petroleum lamp
served for his nightly reading. There was only one spare room which was
turned into a guest room for my mother. We boys were quartered with
a near-by peasant.

There were practically no trees on that island. A strong wind blew
most of the time. The population consisted mostly of fishermen. My father knew most of them by name. At first they had been very reserved,
since Allied propaganda had depicted him as a sort of Frankenstein
monster or even a cannibal. As time went on, however, their reticence
wore off completely. My father learned to speak the local dialect fluently
and gradually won the hearts of these rather poor, hard-working people.
His special friends were the burgomaster of the island, Mynheer Peere-
boom, and his family. The Peerebooms, paragons of Christian neigh-
borly love, did everything possible to make my father's life of isolation
tolerable.

In spite of the cordiality of his Dutch hosts, the five years spent on a
lonely island left a deep impression on my father's mind and soul, which
even time was not able to eradicate. He who had so thoroughly enjoyed
mingling with people became more and more of a recluse as time
went on.[1]

After a fortnight in Wieringen we went for a week to Amerongen,
where my grandparents had taken refuge after their departure from
Germany. Doorn, which the Kaiser had just bought, was not yet ready
for its new owner or his guests to live there.

Although my grandfather with his snow-white hair and the—to us—
unaccustomed goatee struck me as having aged considerably, he did not
give the impression of a broken man. He received us in the same warm,
affectionate manner as always.

My memory of my grandmother on that occasion is a much sadder
one. She mostly lay sick abed and was able to move about only in a wheel
chair. It was the last time I was to see her. She died the following year,

[1] My father has described his experiences on the Island of Wieringen in *Erinnerun-
gen des Kronprinzen Wilhelm. Aus den Aufzeichnungen, Dokumenten, Tagebüchern
und Gesprächen herausgegeben von Karl Rosner.* (J. G. Cotta, Publisher, Stuttgart and
Berlin, 1922.)

1921. Wilhelm and I could witness the burial ceremonies, which had brought an overwhelming number of mourners to Potsdam, only from a window of the New Palace. We had just recovered from illness, and a relapse was feared in case we took part in the burial service.

The trip to Holland in August 1920 was to be the first of a long series of visits I have paid to that sympathetic country. After my grandparents' removal to *Huize Doorn* in 1921, Doorn became a second home for all of us. Especially after Hitler turned Germany into a huge dungeon, I always deeply relished the moment when the train crossed the Dutch border.

Chapter Nine

High-School Days at Potsdam

(1920–25)

MY HIGH-SCHOOL days at Potsdam, which began in the autumn of 1920 after our return from Holland, were much less satisfactory as far as personal happiness was concerned than were my infancy and boyhood. Nevertheless, they were much more important for the formation of my character and my whole outlook on life. The feeling of ease and security which prevailed in my native land up to and even including the first two years of World War I had strongly influenced our *Weltanschauung*. Like almost everybody else we had taken things for granted—our style of living, our position as compared to other people, in short, our whole existence. The question of their meaning or justification had hardly ever entered our heads. I believe, in fact, that a questioning attitude was carefully prevented from creeping into our minds by the guardians of our youth. This lack of a critical attitude towards existing conditions, which in many cases were accepted as unchangeable, is largely responsible for the decline of monarchic government. In my family, for instance, it has been an accepted method since the days of Friedrich Wilhelm I to reduce the ego to a minimum by stressing our duty towards the state on all occasions. Except in the case of the strongest personalities, this concept meant the crushing of self-assurance and self-reliance in the individual. This in turn led to the curious result of an exaggerated confidence in other persons and an over-rating of their abilities.

It may surprise many that my grandfather, too, was not free from this methodically implanted disinclination to decide for himself if confronted with a difficult situation. In the crisis of November 1918, when he had to choose between abdication and exile in Holland on the one hand and sticking it out in Germany on the other, he felt he must be bound by the opinion of his advisers rather than by his own judgment. In fact, he deemed it unpermissible to bring himself to make up his own mind. It was Hindenburg who spoke the final word. At the time and ever afterwards the Kaiser's argument was that he did not want to stand between his country and peace, nor did he want to run the chance of causing bloodshed on his behalf.

It is further true that in many other actions for which he was criticized his instinctive first reaction was that of making the right decision. But his advisers were able to talk him into their viewpoint, which he then accepted reluctantly. Later, it was he and not the advisers who were blamed.

This Potsdam species of pedagogy was disadvantageous also in another direction. The authoritative attitude towards him of those charged with his upbringing resulted in an almost naïve trustfulness in the people who served him as counselors. During his whole life he thought so highly of the human being that he was unable to conceive that some men who had his ear were not as sincere and unselfish as they represented themselves to be.

Though both of my parents had a more practical outlook on life, they were not able to change a system within whose limits they had been brought up. Until November 9, 1918, I, too, had been its captive. Then, with the revolution, it fell overnight. Nevertheless, I felt its existence even afterwards by the way certain people and circles reacted towards my personal development.

My years at high school had, I am sorry to confess, no "democratizing" effect on me. To be sure, the competitive contacts with "normal" children did have a very wholesome effect, but in quite the opposite direction. My self-confidence, underdeveloped until then, was strengthened appreciably during those four and a half years. Wilhelm and I realized very quickly that we would be able to measure up with our classmates. It became evident from the first moment that ours was a solid foundation. Our very first report cards indicated that we were the best of the whole class.

Never having had any audience during the years of our home education, I felt a strong urge to show off before my classmates and at the same time to please my teachers. It was not long before I had the reputation of being a *Streber* (eager beaver). My classmates felt I was breaking the sacred rules of *esprit de corps* by trying to be a model pupil. I now realize I made a grave psychological mistake, which I have tried in later years to avoid. On the other hand I just could not share the viewpoint of my fellow students that the teachers' only purpose and reason for existence were to annoy the pupils and to be annoyed by them.

My brother Wilhelm's position was altogether different. He was the idol of our class and later on of the whole school. This popularity was reflected in a school election. After the revolution of 1918 there was a tendency to democratize the high schools by giving the pupils a form of self-rule. Student councils were established to which each class elected a representative. Each council in turn elected a chief representative who was the spokesman of the pupils in dealing with the principal and the teachers. This well-meaning school parliament, however, did not have the slightest influence on matters of education or discipline.

Wilhelm was elected by a smashing majority to represent our class. He received twenty-five votes whereas I had to be satisfied with the remaining three. After that convincing defeat I once and for all buried all hopes of ever running for any office! My brother later became for two years chief representative of the student body. He was popular with pupils and teachers alike and in most cases put through what his "constituents" expected from him.

How to explain the great difference in popularity between my brother and me? Wilhelm, for one thing, accepted the general antipathy of the pupils as regarded the acquisition of learning. Secondly, he was a great sports enthusiast and advocate of team games such as soccer, football and handball. Sports which up to World War I had occupied a secondary position in the high-school curricula were given a great impulse after the November revolution.

Our teams naturally played against those of the other schools in town and even against Berlin schools. Thus my brother, who took his activities very seriously, became a well-known figure in Potsdam and Berlin youth sports circles.

In short, Wilhelm was a model normal youngster who shared the tastes of his fellow pupils even to the extent of having the usual flirtation with some girl of the *Lyzeum* (high school for girls) with whom he used to bicycle to and from school.

In his class work he excelled in German and history. He wrote good compositions and also had a fine command of the German language. This came in very handy for his activities as chairman of the school parliament. His military interests grew from year to year.

As to myself, I was the opposite of everything I have said about my brother. I liked my school work, tried to satisfy my teachers, did not care for the other classmates, and was a complete dud in anything athletic. I confess that I then regarded gymnastics as vulgar and barbaric. I also had an outspoken contempt for the female sex, to which I gave vociferous expression at every possible opportunity. My blood pressure rose to the boiling point when three girls joined us and remained with our class for three years. At that stage of my development I had not yet learned to appreciate the meaning of the beautiful Spanish proverb, "Courtesy does not prevent courage."

I became further alienated from my fellow pupils in that I had two noncurricular hobbies, Spanish and music, which I cultivated with fanaticism. My liking for the Spanish language dates back to my childhood days and is based on the simple fact that King Alfonso XIII of Spain was my godfather. Each of us princes had several foreign kings as godfathers; thus King Edward VII of England and King Christian X of Denmark also were my sponsors. It was merely a nice gesture and really did not mean a lot.

My enthusiasm for my Spanish godfather was perhaps nourished by my mother's best friend, the hereditary Princess of Salm-Salm—Aunty Christa to us children, who adored her. Aunty Christa was born an Austrian archduchess and King Alfonso's first cousin. She used to go to Spain regularly and always told me about my godfather and the wonderful country he ruled.

A year before the revolution of 1918, I had decided that I must do more than just admire my sponsor and his country. I planned to go and visit him some day. I therefore decided to learn the Spanish language. I bought a Spanish grammar and studied Spanish secretly, mostly at night. I was soon discovered, however. Ditfurth feared I would neglect my other studies and made me deliver my cherished grammar to him. But dear Professor Kappus was my good angel. He supplied me with more Spanish books. The first of these was *Novelas Ejemplares* by the immortal Cervantes. I made written translations which Kappus corrected from time to time. I learned the whole grammar almost by heart. As soon as I was able to write a few sentences I concocted a letter which I sent to my *padrino* (godfather) in Spain through my *madrina* (godmother), my beloved Aunty Christa. It was a birthday letter and contained all expressions of devotion and felicitation which I had been able to assemble from a small dictionary also furnished by Kappus. I filled the letter with titles and royal apostrophes. My pride and gratitude were almost limitless when I received an answer and a beautiful signed photograph from my royal sponsor. He congratulated me on my accomplishments in the Spanish language and asked me to drop all formality, just calling him Uncle Alfonso. This familiarity almost took away my breath. I carried that letter around with me for several months and gave the picture the preferred spot on my night table, ahead even of the closest members of my own family. A regular correspondence developed between godfather and godson. Later, when I met him, Uncle Alfonso told me that he was surprised that any of his foreign relations should take the trouble to learn Spanish.

The deeper I got into the language the more I tried to learn about Spain and her colonial empire. Finally I completely identified myself with the "Spanish cause" and became its fanatic champion. During the geography lessons I rattled off the names of the most unknown Spanish towns, mountains, or rivers. If anybody else did not know them or did not pronounce the words in true Spanish fashion I took personal offense and loudly corrected the violator. My temper grew even worse when Spanish colonization was talked about during history lessons. It was a generally accepted theory that the Spanish colonial system consisted of nothing but lootings and atrocities. The natives were described as demigods and the Spanish conquistadors as devils incarnate. This "Black Legend," as the Spaniards call it, seemed to me to be greatly exaggerated. When our history teacher merely repeated what was written by historians I would forget my usually respectful attitude and accuse him of ignorance and bad faith. As he was, however, a staunch monarchist and admirer of the Hohenzollerns he contented himself with smiling indulgently and saying: "I quite see your point, Prince Louis Ferdinand. During our next lesson we shall be glad to have you give us a little talk about the Spanish colonial system." My classmates were happy—that meant they would not have to recite.

In typically German fashion I even founded a society to foster friendship between Spain and Germany. It soon died of attrition. All through those four high-school years I loved to choose a Spanish topic for the talks which all pupils had to give from time to time. This task was rendered easy for me in that my godfather had sent me a library of two hundred Spanish books containing the best-known selections from the classics to modern literature.

This wonderful present was presented to me on behalf of King Alfonso by Colonel Don Luis Ruiz de Valdivia, military attaché of the Spanish Embassy. It was a gesture of great tact on the part of Uncle Alfonso to choose Valdivia for this mission. The colonel had been assigned to Berlin ever since 1913 and had thus become dean of the military attachés in the German capital. He was as devoted to the Spanish royal family as to the House of Hohenzollern. My grandfather held him in great esteem and during the war had entrusted him with several delicate missions which he brought to a successful end. Though a soldier by profession, Valdivia was a convinced liberal and pacifist. He became a second father to me during those decisive years. His influence on my mental development has been incisive and lasting. To no one do I feel as deeply indebted as to him. More about him later.

As already indicated, my second hobby was music. Two years before World War I ended, I had expressed the wish to play the violin. My brother Wilhelm was already having piano lessons. My request was granted immediately. My mother played the piano well, and my father belabored his famous Amati violin, a gift presented to Frederick the Great by his ambassador in Venice. Papa was not exactly a Paganini as far as technique was concerned, but he played with fine musical taste, which is often rarer than a cold technique.

We children grew up surrounded by the greatest musicians of our day. This was due mainly to my mother's deep and sincere love for classical and romantic music. After her marriage she had become the acknowledged patroness of the fine arts in Berlin. Neither of my grandparents had been very artistically inclined. Mama regularly went to the concerts of the Berlin Philharmonic Orchestra, often attending both rehearsals and public performances.

The great soloists, singers, pianists, violinists, and conductors were regular dinner or luncheon guests at our palace. My parents, unlike many of their fellow citizens, fully recognized the social equality of the artists. A lasting friendship developed especially with two great artists, Bronislav Huberman and Wilhelm Backhaus. Up to World War I both were weekly, sometimes daily, visitors at our homes in Potsdam or Berlin. We children used to admire Backhaus's beautiful shock of hair which seemed to fly all over the place when he got into some *allegro* or *furioso*.

When the war broke out poor Backhaus was drafted. Instead of his impeccable frock coat he appeared in a badly tailored, rough uniform as a simple private. His wonderful head of hair was shorn, and he seemed almost bald. We could not help but break into screams of laughter, in which dear "Backy" finally joined though he felt anything but happy. My father soon had him attached to his private staff. I believe that once, *pour la galerie,* he had to stand on guard before my father's military headquarters for an hour or so. After that his duty was to play the piano in the evenings and give concerts for the wounded soldiers.

Huberman was a Jewish-born Pole and as such a Russian subject. At the beginning of the war he was placed in an internment camp, but my mother intervened and on my grandfather's personal order he was released and allowed to go wherever he pleased.

Another most welcome guest was Professor Karl Klingler with his famous string quartet. Thus the enjoyment of the choicest music executed by top artists became an almost normal procedure for us children. We loved those afternoon or evening musicales. Besides, it meant we were allowed to stay up a little later than usual!

My mother, meaning only too well, had selected Madame Gabriele Wietrowetz as my first violin teacher. She was a very energetic, middle-aged lady and an internationally famed concert violinist, one of Joseph Joachim's favorite pupils. A beginner on the violin perhaps inflicts greater torture upon teacher, pupil, and everybody else within hearing distance than the beginner on any other instrument. This became especially evident in my case. I realized later that the poor lady must have suffered agonies. I am sure she accepted me as a pupil only to please my mother.

My lessons became a constant mutual fight. Madame Wietrowetz treated me like a grownup. I was not allowed to sit down during the half-hour lesson. Once I almost fainted from trying to hold the violin too long just the way she wanted it. I was too proud to admit that my arm did not have strength enough to stand the strain. I did not make much progress, and the lessons were finally called off.

After the revolution a teacher named Ulrich Pfeil-Schneider guided me through the intricacies of violin playing. I loved the lessons and made good progress. During the first year he used to come out to Cecilienhof. During the pauses we often discussed politics. My violin teacher held views slightly on the "pink" side. He was an antimilitarist and sympathized heartily with the Weimar Republic.

During one of the intervals he referred to Bismarck in the most derogatory way. I repeated his words religiously. Suddenly, my mother's angry voice interrupted our conversation.

"Do you want to make a socialist of my son, Herr Pfeil-Schneider?" she asked the little man, towering over him indignantly. "Please concentrate on your music lessons and refrain from now on from spoiling my son. I shall take care of his politics myself." She left the room without giving us another look.

In our Realgymnasium, a students' orchestra was organized while Wilhelm and I attended. I joined as a first violinist and finally rose to the position of concertmaster.

Later, during my university years, I had two more first-rate violin teachers—Professor Brahm-Eldering in Cologne, teacher of Fritz Busch, and Professor Rudolf Deman in Berlin, first violinist of the State Opera Orchestra.

I also took piano lessons from Wilhelm's teacher. I am sorry I did not begin with the piano. I believe that for an amateur the piano is a far more satisfactory instrument, because it offers a much wider scope of possibilities than any other solo instrument.

I enjoyed the first year and a half at high school tremendously. Then, however, I began to be bored, as were my fellow pupils from the very be-

ginning. Two main reasons accounted for this unsatisfactory situation—
one, the indifferent attitude of the underpaid teachers; the other, the
dual character of the curriculum. There was what might be called the
humanistic side, represented by languages, literature, and history; and
there was the material side, represented by the exact sciences, such as
mathematics, physics, and chemistry. It is an often observed fact that
one section in a class is more linguistic-minded and the other more inclined towards mathematics. This meant that during the language lessons the teacher would have to devote his main attention to the mathe-
maticians, who were generally poor linguists, and vice versa during the
mathematics period. One half of the class was always bored for being
left idle and the other because uninterested. Thus much valuable time
was wasted.

While Wilhelm and I were still attending high school in Potsdam,
Mama with her four younger children moved into our castle at Oels in
Silesia, since living was cheaper there. Wilhelm and I remained in Potsdam under the custody of Ditfurth. Our household was cut to the bone.
We lived in a few rooms of the huge building. Wilhelm and I each occupied a bedroom on the second floor, whereas Ditfurth had his suite on
the first floor directly underneath ours. Since it was impossible to use
the central heating system during the winter time because of lack of coal,
stoves were installed in our studies. Our bedrooms remained unheated.

Another room which was never really warm was our dining room,
located in the breezy tower. We always arose at six thirty and at seven
o'clock had breakfast in the cold tower, Ditfurth presiding at the table.
I still shudder when I recall those meager meals in that cold room dimly
lighted by electric light. The dismal atmosphere in itself was not the
worst; it was Ditfurth who at times drove us nearly mad.

I belong to the type of people who are not at their best in the early
morning hours. My mind is usually not completely awake until the
afternoon, when I am in the best mood. My tutor, however, who belonged to the opposite type, chose the breakfast hour for long political
discourses. His favorite newspaper was the *Preussische Kreuzzeitung*.
This newspaper was monarchical and ultraconservative. Its circulation was so insignificant that Foreign Minister Gustav Stresemann once
jokingly remarked to Ditfurth: "The *Kreuzzeitung* appears with the

public excluded." Many a time I found copy of it at my plate with an article, usually derogatory about the present German Government or our former enemies, marked with a blue pencil by my tutor. Ditfurth religiously believed everything he read in it. To him it represented the true German viewpoint. I am sure that his intentions were the best, but his political prophylactic had a devastating effect upon me. I began to hate everything connected with monarchism or conservatism. Out of mere spite I bought the socialist *Vorwärts* and the communistic *Rote Fahne* and placed them on Ditfurth's plate. Instead of trying to find out the truth on both sides, I was slowly becoming just as intolerant of Ditfurth's ideas as he was of mine.

In addition to our high-school program, Ditfurth had worked out a series of courses to be given by specialists who volunteered for the occasion. Once weekly we were taught military history by Lieutenant Colonel Wolfgang Förster, a very brilliant man. He frequently asked us to solve strategical problems based on situations which arose during the Seven Years' War. Wilhelm demonstrated his great ability in this field, whereas I was a complete failure. Only once, to my own and everybody else's great surprise, I found exactly the same solution that my great ancestor had chosen. It was a retreat! After that there was no end of teasing me about my strategical retreat of which I was very proud.

Realizing that our teachers of English and French at the Realgymnasium were only mediocre, Ditfurth had us take lessons in conversation. In addition I had my personal little educational program of two violin and one Spanish conversation lessons per week.

Another course was a political one conducted by Dr. Friedrich Everling, a lawyer and member of the *Reichstag,* where he represented the German National Party, a rightist party with monarchical leanings. Everling was an asthmatic little man who in spite of his poor health smoked cigars incessantly. His lectures, constantly interrupted by coughs, were very interesting. He gave us a neutral, objective picture of the functioning of governmental machinery. He outlined the old Bismarckian and the new Weimar constitutions, comparing them with those of England, France, and America. Nor were current political events neglected. I loved to argue, hence professed to hold leftist theories of socialism and pacifism. Everling, who noticed immediately that my attitude was based principally on emotion, challenged my arguments. With much spirit and wit he generally succeeded in bringing about some agreement by which we met halfway. Everling was a convinced monarchist and loyal to our family. However, he could not satisfy me that a constitutional monarchy would be the best form of government for Germany. I had become a staunch republican, believing firmly in the advantages of the Weimar Republic and the perfection of the Reichstag.

This faith was badly shaken when Dr. Everling one day took me to his "workshop," the Reichstag. He chose a very important session for my visit. The Dawes Plan was to be discussed and voted on. The main bone of contention was the "railway law," which practically forfeited the railways as the main money-making government institution to our former enemies. The leftist parties were opposed to this provision. It depended on the German National Party whether that law and with it the whole plan would be accepted or rejected. The bourgeois parties wanted to accept the Dawes Plan in order to get rid of the inflation and set up a stable currency. Up to the last moment the attitude of Everling's party was not clear.

With my heart beating faster with excitement I entered the temple of German politics. I expected to find an atmosphere such as prevails in a church or in a concert hall.

There was a moment of relative quiet when the *Reichstagspräsident* (speaker) opened the session and gave the floor to Chancellor Wilhelm Marx, who was to report on his negotiations in London and recommend acceptance of the Dawes Plan. The chancellor, a small, gray-haired man dressed in a black cutaway with gray trousers, stepped to the rostrum and began to speak. He had hardly cleared his throat when a deafening noise started from the sectors occupied by the communist and socialist deputies. At first I was unable to understand what they were shouting. The president of the assembly desperately rang his bell, but the shouting would not stop.

Marx tried to continue. I could not understand a word. I only saw his lips move. Finally he stepped back and sat down.

The presiding officer finally managed to restore calm. He pleaded with the deputies please to keep quiet. Marx again stepped forward. But the turmoil resumed the moment he opened his mouth. After a few minutes he again sat down. Again the president implored the deputies to let the chancellor continue. This procedure was repeated several times. Finally Marx gave up. Shrugging his shoulders in a hopeless gesture he left the hall. The session was interrupted for an hour. When Marx reappeared, the uproar started again. He tried for another hour to deliver his speech, but the gentlemen on the left would not let him talk. They yelled and whistled and shouted unprintable imprecations. The session was finally closed and the Reichstag adjourned to the next day.

Everling came up to my gallery to call for me. I was sitting there bewildered and disgusted.

"Well, Prince Louis, how did you like it?" he asked with a sardonic smile.

"Do those people always behave that way?" I asked him.

"Not always, but most of the time," he answered.

For a long time I was completely disillusioned.

During our honeymoon trip around the world in 1938, Kira and I visited both houses of Congress while in session. Our guide was Jimmy Roosevelt, the President's oldest son. We first visited the House of Representatives, where we met Speaker Bankhead. After that we went to the Senate. Senator Key Pittman of Nevada received us at his office and offered us a stiff drink of bourbon. After a peep at the Senate Foreign Relations Committee room Senator Pittman took us into the Senate gallery. In a whispered voice he explained all the details to us. When Senator Robert La Follette, whom I had met in Madison, Wisconsin, years previously noticed us he left his seat and joined us for a while.

It was the atmosphere and behavior which I found in the Senate that restored my faith in parliamentary institutions after my Reichstag experience. I could honestly tell the newspaper men that I was most favorably impressed.

But to return to Dr. Everling: during the years directly preceding the Second World War, I saw quite a lot of my old political teacher. He had meanwhile married a very charming and highly educated wife, who in a very touching way nursed her husband's poor health. During long conversations Everling developed his political thoughts, which had not changed during the intervening fifteen years. On the basis of my practical experience abroad I came to the conclusion that there was a lot more to his line of thought than I had been ready to accept as a radical Potsdam high-school boy with professed leftist leanings.

To get all my work done I often arose at five o'clock in the morning and did not go to bed before midnight. On certain days of the week I had hardly time enough to eat my luncheon, because I had to climb on my bicycle to dash off into town for a music lesson, a rehearsal of the orchestra, or some lecture. Our house was located in the outskirts of Potsdam. It took us about a twenty-minutes' bicycle ride to the center of town. Looking back I hardly believe that nowadays I would have enough energy to do all those things at once, half of which were entirely voluntary. I was busy from morning to night in the true sense of the word. I did not have the slightest difficulty to get along in school. Though—as told before—I kept a lot to myself, I felt perfectly at home in that new world which was beginning to absorb us after the walls of the golden cage had been crushed.

In spite of all my activities I could sometimes not suppress a feeling of acute unhappiness, even of melancholic moods, that followed me for days. The atmosphere of our household was a mixture between a convent and a casern.

We could not expect Ditfurth to be a substitute for both our mother and our father. He did all he could to supervise our education and to steer our lives according to his Spartan and puritanical principles. He wanted to get us used to utmost simplicity and modesty and to impress upon us that we must not expect too much comfort and luxury in life. The household budget at his disposal was certainly very limited and the food situation in postwar Germany during those years distressing. But I doubt whether it was necessary for him to keep our meals at such a low level. Colonel Valdivia, who was one of our rare luncheon guests from time to time, told me after we had become better acquainted that he always got up hungry from our table.

Ditfurth had a high opinion of the value of money. I received an allowance of ten marks a month. On the first of each month I had to render a detailed account of the money spent and of the use I made of it. To my tutor's despair I was never able to balance my account.

The idea that the whole life of a person, especially a Prussian Prince, was nothing but a duty to be performed under any and all circumstances created, in fact, a sinister atmosphere. What was lacking most of all was that simple cheerfulness which makes even the most difficult conditions of life endurable. Things had undeniably taken a bad turn for our family and our country, but this was no reason for being continuously in mourning. Especially in Potsdam as the cradle of Prussian traditions everything was calculated to remind us of our glorious past. Due to that negative attitude, however, we seemed to be living in one of the mausoleums in which my ancestors were buried. I sometimes felt completely choked.

Ditfurth had a natural dislike for the fine arts. Music to him was a poison which corrupted the senses and undermined the strength and virtues of a human. He had nothing but contempt for my mother's musical guests with their long hair and unmilitary behavior. I believe he was honestly horrified and deeply worried that I was showing strong tendencies towards becoming an artist myself.

The austerity of our household was counterbalanced to a certain degree by Dr. Richard Kienast, who joined us during the last two years of our high-school days. Kienast, whose left hand had been badly crippled in the war, was a student of philology and was engaged to supervise our homework. His hobby was German literature. He gave us a much broader picture of the literary achievements of our country than we were able to get during our school lessons. Frequently he, Wilhelm, and I read plays and dramas, each taking a different part. He also included visits to Berlin theatres in our program.

Our religous education up to our Confirmation was in the hands of Pastor Konrad of Berlin. A very forceful character with a striking resemblance to Martin Luther, both physical and psychological, he spoke straight from the heart, sometimes berating his parishioners unmercifully. He had been the favorite preacher of my grandmother. Though he was of rather poor health and was hampered by a clubfoot, Dr. Konrad came out to Potsdam once a week. He taught us religion in a very healthy and natural way without trying to be too philosophical about it. He was a great psychologist and demanded complete honesty. Sometimes he would suddenly embarrass us with such questions as: "How many times have you lied today, Prince Louis?" We all liked and admired him.

One fact easily emerges from the description of our new bourgeois life in Potsdam: the golden cage of imperial days had given way to voluntary self-seclusion. After the November revolution my family went into retirement, so to speak. Our new situation was, however, recognized reluctantly as *de facto* only, not *de jure*. We children thus found ourselves in an atmosphere of resentment directed against all the forces within and without that had actually and presumably led to the downfall of our dynasty. No less than our enemies of World War I were all those who had brought about the ostracized republic. Only people who openly expressed their adherence to our family and to the old Germany were "eligible" to come into contact with us.

I was slowly beginning to realize that we were living in a vacuum completely cut off from the big stream of events. Though our home was hardly twenty miles from the capital, such a condition was possible because of the peculiar atmosphere of Potsdam, whose population was composed to a large extent of pensioned army officers and government officials. Most of these people resented the new state of affairs just as wholeheartedly as did their former ruling house.

We traveled to Berlin only very rarely. One winter we attended a dancing course at the home of old Admiral Count von Platen. The lessons took place every Saturday afternoon. At three o'clock we would crowd into an old brake dragged by the old horse which survived the dissolution of our magnificently stocked stables. At the railway station one of us had to buy the tickets. This was at the height of the inflation. I always tried to get Wilhelm to perform this duty, because I was never able to bring back the correct change and had to spend the whole trip to Berlin counting and recounting bundles of notes stuffed into my pockets.

Besides lanciers, gavottes, and minuets, we were taught to dance a very mild sort of waltz and even a foxtrot. Our partners were Platen's five children and a few other boys and girls of Berlin families. It took us about twenty minutes to walk from Potsdamer station in Berlin to the Princesses' Palace where the Platen family lived on the second floor. Only in very rare cases would Ditfurth hire a taxi. On the whole we liked these expeditions to the capital because they constituted a welcome interruption of our eventless Potsdam life. But aside from the traffic on the Budapester Street or Unter den Linden and on the Potsdamer Platz before the railway station we saw nothing of Berlin, nor did we come in direct contact with the Berliners.

Chapter Ten

Valdivia to the Rescue

(1921)

IT WAS *El teniente coronel* Don Luis Ruiz de Valdivia who penetrated our Potsdam seclusion and successfully broke the shell which was threatening to obliterate my individuality.

Valdivia had been a widower for ten years. He had no children. From the first moment we met he not only became genuinely interested in the young Prussian Prince who was infatuated to such a high degree with his native Spain but soon felt a paternal love and responsibility for me. With his vast experience in all walks of life he immediately sensed my situation and decided to do something about it.

Several circumstances came to his aid. One was the fact that he belonged to a neutral nation which had shown a very friendly attitude towards Germany during the war. The second, almost more important, was his military profession and rank. Ditfurth, who as a rule distrusted foreigners, welcomed my contact with this Spanish officer. He knew about Valdivia's excellent record at my grandfather's court and later on during the war, which earned him the Iron Cross, First Class—an honor hardly ever bestowed on officers of a nation not allied with Germany.

After the first visit which Valdivia paid us in an official capacity to present me with the small library of choice Spanish books on orders of his supreme commander, King Alfonso XIII, he was our luncheon guest from time to time. Everybody liked the elderly gentleman with his emphatic gestures and the loud voice in which he pronounced German words with a typical Spanish accent in spite of the fact that he had lived in Germany since 1913. I always improved the occasion to show off. Not a German word would leave my mouth from the moment I received my new Spanish friend at the door until the moment he left.

Valdivia, after the first few visits, realized that my education, while excellent in many respects, was mostly theoretical and hopelessly out of step with the march of time. It badly needed the counterbalance of practical experience. This could be achieved only by dragging me out of my Potsdam retreat into the broad stream of life flowing in near-by Berlin.

He was too much of a diplomat to communicate his impressions to my tutor, who most probably would have been deadly offended by such criticism. The Spanish military attaché found a more subtle way to reach his goal. He told us he was a great admirer of music, especially of the great German composer Beethoven, and that he devoted most of his free evenings to attending concerts or operas. He said he fully realized that Ditfurth was chained down to his job of running our household and supervising our education. He, Valdivia, would be only too glad to take me to a concert or an opera occasionally to broaden my general education. He even convinced my tutor that such cultural excursions would be extremely useful.

Saturday seemed to be the only convenient day. It was finally agreed that Valdivia should meet me at the Potsdamer Bahnhof in Berlin. Ditfurth said he would take the risk of letting me travel alone from Potsdam to Berlin! My joy was extreme, as was my impatience for the great day to arrive. The event had to be postponed several times, because my tutor did not think the operas billed for the next few Saturdays were suitable for his pupil. He finally consented that the charming *Tales of Hoffman* by Jacques Offenbach was the right choice.

I had my first ride on a subway when Valdivia, after meeting me at the station, first took me to his apartment in the Borough of Wilmersdorf. Here he had prepared an excellent supper for his fourteen-year-old guest, who enjoyed these luxuries as something quite unknown in his Spartan retreat in Potsdam.

A taxicab brought us down to the opera. The fifteen-minute drive through the brightly lighted streets was exciting in itself. Valdivia seemed completely at home in the opera. Everybody, beginning with the stately doorman, greeted him. He had taken seats in the front row of the parquet directly behind the conductor. It was still rather early. The musicians were coming in one by one. They all greeted Valdivia. Many people in the audience, too, came to shake hands or to bow or wave to him.

"You are the center of attention here," I remarked to my host admiringly.

"You see," he replied, "I have been coming to this place almost every night for more than fifteen years. They call me the music attaché. I believe I have earned this title much more honestly than that of military attaché. Believe it or not, I am an anti-militarist. My professional colleagues often are very dull people. I'd rather associate with artists and intellectuals."

The lights went out and the conductor climbed into his seat.

"That's Leo Blech," Valdivia whispered. "He was your grandfather's last Royal Opera conductor. He is one of the best I have ever heard."

Valdivia had certainly not exaggerated. During the first intermission Valdivia suggested we visit Blech backstage.

"I told him I would bring you here tonight," he said. "I am sure he will be glad to meet you."

We were admitted through a special entrance where a sign read, *"Eintritt verboten"* ("Entry forbidden"). After climbing a few flights of stairs Valdivia knocked at a door marked Office of the Chief Conductor. A cheerful voice called, "Come in." It came from a small figure sitting at a simple desk in shirt sleeves, collarless, with a glass of beer in front of him.

"Guten Abend, Herr Professor," exclaimed Valdivia. "I want you to meet a young admirer of your wonderful art."

"I hope you do not mind my informal attire, my dear Herr von Valdivia," Blech said. "But I must put on a new collar after each act. It's so hot down in that orchestra pit." Then, turning to me: "I am very happy to welcome you here in our opera. You are the first member of your family to visit us after that unfortunate November 9. I quite understand your family's reluctance to visit a place which belonged to them and with which they were so closely connected. We are trying our best to keep up the high tradition which won this house world fame under the personal protection of your grandfather. Please come and visit us at any time and feel perfectly at home here. I could not imagine a better musical companion for you than Colonel Valdivia our *Musikattaché*. Will you please excuse me now, gentlemen. I can't very well conduct the second act without a collar. If I did, the Berliners would say, 'Old Man Blech has gone completely crazy.' Well, many thanks for looking me up and *Auf Wiedersehen.*"

This visit to the Prussian State Opera was to be followed by innumerable others. The advent of Hitler unfortunately severed my ties with that great institution of real German culture.

On our way back to the station Valdivia said out of the clear sky: "I tell you one thing, Prince. Some monarchists are sometimes the worst enemies of the monarchy. Especially since the revolution, I have made it a point to associate with people from the extreme left to the extreme right regardless of their political beliefs. I like people for what they are and not for some silly theories or ideologies they cling to. Though Berlin no longer possesses a society in the old sense of the word, there are lots of interesting people living in this city who are worthwhile to meet and to know a little better. Music is always a great tie to bind together individuals in every walk of life.

"Next time I shall take you to one of the Sunday rehearsals of the Philharmonic Orchestra and introduce you to Aunt Luise—some also call her Queen Luise because she completely dominates concert life in Berlin. She is a great friend of mine. I believe she is at least a hundred years old. But nobody would suspect it. Her full name is Frau Luise Wolff. She runs the famous concert impresario firm of Wolff & Sachs.

"Her husband was the founder of the famous Philharmonic concerts which at first were given in a beer garden. She really knows everybody in the musical world. These concerts take place about twice a month. The connoisseurs attend the Sunday morning dress rehearsals. The snobs go to the Monday evening performances. The Sunday concerts start at eleven thirty in the morning. Afterwards we can have a bite at my home with occasionally a few guests.

"Frau Wolff usually gives an exellent luncheon party in honor of the soloist or conductor of the day. I am sure she'll be tickled to have both of us.

"I hope," he added with a little contempt in his voice, "that your almighty tutor at Potsdam won't object to this new strategic plan. On my next visit to Cecilienhof I shall tell him that it is even more convenient than the Saturday arrangement because it will get you back home before sundown and Ditfurth won't have to worry lest you get lost in the dark! I still don't understand why in the world he would let you see the *Tales of Hoffman* and not *Bohème* or *Madame Butterfly*. I was certain he would object to Offenbach because of his Jewish ancestry. The human being is a great puzzle. Isn't it?"

Meanwhile we had arrived on the platform. With a great Spanish *abrazo* (embrace) I departed from my new mentor. Sitting in the train and looking out into the dark landscape I felt that a new world had been opened to me.

During his next visit Valdivia very adroitly expounded the advantages of my proposed Sunday visits to Berlin.

"Opera music is one thing and concert music quite another," he argued. "Prince Louis Ferdinand should get acquainted with both sides of the picture." Skillful old diplomat that he was, he failed to mention that he intended to acquaint me not only with acoustical waves but also with human individuals the very sight of whom would have angered my tutor. The plan was approved without argument.

My concert season was to begin with a program entirely dedicated to Ludwig van Beethoven, Wilhelm Furtwängler conducting the Coriolan Overture and the Fifth and Sixth Symphonies.

Valdivia and I met at the entrance to the venerable concert building. The same friendly attitude of the staff towards my Spanish friend obtained here as at the opera. When we reached a door labeled Box No. 2, Valdivia opened the door and pushed me inside ahead of himself. Its eight seats were still empty with the exception of one which was occupied by Luise Wolff, our hostess. With her black hair and careful makeup she looked middle-aged. She was of small stature and rather stout. She stretched out both her hands, pulling Valdivia and me towards her.

"Please come and sit down, both of you, next to me," she exclaimed with a musical voice which betrayed her Austrian origin.

"My dearest Aunt Luise," Valdivia replied just as fervently, "I want to entrust my young friend from Potsdam to your special care. I am convinced you will introduce him to all the secrets of the musical world, which you so marvelously and completely dominate."

"Nothing would give me a greater pleasure," she answered with obvious sincerity. "I have known this young man's great-great-grandfather and practically every member of his family. I shall certainly obey your command to the letter, my dear Valdivia. Our young friend shall be my guest from now on as long as I run this show."

The old lady kept her word until the day the Nazis snatched her cherished concerts from her clever hands and finally closed her business up altogether. Frau Luise Wolff died in 1935 not only of old age but also of a broken heart.

With the ease of one who has always lived in the great world, Frau Wolff introduced me to her other guests who were arriving one after another: "This is my daughter, Frau Stargardt; this is Herr Georg Bernhard, chief editor of the *Vossische Zeitung;* this is Herr Theodor Wolff, chief editor of the *Berliner Tageblatt;* this is Herr Professor Albert Einstein; and this is His Excellency the French Ambassador, Monsieur de Margerie." She made the introductions as if we were at my grandfather's court. Before Furtwängler appeared on the stage the entire Box No. 2 was filled, mostly with elderly gentlemen. All seemed to know each other quite well.

Accompanied by thunderous applause a tall, lanky figure dressed in cutaway with gray trousers appeared on the stage. He first bowed in the direction of the box of Frau Wolff, then, after a short pause, raised his baton. Throughout the two hours of heavenly music he held both the members of the orchestra and his vast audience spellbound. I heard someone sobbing next to me. It was Valdivia, with tears running down his cheeks.

After the concert I remarked to my friend that my Potsdam tutor would probably get a stroke if he knew that I had met the French Ambassador as well as Theodor Wolff and Georg Bernhard. The latter were journalists of international reputation. Both were staunch supporters of the Weimar Republic and favored collaboration with France. Both were continuously feuding with the organs of the right.

Valdivia observed: "It is none of my business as to whom Frau Wolff invites to her box. These people may not like the monarchy, but they like Beethoven. That vindicates them in my eyes."

Commenting on the fact that Wolff and Bernhard were Jews, he continued: "Most Jews are great lovers of music. Moreover, the Jews have played a very important part in the development of your country. Your own family for centuries has been on the best of terms with them. You have only to remember Frederick the Great, who counted among his closest friends the philosopher and banker, Moses Mendelssohn. Take your grandfather, who had Albert Ballin as one of his closest advisers. Many Jewish families, like the Mendelssohns, the Friedländers, the Oppenheims, the Schwabachs, and numerous others were knighted by your ancestors. These Jews, many of whom have embraced the Christian faith, I regard as among the best citizens of Germany. They have worked for their country and love it perhaps more sincerely than many other Germans. You'll meet a lot more of them. I am sure you will like them and profit by their profound culture and their keen intellects. It was a disastrous mistake of my own country to persecute the Jews during the days of the Inquisition. Many of our best elements were killed or left Spain. The decline of our political power and whole civilization must be largely attributed to that fact."

After the advent of Hitler's Third Reich, Valdivia visited Germany two or three times. I used to remind him of the little discussion we had had about the Jews.

"I am absolutely in despair," he answered time and again. "I cannot understand what has happened to the German people since this Hitler came into power. During all the years I lived in Germany I never noticed any real anti-Semitism. I think it is all inspired and commanded from above. They want some scapegoat. Maybe you and your relations will be next after the Jews have been liquidated."

In 1942 the dear old friend made a special trip to Cadinen, our East Prussian Estate, to implore Kira and me to leave Germany if possible. More than anybody else he foresaw the total collapse of Germany.

When Valdivia was recalled to Spain on reaching the age limit of sixty in 1926, I wrote a letter to Hindenburg, then President of the German Republic, asking him to have Valdivia retained in Berlin.

I received a very courteous letter with Hindenburg's personal signature advising me that he also would love to see Valdivia keep his post. But according to international protocol it was up to His Majesty the King of Spain to decide that question, and not the German Reichspräsident. The letter was mailed to Potsdam in an official envelope. It was discovered by Ditfurth. Though I tried to conceal its contents I finally had to show it to him. He flew into a tantrum. How had I dared ask a favor from the head of the Weimar Republic, which my family so disliked? I had thought it most natural to write the old field marshal whom I considered a dear and old friend of our family. As a retired general he had never failed to call on us at Cecilienhof whenever he came to Potsdam. I was unable to understand why my feelings should change towards our old friend after he had been elevated to the highest position in postwar Germany.

But to return to my education in music appreciation:

For three years until the day I left high school I met Valdivia regularly in Berlin. These monthly or semimonthly excursions remained my only outlet into the big world. Our meetings, at first restricted to concert halls and his own apartment, were gradually transferred to the residences of his friends. As he had predicted, Frau Wolff invited us to her home, a large apartment where she gave luncheons regularly after the Sunday morning concerts. She always had interesting guests. One day I would sit next to a famous musician or opera star, the next time with a celebrated physician or writer. At her house I later met Louis Lochner, who became one of my most intimate friends. All these people from different strata of life, profession, nationality, and race had a common bond in their great love for the queen of all arts.

Under the clever guidance of my Spanish mentor and with the generous help of his friends, mainly "Queen Luise," I became almost imperceptibly a part of the circles which to a large extent shaped and influenced the atmosphere of the capital of Germany in the 1920's. This atmosphere can be termed as liberal, intellectual, and international.

Thus I began slowly to shake off the peculiar atmosphere of my Potsdam surroundings, which turned mainly towards the past. As a consequence, the rift between me and my home environment became more and more pronounced. I decided that, fully recognizing the changed conditions, I would try to lead a decent and happy life as a private citizen, uninfluenced by historical background or political circumstances. Thanks to Valdivia, I was making contacts which no other member of my family had made. I was oblivious of the fact that my Spanish friend was following a twofold purpose. On one hand he was doing everything possible to broaden my outlook on life and the world at large. On the other hand he was doing his best to "sell" me to this very world he was putting me in contact with. He was of course much too clever ever to let me get an inkling of this second purpose. It was only after he left Berlin for good that I found this out for myself.

I was also a frequent guest of the Spanish Ambassador, Don Pablo Soler. The Spanish Embassy was the first foreign mission I ever visited. I was received with great cordiality and enjoyed the typical Spanish hospitality. As Valdivia's "assistant" and because of my personal relations with the King of Spain, I was almost considered a member of the ambassadorial family. This intimate connection was publicly demonstrated during a religious ceremony at the Catholic cathedral in commemoration of Queen Maria Cristina of Spain. The Mass for the Dead was celebrated by Papal Nuncio Eugenio Pacelli, now Pope Pius XII. I had been officially invited by the Spanish Ambassador to attend and had also been delegated to represent my grandfather as chief of our family. The whole diplomatic corps and the German Government were present. As the only foreigner I was asked to sit with the Spanish Ambassador and his staff next to the altar.

As time went on I became acquainted with the majority of the Latin American diplomats. Either Valdivia or Soler invited them to their homes, especially the Argentines and Chileans. It was not until the end of my student days that I came into contact with the diplomatic representatives of the United States. Ambassador Frederick M. Sackett was the first one I met. In those days I was still exclusively sold on the Spanish world!

Chapter Eleven

Spain Beckons

(1925)

B OTH VALDIVIA and I had decided that I was to visit Spain as soon
as possible. I tried to get my family's permission for the trip, but
they argued I was not mature enough for such an important venture. They also feared that an experience of this sort might distract me
from my school work. The six weeks of summer vacation would have
sufficed for an excursion into my "dreamland." But I was unable to talk
them into giving their consent.

To appease my impatience my family promised me a trip to Spain
provided I passed the high-school finals successfully. My dear old Spanish conspirator took charge of the negotiations with the Spanish court.
Early in 1924, I received an invitation from my godfather to visit him
in the spring of 1925.

My mother, who was just as travel-minded as her second son, was
eager for a journey abroad. With the exception of a few visits to Holland
she had not left the country since the beginning of World War I. As she
had previously traveled all over Europe, especially France and Russia, as
well as India, she felt like a bird in a cage. It was decided that she, Wilhelm, and I were first to travel to Tenerife. After that I was to proceed
to Spain, accompanied by our tutor, for a three-week sojourn, after
which I was to meet Mama and Wilhelm at Bilbao for the return trip.
I had desperately hoped that Valdivia might be my chaperon. Unfortunately he could not leave his post for so long a time.

The final examinations at the Realgymnasium went off very smoothly.
I was excused from the oral examinations because the written tests had
been satisfactory.

My parents—my father had been permitted to return from exile while we were students at the Realgymnasium—attended our graduation and sat in the front row with Director Wüllenweber and the Board of Education representative who had supervised the examination.

The exercises consisted chiefly of a musical program which included a Beethoven trio in which I played the violin and a festival overture composed by my ancestor, Frederick the Great. The exercises took place in the Barberini Palace. I considered our little concert, into which we put all we could offer as dilettantes, as a harmonious final chord for the melody of my high-school days.

Our departure was set for April 1, 1925, when the liner *Cap Norte,* on which we were to be guests, was to sail from Hamburg bound for Buenos Aires. It was scheduled to call at Santa Cruz de Tenerife to discharge and take on passengers.

I was almost beside myself with joy and anticipation. My relatives united in a conspiracy to play an "April fool" trick on me while en route to our port of embarkation. I was handed a telegram, signed, "The Chief Master of Ceremonies of His Majesty the King of Spain," which stated that His Majesty would greet me at La Coruña, the first Spanish port of call. The prescribed dress for the ceremony would be a frock coat, regardless of the hour of the day. I burst with pride and showed the telegram to everybody. My friend Valdivia, who had boarded the same train to see me off in Hamburg, was promptly initiated into the secret. He played along for a while but finally put me wise. He did not like the idea that his protégé and his love for Spain should be made fun of. But I certainly had that ribbing coming to me.

The weather was fine until we reached the Bay of Biscay. Then, however, most of us had to pay tribute to Neptune.

There were only a few other passengers, mostly Germans, in our cabin class. I was most eager to meet an Argentine couple I had detected among the passengers, in order to try my Spanish out on them. But Ditfurth would not have it. Especially after dinner I was bored stiff, having always to sit at the same family table.

One evening, however, I decided to break away. I ate my dinner a little faster than usual. Noting that the Argentine couple had also finished their meal, I asked Mama's permission to go upstairs to reserve a table. It was not really necessary to make a reservation, because the steward knew where we sat night after night. When I reached the salon, the Argentines were already at their table in another corner of the salon. I walked up to them and introduced myself in the best Spanish I could muster. The tall, good-looking man, a physician, promptly invited me to sit with him and his wife, who was short but pretty and extremely smartly dressed.

On the fifth day out we entered the harbor of La Coruña. I was standing on the bridge, where I met my first "native" Spaniard, the pilot. He was a tall, husky fellow whose fingernails were anything but clean. Wilhelm claimed that after meeting the first genuine Spaniard, I refused to clean my fingernails for the next few days.

The boat anchored in the middle of the bay. A small motor launch took us to the pier. Wilhelm, who was a better athlete, jumped ashore first. I looked at him furiously for having dared to touch the sacred soil of "my" Spain before I was able to do so. I felt deeply offended and hardly spoke to him for the rest of the day.

I felt so elated at having reached my goal that I shut my eyes to any details that might detract from the halo with which I had surrounded Spain. Wilhelm and Dico took pleasure in pointing out that "there seemed to be a lot of dirt around the place, that there were so many beggars, that conditions as a whole were of course much better in Germany." I bit my tongue in rage.

In Lisbon, I had my first contact with a newspaperman, although I did not know that I was being interviewed. The *Cap Norte* was anchoring in the middle of the Tajo River. On the little steamboat which served as a tender I got talking to a Portuguese gentleman who spoke fairly good Spanish. He seemed deeply interested, and I was delighted to answer his questions. When we returned to the boat after a whole day of sightseeing, the captain with a broad smile handed me a copy of a Lisbon evening paper with a two-column article about the "Democratic Prussian Prince."

Before leaving the ship at Santa Cruz de Tenerife, I went up to the bridge to say good-by to the captain and to the other officers, with all of whom we had made friends during the nine-day trip from Hamburg. I was just having a delightful chat, wishing everybody Godspeed, when

Ditfurth appeared, almost breathless, and in a commanding voice ordered me to come down at once to the smoking room and join the rest of the party.

"Don't you see that I am taking leave of the captain of the ship, and haven't you told me yourself that's the customary thing to do?" I said, enjoying his discomfiture.

"Please hurry up," he urged, "we are in a very embarrassing situation. The governor of the Island of Tenerife has arrived to welcome your mother and you two boys. He has several aides with him. But they do not speak anything but Spanish. You are the only one who can save the situation."

"I am glad that after all these years you admit that my Spanish is good for something at least," I said so loudly that everybody on the bridge could hear me. This triumph was perhaps somewhat cheap, but my pent-up resentment of my tutor had reached the boiling point! He never again heckled me about my Hispanomania.

After ten restless days spent on the beautiful Island of Tenerife, the day for going to Spain finally came with the arrival of the steamer *Cap Polonio,* in those days the pride of the German Merchant Marine. With its 23,000 tons it was the largest German ocean liner and by far the smartest. Neither the *Columbus* nor the *Bremen* and the *Europa* of the North German Lloyd existed at that time. The *Cap Polonio* was the favorite ship of the South Americans, especially the Argentine aristocracy.

It was the peak of the traveling season from South America to Europe. Every stateroom was occupied. I was installed on an officer's cot. Ditfurth had to share his room with the purser.

A new world opened up before me. The boat was filled with more than a thousand dark-eyed human beings who talked incessantly and temperamentally with loud voices and expansive gestures. Children were running around the decks, laughing, yelling, and crying. The scent of rich French perfumes was hanging in the air.

Before I left her, my mother to my great delight had asked Herr Richard Kroogmann, one of Hamburg's most distinguished merchants, and his wife to look after me. "King Richard," as he was called, promised my mother he would keep a good eye on me. During dinner that night at the captain's table he said to me: "Now, Prince Louis, if I were you

I should do exactly as I pleased. I'll keep Ditfurth busy, so don't worry about him," he added with a shrewd smile. He kept his word. During the three-day trip I hardly caught a glimpse of my tutor.

I was enchanted by the South American atmosphere of the boat. All the best-known names of Buenos Aires society, such as Santamarina, Unzué, Alvear, Velar de Irigoyen, Achával, and many others were represented. Though I had practically been a teetotaler until then, I was treated with champagne and *aperitivos* at all hours of the day and night. I never went to bed before three or four o'clock in the morning, a thing that had never happened to me before. I could speak Spanish to my heart's desire.

I had gotten a real taste of the New World concentrated on a few square feet of an ocean liner. The jovial, democratic way of all these people, who seemed to have a natural dislike for formality, was most congenial to me.

Never afterwards in my life have I enjoyed three days as intensely as this trip from Tenerife to Spain on the *Cap Polonio*.

Chapter Twelve

Guest of Alfonso XIII

(1925)

WHEN I left the liner at Portugalete, with the band playing the old Prussian march "Fridericus Rex," I received a hearty cheer from my new friends who were standing at the railing clasping hands and yelling: "See you soon in Buenos Aires."

It was obvious that this time I was my godfather's guest. A smart naval launch flying the Spanish war flag was waiting alongside. I was followed by the commandant of the port, who had welcomed me on the *Cap Polonio* in the name of His Majesty the King. As a farewell, the beautiful ship sounded her deep siren three times. It was difficult for me to control my emotion. Little did I know then that only a year and a half later I would sail on this same vessel on a glorious trip from Buenos Aires to Hamburg.

At the pier I was greeted by two gentlemen, one in civilian clothes, the other in uniform. They turned out to be the *Gobernador Civil* and the *Gobernador Militar* of the Province of Biscay. This procedure, to my dismay, was later on repeated during my whole trip through Spain. We were driven to near-by Bilbao in an official car. Ditfurth, who had resumed his duties of chaperon and looked more solemn and important than ever, admonished me from time to time to be more serious and live up to the situation.

When we arrived at Madrid by overnight sleeper, I was greeted at the station by a middle-aged gentleman in uniform with a long sword dragging alongside. "I am Colonel Obregón," he said in fluent German with somewhat of a southern German accent. "By order of His Majesty the King I am to report to Your Royal Highness and to be at your disposal as long as you stay in this country. I am to welcome you in the name of the King, who at present is residing in Sevilla. His Royal Highness, the Príncipe de Asturias, would have loved to greet you at the station but asked to be excused as he is slightly indisposed. He will welcome you, however, at the palace. If Your Royal Highness so commands, we shall proceed to the royal palace forthwith."

Why on earth did my dear godfather pick this Frankfurt-born German in the uniform of a Spanish colonel to be my watchdog while in Spain, I wondered during the two-minute drive to the palace. My tutor beamed with delight. He had found a kindred soul in Colonel Obregón. Now I have two guides of the same pattern at my coattails, I thought. A feeling of dismay gripped my heart.

When our car entered the huge doors of the palace the sentries presented arms, an honor I had not received since the November days of 1918. At the top of the huge main stairs stood a young man about my age. His face was fair, with blond hair and blue eyes. He was elegantly dressed in a light gray suit.

"Welcome to Spain," he said, giving me a hearty embrace. It was Alfonso's oldest son, the Prince of Asturias, known as Alfonsito in the family circles of international royaldom.

"Papa told me to take care of you and show you the sights of this part of our country until you go down to meet him at Sevilla. He is there with Mama and my sisters and brothers."

Alfonsito fulfilled his task beautifully in spite of his ailment, which bothered him almost constantly. He suffered from hemophilia, inherited from his mother's family of Hesse.

Passing through endless galleries, the walls of which were covered with priceless tapestries, my cousin showed me to my quarters. They were situated in the northern part of the palace and consisted of a suite of half a dozen huge rooms with a beautiful outlook on the Sierra de Guadarrama.

"In about two hours, after you have freshened up and had breakfast, I shall take you to my grandmother," he said. "She wants to see you as soon as possible." His grandmother was the dowager Queen Maria Cristina, who also lived at the palace and held her own court in her son's absence. The relation between my godfather and his mother was a very cordial and tender one. This Austrian archduchess had steered Spain after her husband's death through the troubled waters of the Spanish-American War and the collapse of the once mighty colonial empire of her adopted country. Everybody gave her credit for having saved the throne for her son, the infant king, which otherwise would probably have been lost.

During breakfast, which I had alone with Dico, he asked me why I looked so depressed.

"I am not used any more to royal palaces; you have made a bourgeois of me," I answered curtly.

While I was taking a bath, the Spanish servant came rushing into the bathroom, exclaiming, "His Majesty the King is calling from Sevilla and wants to speak to you." Without even seizing a towel I rushed to the telephone, which was a rather old-fashioned model fastened to the wall. My voice quivering with excitement, I shouted into the phone in Spanish, "This is Louis Ferdinand speaking."

"How are you, Luis, did you get to Madrid all right? Is Alfonsito taking good care of you? How do you like the A.D.C. I sent you?"

I was hardly able to reply when my godfather went on to ask, "How are things in your country? Who'll be elected president?"

I answered that the outlook was none too bright and that there was a certain unrest caused by the sudden death of President Fritz Ebert.

"*Qui vivra verra,*" my godfather commented philosophically, then continued:

"Ena (Queen Victoria Eugenia) and I hope to see you down here in a week or so. I'm sorry I can't be with you, but my king business keeps me here for the moment. I hope you'll feel at home. Good-by, my godson."

"*Adios, padrino,*" I shouted back. This telephone conversation completely restored my mood. The voice of my adored godfather had sounded as friendly and reassuring as if we had known each other since I was born. Still undressed, I strutted into Ditfurth's room, saying: "I just had a long chat with my godfather the King of Spain. He asked about you (here I lied) and sends you his royal greetings." Next I communicated my happiness to Manolo, the servant, whom I called Señor Sanchez after learning his family name.

My manner of addressing him almost caused a small palace revolution.

Ditfurth told me that the chief master of ceremonies, Count del Grove, had let him know through the assiduous Obregón that I was disrupting the discipline of the household, in that it was contrary to court etiquette to call a servant Señor and by his family name. Dico implored me to stop these superdemocratic habits.

The next time I met the count, a strutting old Castilian grandee with a white mustache, I expressed my regret at having caused such a grave incident but added that I failed to understand why I should change my habits even though they might appear a bit revolutionary. Later I told the story to my godfather, who had a hearty laugh.

To my relief I could leave both Dico and Obregón behind when Alfonsito took me to his granny. This was to be an intimate family call.

The queen mother was a lovely-looking old lady in her seventies. Her body was tiny, frail, and slightly bent. Her whole demeanor was extremely aristocratic. Her face showed the characteristic features of the Hapsburgs, an aquiline nose and a slightly protruding lower lip. She embraced and kissed me affectionately on both cheeks, without a trace of the stiffness of Austria's imperial court.

"Come and sit down here next to me, Lulu," she said in gracious Viennese German when she noticed my embarrassment. "How are your parents and how is your dear grandfather, whom I have not seen for so long a time? And how is our mutual friend Luis Valdivia? Couldn't you bring him along?"

"I did my best to persuade him," I replied, "but he said he must stick to his work. He always sings your praise and says he owes his whole career to the queen mother."

"Don't believe the old liar," Aunt Maria Cristina joked. "But he is a first-rate officer and has a marvelous record. He loves music, I know. So do I, by the way. Unfortunately, this is not the concert season. As to the opera house, it has been under reconstruction now for several years but never seems to get finished. It takes a lot of time to get things done in this country. They always say *mañana*. But what can one do about it? It's impossible to change the character of a single individual, much less of a whole people. They take life much easier here than up north, where both of us come from, though you Prussians believe we Austrians are too easy-going. But I have become used to it during all these years, and I love them just the way they are and have tried to make the best of it. I admire their irrepressible individualism, which is frequently misunderstood as a false pride. Here even the humblest illiterate beggar considers himself a *caballero* who does not have to bow to anybody."

I suddenly noticed that it was almost one o'clock and asked if I was not taking up too much of her time.

"It's perfectly all right," Aunt Maria Cristina said. "We shall have lunch in a minute. In my son's absence I always do the honors of the house."

The *comedor* (lunchroom) was richly furnished in sixteenth-century style. The walls were covered with valuable tapestries and several paintings by Velázquez and Murillo.

We were joined by Count del Grove, Colonel Obregón, Ditfurth, and the family doctor. The soup just had been served when the sounds of the "Blue Danube," played by a full-sized orchestra, flowed into the room. I looked at my hostess in pleased surprise. She whispered:

"Knowing that you are a music lover like myself, I prepared a little surprise for you. I have ordered the band of our palace guard to play for us every noon and every evening. I am very proud of them, and they love to play for us." Next to the menu I discovered a neatly printed musical program, consisting mostly of light music.

"At noon I always let them play the lighter genre as hors d'oeuvres," she continued. "In the evening we shall have something heavier. Originally this was a typical military band, but I have transformed it into a real symphony orchestra. I had the band leader study at the music academy.

"Tonight we'll have an American motion picture. I think it's to be 'The Gold Rush' with Charlie Chaplin. As people would not approve my going to a motion-picture theater in town—the emancipation of the female sex is only in its embryonic stage in our country, you must know —I have had one of the salons fixed up as a movie theater. It's perhaps a bit palatial, but it serves the purpose.

"Tomorrow evening, though, I shall have another little surprise for you in the musical field. I promised Alfonso that you should not be bored, even if you have to be satisfied with an old woman like me. I am responsible for your entertainment inside the palace, and Alfonsito will do his best to keep you busy outside."

In the company of Alfonsito I went on several excursions in a radius of about a hundred miles from Madrid. He and I would drive in his private car, a convertible Hispano-Suiza of the latest construction. We both sat in the back of the car, the chauffeur and a footman in front. The next car was occupied by Obregón, Count del Grove, and Ditfurth. Old Grove was, so to speak, Ditfurth's counterpart. He had been my cousin's tutor and now was in charge of his household. We were generally followed by another car, manned by the Guardia Civil, the famous Spanish state police, regarded as the armed body most loyal to the dynasty. The main roads as a whole were excellent, due to the initiative of my godfather who was an enthusiastic automobilist. He had helped to found the famous motorcar firm of Hispano-Suiza.

Alfonsito took me first to Toledo, the most Spanish town in Spain. We visited the cathedral, the Casa del Greco, and the Alcázar.

We also toured the old Castilian towns of Segovia and Avila, the latter famous for its enormous city walls. In Avila we were welcomed and shown about by the local bishop. When I saw that Alfonsito kissed his ring I followed his example. After our return to Madrid, I was severely reprimanded by Ditfurth, who bitterly reproached me for "betraying the cause of Protestantism" by this "humiliating" demonstration. When I saw Alfonsito again at dinner I told him about Dico's complaint. He mollified me by stating that he and everybody else had acknowledged the little gesture exactly for what it was meant to be.

"Tell your German gentleman that we Spanish believe in the proverb, 'When in Rome, do as the Romans do,' " he said.

In Alfonsito's company I also visited the grandiose and lugubrious Escorial and the gay palace of Aranjuez.

During these trips I became well acquainted with my young host. At first he was rather reserved, almost bashful, but after the first two days we became quite chummy. In spite of his precarious health Alfonsito enjoyed life. He had a very open mind and a keen power of observation. The mixture of English, Austrian, and Spanish blood was obvious both in his appearance and character. In his quiet, unassuming way he performed his duties as Crown Prince. He seemed to enjoy great popularity.

Eleven years later I met him in New York, where he was staying at the St. Moritz Hotel with very little money to live on, pathetic in his loneliness and disappointment.

In Madrid, Alfonsito took me to two bullfights. Many foreign visitors were deeply shocked at the cruelty associated with these fights. The horses, especially, with their intestines dragging in the sand presented a most horrible sight. But it is also true that the matadors often give a splendid spectacle of courage, and the combination of masculine vigor and artistic gracefulness displayed by these bull fighters is unique. It is worth while to attend a bullfight alone to enjoy the color scheme and the reaction of the public during the various stages of the spectacle.

In passing I may note that during my visit to Spain in 1951, I also saw a bullfight. This time the horses were protected by a thick blanket, which the horns of the bull penetrate only in very rare cases. I was told that this protection of the horses had been imposed by the Franco régime.

A recital by the famous Negro tenor, Roland Hayes, was the musical surprise which Aunt Maria Cristina had promised me. Hayes, who was a dinner guest, sang Lieder by Schubert, Schumann, and Brahms, and American folk songs. Mr. Hayes, who combined real culture with great modesty, was a living proof for the fact that art is international and in no way restricted to any race or color.

Though I thoroughly enjoyed the days at Madrid and the sightseeing program in Alfonsito's company, I was unable to move about freely. I felt the urge to get into direct contact with the man in the street. I communicated my wish to Obregón. At first he was quite embarrassed, pretending that it was definitely against all rules of court etiquette to let me walk about town all by myself. After consulting with higher quarters, however, he agreed that the two of us would take a walk so that I might come into direct contact with the *Madrileños*. Obregón was utterly conservative in his views and nursed a special dislike for anything transAtlantic, especially South American.

Came the day for my departure for Sevilla. As Alfonsito bade me farewell, he said:

"I'm sure you're going to like it down there. Everything is much gayer than up here in our gloomy Castile. I only warn you not to drink too many cold drinks. It is very warm down there. Most foreigners can't control their thirst and consequently suffer from a very vicious sort of diarrhea. Well, so long then, old boy. Give my love to Papa and Mama."

From the Sevilla station we drove to the Viejo Alcázar, a Moorish palace used by the royal family as their residence during their stay. The

King had come down here to spend the Holy Week, one of the greatest religious events in Catholic Spain.

I had hardly installed myself in my apartment, consisting of two large rooms with enormous windows looking out on a beautiful garden with palm trees, when a servant opened the door announcing simply, "His Majesty the King."

Next I heard a warm, "Good day, Luis, at last we meet personally."

My godfather was elegantly dressed in a light suit. He was tall, slim, and athletic. Though his face was not handsome, because of the protruding Hapsburg lower lip, it nevertheless had great charm. His light brown eyes had a very cordial and lively expression.

After an embrace in the best Spanish style, he showed me a telegram.

"I have just received this wireless from Berlin," he said. "Your countrymen have elected a new president—old *Feldmarschall* Paul von Hindenburg. There is great excitement everywhere because the Germans have chosen their greatest war hero for that position. The French seem to be especially jittery. Some even think that this means a new war. Personally I don't believe that nor does Primo de Rivera, my Prime Minister. I think the old gentleman will serve his country in peace just as loyally as he did during the war. Anyhow, we ought to let your mother know about this important event. I'll send her a cablegram." He wrote a message in perfect German, then continued:

"I heard all about your stay in Madrid. I am sure that Mama and Alfonsito have kept you pretty busy. I only hope that Obregón did not drag you through every church in town. I have never seen such an ardent Catholic in my life. Alfonsito has already told me by phone that you are not any too enthusiastic about him. But it's all my fault. I had chosen him because he is half German. I thought it would make everything easier for you. I didn't know you speak Spanish almost like a Spaniard. I should love to relieve Obregón, but that would break his heart. He really means awfully well. So I'm afraid you'll have to put up with him.

"You simply must see the cathedral of Sevilla, especially because it contains the grave of the great Christopher Columbus. Both Spain and Italy claim him as their citizen, but I don't think anybody knows his real origin. Obregón may take you to that historical place.

"Meanwhile, I suggest you accompany me to our new airport, otherwise you'll think Spain consists only of churches, which is true to a certain extent but not entirely. On our return you will meet the rest of the family. Let's go."

He took me by the arm, led me through the courtyard into the garden, and jumped into a huge open Hispano-Suiza, taking the wheel himself. Used as I was to the little cavalcade of cars during my excursions with Alfonsito, I looked around but could not see any car following us.

"If they want to bump me off, they are welcome to it," the King remarked with a chuckle. "They have already tried several times to get rid of me." My godfather's courage was greatly admired by his subjects. In one instance he had knocked his assailant down with his horse and handed him over to the police personally.

As he drove leisurely through the crowds, people greeted him by taking their hats off or shouting, *"Viva el Rey."*

"They are just having a good time. That's about all they do, especially during the Easter holidays," my host commented. "You'll soon find out for yourself that the Andalusians are about the gayest people in the world. They are always having a *fiesta* of some kind or other."

At the airport, which was quite new with some parts of it still under construction, we were greeted by several officers. We examined all the installations. I was impressed by my godfather's vast technical knowledge. I knew nothing about airplanes and flying, which later was to become my most beloved sport. It was the first time that I came into contact with aviators.

After the inspection we all sat in a big circle at the officers' mess, built in pure Arabian style. All these young men treated their supreme commander like an older comrade. Dico would be deeply shocked, I thought to myself. But he was spared this humiliating sight by having remained behind.

When we were about to depart I pleaded with the King to leave me there for an Andalusian feast.

"If you were a little bit older I certainly would let you stay here," he said. "But I am afraid they might kill you with too much hospitality. I like all these boys, but they are mad as hell, like all aviators." This statement was received by a noise which sounded like a protest but was really approval. In later years, after joining the ranks of those "madmen," I always had to think of these words and their aptness.

When we arrived before the Alcázar we were received by the rest of the family. I was greeted as though I were a member of the family. The Queen, Victoria Eugenia—Aunt Ena to me—was a beautiful, tall, blond lady, whose appearance immediately betrayed her Anglo-Saxon origin. To my great relief she addressed me in very fluent Spanish with only a slight English accent instead of using her own language which in those days would have been considerably difficult for me to speak. With her were three boys and two girls, all a few years younger than myself.

The high points of my five days stay at Sevilla were a visit to a country estate belonging to a Spanish grandee and an excursion down the Rio Guadalquivir on the torpedo boat *Bustamente* with the whole royal family.

The owner of the estate who was a well-known breeder of *toros* (bulls for fights), possessed a small bull-fight arena of his own where the young toros were tried out. The whole performance was nothing but an occasion for everybody to have a lot of fun.

My godfather as a typical Spaniard was a great bull-fight enthusiast and also performed in an amateur way. He knew how to kill a bull, though he did not practice this art in public as his ancestors had been required to do.

I could observe his popularity with the simple people, with whom he conversed in the most natural way without the slightest condescension. Naturally he was very popular with the clergy and the nobility. There was only one class he did not care for and which he neglected during his whole reign, the Spanish intellectuals. This class, small in numbers but rich in outstanding personalities, deeply resented that attitude and constituted a dangerous opposition which eventually became fatal to the Spanish throne. My godfather did not take these people very seriously and was bored by them. He was much more attracted by a bull fighter or a football champion or a simple peasant. He overlooked the fact that intellectual pride and vanity are even more sensitive than pride in physical merit and are just as easily hurt. As he possessed a keen mind himself, it would have been easy for him to win the sympathy of these circles. In this respect he resembled my own father, who unlike my grandfather always had a certain dislike for intellectuals, especially those of the professional type. But history has not been made by boxing champions or bull fighters or baseball players, though in their lifetime their popularity may never have been attained by any other type of individual.

At the fiesta I saw Dico helping himself abundantly to the cold lemonade which was being offered to the guests. The heat was terrific, and nobody could blame him for being thirsty. Possibly he had not been warned as I had been by my cousin. Our departure for Jerez de la Frontera, the home of the famous sherry wine, was to take place two days later.

The next morning my godfather announced with a little bit of triumph in his voice: "Your tutor has broken down completely. He won't be able to accompany you to Jerez. My court physician is looking after him. You will have to get along without him for a while. I suppose you are heartbroken, aren't you? If you don't mind I shall drive you to Jerez and hand you over to the Méritos. They make some of the best wine in the country. I believe you have already met Ricardo Mérito, the second son of the old Marqués del Mérito, at our embassy at Berlin. They want you to be their guest in Jerez and Córdoba as well.

"They are very charming people, but in one sense they are dangerous, I must warn you. When you visit their wine cellar it is their tradition to drink every newcomer, especially every foreigner, under the table. For hours you will have to taste their gorgeous wines. If you empty your glass it will be automatically refilled. It would be extremely tactless to refuse that. The only way to keep sober is to drink very slowly. As long as you have some wine in your glass they won't fill it up again. So if you do not want to be buried the very noon we get to Jerez, a procedure which is absolutely normal, remember this little trick of your well-meaning padrino."

The night before we left for Jerez, I met General Primo de Rivera at a gala performance given in honor of the royal family at the Sevilla opera house. My godfather introduced me to his Prime Minister, who by many was considered the Spanish dictator. He was a tall man in his late fifties, with gray hair and a look in his blue eyes which more than anything else betrayed a great sense of humor. His joviality was underscored by a somewhat Falstaffian *embonpoint*.

"Primo, do you think that I can let my godson go back to Germany with the new Reichspräsident they have?" Alfonso asked. "Had we not better keep him right here if Hindenburg should feel like starting a war?" he added with a teasing voice.

"I am not in the least worried, Señor," the general answered with a delightful Andalusian accent. "I do not see the slightest reason why the prince should not go back if he feels like it and does not prefer our Spanish girls and the Jerez wine to his Moselle, which would of course please me as a born Andalusian. But as far as the old field marshal is concerned, I believe he had enough with the last war."

Primo was the first of six dictators I was to meet in my life, at least up to now. He was by far the most human and the most gentleman-like of the lot, as far as my personal impressions were concerned.

The following morning we left for Jerez.

Again I sat on the front seat with my godfather driving his Hispano-Suiza. Obregón followed in another car. We fell into a discussion of the Prime Minister.

"I had to choose between him and chaos, which would have meant civil war," Uncle Alfonso said. "Our army, unlike the one trained by your ancestors, has always taken a very active part in the political life of Spain. You may say that soldiers ought to have nothing to do with politics, their only purpose being the defense of the country. But I hardly believe it is possible to get politics out of their system in this country.

"Anyhow, the army was thoroughly disgusted with the way the politicians were running Spain, and I cannot blame it for feeling that way. Perhaps you have already heard the term *caciquismo. Cacique* means Sioux Indian chief. Well, practically every village in Spain had its local politician who was running the community as a Red Indian chief would run his tribe. The whole country was in the grips of these little dictators, who were open to every kind of graft. The result was that practically nothing was being done in the way of road construction, railways, telephone communications, schools, and so forth. For the moment, at least, this rotten political system has been broken, and Primo is doing everything to clean up the administration.

"On the other hand, though, I know that this military dictatorship cannot last forever and that we must go back to a constitutional status.

Primo would never stand in the way between myself and my people. When the moment has come he will quit, I am quite sure. It all depends on when that moment will come. I believe it is still rather far off.

"Primo has dictatorial powers, certainly. Fortunately, he is such a balanced individual that he does not abuse them. He believes in the old principle, 'Live and let live.' He may have his little human weaknesses. But he is neither austere nor cruel. He thoroughly knows the mentality of his countrymen.

"From the viewpoint of modern civilization Spain is perhaps the most backward of the Western European countries. But my subjects are frightfully independent and individualistic. They stick to their old traditions, which they are very proud of. In their own typical way they are ardently religious. You will have noticed that the Catholic Church plays a very important part in the everyday life of the average Spaniard. It has always done so throughout the centuries, and I am convinced that it always will. Some of our intellectuals are inclined to be rather atheistic, but they form an unimportant minority.

"Though this country is practically a hundred per cent Catholic, I personally try to follow a course of religious and political enlightenment. I was brought up that way by my beloved mother and by my political teacher, the great Canalejas." He was silent for a few moments, musing, then continued:

"It is rather difficult, though, to follow a liberal course in Spain. You may have noticed yourself that the social differences are much sharper here than in your country. We almost completely lack a substantial middle class such as is the backbone of Germany. On the other hand, the largest percentage of our population consists of peasants who may not be highly educated nor progressive but who constitute a very wholesome element. Spain is essentially an agricultural country. The industrial proletariat, which is susceptible to radical influences, is still relatively small and limited to the industrial regions, especially Catalonia and the mining country of Estremadura.

"We must be very careful in our methods for modernizing our country, because it has remained practically untouched by the social upheaval created by the French Revolution. Do not overlook the fact that it was the Spaniards who were the first to break the power of Napoleon, at least in their own country.

"As a whole," he sighed, "my job is not quite as easy as you might have thought it to be, Luisito."

We had now reached Jerez and stopped in front of a huge white building. "This is the famous *bodega* of the Mérito family," the King remarked. We were met by the whole family, consisting of the old marqués, a gentleman in his early sixties, his daughter Angelita, and two sons, Ricardo and José, nicknamed Pepe, all in the twenties. Pepe was to play the part of cupid two years later by bringing Lily Damita into my life.

We entered the bodega, a huge barnlike structure. Along the walls hundreds of barrels of all sizes were piled up. In the middle, an open space was left for several tables covered with all kinds of hors d'oeuvres, including the biggest lobsters I have ever seen. This wine test was to be strictly a family affair.

"They never have any chairs for these functions," my godfather whispered into my ears. "If somebody gets tight he just drops on the floor. But you had better stick to my recipe."

The glasses were filled for the first time with the wonderful golden liquid known as sherry all over the world. The first glass was drunk to the health of His Majesty the King of Spain. It was promptly followed by a second one, dedicated to my health. In both cases a "bottoms up" could not be avoided.

A short inspection of the whole establishment was suggested by the owner, after which my godfather left for Cádiz to visit the naval base. The rest of us continued the test, which lasted until the late afternoon. Our party was joined by other guests, mostly relatives or close friends of the Méritos.

Among the late arrivals was Colonel Merry del Val, who became a sort of voluntary aide. He combined Andalusian gayety with Irish shrewdness and wit. His uncle had been the famous Cardinal Secretary of State under Pope Leo XIII. Obregón, who had arrived later during the day, kept in the background. Merry told me with a twinkle that the King had given him orders to take Obregón's place unofficially during my visit in Jerez.

Though I tried to heed my godfather's admonition, the combination of sherry and lobster cocktail brought my intestines into a turmoil.

At a dinner given by the Méritos the night before my departure, I delivered my first speech in Spanish. As a relative of the Spanish royal house it was my duty to propose a toast to King Alfonso and his family and also to express my gratitude to the Méritos for their hospitality. Cervantes, Don Quixote, and even Columbus had to serve as backstops for my address.

Our next goal was Granada. My "staff," consisting of Obregón and the driver, was augmented by Ditfurth, who looked healthy and rested. The next day was spent in visiting the Alhambra.

In contrast to the buoyant days in Sevilla and Jerez, where I had met a score of people, all equally interesting and agreeable, I now felt rather lonely. I was given no chance to meet the younger people and was almost glad when we took off for Córdoba two days later.

I fear I was a rather superficial and ungrateful sightseer. I have always been much more interested in the man in the street or the keeper of an ordinary village inn than in historic buildings, churches, palaces, or pictures. Life itself has always attracted me.

The two days at Córdoba were ample compensation for my loneliness in Granada. I was again a house guest of the Méritos, who had returned from Jerez to their main residence at Córdoba. Two nights later I boarded the special train which took the royal family to Madrid. Our party was met by the Archbishop of Madrid and the whole Spanish cabinet. An honor guard presented arms as the band played the "Marcha Real," the Spanish national anthem. King Alfonso told me later that it was a composition by Frederick the Great, who had dedicated it to King Carlos III of Spain. Both monarchs had a mutual admiration for each other, though they never met personally. Both believed in "enlightened absolutism."

Every member of the royal family walked up to the archbishop and kissed his ring. I passed a rather awkward moment not knowing whether to follow their example or not. I finally decided to act as a Protestant, merely bowing to the venerable figure from a respectful distance. This time Ditfurth was all smiles, applauding my "firmness."

The remaining days passed very quickly. Only four days remained before I had to catch the steamer *Sierra Morena,* en route from the Canary Islands with my mother and brother. My godfather decided that I should travel by car in order to see more of the countryside. He suggested I spend a night at Burgos, famous for its beautiful Gothic cathedral and its archbishop, Cardinal Benlloch, the family-confessor of the royal house. He was a true friend of my godfather's and advised him on many things.

My godfather said: "You can't possibly leave Spain without meeting this wonderful man. I am quite sure you will like him just as much as we do.

"It was nice to have you with us. I know you won't quite forget us, Luisito," he said when he kissed me good-by.

"Nunca, padrino" ("Never, godfather") was all I could answer in that moment. As I had to leave Madrid shortly after seven in the morning, he had asked me to come to his bedside before taking off. I was deeply touched by this simple gesture of warm affection.

The visit to the Spanish cardinal turned out to be one of the high spots of the whole trip. The archbishop of Burgos was at least six feet four inches tall. Diplomatically advised by Obregón, he saved me from any embarrassment about kissing his ring by shaking my hand vigorously.

Benlloch was a widely traveled man, especially in South America, where he had officially represented the King of Spain on some special mission. To Obregón's profound embarrassment, this prince of the church indulged in talking about such worldly topics as bullfights and pretty girls. He never even alluded to his own high office and to the important part he was playing as one of the chief representatives of the Spanish church. We got along so beautifully that I was asked by His Eminence to spend the night at his palace and not at the hotel. It was not until the next day that I was shown the beautiful Burgos cathedral.

The departure from the cardinal was exceedingly cordial and ended with a Spanish embrace. "Not quite according to the etiquette applicable in such cases," Obregón, who disapproved heartily of the cardinal's apparent worldliness, remarked sourly.

After stopovers in Bilbao and San Sebastián, I was driven down to Portugalete. The same navy launch I already knew from my arrival took me to the *Sierra Morena*. The Spanish interlude thus came to an end.

Chapter Thirteen

University Days

(1925–26)

"UNIVERSITAS Literarum"—such is the inscription in golden letters over the entrance to the University of Berlin. It had been originally designed as a palace for Prince Heinrich, second brother of Frederick the Great, by the noted Prussian architect Johann Baumann. Built in the neoclassic style, this three-story edifice in its simple dignity is perhaps the most beautiful building in Berlin. During my childhood I could see it across the Kaiser Franz Josef Platz directly opposite our Crown Prince's Palace from the rooms I occupied with my brother Wilhelm.

On a bright May day in 1925, I entered this venerable institution of learning with the firm purpose to earn a doctor's degree before I got through with my studies. Wonderful though my trip to Spain had been, I must confess that I had been looking forward to my return to Germany. I was longing to enjoy the freedom of an ordinary university student. It was not the romantic atmosphere of the famous comic opera *The Student Prince* that I was after. I had a strong aversion to student organizations whose members passed most of their time drinking and dueling. I felt the urge of studying for the sake of studying and to win an academic degree on the basis of my own personal effort, independent of inheritance or tradition.

Once during my high-school days I had felt like quitting and entering the merchant marine. My mother, with her excellent connections with seafaring circles, had made all sorts of inquiries and put me into contact with her friends of the North German Lloyd at Bremen. These experienced people finally convinced me that the profession of a mere sailor would not satisfy me. Fortunately, I followed their advice. My parents had great wisdom not to reject my plan from the very beginning but to let me find out for myself what suited me best.

When I finished high school I had no clear-cut idea as to what profession I wished to take up eventually. I only knew that I was not going to be either a professional soldier or a government official. My decision was supported by the fact that it would have been practically impossible to enter either profession under the Weimar Republic. Though the new regime in Germany had left us unmolested as far as our private citizenship was concerned, even restoring to us a large part of our personal fortune, it certainly distrusted us as far as politics were concerned.

This attitude became quite evident in connection with the Seeckt incident. In 1926 my brother Wilhelm had participated in the summer maneuvres of the *Reichswehr* as a civilian with the full knowledge of General Hans von Seeckt, chief of the German Army. My brother had only played the part of an observer. But the parties of the left used this episode to create a political crisis. Otto Gessler, the minister for defense, was asked in the Reichstag by the Social Democratic Party whether he knew anything about this "shameless" event. He denied and inquired of General von Seeckt. The general retorted that he had given the permission and that he considered it entirely his own affair, for which he took full responsibility. The controversy finally led to Seeckt's resignation. This incident once and for all spoiled my brother's hope to be an active officer in Germany. In Wilhelm's case Hitler inherited the republic's distrust and never permitted him to enter his army as an active officer. When World War II came Wilhelm was nevertheless drafted and died from wounds received on a battlefield in France. He had attained the rank of a first lieutenant of the reserve army.

I was seventeen and a half years old when I graduated from high school. There was no need to be in a hurry about a profession. The best thing was to mark time and grow a bit older. I hoped to work in some commercial field which would give me an opportunity to travel and bring me in touch with the great world outside the boundaries of my own country.

Economics appealed to me more than any other branch of learning. On entering the university I therefore chose political science as my major. I proudly had *Stud. rer. pol.* printed on my visiting card with the hope of changing it one day to *Dr. rer. pol.* (doctor of political science). My degree eventually turned out to be a *Dr. phil.* (Ph.D.) for reasons which I shall mention later.

From the first lecture, I noticed the almost radical difference between the atmosphere of the university and that of the high school. Until now I had been a pupil, subject to a strict discipline of following a fixed program. From now on I was a real *Student* enjoying the academic freedom for which the German universities are rightly famous, even today. I was free to choose my teachers and the subjects they were teaching, free to listen to what they taught, but also free to absent myself if I felt like staying away. I was free to express my feelings. If the professor's remarks pleased me I could express my satisfaction by tramping; if he displeased me I could scrape the floor with my feet.

The atmosphere of the University of Berlin differed greatly from that of other universities in that it was an institution to which students flocked in order really to learn something. To get a degree there they had to work very hard. If they wanted to have fun they went to universities in smaller towns where student life dominated. As Berlin was a cosmopolitan metropolis with several million inhabitants, university life outwardly passed almost unnoticed in the turmoil of the German capital. The student did not play any special role.

The university also had some student fraternities whose members fought duels and drank a lot of beer. But they were in the minority.

I religiously attended every class scheduled for me. I soon found out that I had a pronounced aversion for the lectures on law, also, that I had enrolled in too many courses. I spent most of the time of my first semester within the walls of the university, with the sun shining and the birds singing outside. I returned to Potsdam late every night and left early again in the morning to attend my first lecture.

It was again my old friend Valdivia whose guiding hand led me on to a broader road. One day he asked me whether I knew his friend Professor Ludwig Bernhard. "He is not lecturing this semester," he said. "But once a week he has an office hour at the seminary for social sciences. I shall introduce you to him next Friday at six o'clock."

Professor Bernhard was in his early fifties. He did not look at all like a typical professor but gave the impression of being a man of the world, at home in the smartest hotels of Berlin, Paris, or London. He was tall, slim, and tanned, had a lean face with closely cropped dark hair, and a nicely shaped nose which slightly indicated Jewish ancestry. There was something very youthful about him. His blue eyes reflected a great joy of life. Bernhard was the idol of his students. He was more of a practical educator than a theoretical scientist.

I proudly showed him my schedule of courses. One look at it and he exclaimed:

"For heaven's sake, Prince Louis Ferdinand, this is the program for a student in the seventh or eighth semester who is about to come up for a degree! There won't be anything left for you to learn if you go ahead at this pace," he added, mockingly. "My old friend Valdivia brought you here to get my advice. Well, here it is."

He took a red pencil and eliminated every course with the exception of one on Beethoven by Professor Max Friedländer and one on the philosophy of history by Professor Eduard Spranger. Enjoying my amazement which was visibly mixed with hurt pride, he continued:

"You still are very young. Why don't you enjoy yourself? I want you to forget all about your doctor's degree. There will be lots of time for that later. For the present go and listen to my colleagues who talk about history, philosophy, music, or whatever else you like. This is a university, you know, and not a 'prep' school. And there are many things you can do outside this building. If you feel like coming back in a year or two we can then talk shop."

The summer semester was practically over. I therefore followed Bernhard's advice and hardly went near the university.

For the month of August my parents had planned a trip to East Prussia. They had not been to that part of Germany since the Treaty of Versailles had cut it off from the rest of the Reich by the Polish Corridor. They had many friends there, especially among the landowners.

This trip also had a political purpose. The population of this province was regarded as particularly loyal towards our family. Herr von Berg, the administrator of the Hohenzollern household, was an East Prussian and had warmly recommended this journey. Wilhelm and I were to accompany my parents.

In order to avoid the corridor we traveled on an eight-hundred-ton steamer from Stettin to Pillau. It was the worst crossing I have ever experienced. The Baltic Sea with its choppy waves can be much worse than any of the great oceans.

In East Prussia, I had my first contacts with the so-called *Junker*. We visited at least half a dozen large landowners. Most of them turned out to be highly educated people, well read and much traveled. Some of their homes were built and furnished with exquisite taste.

At Königsberg, where my ancestors had been crowned as kings of Prussia, my parents were cheered by a great crowd. I thoroughly enjoyed the people, their style of life, and the country itself. The thought that this lovely part of Germany is to be lost for all times is utterly intolerable for me, as it is for the great majority of my countrymen.

This trip, a success from several points of view, had one bad result as far as I personally was concerned. Many of our East Prussian hosts belonged to a student fraternity at Bonn called the *Bonner Borussen*. My grandfather and father had belonged to it.

Both the older men like Herr von Berg as well as the younger generation who were still enrolled at Bonn implored my parents to have Wilhelm and me join the traditional fraternity for the members of our family. It was not easy to persuade my father. While at Bonn he had objected to some of the fraternity customs, especially the exaggerated drinking. Also, neither my father nor my grandfather had fought any duels, because duels were officially forbidden though unofficially tolerated by the state. It was felt that the members of the ruling family could not break a law even though that was done by other people as a routine.

The main argument was that this fraternity would be a good substitute for the military training which we would have to forego. Comradeship and new contacts were also given as reasons in favor of this plan. To me it appeared preposterous from the very beginning.

It was tentatively agreed that Wilhelm and I should go to Bonn for the following summer semester, half a year hence. I hoped my parents would meanwhile forget the whole scheme. I was sadly mistaken.

During the ensuing winter semester, following Professor Bernhard's advice, I attended only lectures which had nothing to do with economics. There was hardly a night that I did not go to a theater, the opera, or a concert. Berlin then was second to none as a cultural and artistic center.

I also joined the Academic Orchestral Association, an amateur body consisting mostly of students. We gave several concerts during the winter season. I was busy from morning till night in Berlin, which I grew to like and admire, and saw little of Potsdam, where I merely spent the nights.

As the semester drew to a close my hopes to evade the Bonn plan dwindled. During the Christmas holidays in our castle at Oels in Silesia my parents told me that they had definitely made up their minds. I was to study for a few semesters at Bonn and join the Bonner Borussen. I argued in vain. I would gladly have gone to Bonn for a change of atmosphere. Many students attended various universities before taking their examinations. But the thought of having to join the *Corps* was maddening. The possibility of having my face cut and left scarred for the rest of my life made me furious. My question as to what my grandfather thought about the dueling angle met with the rejoinder that Berg had obtained the Kaiser's approval.

At the age of eighteen I was not free to make my own decisions. To disobey my parents, who both meant very well, did not enter my head.

"A little discipline and dueling will do you a lot of good," Mama reassured me. "You'll get used to it and perhaps even like it after a while. So be a good boy and go to Bonn." I finally yielded—there was nothing else to do—but hoped that an opportunity would present itself to leave Bonn soon. I had hardly said yes, when a chance for my early escape presented itself. At a luncheon a few days before my departure for Bonn, Valdivia introduced me to Dr. Enrique Telémaco Susini of Buenos Aires with the words: "This man will arrange a trip to Argentina for you." Susini was a throat specialist, but his main interest was music, especially opera. He had spent several years in Vienna and spoke German fluently. Valdivia had mentioned to him that I was longing to travel to Argentina.

"All you have to do is to get there," Susini said. "I shall take care of the rest. The autumn vacation which lasts almost four months will suffice for an enjoyable round trip. You will be able to spend about six weeks ashore, which is better than nothing. You can always repeat the trip later," he added with a smile. Both Valdivia and Susini shared my misgivings about the Bonner Borussen.

"Please your parents by going to Bonn and get them to let you make that trip to the Argentine," Valdivia counseled. "That's the wisest thing you can do right now. I shall do my best to convince them that our friend Susini will take perfect care of you and that I assume full responsibility for the plan."

Our little plot worked out much better than I had dared to hope. I wrote to my mother about Susini and the prospect of visiting Argentina. She was very much in favor of it. I left for Bonn almost in a cheerful mood.

I went there with a strong prejudice, not towards the university itself, which ranked among the best in Germany, but against the institution of the *Schlagende Verbindungen* (dueling fraternities). I left Bonn six months later with an even stronger feeling, that of thorough disgust. Now, I am fully aware that thousands of Germany's best sons count their student days as the happiest in their lives—days and years inseparably linked with these fraternities. I am ready to admit that these fraternities fulfilled a great patriotic and historic task in an earlier period when they fought for liberal and broad-minded principles as well as for German unity.

As far as the Bonner Borussen were concerned, they were hopelessly out of date. I was amazed to realize that Ditfurth's narrow-mindedness seemed almost like cosmopolitanism compared with the class snobbishness cultivated there.

My fraternity brothers belonged exclusively to the nobility. They were nice fellows, some of them highly musical and intelligent. Though their outlook was much narrower than that of Wilhelm and myself, even they were for the most part bewildered by the doctrines preached by the older *Corpsbrüder* (fraternity brothers) to whose care we were entrusted. Only two or three other fraternities in Bonn belonged to our exclusive group. Only with their members were we allowed to speak or even exchange greetings in the streets.

The main idea underlying our fraternity concept was to make the novice feel that he was an absolute nonentity, that he must obey blindly, carry out all orders coming from his seniors. This "education of the character" aimed at proficiency in two accomplishments, drinking and dueling. The novice, it was held, would reveal his true nature when completely intoxicated. He would demonstrate his self-discipline and courage during duels. Only if he proved a satisfactory guzzler and duel-ist could he be admitted to full membership and receive the *Burschen-band* (ribbon).

I hold that self-discipline and courage can be tested without slashing one another's faces. As to drinking, I believe two or three tests should suffice to find out how a person behaves when inebriated—if indeed such a test is desirable!

We had three *Kneipen* (drinking bouts) a week, one of them formal with guests. The liquid provided for such cases was beer. Owing to the general economic depression, wines or champagnes were not served as they had been during the "good old days." The advantage of beer was that one could get rid of it much more easily than of any other alcoholic concoction. The drinking started during dinner. It was useless to eat anything. It only meant an additional burden for the stomach. The pro-cedure was very simple. We *Füchse* (freshmen) sat at the lower end of the table, the *Burschen* (older students) and the *Alte Herren* (alumni) at the upper end. The *Erste Chargierte* (president) was at the head of the table, flanked by the second and third presidents, who took turns as masters of ceremonies.

Each member of that "Upper House" would drink the health of the freshman, who always had to empty his glass. Only when the other fellow said *"geschenkt"* ("forgiven") was he allowed to pass up empty-ing the glass. Rather small beer glasses were used for these purposes. This ritual might have been innocent fun had one been allowed to stop according to one's own capacity for drinking. But that was exactly what was taboo! The whole point was to make us drink far beyond our capacity.

Besides these fixed drinking bouts, visiting alumni like our Herr von Berg would throw a party which would start at noon. For these purposes generally a *Bowle,* a mixture of wine and champagne with a certain amount of brandy in it, was donated by the guest. The result was usually devastating. The guests believed they were doing us a special favor. We hated them for this act of cruelty.

Even with that minimum program of three Kneipen a week, one just had time to sober up from one bout for the next. I was constantly in a haze, tumbling from one hang-over into another. I was never completely sober during those months. It was useless to attend classes, because one was in no mental condition to listen to lectures. After about two months I got weary of feeling sick all the time and consulted Professor Adolf Hirsch, a well-known *Internist* of the university. He promptly diagnosed that my kidneys were badly affected.

"I thoroughly understand your position," he said, with a twinkle. "You cannot go on like that. I am very sorry, but I must strictly forbid you to drink liquor in large quantities. I suppose now you will be very angry at me for spoiling your fun?"

I left his office armed with a strongly worded statement as to my physical condition. I knew that this meant my death sentence as far as the convivial side of my fraternity was concerned. Its president, Count Eulenburg, shrugged his shoulders in disdain when I showed him my doctor's orders.

"If that's your way of dodging the rules of our fraternity I cannot help you," he remarked.

"If your rules are meant to destroy a person's health for life, you can have them," I snapped back.

Dueling was a different problem. There was no decent way to get out of it, because it would have been considered an act of cowardice.

Every novice had to fight at least one so-called *Bestimmungemensur* (prescribed duel) to be admitted as a full member. The first duels had been set for my brother and myself for the last month of our first semester at Bonn. Each day in the mornings and afternoons we had to take one hour of fencing practice. For these, the face was protected by a mask and the swords were not sharpened. I had no difficulty learning how to fence. From playing the violin I had developed a supple wrist.

Once or twice a month the seven Corps of Bonn met at the *Paukboden* (dueling floor) for the duels. These events lasted from seven in the morning until three in the afternoon. This was about the only time we met the members of the other fraternities. The Paukboden was a hall of an ordinary beer garden.

The fighting was done according to set rules. There were several doctors present to take care of the wounded, who were treated in a special room in the cellar. The main thing was that the duelist must not move or wince, even though he received heavy blows or cuts. If he did, he was counted out. If he behaved the same way a second time, he was excluded from the fraternity. This happened only in very rare cases.

The fact that Wilhelm and I were to fight our first duels was to a certain extent sensational, because never before had a member of our house been allowed to do so. The whole city, which lived almost entirely off the students and the university, was curious to know how these two Hohenzollerns were going to pass the test.

These duels were not based on any personal animosity for the assigned opponent. My opposite number was the son of the mayor of Bamberg, a nice chap, not quite as tall as myself. The final date was set. But unwittingly I almost spoiled the whole show.

About a week before the duel was to take place I went to Doorn to obtain my grandfather's permission to visit Argentina. He already knew about the plan, but I explained it in detail to him. When I finished, he answered gravely:

"My dear Lulu, I have been strongly advised by several people not to let you make this trip. They fear that you are much too young, that you do not have a proper traveling companion, and so forth. I think they are wrong. I always wished to go on such a long voyage myself when I was your age. Unfortunately, I was never given the chance. Now, since this unique opportunity presents itself to one of my grandsons, I not only permit you to go but I definitely want you to make that trip. You have my full blessing."

I happened to mention that I was going to fight my first duel when I got back to Bonn. My grandfather was thunderstruck. His face went quite pale. For a few moments I thought he was going to faint. Breathing heavily, he murmured: "Are you crazy? Who has permitted you to fight a duel?"

Now it was my turn to be baffled.

"But didn't you approve of our joining the Borussia Corps and to fight duels?" I asked. "Herr von Berg told me that you know all about it."

The Kaiser, who had meanwhile regained his old poise, with sparkling eyes said angrily: "Nobody ever told me that you were going to fight duels. I never would have allowed it, and I am not going to, either."

Without the slightest intention, I had created a very awkward situation. Although I hated dueling, I begged my grandfather to let me fight this one duel. Both Wilhelm and I would be branded as cowards if we reneged. But the old gentleman was adamant.

"Go back and tell them that this sort of thing is against all Hohenzollern traditions. I don't care what anybody says. I cannot let you go to South America with a fresh scar in your face," he closed the conversation.

When I reported my grandfather's decision to Count Eulenburg, there was general consternation. Everybody was furious, suspecting—as I feared they would—that this whole situation had been cooked up by the treacherous Louis Ferdinand.

Frantic telegrams were sent and telephone calls made to Berlin and Oels, where my parents were living at the moment. Finally, Herr von Berg was ordered to report to my grandfather, who did not give him a very cordial reception, judging by what I was told later. But he succeeded in obtaining my grandfather's consent for this one duel each for Wilhelm and myself, and no more. Thus our faces would be saved.

Wilhelm and I fought to everybody's satisfaction. Nobody was hurt. I felt like the luckiest person in the world and took off for South America. This was in the spring of 1926.

Chapter Fourteen

Interlude in Argentina

(1926)

I OWE THAT first overseas trip chiefly to my mother. True, my stay in South America was cared for by the invitation of Dr. Enrique Susini, but how was I to get over there?

My monthly check as student was by no means sufficient to buy a round-trip ticket to Buenos Aires! Our family fortune was still in a state of animated suspension, since no settlement had as yet been effected with the Prussian State.

Mama relieved me of my worries. She wrote a letter to her old friend, President Philip Heineken of the North German Lloyd, asking whether I might hitch-hike my way on one of the steamers of his line. Heineken was most co-operative and even though the SS *Madrid,* on which I was booked as guest of the line, could not be called a luxury steamer, this fact was not the fault of the company but rather of my university schedule.

As a matter of fact, my journey took on added color, for the *Madrid* was an emigrant ship, filled to the last berth. In this way I came in direct and immediate contact with the problem which I was later to analyze in my thesis for the doctor's degree. The object lessons I gained were drastic. Meals had to be taken in three shifts. The mixed nature of the passenger list led to tensions which resulted in explosions and even shooting affrays. When I expressed my astonishment to kindly Captain Block, he tried to calm me by stating that was part and parcel of a regular voyage to South America, especially as the tropical nights affected the senses. Even I, inexperienced as I then was, realized what passions were at work during the long voyage of four weeks, with many stopovers. I was down with a fever for part of the time, hence in no condition to enjoy the breathtaking approach to Rio de Janeiro. Not until our arrival in Buenos Aires was I my normal self again.

The impact of the New World upon this upper teen-age Berlin student was an overwhelming one. Not only was Europe far away, but I was on my own, with no Dico to hover over me as had been the case during my sojourn in Spain the year before. Dr. Susini was my only acquaintance on this hemisphere. He did everything possible, however, to introduce me to Buenos Aires society and even arranged for me to be received by President Marcelo T. de Alvear, a man who was considered anything but pro-German—rather, pro-French.

Susini also persuaded the President of the Republic to give an evening party in my honor, in the course of which his wife, a celebrated former Italian opera star, sang several arias and lieder. As she had not sung publicly since taking leave from the stage, this was interpreted as a special indication of the presidential couple's favorable disposition towards me.

This incident, as well as the publicity given it by the press, converted my visit into a semiofficial one without my having in any way intended it as such. The German diplomatic mission had no part in it—on the contrary, these circles were at first extremely cautious. During the races for the *Gran premio nacional,* one of the greatest society events, the Argentines had draped my box with the old imperial colors. Only after having witnessed this manifestation of sympathy did the German diplomatic set dare invite me into their club and their private homes.

When Dr. Susini noticed that my health was not equal to the lavish Argentine hospitality, he suggested a side trip to the northern part of the country, to Misiones. The territory of Misiones forms the northeastern tip of Argentina. Jesuit missions, as the name indicates, for several centuries had done a remarkable piece of colonizing until the order was expelled in the eighteenth century. Nobody continued their great cultural work. Only a few ruins give testimony to their unique effort.

Arrangements were made with Don Adolfo Schwelm, head of a subsidiary of the Tornquist Bank, which was engaged in colonizing vast areas of the territory of Misiones mostly with German immigrants. Enrique Susini and another friend, Ricardo Frers, accompanied me.

The first leg of our journey was made in the private carriage of Don

Ramos Mejía, the president of the North-Eastern Railway Company. On reaching the Paraná, we changed to a steamer. A most interesting trip began through the enormous delta of the Paraná River with its countless islands and canals. In the early hours of the following morning we reached its eastern shores. Again we traveled by train, now across the province of Entre Ríos.

After two more days we reached Posadas on the Upper Paraná, the terminal of the North-Eastern Railway. There we boarded the *Cuidad de Posadas,* a floating contraption which was so small that we feared it might capsize whenever Susini, who weighed 250 pounds, decided to lean over the railing. On the third afternoon we finally reached Puerto Eldorado.

Don Adolfo Schwelm, a man in the fifties, was standing on the beach in a perfect, London-tailored gray suit. "Welcome," he said in a deep baritone voice. We climbed up the sandy embankment to his house, a simple wooden bungalow containing about five rooms and a porch which extended over the whole length of the house. Our hostess, Doña Elena, awaited us on the porch. The word charm fitted this young woman better than any other. She was at least twenty years younger than her husband. Her small figure expressed a touching helplessness. Her face could change abruptly from one of extreme gaiety to one of pathetic sadness and resignation. She was flanked by her three children, two boys and a girl.

"These will be your royal quarters for the time being," Don Adolfo remarked with a grand gesture as he showed me my room. "If you don't mind we shall leave you to yourself for the moment to clean up a bit. Elena will meanwhile look after our supper, and I'll see to it that your luggage is brought up from the puerto. Auf Wiedersehen, my dear prince."

When I emerged from my room, quite refreshed, Don Adolfo was sitting in an easy chair out on the porch. In his hands he held a glass with a brown liquid. A whiskey bottle, a water jar, and other glasses were on a small table.

"Come, have a drink," my host said. "After that long voyage you need one. Don't mind the brown color. It's because the water contains a lot of iron."

My two traveling companions joined us a few moments later.

Adolfo Schwelm was a remarkable personality, with a certain amount of mystery woven around his life. Some people said his father had been secretary to the famous English Rothschild. Don Adolfo, though of Jewish extraction, had been brought up partly in Germany, partly in England, as a Catholic. He was a British subject but also spoke German, Spanish, and French fluently.

To the colonizing project which he carried out for the Tornquist Bank, Schwelm had given the beautiful name of Eldorado. At the time of my visit the population of the settlement was several thousand, and it covered about 50,000 acres. Every strip of land had to be carved out of the virgin forest. The main product was the *yerba mate* which produced a bitter tea drunk by a large part of the Argentine, Uruguayan, and Brazilian populations. The settlement seemed to be pretty much self-supporting after several initial years of struggle, during which the woods had been cut down and the soil cleared for the yerba plantations.

Our host ruled his "golden land" from his chair on the porch.

"I have an office down in Buenos Aires," he said. "But up here in this wonderful climate I don't see the slightest reason for shutting myself up in a sticky room and sitting behind a desk. Out here in the fresh air my mind works much better."

From time to time a well-mannered young Argentine appeared in this open-air office to take orders. He had a bureau in a small barracks in "town," meaning in the settlement of Eldorado, which was about half a mile from Don Adolfo's bungalow. Once in a while a settler came up on the porch to complain about some neighbor or to ask for help. My host had a very diplomatic way of handling these cases. The colonists usually left with the feeling they had received sound advice. That pepped them up considerably.

With the exception of these open-air "audiences," Don Adolfo did not see much of his "subjects." Perhaps to avoid the impression of favoritism he limited his personal contacts with the Eldorado population to a minimum. We went out into the colony with him only two or three times, always riding along the main road on our ponies for an hour or so, then turning to go back the same way. This main "highway" was an ordinary path running due east for about sixteen miles. At several intervals the wood had been cleared completely in a width of one to two miles. There

The Prince (behind Henry Ford) on an outing with the Ford family.

In Los Angeles with Will Rogers.

the highway was cut by smaller paths which led to the homes of the settlers. With the exception of a physician, we never visited any of them, much to my distress, because I was very anxious to see the immigrants in the flesh.

Although my host seemed reluctant to have me mingle with the immigrants, or at least to observe at close range how they were living, it was he to whom I am indebted for suggesting the theme for my doctor's thesis. The result was my dissertation: "Theory of Immigration as Exemplified by Argentina."

Our return trip to Buenos Aires differed in one important respect from our journey out: In one of the harbors of the lower Paraná there awaited us the luxurious private yacht of the Argentine banker Carlos Alfredo Tornquist, whose connection with the Misiones project I have already indicated. I had become acquainted with this much traveled gentleman through my good friend Susini.

When he learned about my enthusiasm for Argentina, which not only determined my choice of theme for my Ph.D. dissertation but also my decision to return to the Argentine perhaps for life after obtaining my degree, he suggested:

"I shall soon have to go to Europe and shall then visit your parents. I shall then suggest that you take a job in my bank."

This little plot functioned perfectly, as we shall see later.

After another series of social engagements it was high time to think of my return journey. But my Argentine friends would not have it thus. They insisted that I must wait for the luxury liner *Cap Polonio* as more befitting my station in life. The *Cap Polonio* was the swankiest ship of the Hamburg-Süd Line and was due two weeks later. As this was the off-season, the passenger list was small and it was easily possible to accommodate me in a luxury cabin, again as guest of the line.

My departure was in the nature of a pro-German demonstration on the part of my Argentine friends. Tornquist and other prominent Argentinos accompanied our vessel for a while on the La Plata in their gaily beflagged yachts, with the imperial colors—black-white-red—on the top of the mast, a gesture which touched me deeply.

I had lost my heart to the New World.

Chapter Fifteen

The First Ph.D. in the Family

(1926–29)

M Y FIRST trip to Latin America had two immediate results: first, from Argentina I brought home the idea for my doctor's thesis; second, I was able to quit the loathed Bonn fraternity and return to Berlin to complete my university education.

From the *Cap Polonio,* I had mailed a long letter to my grandfather, giving him details about my stay in the Argentine and developing my plans for the future. I wrote him that I was eager to return to Berlin and study seriously so as to earn my doctor's degree in the shortest time and then return to South America. At the end of the letter I asked for his consent and moral support to quit Corps Borussia.

When I arrived at Potsdam a week later I was happily surprised to find a telegram reading: "Fully approve of your plan, (signed) Grosspapa Wilhelm." My parents were not very happy about my decision, but they did not oppose it.

I went to Bonn, handed in my fraternity ribbon to Count Eulenburg, and left the same day. In the eyes of all the Borussia members and also the other fraternities I had committed a great crime. These circles interpreted my action as a breach of loyalty. It was unheard-of that anybody should leave the smartest fraternity in Germany just because he did not like to belong to it. It was branded as an affront to all the dueling fraternities of Germany. Herr von Berg gave expression to this general resentment: "In my eyes by your action you are definitely lost for your family and all its supporters." His intolerant attitude was typical of our court people, who showed themselves "more papal than the pope."

A few days later I was cordially received by my grandfather. When I mentioned to him that from now on I would be considered a sort of out-cast by some people in Germany, he remarked ironically: "As far as I know you, you will be able to live down the resentment of certain narrow-minded people who have never been able to look further than their own noses. You go back to Berlin and get your doctor's degree and forget about the rest. If anybody should get tough with you, I shall get tough too."

I left Doorn greatly relieved and deeply grateful to this old gentleman to whose strong support I owed my victory in the battle against backwardness and prejudice. He had shown himself to be the most common-sensed and modern-minded of them all. Nobody dared to challenge my grandfather's authority in family matters. Without his support I would never have been able to achieve my goal. I most certainly would have been compelled to spend at least two more miserable years at Bonn, probably spoiling my health completely and having my face scarred for the rest of my life.

My rebellion saved my two younger brothers from having to join a fraternity. Wilhelm was able to adapt himself to the atmosphere of Bonn and made himself liked and honored by everyone. He tried his best to modernize an institution that had outgrown such usefulness as it may once have possessed. He became an excellent swordsman and fought at least a dozen duels. After having overcome his aversion to drinking bouts he became accustomed to fraternity life and thoroughly enjoyed his student years at Bonn and several other German universities.

On my return to Berlin late in 1926, I immediately called on Professor Ludwig Bernhard.

"So you rather like our old university," he remarked with a smile. "Do you still want to get your doctor's degree here?"

"Most certainly, Herr Professor," I answered proudly. "I have found a theme for my doctor's thesis while in the Argentine, and I would like for you to be my *Hauptreferent* (main professor, responsible for the thesis and the doctor's examination)." I told him about the Bonn incident. "Now I want to show Herr von Berg and his clique that I mean business," I added emphatically.

"If it is as serious as that, we shall have to do something about it," Bernhard answered.

I told him I wanted to write my thesis on the Argentine immigration problem. During my visit I had been impressed by the fact that such a rich country had only so small a population. It would be my task to find out the reasons for such a phenomenon.

Professor Bernhard had no objection, especially because he said this question was still more or less scientific virgin territory.

"We never graduate anybody here before his eighth or ninth semester," he reminded me. "That will give you plenty of time to write your thesis and prepare for the oral examination." We also decided that I should prepare for a Ph.D. degree and not for *Dr. rer. pol.,* which would mean concentrating more on law, for which I had no desire. I chose economics as my major and philosophy and history as my two minors.

"Now, don't work too hard," Professor Bernhard said at the end of our conference. "You still have plenty of time." I was extremely happy. In high spirits I went to see my old friend Valdivia to report on my successful trip to the Argentine and my plans for the future.

To my great disappointment Valdivia told me he was about to leave Berlin for good. Besides, he had become engaged to a niece of his. I tried to persuade him to settle in Germany. He replied that he had already thought of that himself, but his future wife would not like to live anywhere except in Spain. He promised, though, to visit me frequently. This marriage turned out to be a very happy one. The Valdivias kept their promise and came to Germany at least once or twice a year. "Filo," as he called his second wife, was considerably younger than her husband, who idolized her. She was pretty, intelligent and kindhearted. Unfortunately, she died shortly before World War II, leaving her husband behind, for the second time a lonely widower.

In order to avoid the waste of time caused by commuting to and fro between Potsdam and Berlin, I rented a room from Count Platen-Hallermund. Wilhelm and I, as already related, had attended dances there during our high-school days. The old count, a former admiral of the Imperial German Navy, had been court chamberlain to my grandmother, the Empress Augusta Victoria. My parents were quite happy about this choice. They were certain that I would be treated like a member of the Platen clan, who at the same time would keep a watchful eye on the young "rebel" to prevent his getting into mischief.

Among the frequent guests of the Platens were Joachim von Ribbentrop, later Hitler's Foreign Minister, and his wife. In those days the Ribbentrops played a prominent part in Berlin society, entertaining lavishly with lots of champagne. Ribbentrop then was a champagne salesman for a firm belonging to his father-in-law. At that time Ribbentrop impressed me as a man of international broad-mindedness with slightly "pink" political tendencies. He was a great lover of music and played the violin remarkably well for an amateur. He knew many of my Jewish musical friends in Berlin. In those days I thought quite highly of him. It was not until he had become Hitler's special ambassador that our acquaintanceship was completely severed.

Looking back upon this period I realize that I was extremely unsociable. The thought never entered my head, for instance, that I ought to take one or all of Platen's three attractive daughters to a show or to some night club. Anything connected with movies, dancing, or night life was then held in contempt by me.

Whenever I went to a theater or concert I went by myself or in the company of older people. Even my parents tried to induce me to have a fling at the lighter side of life once in a while, but all in vain. I clung persistently to a narrow, ascetic attitude, believing it to be in true harmony with a life mainly dedicated to the purpose of acquiring a scientific degree.

I would quite likely have developed into a bookworm and a sour puss at that had I not met someone at this juncture who put my life on a new plane.

Rather reluctantly one day in the spring of 1927, I had accepted a dinner invitation from Antonio Vargas, a young attaché at the Spanish Embassy. He was known as a "man about town." Only on very rare occasions could I be persuaded to dine out at any of Berlin's smart restaurants. For reasons of economy and of my total lack of culinary appreciation I usually patronized eating establishments which served meals for one mark (twenty-five cents) or even less. In this case, however, it was difficult to decline the invitation, because it really came from Pepe Mérito, who had been my host during my visit to Jerez and Córdoba. Pepe was spending a few days in Berlin and was eager to see me again. I was to meet my Spanish friends at 8:00 P.M. at Forster's Restaurant.

From 5:00 to 7:00 that late afternoon I attended a seminar on the philosophy of the eighteenth and nineteenth centuries, with the Categoric Imperative by Immanuel Kant as the theme. The seminar was conducted by Professor Max Dessoir, a world-known philosopher of aesthetics, who enjoyed the reputation of being the best-dressed faculty member of the University of Berlin. Noticing that I had donned a black jacket, gray trousers, and a stiff white collar, he whispered into my ear after the lesson: "Are you going to a wedding tonight or a late funeral? Or did you want to express your admiration for the immortal philosopher of Königsberg by dressing up in such a formal way?" he added with a fine sarcasm, for which he was famous.

"Nothing of the kind, Herr Professor," I retorted, slightly offended. "I am only meeting Antonio Vargas and Pepe Mérito at Forster's Restaurant tonight."

Dessoir could not refrain from teasing me: "Well, Prince Louis Ferdinand, as far as I can judge the situation, you are not going to a stag party. Watch your step and don't fall in love with one of the girls these two young men are known to attract. I have been told that Vargas has very good taste as far as women go. I wish you a very good time. Tell me all about it at our next meeting."

"You may rest assured that I wouldn't fall for any of their tricks, Herr Professor," I answered with complete self-assurance.

At the Forster establishment the proprietor took me to a table in one of the corners. "Mr. Vargas and his friends will be here in a minute or two," he said. Five empty chairs were placed around the table. This looked decidedly suspicious.

After a while Antonio Vargas and Pepe Mérito appeared on the scene, accompanied by two young ladies. "Please excuse us," Vargas exclaimed, as he gave me the customary Spanish embrace, "but these ladies kept us waiting as usual. You already know Pepe. This is Mademoiselle . . . (I have forgotten the name) and this is Mademoiselle Lily Damita, the great French motion-picture star." After a few seconds several waiters were hard at work serving most delicious food and filling our glasses with champagne.

"What have you been studying today, Louis?" Vargas asked me in a slightly patronizing way.

"I hardly believe that the topic of our seminary is of any interest to you," I snapped back. "But I begin to believe that philosophy professors are endowed with second sight." I told them about Dessoir's prediction that this was not going to be a stag party as I had hoped.

"And now you are very much disappointed, *Príncipe* (Prince)," Mademoiselle Damita said in correct Spanish with a Portuguese accent.

"I am not so sure about that any more, señorita," was all I could answer at that moment. While chatting with Vargas and Mérito about Spain and our mutual friends, I could not help but look at this French actress sitting opposite me. "She is extremely attractive," I confessed to myself. "Especially that combination of brown eyes and blond hair and that infectious smile of hers." In contrast to her companion, who gave the impression of being a rather dull person, she acted in a most natural way, displaying lots of temperament and personality.

Born of Portuguese parents, she had been brought up in France. One day at the swanky ocean resort of Deauville, King Alfonso XIII of Spain had met her and nicknamed her Lily Damita (*damita* means "little lady" in Spanish).

Pretty soon I found myself talking to her only and forgetting everybody else. After some time we were the sole guests left in the room. The orchestra was playing languid gypsy music to add to my enchantment.

Well, it was love at first sight as far as I was concerned. I wonder if Lily Damita ever loved me. I have never found out. But at least she did not destroy my illusion. I had never been interested in a woman before. My affection for her was that of a completely inexperienced young man who was full of romanticism. She never tried to take advantage of my "handicap." Perhaps her feelings were more those of an older sister than that of a young woman in love. Without hurting my pride, she slowly convinced me that up to now I had been having a single-track mind. She approved of my intellectual ambitions, even admiring them to a certain extent, but she also showed me that there were other things in life besides books and classical music, things which up to now I had ignored.

I slowly began to reform my exterior appearance. My wardrobe was brought up to date. My hair was cut more frequently, my fingernails were manicured for the first time. I visited her at the Tempelhof Studios where she was working on a new film. We went to the movies with

Vargas or just the two of us. She advised me to go in for physical training so I would look healthier and more like a man, not just like a student. She even induced me to go to a few night clubs and dragged me out on the dance floor, where she tried patiently to teach me some of the modern dances. She merely laughed when I stepped on her toes most of the time. After three happy weeks during this midsummer of 1927, Lily Damita left Berlin to do a picture in Spain and afterwards one in France. She promised to be back for the winter season.

Meanwhile, I did my best to live up to her expectations. I played tennis by the hour, went swimming several times a day, and even took boxing lessons. The result of these concentrated athletics was a collapse of the heart which kept me in bed for over two months. I felt like a hero of the Middle Ages who had sacrificed himself for his ladylove.

I used my involuntary leisure to brush up on my French. My effort to consume French literature almost by the ton was amply rewarded by frequent letters from Lily Damita, who expressed her satisfaction about the improvement in style and grammar of my correspondence.

I wrote a long and enthusiastic letter to my old friend Valdivia, explaining my adventure in every detail. I asked him as a great favor to travel from San Sebastián, where he always spent the summer, to Barcelona to have a look at my lady friend, who was doing some outdoor scenes there.

To my greatest disappointment I received a negative answer. Valdivia expressed gravest concern about my falling in love with a moving picture star. It was altogether wrong, he wrote, and he would not even think of wasting his time by traveling all the way from San Sebastián to Barcelona.

"If it were for some constructive purpose," he finished his letter, "you know that I would go to the moon for you."

After my wedding ceremony in 1938, at which old Valdivia was a guest of honor, he said teasingly: "Have I made up today for not going to Barcelona eleven years ago? The distance from Madrid to Potsdam is about three times greater than that between San Sebastián and Barcelona."

"Is this a constructive occasion?" I shot back.

"I shall tell you at the christening of your first boy," he replied in a commanding voice.

One evening out at Cecilienhof, soon after meeting Lily for the first time, I confessed first to my mother and then to my father about the novel turn my life had taken. Both took a very broad-minded and lenient attitude. I gave them the assurance that this was merely a friendship and that the thought of marriage was completely out of the question. I know that my father had a heart-to-heart talk with her soon thereafter, during which he assured her that he did not mind at all that she was trying to make more of a human being of me, but at the same time warned her that he would not stand for any "marriage nuisance."

I also reported my great adventure to my philosophy teacher, Professor Dessoir. I offered him a small amateur photo of Lily Damita and myself taken at the Tempelhof Studio. He accepted it gracefully, expressed satisfaction that my taste was up to aesthetical standards, but sounded a slight warning note, remarking: "If I were you I should not let my psychological interest get the better of me and rather concentrate on the physical," whereupon Mrs. Dessoir, known for her refreshing bluntness, corrected her husband: "My dear Max, you had better keep your nose out of our friend's personal affairs and stick to your duties as a professor of philosophy."

"This advice was meant only in a purely academic sense," he replied apologetically. In his memoirs, published in 1946, my venerated teacher disclosed to my greatest surprise that in 1934 he used to take my former girl friend out in Paris! He mentions her as being pretty, also without *maquillage,* and sensible at that. Neither he nor she had ever mentioned their contacts in Paris.

Unbelievable as it may seem, my interest for Lily Damita never was anything but Platonic. I suppose that was the main reason why it took me such a long time to get over it.

To recover from my heart attack I spent several weeks at Bad Kreuth as a guest of the Duchess Marie José of Bavaria. She was a magnificent old lady, born a Portuguese princess of the House of Braganza. She nursed me back to health in a very touching way. At her home I met the old Duke of Urach, nicknamed *Onkel Wilhelm,* who was related to the House of Monaco and spoke beautiful French. He convinced me that I needed supplementary treatment on the Italian Riviera and recommended a small boardinghouse in the little fishing village of San Michele di Pagano near Rapallo.

It was my first visit to Italy. I spent four restful weeks there. My daily expenses amounted to about thirty cents, three meals included. The population of San Michele consisted of about four hundred inhabitants, mostly poor fishermen. They told me they were Communists who hated Mussolini but loved the House of Savoy—indeed, a strange brand of royalistic communism!

At Milano, I heard Arturo Toscanini for the first time as he conducted Beethoven's *Fidelio* at the famous La Scala opera house. To be admitted I had to borrow tails and a white tie from the head waiter of my little hotel. "A dark suit won't do, you will be turned back," he remarked proudly. "At La Scala only people in formal dress are admitted." I was almost disappointed that nobody took me for a professional waiter. But I was admitted without any further difficulty. It was a most impressive opera performance.

As I was a foreigner I was in no way molested by the Fascists. But from many conversations I gathered that the majority of the people disliked the system. To Fascists who tried to sell Mussolini's achievements to me, I used to answer: "In Germany we do not need a dictator to make our trains run on schedule or to keep the streets clean." (After Germany got her dictator neither did our trains continue on schedule nor were the streets any longer kept clean.)

During the winter season of 1927–28, Lily Damita put in several meteoric appearances in Berlin. She was at the height of her career in Europe and ready to take off for Hollywood. She worked hard at several Berlin studios. Her spare time had to be divided between various admirers, all of whom were in a much better position than I to entertain her. I had a feeling of hopeless and jealous resignation. How could I compete with my $150.00 monthly allowance and a rented room at the Platens? Once in a while I invited her to some restaurant with good bourgeois cooking. Lily, noticing my dejection, tried to cheer me up.

"In due time," she said, "you also will have all the advantages these rich boys now have. They will then be fed up with life whereas you will not even have started to enjoy it. That's your great advantage. At any rate, I don't see why you should not have a motor car," she added quite casually. "Why don't you ask your grandfather to give you one? If you have a car by next summer, we can take nice trips together." This seemed like a grand idea.

My university studies were meanwhile drawing to a close. My affair with Lily Damita did not have any adverse effect on them—quite the contrary. After she left Berlin for good in the spring of 1928, booked to go to Hollywood during the ensuing winter, I worked harder than ever.

As a matter of fact, the idea of marriage was beginning to take hold of me.

The first version of my doctor's thesis, presented in the summer of 1927, had been a flop. Bernhard returned it to me with the caustic remark: "I did not ask you to write a pamphlet for some Argentine national jubilee. Why don't you try to develop an immigration theory which stands on its own merits and then apply it to the Argentine as a practical demonstration? That will give you an opportunity to prove that you possess the scientific spirit which we are trying to cultivate at our universities."

After another twelve months I again called on him, armed with a new manuscript. A month later he rang me up and said: "Well, Prince, this time I am almost satisfied. Write me one more chapter, enlarging your thoughts just a bit more. Then I can take your thesis to the faculty and we shall fix a date for the oral examination." This was at the end of the summer semester of 1928. Despite several redrafts I did not satisfy him until almost Christmas of that year.

During the summer vacation of 1928, I drove to Doorn in my new two-seater car which I had practically extorted from my grandfather. I simply bought it in Berlin and on my arrival at Doorn said to the donor:

"Grosspapa, now I want to show you the wonderful car you promised to give me on getting my doctor's degree."

"But you haven't got the degree as yet," he protested.

"I shall get it during the winter semester. I thought the car would be very useful during the summer."

My grandfather loved to tell his visitors the motor-car story. He would then add:

"Lulu also chiseled a fur coat out of me. If he goes on like that I shall be broke before long."

On this trip I was accompanied by a young Spaniard, Dr. Juan Terrasa, who held a scholarship at the University of Berlin. We had met in Professor Dessoir's seminar. Juan became one of my most intimate friends.

As the time for my examination approached I almost had a nervous breakdown from fear lest I might not pass. My professor's sudden toughness about my thesis—he who until then had always behaved like an older brother towards me—upset me. Later I found out that his behavior was in line with the educational tradition of our university system, by which the student at a certain moment is to be impressed with the fact that the more he studies, the less he really knows.

My mental equilibrium was restored, however, when Bernhard finally told me to have my dissertation typed in the three prescribed copies. During the last two months before the examinations I did hardly any studying. I went to many gay parties and drank Bordeaux wine to counteract the coldest winter in a hundred years.

My examinations took place in February 1929. The moment when I was informed that I had passed will always remain one of the most glorious in my life. My examiners were Professors Bernhard and Friedrich von Gottl-Ottlilienfeld in economics, Erich Marcks in modern history, and Max Dessoir in philosophy. Dessoir had planned the traditional *Doktorschmauss* (doctor's dinner) for a Friday following the examination. Hence, when he said to me: "Until Friday evening," after having examined me, I felt that the battle for the degree was won. Nevertheless, there came some terribly long minutes of waiting outside the room in which my fate was being decided by the whole faculty. Finally, I was informed that I had passed *cum laude*. In a warmhearted speech Dessoir congratulated me on being the first member of the Hohenzollern family to qualify for a doctor's degree at the University of Berlin, founded by my ancestors two centuries ago.

Professor Bernhard, with whom I drank a bottle of champagne immediately after the faculty session, told me that a *magna cum laude* had been proposed. But to avoid possible political criticism I had finally been graded one mark lower—*cum laude*—to make sure nobody would say a Hohenzollern had been given preferential treatment in the German Republic.

Anyhow, I was extremely happy and definitely proud of myself (excusable at the age of 21!). I shall always remember my university days with the greatest gratitude and respect for my teachers and our German university system. The chief purpose of our academic training then was not so much to acquire detailed knowledge as it was to learn how to think, how to maintain an objective outlook on things. Science was taught for the sake of science and not of some Weltanschauung or political creed, as was later ordered by Hitler and his Soviet counterparts.

But although I had passed my finals, the actual conferring of the Ph.D. degree took place much later. My thesis, it will be remembered, dealt with the Argentine immigration problem. Before having it printed I wanted to check on my scientific product by on-the-spot observations and research.

In 1928, Carlos Alfredo Tornquist, the Argentine banker who had been so kind to me during my first sojourn in his country, kept his promise of visiting my parents and me. When I had told him of my plan he had offered me a job with his firm, which held large interests not only in Eldorado but also in other parts of Argentina. By joining his firm, he pointed out to my parents, I would be able to combine my research work with practical experience and a thorough knowledge of the country's economy.

This plan looked very promising to my parents, my grandfather, and me. It was therefore agreed that I was to leave for Buenos Aires after passing my examinations for my Ph.D.

Following Tornquist's visit, however, Lily Damita had agreed to go to Hollywood during the winter of 1928–29. It was obvious to me that she would not return to Europe for a long while. I therefore conceived the plan, which I kept entirely to myself, to visit the United States on my way to South America.

I simply *must* see Lily!

Chapter Sixteen

My Non-Discovery of America

(1929)

I AM giving this strange title to this chapter because, during my first trip to the United States, I did not discover the real America. In fact, when I sailed from New York, South America bound, in the summer of 1929, after three months of extremely interesting travel from coast to coast, I was nevertheless disappointed and had no wish to return. My special grudge was against the American press which had definitely "taken me for a ride." Of this more anon. I did not realize then that my unhappy experience with the Fourth Estate had all been my own fault. Later I found my dearest friends among the newsmen—friends who remained such throughout World War II.

But let me tell how it all happened:

A short time before my university final examinations I told Professor Bernhard about my intention to visit the U.S.A. on the way to South America but refrained from disclosing what I really had in mind. I asked his help to obtain my grandfather's permission and financial support for this detour. I knew that Grosspapa regarded Bernhard very highly. The professor obligingly wrote to Doorn.

Some days later I started out for Doorn. On the way I noticed that I had left my passport behind! I got off at Hannover and telephoned to my apartment in Berlin to have it sent along on the next train. Four hours later the conductor of the Hoek van Holland Express handed me an envelope with the vital document. This little incident was again proof of the friendliness of German railway employees towards the Hohenzollern family which we experienced throughout the Weimar Republic and the Nazi regime.

I was quite embarrassed when I arrived at Doorn in the evening, because my grandfather had been kept waiting for four hours. But he was in a forgiving mood and amused. He said:

"If you always forget your passport and must have it brought after you, you'll never even get across the English Channel."

He was highly pleased to have a Ph.D. among his grandsons. He had always held scientific work in great respect. During his reign he had given research every possible help and had founded the Kaiser Wilhelm Society for the Advancement of Science in honor of his grandfather Wilhelm I. During the years of his exile he had founded the *Doorner Arbeitsgemeinschaft,* which brought famous scientists from Germany and other countries to Doorn once or twice a year as his guests to discuss learned topics, especially archaeology. The days with the savants were the high points of the year for him.

The following day I developed my traveling plans. The letter from Professor Bernhard had arrived and I read it to my grandfather. Bernhard wrote that my knowledge of the New World would be utterly incomplete without personal acquaintance with the most important republic of the Western Hemisphere. A three-month stay, according to his view, would be the shortest advisable length for a coast-to-coast visit of that country.

The Kaiser listened with great interest and then, with a twinkle in his eye—did he suspect something?—said: "I think your professor is quite right. I gladly give you my permission for this detour. I'm sorry I was never given that chance. I see no reason why I should not let you have it. There is only one thing I want to warn you about: Keep away from Hollywood. That's no place for an inexperienced youngster of your age. If you want to go to the West Coast, you can stay with some of my American friends."

I still feel thoroughly ashamed of myself for not having told him the truth and for having instead abused his grandfatherly love and confidence. He later on forgave me this breach of trust. That is why I am able to tell this whole story.

At the moment I felt gloriously happy and grateful for his magnanimity. When we came to discussing details of my North American visit, Grosspapa said: "As you don't know a single soul in that vast country, I shall announce you to my old friend Poultney Bigelow, who lives at

Malden-on-the-Hudson like a hermit. He knows all the most important and interesting persons in the States. We used to play together at Potsdam about sixty years ago. His father was American Ambassador to Napoleon III under Abraham Lincoln. After resigning his post, Bigelow, Sr., and his family came to Berlin, where they met and became good friends of my parents.

"Poultney, who was older than I and my brother Heinrich, used to stand us up against a tree and shoot at us with bows and arrows. We therefore called him the Red Indian."

The days at Doorn passed rapidly. I departed from my grandfather with his blessings for the trip. Back home I surprised my parents with the new plan to visit the United States. They were not overenthusiastic! Perhaps they had an inkling of adventurous dangers lurking. But they, too, finally gave their approval. I then booked passage for the second half of March.

My personal contacts with the U.S.A. until now had been practically nil. My knowledge of the North American continent and its history was very limited. The Anglo-Saxon world held no particular attraction for me. In my youthful opinion it lacked color and temperament. Moreover, since the beginning of the First World War, I had made little practical use of the English language. I had all the usual prejudices held by most Europeans about America. America connoted lack of refinement and tradition, idolization of technical achievement, overemphasis on business and the acquisition of money—in a word, materialism. Skyscrapers, motor cars, and motion-picture stars projected against the romantic background of James Fenimore Cooper's novels rounded out my more than primitive notion of America and the Americans.

The day for my departure finally dawned. Professor Bernhard came to see me off at the Berlin Friedrichstrasse station. I was deeply touched by this gesture. *Geheimrat* Köhler, an old secretary of our family administration, also put in his appearance. During all these years he had been in charge of my personal finances. Sometimes it was difficult for him to balance my budget, but he generally succeeded in drawing upon some secret source to keep me solvent. Juan Terrasa joined us to accompany me on the SS *Berlin* as far as Cherbourg.

A grand surprise awaited me at Bremen: I was to be the guest of the line!

This was not my first ocean voyage and by far not the last. But at every departure I experienced that strange sensation which only a boat leaving port can offer. There is an expectation of the unknown. On this cold March evening my departure took on a new significance. It meant farewell to boyhood and student days. It might mean good-by to Europe. For, my intention then was to settle down in Argentina permanently. Would I be able to carry it out?

The *Berlin* did not carry many passengers, as this was the off-season. Outstanding among them was Mrs. Charlemagne Tower, widow of the late American Ambassador to Germany. This charming old lady, who had known my grandparents and indeed my whole family well, cordially invited me to visit her in her home in Pasadena, California. I was silly enough not to follow through. Had I done so, I might have spared myself and others a lot of trouble.

Among the German passengers there was Edward Messter, owner of a big optical business, with his wife. He had a moving-picture camera with him and decided to make a movie with a plot. That kept virtually all passengers busy during the entire trip. None of us knew anything about scenarios, scripts, or stage management. The high spot of the whole effort was to be a love scene between the attractive young Mrs. Messter and myself, to be climaxed in a long kiss. The photographer-director somehow did not insist on redoing this scene, although other scenes were repeated over and over! Nor did the hero and heroine mind —both were meanwhile suffering from seasickness. A year later the Messters came down to Buenos Aires, where they showed me the picture. We laughed heartily at our amateurish effort.

Among the passengers, I also remember Willy Messerschmitt, who later became one of Germany's most important airplane constructors. He seemed to be a rather shy person, as he kept mostly to himself.

The night before reaching New York harbor there was the usual farewell dinner and dance. Everybody drank as much as possible because we were heading for a dry country—at least that is what I as a typical greenhorn believed. My American fellow passengers warned me very seriously that I would not get anything but water during my whole stay in North America.

It sounds almost like sacrilege if I confess that I was at first disappointed at New York's famous sky line. My initial impression, however, yielded more and more to one of admiration and wonderment the closer we drew to the docks. My excitement grew every minute.

But I was not left alone with my thoughts for very long. A gentleman walked up to my hideout on the upper deck, shouting: "Hello, Prince, how do you like America?"

This approach to a problem did not quite correspond to the scientific methods I had been taught at the university. But my good angel told me that a logical procedure in this case would be out of place and that instinct would be the only reliable guide in the emergency. The gentleman's purpose apparently was not caused by merely social reasons, nor did he seem to have come to meet me in an official capacity, because he looked neither like the *Chef du Protocol* of the White House nor like the German Ambassador. So I answered with as much determination and conviction as possible, "I think it's grand."

My interrogator seemed to be satisfied with the answer and introduced himself as a representative of the press. He was joined by several colleagues. I suggested that we all go down to the smoking salon to drink some German beer. Nobody protested, and we sat down for an amicable chat.

I had to answer many questions about my grandfather and his life in exile. I did this with great gusto. Fortunately, there was no mention of Lily Damita. Our round-table conference soon broke up. My guests had to get back to their desks. They left me in a cheerful mood, which was increased when I read their stories. My first contact with the American press had come off surprisingly well. I enjoyed the informal approach and the originality of the questions, so unlike anything I had experienced in Europe.

Before going ashore I went to say good-by to the captain. In his cabin I was handed a note from Poultney Bigelow:

"I shall be very happy to make the acquaintance of a grandson of my dear friend Emperor William II. I expect you to be my guest today for lunch at the Players Club, Gramercy Park. God bless you.

Poultney Bigelow."

The great moment had finally arrived. For the first time in my life I was on North American soil.

The customs official hardly looked at my trunks, except to remark that to judge from the amount of my luggage I apparently wanted to spend the rest of my life in America. He did, however, rivet his eyes on an odd item of baggage—a canoe. This canoe had accompanied Bigelow all over the globe. Forty years previously he had given it to my grandfather for training his sons as oarsmen. Now the Kaiser had entrusted me with the mission of restoring it to its former owner. It took some time for the inspector to decide whether it was dutiable. Finally he said, laughingly:

"You see, people generally do not import canoes into this country. But as it's an American product and evidently has been used a lot, I suppose I can let it go at that. Please give my regards to Mr. Bigelow. I have read some of his books."

This conversation was quite encouraging. I felt important at the thought that even the customs officers knew my grandfather's old friend.

I registered at the Ambassador Hotel on Park Avenue. The manager showed me into a beautiful suite of rooms, evidently presupposing a very substantial checkbook in the possession of a Hohenzollern Prince. Later, when the bill was presented, the rooms caused a very painful drain on the travel money my grandfather had given me to take me across the United States and all the way down to Buenos Aires.

For the moment, however, I had but one thought—to meet Poultney Bigelow.

The drive in an open taxi from my hotel down Park Avenue to Gramercy Park was like a dream. Gliding through this valley of gigantic stone buildings was a strange sensation, almost awe-inspiring. When I reached Gramercy Park the skyscrapers suddenly vanished. I had the impression of being back in London. The taxicab pulled up at an old building which looked like a private home. A fine-looking old gentleman with a white beard stood at the entrance. His resemblance to the Kaiser was astonishing. He was very smartly dressed in a black redingote and gray trousers. In his left buttonhole he wore the red ribbon of the *Légion d'honneur.* This must be Poultney Bigelow.

Before I could utter a word the old gentleman gathered me into his arms and gave me a hearty hug. *"Willkommen,"* he said in perfect German. "Willkommen, son of my dear Kaiser." I had to explain, apologetically, that I was only one of the Kaiser's many grandchildren, whereupon Mr. Bigelow exclaimed:

"*Ach Gott,* you are so young and it seems only like yesterday that I played with your imperial grandfather at Potsdam when we were both children—and that was sixty-five years ago."

His first question was: "How is your grandfather?"

I answered that his friend was enjoying the very best of health and that I considered myself to be his special envoy with strict orders to place myself under the protection of the "aggressive Red Indian of Sans Souci Park."

Bigelow shook with laughter and replied: "I have always warned your grandfather not to trust Red Indians, especially not those of the Bigelow tribe. But, my dear Prussian eagle, I believe it is high time for a welcoming drink. Let us go to the bar and then have lunch. We have a lot to talk about."

On the way to the taproom Bigelow explained the history of the Players Club. "Here you will find the real elite of our country," he continued, "not those dirty politicians or those cold-blooded, dollar-hunting money makers called businessmen."

At the bar he ordered two highballs, which were immediately followed by two more. When I asked where prohibition came into the picture, he thundered: "This so-called prohibition is the d——st nuisance ever invented. Nobody pays the slightest attention to this law. There is nothing like a good drink once in a while. The trouble is that nowadays you never know what you get. Many people go blind or insane or even die from bad liquor. So be very careful and don't drink everything people offer you over here. You'll be offered plenty, I tell you."

So this was my first lesson in "Americanibus"! Old Bigelow expressed his thoughts in such a convincing way and in such picturesque language that I hardly ate anything. I preferred to listen to his outbursts, ranging from the most classical vocabulary to expressions not generally used in drawing-room conversation.

During the meal Bigelow asked me if I had any plans for the immediate future. I mentioned that a number of invitations from German societies and groups had reached me on the ship. When I confessed that I had accepted them he exclaimed quite angrily: "You are not going to do anything of the kind. You did not come over here at your grandfather's expense to be entertained by your countrymen. I want you to meet Americans and forget about the Germans for the moment."

My protests that I would offend my would-be hosts were of no avail. The old gentleman was adamant. "I have an entirely different program for you," he said. "At four o'clock this afternoon a train leaves for Malden. I've got to get back to my home and shall take you with me. In this city of stone pyramids you won't be able to form a single decent thought. In the quietude of my village on the shores of the Hudson, I shall tell you whom you ought to meet. I know some people,"—here a twinkle came into his eyes—"who are quite worth while meeting. After such a mental preparation you may go back to New York and do the town if you feel like it.

"But before departing I want you to meet my sister, Mrs. Tracy. She lives almost next door. She will give us a good cup of coffee and perhaps some cognac to go with it."

Mrs. Tracy, a charming, gray-haired lady, almost threw a fit when her brother Poultney told her of his intention to take me up to Malden immediately.

"It's preposterous," she protested, "to rush the poor boy, hardly off the boat, on a Saturday afternoon up to your wretched country house in those overcrowded trains. Why don't you both spend the night here with me and then go to Malden in the morning, if you must?" she asked.

But her brother's mind was firmly set on leaving that afternoon. He was finally persuaded to concede me one night in New York. I was to join him the following day, taking the noon train. He could not refrain, however, from remarking in a pained voice: "As you are my older sister and as I hope some day to inherit your fortune, I guess I shall have to capitulate. Keep your Hohenzollern grandson, but do not spoil him too much."

The old lady replied with a chuckle, "Poultney, you are terrible, but nobody can ever stop you from making nasty remarks."

My new tutor, after another embrace for both of us, rushed out of the room and down the stairs. I ventured to ask his sister about his age. Mrs. Tracy answered: "Poultney must be seventy-five years old or something of the kind. We all envy him for his youthfulness and energy. You will be surprised at what kind of a life he leads up at Malden. It is certainly very wholesome, but rather strenuous. I hope he will not overwork you. But I don't want to spoil my brother's fun by telling you everything in advance. You must find out for yourself. Now, my boy, you had better have a nap after all these exciting talks. Then we shall have tea and later on you'll dine with me alone, if it does not bore you to spend an evening with an old woman. I have, by the way, a very capable French cook and some good German wine which may help you feel more at home in this new world."

Mrs. Tracy certainly had not exaggerated the achievements of her chef and the qualities of her cellar. The dinner could not have been better in the best Paris restaurant. We spent a delightful evening together, in the course of which I learned a lot more about her brother Poultney and her own life. As midnight approached I left my hostess in a very happy mood, thoroughly satisfied with my first day in the United States of America.

Chapter Seventeen

F.D.R.

Two Americans have had a strong, abiding influence upon my life —Franklin Delano Roosevelt and Henry Ford. I have liked and admired them both equally, although Henry Ford was an uncompromising opponent of President Roosevelt, and I am proud and happy that I can claim them both as my personal friends. Totally different types though they were, both had great human hearts and souls.

As Poultney Bigelow and I sat on the porch at Malden a day or two after my arrival, after a six o'clock morning swim in the Hudson River, my host observed:

"Well, my dear Hohenzollern, I succeeded in kidnapping you from your well-meaning compatriots. But as I have already said, I want you to meet some real Americans, because if you do not, I am sure your grandfather will be very angry with me and I shall not dare visit him at Doorn.

"There are two people I want you to meet: Franklin D. Roosevelt, the Governor of the State of New York—he will be the next President of the U.S.A.—and Henry Ford, who quite likely will be your next boss."

I asked Mr. Bigelow if he were a fortune teller or perhaps an astrologist, because he made these statements as though they represented indisputable facts. He merely chuckled, then continued:

"Today I am going to phone to Albany and ask Governor Roosevelt when we may call on him. Mr. Roosevelt rarely misses a week end at his ancestral home at Hyde Park, now the property of his mother Mrs. Delano Roosevelt. She is only a little younger than I. We were playmates. I've known Franklin ever since he was a child. The Roosevelts belong to our real aristocracy—not to those moneybags about whom you read in the papers all the time. I think they are grand people and am sure that you'll find them delightful.

"I have also written to Mr. Ford's secretary, announcing your visit, and expect to get an answer almost any day."

Old Poultney soon rang up the governor's mansion. Mr. Roosevelt said he would be very glad to have us come to Hyde Park for lunch the following Saturday. The appointment had hardly been made when a letter arrived from an old friend of Bigelow's, urging me to come to Florida that same week. To my great surprise Poultney again rang up Mr. Roosevelt and asked him to postpone our visit for a week, as he wanted to go down to Florida. Such informality was not customary in Germany! The governor, who was very fond of yachting himself, said he didn't mind in the least if we came some other day.

The next day, however, the daughter of the old commodore rang up from Florida, saying that her father was much too ill to have any guests. Bigelow was quite annoyed at this interfering lady. Then, however, in a most casual manner he asked Governor Roosevelt to change the Hyde Park date back to the Saturday originally agreed upon. The governor, without being hurt in the least, agreed. This little incident made a deep impression upon me.

The Hermit of Malden of course did not own a motor car. "I am much too poor a man to indulge in such a luxury," he told me, "and besides, I don't like these modern contraptions. I have enough friends here to drive me about."

At ten o'clock on the morning of the appointed Saturday a retired schoolteacher, apparently one of those friends who served Bigelow as voluntary chauffeurs, drove up in his ancient "tin lizzy." Bigelow, noticing my sheepish look, explained angrily:

"This car is perfectly all right, and if we were driving to the White House, it would still be all right."

We all climbed in, Poultney and I sitting in the rear seat. The hermit struck a very dignified pose, in keeping with the importance of this journey. Mr. Sutton, our gentleman-chauffeur, took up his post behind the wheel and after a little backfiring and other deafening noises managed to start the motor.

A few minutes before one o'clock we pulled up before the Roosevelt home. Bigelow said proudly: "You see, we are absolutely on schedule with true Prussian punctuality. You must report that to your grand-father in the letter which you have been too lazy to write up to now."

Evidently aroused by the noise of our car which came to a halt with one more noisy explosion, two or three tall young men, elegantly dressed in riding clothes, emerged from the house and darted down the steps. They were the governor's sons. They immediately took hold of my venerable chaperon and hoisted him out of the car, ignoring his protests that he did not need any help from anybody. They were joined by Mrs. Roosevelt, who burst into gay laughter as she said: "Congratulations on your beautiful new car, Poultney. I am sure that your guest never had such a marvelous ride in his life."

Bigelow, as though acting in a Shakespearean drama, replied with a courtly bow: "Madam, you flatter me indeed, but this automobile of latest make unfortunately does not belong to a poor man like me but is owned by my good friend and neighbor Mr. Sutton, who has been kind enough to take me and my Hohenzollern offspring to Hyde Park to enjoy your most charming presence and hospitality."

We now all went inside. Near the fireplace of the comfortable living room the governor was seated in an armchair. Taking me by the hand, Bigelow walked up to Mr. Roosevelt, who greeted us with a big smile, shook hands, and said:

"Hello, Poultney, I'm glad you came down here and brought your German guest with you." A cocktail was served, and then a servant announced that lunch was ready.

Mr. Roosevelt invited me to sit next to him. "Louis," he said, "I hope you don't mind that we are completely *en famille*. But on purpose we haven't invited anybody else, because you must be sick and tired by now meeting new people all the time. Today you'll have to put up only with the Roosevelt clan."

After a few minutes it seemed as though I had known the governor all my life. I could not help feeling a deep affection for him. He could have been a close relation of mine—one of our foreign relatives in England, Denmark, or Sweden. Somehow he must have guessed my thoughts, because he said: "You know, there is a strange similarity between your family and mine. I was born the same year as your father.

We were married the same year. We also have four sons, all about the same age as you and your brothers."

Mr. Roosevelt then talked about Germany and told me that, as a boy, he had visited my country almost every year with his parents, who regularly took the cure at Bad Nauheim. He used several German words and said he could understand my mother tongue quite well. "But Mother," he added, "speaks it fluently."

He also referred to his frequent trips through France, Italy, and England. Then he asked me about my own life and plans.

Poultney Bigelow gave him a vivid description of how he kidnapped me from my compatriots in New York and unfolded the program he had laid out for me.

"I see that our young friend seems to take a keen interest in our country," the governor said. "Poultney, why don't you bring him up to Albany? There I'll give Louis a lesson on American politics and the constitution."

"My dear Franklin," Mr. Bigelow answered with evident satisfaction, "who could be more qualified to give such valuable instruction to a grandson of my dear friend Emperor William II!"

Then Poultney suddenly got up, exclaiming: "Oh Lord, it's already four o'clock; we have been keeping you much too long, and I must be home before night." I squirmed at my old friend's abruptness. But the Roosevelt family seemed to be used to his eccentricities. The governor, shrugging his shoulders, flashed another charming smile and said to me:

"We should like to have you stay with us a little longer, but nobody, not even God Almighty I assume, is able to talk our friend Poultney Bigelow out of anything once he has made up his mind." Then, turning to Poultney he added: "I really can't understand why you are in such an awful hurry, because with your super-modern car you ought to be able to get back to Malden in no time."

As we took leave, the governor said: "Now don't forget to attend that lesson. I expect both of you. Poultney also needs a little brushing up on his history, even though he hasn't been doing anything else for the last seventy years."

Poultney snapped: "But I am always ready to acquire more knowledge."

Grunting all sorts of protests, Mr. Bigelow was again heaved into the car by the Roosevelt boys. I kissed Mrs. Roosevelt's hand in German fashion and shook hands with all of the young Roosevelt generation, who patted me affectionately on the shoulders. The wheezy engine was started by Mr. Sutton. Through the roaring backfiring we could hear the shouts and taunts of the Roosevelt clan.

My main impression of the Roosevelt family was that these people were aristocrats in the best sense of the word. The charm of Mr. Roosevelt was irresistible. I had the feeling that it was sincere. The governor's lack of pose and affectation, combined with a very easy and worldly manner, gave me the feeling of being with a real *grand seigneur*. He approached and explained the most involved problems in a simple, human way coupled with a keen sense of humor. My initial impression was deepened and strengthened anew each time I met him. His infirmity was completely overshadowed by his personality.

During a period of nine years I met Franklin D. Roosevelt at least a dozen times. To call on the Roosevelt family became almost a habit. Even after he had become President, Mr. Roosevelt did not change his attitude towards me in the least. Quite the contrary, he became even more cordial, treating me as a father would treat his son.

About a week after our Hyde Park visit, Bigelow and I, again piloted by the friendly Mr. Sutton, drove up to Albany. We found Governor Roosevelt at his desk in the state capitol.

"So you've come to have your lesson," he greeted us, again with a cordial hand clasp and smile. Taking up a book from the desk he continued:

"This is the American Constitution. Let's plunge into it right away." He first gave me a short historical résumé as to when and how the constitution was created, then concisely outlined its contents, illustrating several points with vivid remarks and examples. The "lesson" lasted more than an hour. It was very easy to understand because of the simplicity of the governor's diction. I could easily have listened for another hour. Several times I interrupted my teacher to ask questions, which he readily answered.

When he explained the powers of the Chief Executive, Poultney Bigelow interrupted with: "To my mind, the President of the United States has more power than my poor exiled friend, Emperor William II, ever had during his whole reign. This will of course apply to you, too, Franklin, once you are in the White House. Am I right or not?"

"You know you always are, Poultney," F.D.R. replied with a hearty laugh.

The governor's secretary entered to remind the governor that important scheduled visitors were waiting outside. Mr. Roosevelt laid the book aside and said: "I'm sorry, but that'll have to do for today. I hope I gave you a general idea of our constitution. I know it is not the most modern one. Your new German Weimar Constitution, for instance, is much more up to date theoretically. But the main thing is that ours works, and we could not very well do without it. The next time you visit Poultney don't forget to look us up. Then we can continue with our course. Meanwhile, I wish you a nice trip out West. I am sure you'll have a hell of a good time out there."

Back in Malden, as I landed in the ancestral double bed of the Bigelow family, my head was in a swirl. My two experiences with F.D.R. seemed all the more fantastic in view of what Poultney now told me about the governor's earlier career. All I had known hitherto about the Roosevelts was what my grandfather and my parents had told me about the Teddy Roosevelt with whose children my father had played in the New Palace in Potsdam thirty years ago. Now Poultney Bigelow informed me that the governor of New York had been one of the most important enemies of Imperial Germany. As assistant secretary of the navy he had organized the gigantic fleet that carried millions of young American men to Europe, thus contributing largely to the winning of World War I. Yet, just a few hours ago the man who was thus largely responsible for the downfall of the Hohenzollern dynasty had taken the trouble to teach a member of this deposed family the constitution of his country!

I shall now interrupt the chronological sequence of this narrative to record several other meetings with the late President and also to yield the floor to my beloved Kira for her impressions of her meetings with the Roosevelts.

My next visit took place in September 1932. Three years had elapsed since that "lesson" in Albany. They had been filled with events which had taken me to three different continents. F.D.R. had meanwhile won the Democratic nomination for the presidency.

My youngest brother Friedrich, called Fritzi, had expressed the wish to visit me and attend the Olympic Games in Los Angeles. From the dock in New York we drove straight to Malden, following Poultney Bigelow's example of three years ago. This time I was the proud owner of a new V-8 Ford coupé. From Malden we planned to start for the West via Detroit. Bigelow insisted we must not miss the opportunity of calling on the presidential nominee at Albany. As usual he telephoned to Mr. Roosevelt:

"Hello, Franklin, is that you? I've got two Hohenzollerns with me right now. They have strict orders from me and their grandfather to call on you. One of them is Louis, the other his youngest brother Friedrich. They'll be in Albany at nine o'clock because they want to get to Detroit in daytime. Can you see them? Very well, then. God bless you, my future President."

Prompt to the minute, we drove up to the governor's mansion. Jimmy Roosevelt met us at the entrance: "Mother and Father are having breakfast, won't you join us?"

Mr. Roosevelt received us with: "Please sit down and have a bite with us. We know Poultney's Spartan habits. He probably got you out of bed at five o'clock and didn't even feed his guests. We don't want you to arrive at your destination half starved."

The governor was in the best of spirits. I congratulated him on his nomination and told him I had listened to his acceptance speech in my car driving from Detroit to Chicago. "You seem to have become quite Americanized," he remarked laughingly. "You certainly did not speak with a Middle Western accent when I met you first three years ago."

After breakfast we all went over into the living room. Suddenly, Roosevelt asked us: "Do you mind having your picture taken with us? You know, we are at the height of the campaign, and it is almost impossible to keep the photographers away." An informal group was formed by F.D.R., his son Jimmy, and Fritzi and me. I used this opportunity to brag about my new Ford car, with which I had made the trip from Detroit to New York in ten hours.

"If you don't break your neck," the governor said, "which is very likely to happen if you don't watch out, you ought to get a transfer to the Ford sales department. I'd suggest that to your boss myself, but as he does not seem to like me very much, I shall leave it up to you."

"If I could sell you a Ford car, I'm sure he'd change his opinion," I shot back. (Six years later President Roosevelt actually drove a Ford car over the grounds of his Hyde Park estate with Kira and myself as his passengers.)

The next morning we found our picture with the Democratic presidential nominee in all the newspapers.

Before taking my brother back to New York to sail for Europe three months later, we again were the guests of the Roosevelts. This time we were invited for tea at Hyde Park. Everybody was in a high spirit of expectation, the presidential election being only three weeks off. With a twinkle in his eyes the governor remarked:

"In case I should be elected President we'll have another picture taken together. You will not need any ambassador for that purpose, and Poultney won't even have to write an article in the *Times*."

My host was referring to a "diplomatic incident" of which I had been the innocent cause three years previously. Poultney Bigelow had deemed it desirable that I present my respects to President Herbert Hoover. I had disagreed with him, saying I was not traveling in any official capacity whatsoever and was trying to avoid any steps which could be interpreted as political. Bigelow nevertheless had written to Mr. Hoover, who promptly sent word that he would be glad to receive me but that in such cases the White House etiquette required that distinguished foreign visitors be presented by the ambassadors of their respective countries.

Bigelow then ordered me to write immediately to Ambassador Friedrich Wilhelm von Prittwitz und Gaffron, asking him to take me to Mr. Hoover. I was extremely reluctant, but Poultney would not tolerate any argument. So the letter went off a few days later. The reply was negative. The ambassador wrote that he would take German guests to the White House only in special cases and was convinced I would readily understand that I was not a special case. I showed the letter to Poultney, who said something about "d——d foolishness" but then forgot all about the matter.

About a week later to my amazement I discovered a headline in the *New York Times:* "German Ambassador Snubs Grandson of Kaiser." The detailed article ended with these words: "History repeats itself. Half a century ago a very distinguished American citizen during a visit to Germany asked his ambassador to be introduced to Kaiser William II. The ambassador refused to do so. But the Kaiser had heard of this American visitor and met him at some private Berlin house. The visitor's name was Mark Twain." The article was signed Poultney Bigelow. It was to this incident that Governor Roosevelt referred.

At this tea party, Mrs. Sarah Roosevelt, the governor's mother, acted as hostess. She spoke German fluently.

"If you provoke me, I shall recite all of Goethe's *Faust* by heart," she said jokingly. In spite of her age she walked very upright, her movements were vivid, her spirit sparkling.

Three weeks later my Hyde Park host was elected President by a landslide majority. I spent the evening of November 8, 1932, at the Grosse Pointe Yacht Club near Detroit. My birthday was due the following day, and I had made up a little combined election and birthday party with some Detroit friends of mine. Roosevelt's election had meanwhile been conceded. We all got up, clinked our glasses in German fashion, and drank to the health of America's new President, who had been elected on a dripping wet platform.

In September 1933, I received my first invitation from the new President of the United States. The circumstances were rather odd. I was still working for the Ford Motor Company, no longer as mechanic but as a free-lance roadman, a job which had been created specially for me. I had established my temporary headquarters at the Bismarck Hotel, Chicago. One afternoon I received a wire from Poultney Bigelow, reading: "Are both invited by President to Hyde Park for tomorrow afternoon. He counts on our coming." I was in very high spirits. Hardly had I set foot on American soil again after a quick trip to Europe, and already my friend in Hyde Park sent for me! This time I would be the guest of the President. I was so excited that I confided my good fortune to several co-passengers.

At Albany a Ford limousine awaited me. A young man, elegantly dressed, asked, "Are you Dr. Ferdinand? I have orders from head offices to be at your service for the time you are here." During the trip to Malden he remarked: "Are you one of those big shots who come over from Europe and whom we must drive around?"

I explained that I was nothing of the kind, just an ordinary free-lance roadman of the Ford Motor Company.

"Henry must have invented this new job," he commented. "Never heard of it before."

When I told him I was going to Hyde Park in the afternoon, he said, dryly, "I see the guys in Detroit want to make a good impression on the President."

Poultney greeted me with feigned outrage in his voice: "What do you mean driving up here like an Indian Maharaja?"

"I would have come on foot," I answered, "but these are Henry Ford's orders. I don't want to be fired yet. My salary has just been raised to $250 a month."

"I certainly don't want to spoil your chances of becoming a millionaire," he grunted as he gave me a hearty kiss and pulled me into the house.

This time we were received at Hyde Park by one of the President's secretaries. After an exchange of congratulations—the President to me for having been promoted to a Ford salesman, I to him on his elevation to the presidency—we proceeded to the living room.

Besides Mrs. Roosevelt, there were only two other persons in the room. The President made the introduction: "Louis, I want you to meet Mr. Montagu Norman and Mr. Henry Morgenthau." I shook hands with both of them.

Mr. Roosevelt directed me to sit next to him. I had to tell him about my trip to Europe and my new activities with Ford. I also confided that I had spent several months with my grandfather at Doorn, who had put me on a dry regime because I had been drinking too much bathtub gin and other doubtful liquors in prohibition-ridden America.

"In a few months the people are going to vote on this question," the President said, "and I am sure that the Eighteenth Amendment will be repealed. After the repeal I shall mostly serve California wines to stimulate our wine industry."

The President then spoke about my brother Wilhelm's marriage to a

Returning to Detroit in 1933 to work again for the Ford Motor Company.

Grand Duchess Kira of Russia at the wedding of the Duke of Kent and Princess Marina. She is shown standing

commoner and asked me whether this would have any bearing on my own future.

"Unfortunately it will," I answered. I explained that my older brother had given up all his rights of a first-born and that these had been transferred to me. What this involved will be explained in a later chapter in its proper chronological place. Suffice it to say that it meant my Ford career was nearing its end.

The President listened with great patience to my recital of Hohenzollern family problems. Montagu Norman seemed rather annoyed. Apparently he felt neglected.

"Before you return to Europe for good, come to the White House and tell me all about your sales trip," Mr. Roosevelt said as we took leave.

The next morning I read this headline in a Chicago newspaper: "President Stalls Talks with Montagu Norman by Inviting German Prince." Here was the explanation for Mr. Norman's annoyance.

Six months later, to meet the schedule agreed between my grandfather and me, I flew to New York from New Orleans to catch the SS *Europa*. I did not have the courage to ask for an appointment with the President on such short notice, but the Walter Trumbulls with whom I was staying in New York were close friends of Louis Howe, and they requested him to let Mr. Roosevelt know I was about to embark for Europe.

The White House replied that the President would see me at five o'clock the following afternoon. I went to Washington that same night.

A few minutes before the appointed time I drove up to the main entrance of the White House. Getting out of my taxi, I saw a lot of other people heading for the same destination. On entering the gate I was asked by a guard what I wanted.

"I have an appointment with the President," I answered proudly.

"You got out at the wrong entrance, Sir. This is Mrs. Roosevelt's reception. You'll have to go to the annex, where the President has his office."

The guard gave me a few cryptic directions which evidently were beyond my comprehension. I was quite nervous, as I did not want to be unpunctual. I got lost. In desperation I jumped a fence. Finally, sweating and completely out of breath, I reached what appeared to be the White House annex. Entering the first door I could find, I almost collided with an old, dignified-looking Negro doorman.

"Could you tell me the shortest way to the President?" I gasped, all out of breath. "I have an appointment with him and am already several minutes late."

The doorman must have thought some lunatic was trying to see his boss, but he politely concealed his misgivings.

"Please step in here for a moment," he answered in a friendly, reassuring way, and ushered me into a medium-sized room with a desk, a comfortable red leather sofa, and a few chairs. Turning to a gentleman behind the desk, he said: "This gentleman wants to see the President."

I introduced myself, whereupon the man said: "I'm Steve Early, the President's secretary. I think we already know each other from Hyde Park. I believe there is a little mistake. Please wait here. I shall tell the President you're here."

I was almost in a state of hysteria. I feared I had made some awful *faux pas*. After a few minutes, which seemed like an eternity to me, Mr. Early returned, announcing with a smile: "The President is ready to see you, please come this way."

I followed him into a room lighted only by a lamp standing on a big mahogany desk. Behind this desk sat President Roosevelt.

"I suppose you want to find out whether I am keeping full working hours," he said with a big grin. "My wife is expecting you over at her party, which I am to join later in the evening. But this gives me a good excuse for not attending. Sit down and let's have a chat right here."

Early had left the room. We were alone. It was a great moment in my life.

"I have heard quite a lot about your sales tour," F.D.R. remarked. "You seem to have quite a good publicity manager. I read in the papers that you have become a Rooseveltian. What's that? Do you mean to start a new party?"

I explained that I had been asked by a newspaperman whether I was a Republican or a Democrat. "As a foreigner, I can be neither one nor the other, but I am a Rooseveltian anyhow," I had answered.

We also talked about my experiences as a Ford salesman. "Henry Ford thinks that I am the big bad wolf," the President said. "It would be splendid if he or Edsel would come down here and see me. A lot of misunderstandings could be cleared up."

As we finished our hour's chat, the President said as he bade me good-by: "Though you must carry out your grandfather's wishes and return to Europe, I'm sure you won't forget us over here completely. We shall always be glad to see you. And now I wish you *bon voyage* and happy landings."

My next visit occurred during Kira's and my honeymoon trip in May 1938. Here is how Kira describes our visits to Hyde Park and to the White House:

KIRA'S STORY

"You are invited to spend the week end at Hyde Park with President Roosevelt and his family," Poultney Bigelow informed us shortly after we arrived in the States on the first lap of our honeymoon trip around the world.

Louis looked forward to meeting again an admired friend, and I was frankly excited at the thought of getting to know the famous F.D.R.

As we approached the President's ancestral home, I rather expected to notice some outward signs that a very important personage lived there. But no. We turned into the park and were already within sight of the house before I saw two stalwart figures in plain clothes, most unobtrusively stationed behind some lilac bushes.

We were warmly welcomed by the President's mother, Mrs. Delano Roosevelt. Her whole appearance and the charming simplicity of her manner personified to me the American mother and hostess of tradition. She won my affection at once. She led us through the hall and a beautifully proportioned big living room to a smaller room at the end of the house, opening into the garden.

Here our host was waiting to greet us. I remember vividly my first impression of the American President. He was seated in a low chair, facing the open windows; a table with flowers, books, papers at his elbow. He wore a loose, light gray suit. His strong face, a little tanned already by the early summer sun, the whole big figure of the man gave such an impression of health and force that for a moment I forgot his infirmity entirely and caught myself wondering why he did not rise to meet us. Then

I was seated beside him, giving an account of myself and Louis and our wedding trip so far.

The President made us feel very welcome; I think his pleasure at meeting Louis again was as genuine as Louis's own. Poultney Bigelow, who accompanied us, and F.D.R. said rude things to each other and were very hearty in their greetings, two good friends of old standing. Conversation over the tea table was animated, punctuated with many jokes at our expense as a honeymoon couple.

Later the President's mother took us up to our rooms and saw to it that we had every comfort.

For dinner, a number of guests were invited, among them Mr. Steinway of piano-building fame. Of the Roosevelt family, Jimmy and his attractive wife were present and one or two of his younger brothers.

Mrs. Eleanor Roosevelt was just back from performing some public duty, and I met her that evening for the first time. She struck me as highly intelligent, an excellent hostess, and also a very busy woman. "Mother is always away!" as her young son remarked to us.

At dinner I sat next to the President and we talked at length about Germany. Our host spoke of the trips he had made there with his mother as a young man, of his affection for Heidelberg, of an adventure on some bicycle tour he had taken through southern Germany in the course of which he had managed to get himself arrested six times for infringement of traffic and other rules, of the many pleasant memories he had kept of the country and its people. F.D.R. could still speak some German and quoted astonishingly from classical poems.

We spoke of my family and Louis's, of our marriage in Doorn, of Louis's grandfather, of his generous wedding gift. Then I sketched out our proposed tour. F.D.R. was keenly interested and made several suggestions as to what we must be sure to see and do. When I told him of my father-in-law's apprehension that a honeymoon trip of six-months' duration, entailing all the strains of constant traveling, was not the best way to start married life and would probably end in our quarreling violently, my host disagreed and assured me that, having seen Louis and me together, he did not entertain the slightest fear for our future happiness.

Next day, Sunday, we all drove to church in the morning. After the quiet service in the simple but pretty little church, our party was photographed on the porch of the house of worship.

In the afternoon our host invited us for a ride, driving his specially built Ford car himself. I confess to having felt a slight nervousness at first, but as I sat beside him I could only marvel at the dexterity and speed with which he drove.

The President took us over the estate, showed us the improvements he was making, which included road building and reforestation. On a hillside he pointed out the place where he hoped one day to build himself a simple log house. "To retire to, when I am through being President," he said with a laugh.

Before our departure the following day, the President's mother showed me her son's room. I was touched by this manifestation of a mother's very great love for her offspring.

Louis and I had not expected to see the President again before leaving the States. But an unexpected turn of events brought us to Washington ten days later.

This trip to Washington was not on our schedule. We had purposely avoided the capital so as not to embarrass the German Embassy with the problem of whether or not to entertain us.

As things turned out, Ambassador Hans Dieckhoff finally almost begged us to come to Washington to avoid the impression of a snub. Hearing of our visit in Hyde Park, of the many other affairs given in our honor, the German Ambassador issued a pressing invitation. It upset our plans but gave us a certain wicked satisfaction crowned by an unexpected summons from F.D.R.

In the middle of luncheon a surprising call came from the White House conveying a message from the President for Louis and myself to call upon him at two o'clock that afternoon. This mark of the friendly informal relations between President Roosevelt and ourselves caused consternation. I am afraid we broke up the luncheon party, but our hosts were very gracious about it and hurriedly ordered the car. Soon we were on our way to the White House for our second and, alas, last meeting with the President, who received us in his study seated at his famous writing table.

The same dignified porter whom Louis already knew showed us in. There was no formality, no "passing us along" from one official to another before reaching the "Presence," as would occur in any European city when visiting the head of the state.

Noticing the many gadgets littering the President's desk (among them I remember especially the donkeys) I gasped over the bewildering set of push buttons at his right hand. The President laughed and said it reminded him of his first day in office, when, as he sat down at that desk, he wondered what he should do first. Catching sight of the push buttons he decided to ring all bells at once and see what would happen. I forget what did happen, but the result was evidently satisfying!

Before saying good-by we were joined by Jimmy Roosevelt, who was to show us over the White House. Had we known that this good-by was to be the final one, Louis and I would have felt very sad. Sadder still had we been able to foresee that soon this great man and our friend was to be considered Germany's bitterest enemy. Within a year my husband was to get into serious trouble with the Nazi authorities for daring to send President Roosevelt a cable of good wishes for the New Year.

This story, however, as well as that of a delicate mission with which the President entrusted my husband, can best be told by quoting from an article by our friend Louis Lochner of the Associated Press:

When Prince Louis Ferdinand and his bride went on their honeymoon trip around the world in 1938, they were house guests of the Roosevelts and had many chats with the President on the dangers of Nazism and its imperialistic and militaristic threats. The President and the Prince found themselves in complete accord.

Before the young couple departed for Germany, Mr. Roosevelt, as was sometimes his practice, by-passed official channels to convey a delicate proposal, which on account of its unofficial nature could at any time be disavowed by either the proponent or recipient.

He entrusted Louis Ferdinand with sounding out Ribbentrop on the possibility of a personal heart-to-heart meeting of the American President, the German Führer, the Italian Duce and the British Prime Minister, possibly on the Azores.

"Ribbentrop, of course, was to take the matter up with Hitler," Louis Ferdinand said. "If he reacted favorably, the proposal could then be transformed into an official one through the customary channels."

Returning to Germany late in the autumn of 1938 the Prince prepared a careful memorandum to Ribbentrop setting forth, without revealing details, that he was charged with communicating certain information from the American President unofficially to the German Government.

Ribbentrop had not even the courtesy to acknowledge its receipt.

Weeks passed. Through various channels Louis Ferdinand pressed for an answer. There was stony silence.

Then a reply revealing Hitler's attitude toward the President came in quite a different manner from the one expected. Christmas was approaching, so the young Hohenzollern couple sent a message to the Roosevelts thanking them for their hospitality and extending the season's greetings.

Hardly had the cablegram been handed in, when a *Luftwaffe* officer appeared. Louis Ferdinand was then serving with the German airforce as a reserve officer. "I have been sent by Marshal Goering to demand how you dared communicate with our Führer's greatest enemy," the officer said. "Our Führer personally ordered the Marshal to investigate. Unless you have a satisfactory answer you will be discharged from the *Wehrmacht* in disgrace, with other consequences as a possibility."

"What saved my skin at that time," the Prince recalled, "was the fact that Kira and I had sent messages not only to the Roosevelts but also to statesmen in other countries in which we had been entertained. That knocked the bottom out of the allegation that my cable was sent with the deliberate intent to commit an affront against the German Chief of State."

After this episode, Louis Ferdinand ceased pressing Ribbentrop for a reply to his memorandum, as the depth of the cleavage between the American President and the German Dictator now was revealed fully.

Chapter Eighteen

Fordland

(1929)

FTER THIS digression on later meetings with President Roosevelt, I now return to my first visit to the United States in 1929. When Poultney Bigelow, during one of his 6:00 A.M. chats on the shores of the Hudson, informed me in a matter-of-fact way that "Henry Ford will quite likely be your next boss," his forecast seemed to be far beyond the realms of probability. I had left the university only a month before, had never had a boss in the ordinary meaning of the word, and if I was to get one, took it for granted that he was waiting for me in Buenos Aires. The thought of working in a motor-car factory certainly had never entered my head. Although I had studied social science and was familiar with Mr. Ford's autobiography, my interest in the Ford empire was entirely theoretical.

I had no desire to get dirty hands and breathe the unwholesome fumes I associated with all industrial establishments. I had no intention of joining the proletariat. Such an experience, of course, is an ideal testing ground for the social and economic theories taught at the university, but at this stage of my life such a logical thought was foreign to me. I was still an intellectual snob who preferred doctrines and maxims to realities.

Hence, when old Poultney informed me that Henry Ford was to be my boss, he did not find me in a receptive frame of mind. I was out for adventure and was definitely heading for Hollywood with my thoughts centered on a certain motion-picture star. Naturally Bigelow could not know that! I was willing, however, to go along with whatever plans he might make so long as they would carry me in the general direction of the Pacific Coast.

Shortly after my first visit to Hyde Park my mentor received the expected invitation for me to come to Dearborn and Detroit. He accepted and set the date without even asking me.

From his porch I had been watching the express trains roaring by day after day. The huge locomotives fascinated me.

"You seem to be a sort of Aladdin who can make everything possible," I said to my host. "Do you suppose you could arrange for me to ride on a locomotive like those racing along the river?"

"It would please me more to see you pushing a wheelbarrow or doing something else more useful," he grumbled, "but if you want to ride on a fire horse I will see what can be done about it."

As usual he was as good as his word. He wrote a note to David Crawling, president of the New York Central Railroad, and when I called at the latter's office the day I set out for Detroit, all arrangements had been made for me to gratify my wish. Mr. Crawling seemed vastly amused at the thought of a Hohenzollern Prince riding on one of his mighty engines. As for me, I was as pleased as a twelve-year-old boy. His parting advice was that I had better buy a pair of overalls.

As soon as I got to my compartment on the train I changed into my new outfit. At Harmon-on-Hudson I followed the conductor up to the locomotive. He introduced me to the engineer and the fireman. Both shook hands vigorously.

Presently the engineer threw the switch or whatever it was that started the machinery functioning, the huge monster began to pant and tremble and move, and before long we were roaring along at full speed, splitting the blackness of the night like an eerie comet. Two technical achievements impressed me particularly. One was the fact that the boiler was automatically stoked with coal, and the other was that water was scooped up while the train was careening along at top speed. To my knowledge, such devices did not exist in Europe at that time.

At Albany, I got off the engine. When I returned to my sleeper some jovial fellow passenger dragged me into his compartment where I met several other gentlemen. As my face was covered with grime and my overalls were smudgy, I was received with great laughter. I was immediately offered a drink poured from a hip pocket flask—to me a sign of the "respect" the average American citizen seemed to have for the Eighteenth Amendment.

At the station in Detroit the next morning I was approached by a young man who asked me in a most jolly and friendly manner if I was Prince Louis. He introduced himself as Ben Donaldson, assigned by Mr. Ford "to follow you around as long as you are here." We became friends instantly. His first assignment was to deposit me at the Dearborn Country Club and later to take me to the Dearborn Laboratory to have lunch with the boss. Meantime, we would have a drive about town, during which he gave me a thorough briefing on Henry Ford, his business enterprises, his eccentricities, and many other matters, all of them of intense interest to me. He explained, for instance, that Ford's anti-liquor stand had done the business considerable damage. So also had his anti-Semitism.

I was more than a little astonished at his frankness. That a young Ford employee, only slightly older than myself, should have the temerity to criticize his boss without hesitation in the presence of a complete stranger who was a guest of this same boss was incomprehensible to me. That sort of thing wasn't done in Europe. I admired Ben for it.

Later, when I became a member of the Ford organization, I discovered that Ben belonged to a type which unfortunately was neither numerous nor especially popular in a concern which looked with considerable distrust on anyone who had been tainted by a college education or by anything resembling intellectualism.

Ben deposited me at the Dearborn Country Club. A hot bath revived me after the night spent on the locomotive and the train. I now felt prepared to meet Henry Ford. At that time the name of the automobile king meant more to the average European than that of almost any other American. I was nervous and showed it. Ben, noticing it, steadied me somewhat by saying: "Don't be nervous, Louis. Henry is a swell old boy."

Our car pulled up before the laboratory. At the sight of the low buildings with the huge windows, the well-kept lawn, and a lovely little lake I felt greatly relieved. Henry Ford at least did not have his office in one of those formidable skyscrapers which seem ready to fall down on you and crush you.

The great industrialist, whom I immediately recognized from his pictures, was sitting comfortably on a big desk, dangling one leg nonchalantly. He was chatting with a man in the thirties with black hair and warm brown eyes, his private secretary, Frank Campsall. This was Frank's office.

Mr. Ford had a private office in another part of the building, but seldom used it. He was much too dynamic to be pinned down to one particular place. He preferred to sit at some rough table in one of the laboratory rooms where he tried out the newest gadgets for his cars. Or, he would lie down on the floor under a car, thus forcing his collaborators to do likewise. The more stuffy ones did not appreciate this informality, but others with a sense of humor did.

As I entered the room I made a deep, formal European bow. Mr. Ford swiftly came up to me and exclaimed: "Well, well, this must be the young man from Germany." Then he shook hands very cordially and looked me straight in the face with his steel-gray eyes, one of which drooped slightly. They were kind and bright eyes, revealing a natural shrewdness which I have often found in the eyes of farmers and other simple folk. He seemed to look right down into one's soul. There was lots of fire in those eyes, and this produced a certain hypnotic effect, at least on me. Henry Ford impressed me as quite slender, rather small, but extremely wiry. His movements were those of an eighteen-year-old youth and not of a man of sixty-five. He seemed nervous by nature. His soft voice was pitched so low that it often seemed almost like a whisper. A certain shyness was obvious. All in all, I had never imagined that the richest man in the world, head of an industrial empire, would be like the man I saw here.

About half a dozen dignified-appearing gentlemen were standing in the little dining room in which we were to have our lunch.

"I want you to meet my general staff," my host whispered to me with a mischievous grin. "But these men do not plan for war; they merely help me build motor cars."

I shall attempt a short characterization of each of the men present, based largely, of course, on my later association with them. First there was C. E. Sorenson, at that time probably the most influential man in the organization. He was a tall, handsome man, but with rather stern, cold eyes. Coming to the United States from Denmark as a small child, he had started with Ford as a simple mechanic and had risen, along with his employer, to a position of wealth and influence. It was apparent that he enjoyed his position and realized his power. He was a hundred per cent production man, with a deep contempt for the sales end of the business and rather suspicious of anything that resembled culture or education. He was utterly loyal to his boss.

Pete Martin, also in charge of production, a man of small stature and dark complexion, was a French Canadian with amiable manners and a kind heart.

The famous Bill Cameron, Ford's public relations man, was a jolly fellow with a red face, who resembled a country gentleman in an old English print. His watery blue eyes revealed much wisdom and kindness. I was not at all surprised to learn that he conducted nonconfessional Sunday school services in the near-by Greenfield Village church built by Ford. Cameron was the intellectual center of the Ford empire, outranking his colleagues by the force of his spirit.

William Cowling, the general sales manager and a former lawyer, was a big, husky man with a large eagle's beak for a nose, and a deep, ringing voice.

Ernest G. Liebold, general secretary, was the last to shake hands with me. It was quite apparent that he was very proud of his German origin. He greeted me with the words, spoken with an American accent: *"Guten Tag, wie geht es Ihnen? Ich freue mich, Sie kennen zu lernen"* ("Good day, how are you? I'm glad to meet you"). From the first moment we met, Mr. Liebold assumed the part of chaperon and paternal friend to me. He is the Ford organization man with whom I had the closest associations, especially in regard to my private affairs. He had many powerful enemies, among them Charlie Sorenson.

Another guest, Albert Kahn, the great American industrial architect, was a pleasant elderly gentleman who impressed me as a man of great ability and education.

I sat on Mr. Ford's right. In those days my English vocabulary was very limited, and it was necessary for my host to help me with my ordering. As the meal progressed, my host touched on a score of subjects. At times it was difficult for me to follow the trend of his conversation. But every word he spoke revealed his deep interest in human nature.

"I think," he said to me, "that a person can only be happy when he creates."

I expressed the opinion that real creative happiness is reserved to geniuses. His answer was that "everyone is able somehow to create something. It depends on himself to develop his creative powers."

Then he talked about my country. "I like Germans," he said. "They are talented and thrifty people. When I was a boy I worked for a toolmaker from Germany. He taught me a lot of useful things. In our factory, many of the toolmakers were born in Germany.

"It was a great pity that Germany got into that last war. I hate wars and am a confirmed pacifist. I therefore refused to turn my shop into a munitions factory, although when the United States entered the war we did what we could to help our country.

"The whole world laughed at my Peace Expedition, I know. But it would have been far better if they had all gotten out of the trenches instead of going on fighting. I really can't see why there is so much hatred and jealousy among the different nations. Your country is very fortunate because it has no large army to maintain. The Germans now can concentrate on more useful things than training soldiers. I wish all other nations would do the same."

This line of conversation struck a responsive chord in my heart. From my early childhood days I had never evinced any enthusiasm for military things. In later years, it is true, I discovered that military service, if properly managed, can be used as a good instrument of general education and bring out valuable human qualities, especially that of good comradeship. But I still believe that war is the greatest curse humanity ever invented.

My host expressed an idea that seemed to be shared by many Americans, that is, that politics is a dirty business in which they did not wish to participate and that everything connected with government work is under suspicion. This attitude was totally opposed to what my ancestors had developed in Prussia over several centuries, where it was considered a great honor to serve the state, even though the position might not offer strong inducements by way of remuneration.

After luncheon Mr. Ford took my arm and said he wished to "show me around a bit." As we walked along I was certain that somewhere I heard the strains of the "Blue Danube." This amazed me. I could not believe that the most famous car manufacturer was also the proprietor of a conservatory of music or perhaps a dancing club. I expressed my surprise. Mr. Ford's eyes lighted up and his thin mouth contracted mischievously as he told me to "keep my shirt on," he would explain everything presently.

We walked to a door which my host threw open with a grand gesture. I was astounded. About sixty boys and girls from six to twelve years old were dancing to the tune of the famous minuet by Boccherini. The "gentlemen" made deep bows and the "ladies" responded with deep curtsies. An atmosphere of solemnity pervaded. For a moment I believed myself transported to a ball given by some ancestor of mine two hundred years earlier.

Presently the music stopped. The little dancers went back to their chairs after one more "reverence." I was introduced to Mr. and Mrs. Lovett, the dancing teachers. My host seated himself on one of the steps leading to the platform for the orchestra. He seemed to have an aversion to chairs. Apparently he knew every child by name. Several of the young couples paused as they passed him and got a pat on the shoulder or sometimes a quick embrace. They showed no bashfulness or timidity.

"All this must seem rather strange to you," Mr. Ford said suddenly. "And I do not blame you in the least if you think I am crazy. You would not be the only person who does," he added somewhat ruefully. "I have always indulged in a few hobbies, and this is my favorite one.

"You see, our modern life with all of its technical progress lacks one essential thing—I mean gracefulness. I am a great friend of old traditions, which we neglect almost entirely over here. I suppose in Europe you are much better off in this respect, although you may have too much of what we have too little.

"Now then, these square dances are as fine an American tradition as we possess. Formerly they were danced everywhere, but now they are almost unknown. I heard of Professor Lovett as being the foremost specialist in old-time dances and asked him if he would help me to revive them."

Mr. Ford told me how he had advertised in the papers asking for old square dance music and offering to pay handsomely for what was accepted. Some music was even submitted from foreign countries.

"The music finally started coming in by the truckload," he chuckled. "Everything submitted was carefully studied until we had built up a considerable library, and now we have the largest collection of such music in the world, all carefully catalogued."

Mr. Ford explained how his original idea had expanded to include his friends and employees in weekly square dance evenings and then had grown into a regular Ford institution. Finally the children had been included—even blind and deaf children.

Before excusing himself after having given me four hours of his time, he invited me to attend a dance for grownups the following Friday night. Later that evening, again with Ben Donaldson as my guide, I visited the Scarab Club, where I met such artists as Ossip Gabrilowitsch, Dr. Francis L. York, Paul Honore, Dr. Valentiner, and many others renowned for their achievements as artists, musicians, or scientists. I was called upon for the first speech I ever attempted in English—a terrifying thought. Somehow I seem to have managed. I got out of the affair by dubbing the toastmaster, Fred Black, a German spy whose real name was Fritz Schwarz. This name stuck to him!

Next day I took a dancing lesson at the Lovetts in preparation for the Ford party. No Prussian drill sergeant could have been more exacting in the training of a recruit than were Mr. and Mrs. Lovett in teaching me the steps of the square dances.

After the lesson, Ben showed me the Dearborn Inn, another Ford institution. He explained that Ford foreign managers were supposed to stay there when they came to Detroit, "at least Henry wants it that way. But the place is too quiet for these gentlemen. They usually stay at one of the large Detroit hotels where they can get something to drink and enjoy other frivolities those places have to offer."

My introduction to Harry Bennett, chief of the Ford private police force, was as unconventional as the man himself. He had his office in some remote basement section of one of the large buildings of the Ford institution. I walked into his office with Ben Donaldson leading the way. It was about the size of, and resembling, a cell in a penitentiary. I was startled to hear Ben let out an emphatic curse just after we had crossed the threshold. Meantime, I had heard two gun reports and a roar of laughter coming from a small man sitting with his feet resting on the top of a desk.

Ben was staring ruefully at his brand new straw hat. He pointed at two small holes in its otherwise immaculate surface.

"Now," said the man, "that will teach you to take off your hat when entering the sanctified office of a gentleman. Besides, you know I detest straw hats. Better get yourself a derby like the prince is wearing."

Following these formalities, I was introduced to this practical joker whom Ben described as "the most powerful and most wicked man in the entire Ford organization."

"You've only got to say that I'm Al Capone's brother," Ben was corrected, "then Louis will know all about me that's necessary."

This, then, was Harry Bennett. He was then about thirty-five and small but athletic. His eyes were steel gray, revealing a great deal of energy and cunning—the eyes of a man accustomed to take the measure of a person in a few seconds. A native of Ann Arbor and a graduate of the University of Michigan, he had served in World War I and been light-weight boxing champion of the U.S. Navy. In the early twenties, Henry Ford was looking for someone to protect his grandchildren from kidnappers. He found his man in Harry, who soon became the bodyguard of the entire Ford family, including the old gentleman himself.

Bennett took over the operation of the so-called service department which actually was Henry Ford's private police. These "service men" were distributed all over the plant. Some were disguised as workers, taking their places on the assembly lines along with the others. Through these agents Bennett always knew what was going on. This system was criticized violently by Ford's enemies and compared to the Russian GPU.

Harry was also obliged to keep a watchful eye on more than two thousand paroled convicts whom his boss had taken on after they left jails and penitentiaries to try and readjust them to the ways of law-abiding citizens.

This courageous, but frequently reckless, man who idolized his boss had a strong sense of justice and would go out of his way to help people in trouble. Harry later became one of my closest and most loyal friends.

If I had any problem, I dropped in on him in his cellar office where he never failed to cheer me with his help and sound advice. He was certainly the most interesting person in the Ford inner circle.

One noon after this first experience in Fordland with Harry Bennett, I had been scheduled to have lunch with him, when at the last minute Henry Ford himself appeared to take on the assignment. I was much impressed when he personally drove me to his home in one of the new Model A cars. He told me he still liked the "tin lizzy" (Model T) better than the new model, "but most people want to have something more comfortable and luxurious. Farmers like the old cars better, too."

Mrs. Ford, whom her husband called Clara, greeted me cordially in a loud voice with a slight English accent. She had been born in England, a fact which had a considerable effect on the Ford policy in that country and in Europe.

There were only three of us at luncheon, and I was amazed to find that excellent port wine was served. Prohibition was still in effect! Mr. Ford evidently was quite amused at my stupefaction. "Do you like my port?" he asked, slightly ironically.

"I think it is absolutely delicious. But the idea that Henry Ford, the champion of teetotalism, should actually drink my health with his own wine is even more so," I answered with great emphasis.

"I don't like the stuff myself any too well," Ford said, "but I don't see any reason why other people should not go for it. I am glad that you enjoy it. And after all," he added with his twinkle, "I could not very well drink your health with water. That would not mean good luck for the three of us. I am a little bit superstitious, you know.

"I am not quite as bad in this respect as my boys may have described me. They sometimes exaggerate. But that does not hurt me. Young people are inclined to do that."

Both Mr. and Mrs. Ford—this must be said to keep the record straight —merely sipped from their half-filled glasses.

Mrs. Ford talked about her experiences as a schoolteacher and wanted to know all about my early education. With delightful simplicity, her husband told me about the tricks he had played on his comrades as a poor and barefooted little fellow in the country school I had visited in Greenfield Village the day before. The barefoot experience, he said, was forced on him by necessity because he came of "such poor people."

I had just explained my projected trip to the West Coast and South America (omitting the name of Lily Damita!) when Henry Ford suddenly asked me out of a clear sky:

"Would you like to work for me?"

"This is a most flattering offer," I replied, completely taken by surprise, "but I really am not interested in technical matters at all, and I am completely ignorant of everything connected with the motor-car industry."

"You are just the type of person we can use here," Mr. Ford assured me with a smile. "The less you know, the more quickly you can learn."

I repeated that I wanted to go into the banking business. "You need not decide now," he commented, "and if you do change your mind and want to work for us, just let me know. You are still a very young man. It would perhaps be a very useful experience for you."

On the way back to the country club I thought about Mr. Ford's offer but discarded even the possibility of giving it further consideration, even though it came from the most successful industrialist on the globe. I was going to be a businessman and not a motor-car mechanic, which I understood was the position he had in mind for me.

Next evening came the Ford "Court Ball," or dancing lesson, as it was called. For the first time I got into a tuxedo I had specially tailored in Berlin for my foreign tour. Accompanied by Ben Donaldson, we entered the ballroom just as many of the guests were beginning to arrive. I created a mild stir by kissing the hand of Mrs. Ford. Incidentally, I have found that once the first shock is over, most American women appreciate that little courtesy.

For the first time I met Edsel Ford at this party. I liked the Crown Prince of the Ford dynasty instantly. He was considerably shorter than his father although they had a certain resemblance. He was certainly as diffident as his sire and had prepossessing brown eyes. The fact that, after a manner, he lived in the shadow of his great father seemed to have left visible traces on his sensitive character. In my thoughts I have often compared Edsel's situation with that of my father. Both were crown princes who were beaten out of their heritage, one by the course of world history and the other by his untimely death. And both tried hard to modernize the sales policy of their respective empires without being able to penetrate the barriers set up by a circle of advisers surrounding their respective fathers.

In both cases their efforts were more or less frustrated. In my father's case the downfall of a royal dynasty resulted. In Edsel's case a dangerous financial situation developed that was finally averted.

At this dance I had my first experience with an American reception line. My future boss practically ordered me to stay by his side to meet all his guests, who included most of the key Ford men and their wives, with the notable exception of Harry Bennett, who kept very much to himself and had the privilege of not attending. To most other invited Ford employees these affairs practically amounted to a "command performance."

Yet it was a truly democratic crowd with secretaries, typists, nurses from the Henry Ford Hospital, telephone operators, and many others present. I was very much impressed.

When Professor Lovett mounted the orchestra platform and directed: "Gentlemen, get your ladies," I walked boldly up to Mrs. Ford and invited her to dance with me as I made a very deep—and to the other guests present no doubt an unnecessary—formal bow. She accepted, although rather startled, encouraged by an approving nod from her husband.

A square was formed in the center of the floor, which consisted exclusively of members of the Ford family, myself excepted. Mrs. Ford and I took our places with our backs to Professor Lovett, who was calling out the dance commands. Henry Ford and Mrs. Edsel Ford were the opposite couple. The other two positions were taken by Edsel, his sister-in-law, Mrs. Kanzler, Mr. Kanzler, and a young lady who was a distant relative of Mrs. Ford.

Professor Lovett announced the first tour, the musicians began to play, and the *quadrille à la cour* had started. Thanks to the special lessons I had had from the professor, I managed to get through the ordeal in a reasonably creditable manner, even though I was in the company of experts in this business. The Ford invitees were as well drilled as the dancers at one of my grandfather's court balls in Berlin.

After an hour's continuous dancing, there was an intermission of fifteen minutes. No refreshments were served. No one smoked. The dancers could get a glass of water at an ordinary water tap if they so desired.

Now, I thought, the moment had come to attack my host on the subject of visiting the Rouge Plant.

"Mr. Ford," I said, "I am leaving tomorrow afternoon, and I have not seen the Rouge Plant yet. At home everybody will laugh at me if I tell them about my interesting visit to Detroit without having seen that world-famous cradle of the Ford car."

"There are cradles, Prince Louis, which to my mind are more worth looking at than the one you seem to be so anxious to see," the old gentleman said, "but I quite understand your feelings. Anybody who goes to Detroit has to see the River Rouge Plant, I guess."

He called Sorensen: "Charlie, our young guest from Germany is going to leave us tomorrow. I want you to take him through the Rouge Plant. He says he is forfeiting the happiness of his soul if we don't show him how we make our cars. But the inspection can't be any too thorough, because his train leaves at three o'clock for Chicago." Then, turning to me: "Don't let Charlie put you on the assembly line right away. He likes to do such things to our foreign visitors."

A few minutes later, while I was talking to one of the musicians, Mr. Ford asked me to play something. Struggling against my embarrassment I grabbed a violin and started the barcarole from the *Tales of Hoffmann* by Offenbach. Mr. Ford immediately grasped Mrs. Ford about the waist and began to waltz. Many others followed this example. For a few minutes I had the job of being Henry Ford's chief musician.

The evening ended with a polonaise, when I again had Mrs. Ford as my partner. Around ten o'clock the party came to an end.

It was also time for me to part from my hosts. When I tried to express my gratitude for all the kindness they had shown me, when I shook Mr. Ford's bony hand and looked into his gray eyes, I had a lump in my throat. He told me that a car would be furnished me in California and that I should not forget what he had said to me about working for his company.

Before departing next day, Charlie Sorenson showed me through the gigantic plant at River Rouge where they were turning out nine thousand cars every twenty-four hours. I saw the famous conveyor system in action. The name of Henry Ford and conveyor system were synonymous in Germany, and the system had been the subject of numerous books and heated public and private discussions. It was admired by many and hated by others as a diabolic invention for slave-driving. Many of the men working on that line were my pals two years later. I learned from these men and from personal experience that the conveyor system, which requires the individual worker to do only a single job over and over again, did not necessarily have stultifying effects on the laborer. While your hands are busy, your mind is free to go wandering where fancy pleases. Many workers expressed it to me this way: "So long as I must work for a living, I don't give a damn how I earn my daily bread. The less effort I have to make, the better I like it."

This simple statement should be weighed against the arguments that were once used to attack what was described as "Fordism." Nevertheless, I never liked the work on the assembly line. I was always more or less overwhelmed by so much system and so much mechanism.

Many of my newly acquired friends saw me off at the station. The last to leave the observation car was Ben Donaldson.

"If you get into trouble with any of those dames in Hollywood, send an SOS for me," he whispered in my ear. "I'll gladly come to your rescue."

A few seconds later the train was on its way to Chicago.

Chapter Nineteen

Rendezvous with Lily

(1929)

A S I SAT on the platform of the observation car watching the continuous change of the view, my mind leaped forward, outdistancing
the flying train which, with every spin of its wheels, was carrying me closer to my goal on the Pacific Coast.

My travel was to take me to Los Angeles by way of Chicago, St. Paul,
Minneapolis, Seattle, and San Francisco. My route West had been suggested by a son-in-law of Louis Hill, Sr., of St. Paul, a descendant of the
famous James J. Hill, the "Empire Builder." I was assured that by making this detour I could probably manage to ride on the engines of the
Great Northern Railroad all the way to the West Coast. This last point
quite won me over, even though it meant a few days' delay in reaching
the object of my affections.

The puritanic life I had led for six days in Detroit was more than compensated during the three days I was in St. Paul. Louis Hill, Sr., was
determined to make up for the "boredom you must have experienced
with that old moralist, Henry Ford, with his old-fashioned dances and
other crank notions." I was dined and wined and entertained without
interruption.

Most vividly in my memory there stands out a "Dance Marathon" held
in the great municipal auditorium in Minneapolis. It was interesting to
observe the attitudes and states of mind of the different couples. Some
danced quite normally. Others dragged their feet about in almost complete exhaustion, their faces dull and lifeless like persons in a trance.
Others had fits of hysteria and screamed like animals.

Louis Hill, Jr., offered to take me out to the West Coast in his motor car, but I refused to accept. His father had given me permission to ride on his locomotives whenever I liked. Louis, Jr., was quite disappointed at my stubbornness. Had I accepted his invitation I would certainly have seen more of the country and the people than I did.

As I was packing my things for the trip West, I found two beautiful, sizable perfume bottles, neatly wrapped in paper, standing on my night table. It did not take me long to discover that the "perfume" actually was a fine brand of old Scotch whiskey. But my German inbred respect for the law was so strong that I did not dare take the two valuable bottles with me. Prohibition was still on the statute books! I continued to refuse despite the urging of my hosts.

With the instructions of Louis Hill, Sr., wired all along the line, I was treated by the railway personnel as though I were an ambassador of some great country. Most of the day I spent in the locomotives.

In Seattle, I had to face a battery of press photographers. The publicity department of the Hills had been given their orders. I had to pose in my overalls, which by now were so begrimed that they gave authenticity to the pictures. Armed with a huge oil can, I had to pretend to be greasing the wheels of the locomotive. When I mildly suggested that this seemed like somewhat of a "fake," everyone assured me that it was quite all right.

My entrance into San Francisco the next day was anything but triumphant. I had left the train at Oakland and boarded the ferryboat to cross the bay in a heavy fog. For some unexplained reason I had a bad attack of nosebleed. Hence, instead of watching the grandiose panorama that unfolded as the sun dissolved the mist, I spent the twenty minutes flat on my back reclining on one of the benches on the upper deck.

The bleeding had fortunately stopped when we reached the San Francisco side of the bay. A stiff breeze was blowing from the Pacific, and the Golden Gate was putting on one of its most gorgeous shows. Together with Rio de Janeiro, San Francisco is the most beautifully located metropolis I have ever seen.

As I look back, I now know that I should have gotten far more out of this trip than I did. I was in such a blind, heedless rush that I was oblivious of my opportunities. Here I was, a youngster, scarcely of age, given the unique chance of crossing the United States, of being entertained by so many people who combined great hospitality with culture, wealth, intelligence, and influence from coast to coast. Any normal person would have reveled in this unusual experience. But a young man who fancies himself in love can hardly be called normal! During the next three weeks I caused a lot of unnecessary headaches, more to other people than to myself, perhaps. But in the end, everything came out all right and no one was permanently hurt.

When I arrived in Los Angeles the next morning on the San Francisco-Los Angeles Express, it was again a bright and sunny day. But my heart thumped wildly, and I had a strange feeling in the pit of my stomach.

Now that I had reached my destination after traveling about ten thousand miles since leaving Berlin, I suddenly was stricken with a dreadful thought: what if the "quarry" I was seeking had vanished—had moved elsewhere? I had not announced my intended visit.

And then the problem of secrecy began to torture me. I hoped to remain unnoticed by the press. No reporter or photographer had met me at the station. So far, so good, I said to myself.

At the Ambassador Hotel, I was quickly installed in an elegant suite of rooms. I was too excited to inquire about the cost—cost meant nothing at this point in my life. I was about to lay my heart at the feet of the lady of my choice, and any consideration of financial matters would certainly lack chivalry.

The moment the solicitous manager of the hotel had departed, I rushed to the telephone and grabbed the receiver.

"Please connect me with the Roosevelt Hotel," I demanded, almost breathless with excitement. Then, to the operator at the Roosevelt: "Please give me the room of Miss Lily Damita." After a pause, which seemed to run into eternity, a voice answered: "I am sorry, but there is no Miss Damita on our hotel list."

My heart stood still. "Will you please inquire of the manager?" I pleaded. "I am certain that Miss Damita lives at your hotel (my information was about five months old)." It then turned out that Miss Damita had left the Roosevelt some weeks before and was staying at the Chateau Elysée—would I try there please?

When I finally got connected with the Chateau Elysée, the ardor-dampening information was given, "I'm sorry, but Miss Damita does not wish to be disturbed; it is only eight o'clock."

"I quite understand," I pleaded, "but please make an exception today. I am a very close friend of hers and have just arrived from Europe. Please tell her that."

I heard a telephone ring for a long, long time. Finally, a sleepy voice with a French accent asked, "Who is calling?"

"Lily, this is Louis," I replied in highly emotional French. I could say no more.

"Louis! Where are you—you're not here in Los Angeles?"

I believed I detected genuine pleasure in her manner.

"Certainly I am," I said. "I have come all the way from Berlin to meet you again. When can I see you?"

After a pause—which seemed a bit too long—she said: "Come to my apartment at eleven o'clock. That will give me enough time to get ready. Sunday is the only day in the week when I can sleep late. I am working very hard right now on a new picture."

As in a dream, I slowly put down the receiver. Three more hours, and I would be with her! If her eagerness to see me was something less than my eagerness to see her, it was a circumstance that escaped me entirely. I was too blindly in love to notice.

In a sort of heavenly trance, I had boiled eggs and California sunshine on the terrace. Presently, the telephone rang. I was annoyed—my thoughts were too far above such earthly things as jingling bells.

"This is the desk," a masculine voice said. "There are several gentlemen of the press who want to see you—and photographers. Shall I send them up?"

"Please ask them to wait until I finish my breakfast," I answered, vaguely sensing that a small but black and ominous cloud was appearing on the horizon. What were these men going to ask me? Did they have an inkling of the real reason why I was in Los Angeles?

In later years, when painful experience had made me somewhat wiser, I never asked a newspaperman to wait, not even for a minute. I have been interviewed even in bed and in the bathroom.

When I arrived downstairs in the lobby, two reporters and two photographers were waiting. I posed for pictures in the garden of the hotel and then the reporters went to work on me. I talked on and on about my experiences since I had left home, hoping to give them so much "copy" that they would overlook a certain question. But it came—one of the reporters asked quite casually:

"By the way, Prince, are you going to visit Miss Lily Damita while you are here? There is a rumor going around here that there is a romance between the two of you."

There it was—the question I had been anticipating and fearing ever since I had left Doorn. My bad conscience writhed within me. That very morning I had received a letter from my grandfather sending me his love and expressing the hope that I would have a wonderful time at the home of Mrs. Charlemagne Tower in Pasadena, again advising me against the wickedness of Hollywood. (I had told him that I was to be Mrs. Tower's guest as an excuse to get to Los Angeles.)

"Such a rumor is entirely false," I lied, with a considerable degree of irritation. "Miss Damita and I are just good friends and nothing more."

With that my tormentors departed.

My concern over the possible consequences of the interview vanished when I got into a taxi and, with a singing heart, ordered the driver to head for the Chateau Elysée. I left the car in such a hurry that I forgot to pay my fare, of which I was quickly reminded by the driver.

My spirits mounted when the hotel clerk told me that Miss Damita was waiting for me.

I will spare the reader a detailed description of the reunion after a year of separation. He can use his imagination. For me, at least, it was an ecstatic moment.

When Lily expressed her surprise that I had come to Hollywood, I reminded her of my promise, made in Berlin, that "I will follow you to the end of the earth."

In her white beach dress she seemed more lovely than ever to me. Her skin, tanned by the California sun, stood in exquisite contrast to her flowing blond hair. Her brown eyes and full lips accentuated her charms. Her smartly furnished two-room apartment set off her Parisian chic to its best advantage.

With a combined rush of words, we told each other of the events that had taken place in our lives since our tearful parting in Berlin. Lily ex-

plained that after the first critical months she had been able to win success in Hollywood.

She proposed a day on the beach at Santa Monica and I cheerfully accepted—anything to be in her presence. For several hours we lay in the
warm sand talking about the future, which I was secretly determined
we would spend together. I told Lily about my South American plans
but explained that I certainly would not embark on that expedition until
I had spent at least three months in Hollywood. If she inferred—and I
am convinced she did—that I intended spending these ninety days engaged in ardent wooing with herself as the object of my desires, she was
quite correct.

Under the spell of my beloved idol, I then did a very silly thing on my
return to my hotel: I wrote a long letter to my father, telling him everything short of my determination to marry Lily. I did not or would not
remember that my father in a private talk with Lily had approved of our
friendship but had categorically ruled out matrimony. This letter created something of a stir at home and called for immediate action from
those who read it.

That night the papers published a story about me, but there was no
mention of Miss Damita. I felt quite reassured. But when I opened the
Los Angeles *Examiner* the following morning, I found an item that re-
counted in considerable detail how I had spent the day on the shore of
the Pacific, how Lily and I had eaten in a little nook, and what else had
taken place. My appetite was completely spoiled and my mood was anything but "pacific." I was deeply alarmed. The cat was out of the bag,
and thereafter it would be impossible to convince anyone that there was
no romance in the air. This story would certainly find its way into the
European press. My beloved grandfather would feel deeply hurt and
thereafter despise me as a cheater and a liar.

In addition, a horrible doubt began to creep into my mind. Could it
be possible that Lily herself had something to do with that story getting
into the papers? Wasn't I in Hollywood, where publicity was everything? I instantly rang up the Chateau Elysée but learned that Lily was
at the studio and would not return until late in the afternoon. I don't
remember how I got through the day. When I arrived at the Chateau
Elysée that evening my nerves nearly gave way. However, the news-

paper article didn't disturb Lily in the least. She merely laughed at my distress and my reproaches.

"My dear, you were silly to believe that you can remain incognito here in Hollywood of all places in the world," she said. "Don't worry about that harmless little story. It doesn't mean a thing. After a few days the press will go searching after some other novelty, and you will not be bothered any more."

And so she renewed my confidence and restored my mental equilibrium. In my fatuous devotion I neglected to discover whether or not she had tipped off the press to my presence in Hollywood.

We decided between us that I should move to the Villa Carlotta, which was immediately across the street from the Chateau Elysée and not nearly as expensive as the Ambassador. A kindly negro named Elmer, attached to the establishment, was to be my valet, butler, and secretary all in one. We became great friends.

Lily also arranged that my food situation be well cared for by introducing me to Henry Bergman, proprietor of a small restaurant on Hollywood Boulevard. Henry had been born in Germany, had once been an opera singer, and somehow or other had managed to arrive in Hollywood where he played a few small parts in films. One of his closest friends was Charlie Chaplin, who, Lily told me, had presented him with this restaurant which he had developed into a great success.

So my life appeared to be quite ordered—a suitable apartment near my *dulcinea,* good food assured, and little to do except to carry on with my wooing. No alarming news came out of Berlin, greatly to my relief.

Through Lily, I began to circulate among Hollywood celebrities. I was a guest of Douglas Fairbanks, Sr., met Charlie Chaplin and many others.

One night I was invited to a huge dinner party given by Carl Laemmle in honor of his son Carl, Jr. I was asked by the master of ceremonies to make a speech. Taking this honor very seriously, I told the birthday child and the guests that "we Europeans have a great respect for American movies. In your position, you have a tremendous responsibility towards the entire human race. In the name of thousands of German movie-goers, I wish you great success," I shouted with conviction and enthusiasm.

My after-dinner effort seemed to be satisfactory to those present, judging by the applause, but it did not go well with certain German news-papers (the Nazi press in particular), I learned later. I was severely criticized because Universal Pictures, of which Mr. Laemmle was presi-dent, had some years ago produced several films based on World War I, which were violently anti-German.

I did not see much of Lily, because she was spending most of the day at the studios and could not go out often in the evening, her work re-quiring that she get up early in the morning. One night we dined to-gether at the home of Marion Davies. Adolphe Menjou was also present. In any event, my friendship with Lily was anything but a secret.

Several people told me in "strict confidence" about how my cousin George of England, the Duke of Kent, had "quite a time of it" in Holly-wood. According to this story the duke had been almost forced to tear himself away from a very magnetic person and return to his battleship, which was anchored in the harbor at San Pedro. From certain allusions, I gathered that this person was the same one who was absorbing my attention at this particular minute!

Time passed rapidly. I started taking flying lessons and spent most of the day at an airfield. By now Lily had more free hours, and we spent them together. There were no further references to her and me in the press, and no adverse news arrived from my family.

Then one afternoon a reporter from the *Los Angeles Times* came to see me. He spoke Spanish, which prejudiced me in his favor, and pres-ently I was telling him all about Lily and myself, what she meant to me, and other indiscreet things. I finally gave him a few amateur shots of us that had been taken in Berlin. I trusted this reporter so blindly that I even asked Lily to come over and join us, which she did, and there was more talk in Spanish. A photographer was called in, and he made a pic-ture of us seated together in an armchair in my room.

An inner voice told me that this was a reckless thing to do, but I be-lieved the picture couldn't do any harm. It might force us to make up our minds about marriage and might be interpreted as an engagement picture, hence obviating a possible scandal about us of which I had heard hints.

That same evening, out on the beach, I made quite a long and eloquent speech to Lily in which I said, in addition to my protestation of undying love, that I could no longer endure the idea that people were talking about us as though our relation were not proper.

"You're nothing but a big child," she said, "but since we are in love with each other, why shouldn't we get married? We can go down to Tia Juana. It's easier to get a marriage license in Mexico than here."

Now that the decisive words had been spoken, the great question asked and answered in the affirmative, I felt greatly relieved. Though I did not dare to think of the consequences at that moment, I did realize that the step I intended to take would completely change the course of the life I had planned for myself.

I knew that my family would make a united effort to prevent this *mésalliance* or, in case it was actually consummated, to have it annulled. In the eyes of my grandfather and my parents I would have disgraced myself. My father, too, in spite of all his "broad-mindedness" in matters concerning the female sex, would never give his consent to this betrothal, even though he had nothing personal whatever against Lily.

All of these problems, I realized, would have to be faced in due course. It was the present and the immediate future which had to be dealt with by both of us. Lily's situation was practically unchanged. She had her contract with Warner Brothers, and she was not going to give up her profession—not, in any event, until I was able to support her, which did not appear very likely for some time to come.

The necessity to look for a job would arise very soon. My money reserves were dwindling rapidly. Under the circumstances, it wasn't to be anticipated that my family would be in a mood to advance more funds to enable me to remain longer in Hollywood.

Suddenly, I remembered Mr. Ford's offer, made at his home in Dearborn at the family luncheon get-together. I decided to discover whether or not this offer was still good. Lily agreed it was a splendid idea.

On the front page of the *Los Angeles Times* the next day appeared the story of my indiscreet utterances to a Spanish-speaking reporter, with plenty of pictures. I now realized what a fool I had been. I began to feel miserable and at the same time furious.

Nevertheless, while waiting for the expected lightning to strike, I dropped in at the Ford branch in downtown Los Angeles and after its manager had checked with Detroit, was informed that a job as an ordinary laborer was waiting for me. That was good enough for me. The important thing was that I had a job and could stay on in Hollywood under my own financial steam. Besides, I hoped that the fact that a Hohenzollern Prince wasn't too proud to become a simple working man might improve the opinion Americans had of me since reading of my affair with Lily.

The next morning, clad in my "locomotive overalls," I punched the clock at the Ford assembly branch, with a tin badge on my chest bearing the number 113 in the same relative position where I once wore the Order of the Black Eagle on my frock coat. Thus I had joined the largest army in the world, that of the industrial worker, or, putting it in European terms, I had become a proletarian.

I believe that my decision to become a Ford worker was a step in my life second in importance only to the one I took eight years later in 1937 when I proposed to Kira under the Christmas tree.

I was entered on the Ford payroll as "Dr. Ferdinand" and kept that name as long as I was with the organization. At least my college degree served me to one good purpose! My routine involved getting up at five in the morning in order to punch the clock at six thirty. When I walked out of the lobby of the Villa Carlotta, the night clerk always greeted me with: "Well, Dr. Ferdinand, you have beaten the milkman again this morning."

Usually I did not get back to my room until six, and after a dinner at Henry's and perhaps a short ride in the Ford coupé which the Los Angeles branch had placed at my disposal on orders from Detroit, I was ready for bed. Not being accustomed to physical work, I was very tired and eager for sleep.

What became of the trip to Tia Juana? I went there all right, but not to be married. I spent a week end there with two of my pals from the Ford plant.

And what of Lily Damita and the marriage plans?

Nothing. This does not mean that I suddenly gave up the idea, but slowly sanity began to return to my romance-addled head. This tendency towards a restoration of reason was greatly expedited by Henry Bergman, my restaurant-keeping friend. One evening he served as father confessor to me, after I had told him my troubles.

"It wouldn't ever work, Louis," he told me. "You must promise me that you will not do this foolish thing. You may not like me for telling you the truth. I know Hollywood inside and out after my thirty years here. Even disregarding your parents and your grandfather, whom you are not treating with much consideration, you would not be happy.

"Miss Damita is an actress; she loves her profession, and she needs the public. I do not say she is using you for publicity purposes, but her publicity manager is certainly doing exactly that thing to you in his client's interest. She would be very foolish, and act entirely against all Hollywood tradition, to object.

"Some day you will want to have a wife and a home. Do you want that home to be empty? I visualize you among a whole flock of little ones just as most of your ancestors had them. I don't believe Miss Damita would be eager to have a brood of children. That would hardly go with a movie career. Actresses are afraid of losing their figures."

I had sadly to admit to him and to myself that probably he was speaking the truth. Today I am certain that he was right, and I am very grateful to good old Henry for the sound advice he gave me in a quiet corner of his restaurant.

Presently, the stories about Lily and me had reached the European papers, touched up with a dash of scandal. A flood of wires began to arrive. The first to reach me was from my father's old aide, Herr von Mueldner. Then wires came from my father, himself, and from my mother. None came from Doorn. All gave me verbal lashings and admonitions as to my future deportment.

I did my best to soothe my family with honeyed fabrications. I begged my father and mother to have confidence in me, assuring them that I did not intend doing any of the foolish things that had been ascribed to me in the newspaper articles. But apparently I was not convincing, for they started issuing orders. I should quit Hollywood immediately and continue on my voyage to Buenos Aires. Nor did my reference to my job with Ford help my case in the least.

"Go to Buenos Aires at once," said a wire, signed "Papa." It was an order. But the more wires I received, the more stubborn I became. I refused to obey my father's mandate. I might decide it was best to give up Miss Damita by my own volition, but in this affair of the heart I reserved the right to make my own choice. My answer to the order was that regardless of consequences I would stay "put." I would not capitulate.

The flow of trans-Atlantic wires suddenly came to an ominous halt. Then, the blow that could not be parried came from an unexpected quarter. I received another wire, but not from any member of my family.

"Dear Dr. Ferdinand," it read. "Advise you to go to Buenos Aires. You can work at our branch there. Come back to the States in a year or two if you wish to do so. You are still a very young man. Best of luck.
(Signed) Henry Ford."

Now I was really up against an insurmountable hurdle. If I did not accept the conditions offered by my boss, I knew that he would be through with me for the rest of my life. I accepted his terms, vowed eternal devotion to Lily in a tear-splashed farewell, and boarded the Union Pacific for Chicago two days later.

The Spanish-speaking reporter of the *Times* was on the platform to bid me good-by—or so he claimed.

"I have come to wish you a very pleasant trip," he said.

"It's because of your d——d story that I have to make the trip," I retorted with considerable heat.

He has long since been forgiven. I know now that if I had not been so gullible and had frankly asked him to tone down his story, or perhaps forget the matter entirely, he probably would have done so.

Anyway, the Hollywood dream, now turned into a tragedy as I then fancied, had come to sudden end. "Much ado about nothing" no doubt, and yet the hurt to me was extremely poignant.

What did it all matter? A little gossip more or less meant less than nothing in Hollywood. Some free publicity for a member of the movie colony. A few headaches to my family and to myself. Besides, it was a very wholesome lesson for a conceited young man, who suddenly discovered that he was nothing but an inexperienced greenhorn who had made a fool of himself.

As I headed for Chicago my mood was in sharp contrast to what it had been when I arrived in Los Angeles only a few weeks previously. Expectation had turned to disappointment, enthusiasm into discouragement, and pride into shame. In a word, I was suffering from a gigantic moral hang-over, as we call it in Germany, which, unfortunately, was not caused by alcohol. That sort of hang-over usually grows less by the hour. Mine got progressively worse.

What goal was there left for me in life? With every minute, the distance between myself and the object of my love was increasing. Would I ever be able to forget? Never, I moaned to myself!

In this despondent mood I traveled back to New York. When the train stopped at some of the larger stations along the way, newspapermen wanted to see me. I did my best to hide, feeling like a schoolboy who had been scolded. I had acquired claustrophobia in an acute form.

Before sailing for Valparaiso on the Chilean steamer *Tenu,* I made one more pilgrimage to the Hermit of Malden. Old Poultney Bigelow listened to my explanations very patiently.

"You do not have to make excuses to me, my dear boy," he said. "The only thing I regret is that Miss Damita did not become your mistress. I hope you will be wiser next time. Now be a good boy and go down to Buenos Aires and cool off."

To my intense surprise and consequent irritation he told me, his face beaming with a mixture of joy and mischief, that it was he who had caused Mr. Ford to issue his "evacuation order," as he described it.

At my grandfather's request he had written to Mr. Ford, calling attention to the fact that I had "gotten completely out of gear" under the seductive influence of some Hollywood siren, and appealed to him as a great humanitarian to assist a sorrow-worn grandfather who was pleading for his grandchild's future. Everything indicated, he wrote Mr. Ford, that, as the young man's employer, he was apparently the only person who could rescue the victim from the claws of vice and complete moral ruin.

I admit that, despite my initial displeasure, my grief subsided slightly after Poultney's explanation of the part he and Mr. Ford had played in this antiromance plot. It was flattering to think that the great automobile manufacturer had cared enough about me to concern himself with my personal affairs.

The Hollywood incident had affected my whole attitude towards the United States. In the face of all the wonderful hospitality I had enjoyed everywhere, my resentment and disappointment got the better of me. I was especially displeased with the press for exposing my private life in such a heartless manner, even to the inclusion of happenings during the last day I had spent in Hollywood, hinting that I had been ordered home by Grosspapa.

Driving through the almost deserted streets of Manhattan on a Sunday afternoon to board the *Tenu,* which was docked at Brooklyn, I swore to myself that I would never return to this country where I had endured such humiliations. After cooling off in the Argentine for a year and a half, this dire oath was entirely forgotten.

Now, if I were a mythical prince contrived after the manner of one of George Barr McCutcheon's dashing heroes, this dismal account of my first experience in the United States would be amended to read that on my way back to New York, I suddenly left the transcontinental flyer at North Platte, Nebraska, took the first train—or first opportunity to hitch-hike—back to Hollywood to throw my heart once again at the feet of Miss Damita and dramatically renounce all pretensions to a title and fortune.

But, as my mother used to say, "there was always something the matter with Louis!" I actually went on to marry a genuine princess and have many young princes and princesses, with every assurance that we will "live happily together ever afterwards."

Chapter Twenty

Via the Panama Canal to Chile

(1929)

WELL, I WAS off again, this time south bound. For the first time I was sailing on a boat which was not run by Germans. The SS *Tenu,* formerly a German vessel, now belonged to the Chilean States Lines. It was not modern, but comfortable and solid —a glorified cargo boat with a limited number of passengers.

This trip had been planned a long time beforehand. I had frequently visited the Chilean Legation in Berlin. Count Porto Seguro, the Chilean Minister, and his wife became great friends of mine. There was almost such a thing as a family relation between us. For, the count's real name was Varnhagen. Among his ancestors was the husband of Rachel Varnhagen, lady friend of my ancestor Louis Ferdinand!

After my first trip to Argentina, the count had told me that his countrymen had somewhat resented my failure to visit them. This may sound rather conceited, but it is a fact that my family had many friends among the Chileans, who were often called the Prussians of South America. Their army had been organized by the German General Körner. Germans were also prominent in Chilean trade.

I had gladly accepted Count Porto Seguro's suggestion that I travel from New York to Valparaiso and then on to Buenos Aires.

The *Tenu's* crew was made up almost entirely of *Chilenos.* My command of the Spanish language enabled me soon to become acquainted with most members of the crew. Though most Latin Americans are strong individualists, passionately fond of animated argument, they seemed united in their resentment if anyone spoke of the inhabitants of the United States as "the Americans." These Chileans were no exception.

In spite of the unique experience which the trip through the Panama Canal offered, I felt immensely relieved when the first fresh breeze from the Pacific made itself felt. For, the terrible heat impressed me more than anything else about this link between the two mighty oceans.

During that first week aboard the *Tenu* my romantic hang-over slowly receded. The gay atmosphere of the boat and the delectable Chilean wines helped considerably to improve my psychic condition. Also, the prospect of seeing new places and meeting new faces began to arouse my curiosity.

After Panama, the next port of call was Callao, the main harbor of Peru. This South American republic was under the iron rule of its multi-term dictator-president Augusto Bernardino Leguía. The chief of staff of the Peruvian Army was the German General Wilhelm Faupel, whom I had met three years previously in Argentina where he had been an instructor at the military academy near Buenos Aires. He was now the second most powerful man in Peru.

Hardly a day out of Panama I received a very hearty welcome by wire, signed, "Faupel, general and chief of staff of the Peruvian Army."

Together with the port authorities, General Faupel boarded our boat in Callao Harbor. To my surprise he came in modest mufti and without any military aide. He took me ashore in his private motorboat, then drove to the suburb of Miraflores, where he lived in a small but comfortable furnished house.

Faupel informed me that he would introduce me to the President of the Republic and several cabinet ministers in Lima in the course of the following morning and would also show me some of the military installations to give me an idea of the Peruvian Army. For the afternoon he had arranged a cocktail party at which I was to meet many Peruvians and members of the German colony.

"But, General," I dared interject, "the *Tenu* is to sail tomorrow afternoon. I cannot very well miss the boat."

"Don't you worry about the ship," he replied proudly. "She won't sail without you. Of that you may be sure." The *Tenu* did not sail the next afternoon!

We drove out to the country club. After introductions all around, Faupel, with slight embarrassment, said: "Now, my dear Prince, I beg to be excused. For the rest of the evening I'll turn you over to my friend Mr. Schröder. I still have some preparations to make for tomorrow. I am sure that these nice people will show you an excellent time. I shall call for you at the pier at nine o'clock tomorrow morning."

I asked Schröder, a retired German officer, whether he could explain why the general had so suddenly left us, and why his embarrassment.

"As you know, Peru is a democracy," Schröder replied, "but only by letter, not in spirit. Putting it bluntly, we have been governed for the last twenty years by a dictator. Compared to Don Augusto Leguía, your imperial grandfather, in whose army I had the honor to serve, was practically powerless. Leguía, himself of modest origin, claims that his is a popular rule. He hates the old ruling class of this country, which derives its origin from the Spanish conquistadors. He has banished most of his opponents to the Island of San Lorenzo. There they live under more or less tolerable conditions. A few of his enemies are still walking about in relative freedom but must expect to be arrested any moment for any reason or no reason at all.

"Leguía, who knows his countrymen inside out, does not trust anybody. Therefore, he engaged Faupel, who came here as a stranger and has practically no ties to any side. Leguía can be sure that Faupel will never provoke a *pronunciamiento* (military revolution), because former German Army officers do not go in for such old Spanish customs. Naturally, Leguía closely watches his chief of staff just as he spies on everybody else. Faupel, therefore, has to be very careful in the choice of his social activities.

"On the other hand, he is decent enough to let you meet also our side of the fence. I always see him privately. He could not very well have come with us to the Club de la Unión, where I shall take you now for dinner. There you will meet a few more of the outlaws."

Half an hour's drive took us to Lima. Night life seemed to be in full swing in the Peruvian capital. The traffic lights, the street cars, and the automobiles contrasted strangely with the beautiful old sixteenth- and seventeenth-century buildings in pure colonial Spanish style.

We stopped before a huge white building and entered a large hall with a pompous marble staircase. "This is the Gallinazos Club," Schröder said, as he presented me to a number of middle-aged and older gentlemen. During the exquisite dinner a distinguished old grandee proposed a toast to me. From time to time a fellow diner left the room and returned after a short time. There was an atmosphere of restlessness and nervousness about the whole party. 1 whispered to Schröder, asking why his friends interrupted their meal so frequently.

Schröder laughed heartily: "Most of my friends here suffer from an ailment, but it's not physical, it's a political disease, the 'Leguíaphobia.' All these men have been prominent in public life. They are lawyers, doctors, businessmen, and politicians, all of them distinguished representatives of the opposition. They are always on the verge of being arrested by their common friend. Therefore, they have to keep a watchful eye on the main entrance of this building in order to disappear in case Leguía's henchmen are after them. They have formed this little club because they still want to be together once in a while and have a good time. As symbol for their own fate, they have chosen the gallinazo, a bird which lives in the Andes. It's just an oversized crow, always sad and mournful."

"These gentlemen must have a great sense of humor to make fun of themselves in such a situation," I remarked with admiration.

"They are certainly worth admiring," Schröder answered, "because they are not sure of their lives; nobody in fact is, in this unfortunate country. Leguía has done many things to develop this country, which was very backward in many respects. But he has completely suppressed the freedom of the individual.

"His enemies, and there are plenty of them, claim that he is paid by the United States, because he mostly favors American big capital. Well, sooner or later he will himself end up on San Lorenzo Island or in a place from which people do not return."

I was deeply impressed by this conversation and the whole scene. I knew that in Soviet Russia people had constantly to be afraid of being arrested and suddenly banished by the GPU. Nor were contemporary Italy and Spain countries in which the freedom of the individual was overemphasized. But up to that meeting of the Gallinazos Club in faraway Lima, I had never had a practical demonstration of what the abolition of personal freedom really meant.

Time and again during the years I lived under the Hitler dictatorship I remembered that evening at Lima. Now it was my friends or I who had to keep an eye on the door, expecting the unwelcome visit of the *Gestapo*. But when I hear the opinion expressed that the Hitler dictatorship was possible only in Germany, that he never could have succeeded in any other country, I always tell of my experience at the Gallinazos Club, which happened in 1929, when most people including myself had not even heard the name of Hitler. I ask them to look south of the Rio Grande for proof that there is fertile soil for dictatorship elsewhere.

On the following morning General Faupel arrived in a huge car in the full splendor of his military regalia, accompanied by his aide, a young Peruvian captain who spoke German fluently. Forgetting that I was not in a free country, I began to tell Faupel all about my experiences with the Gallinazos. With an ominous glance in the direction of the captain, who sat next to the driver, he quickly changed the subject.

There was not the slightest doubt that this was Señor Leguía's town. Streets, squares, theaters, movie houses, libraries—everything but churches had his name written, pinned, or pasted on in large letters.

Government House—Francisco Pizarro's old palace—was one of those typically Spanish buildings which look unprepossessing from the outside and reserve their beauty for the inside. Through a doorway still adorned with the coat of arms of the Spanish crown, we entered a large patio with a huge fig tree in the center, said to have been planted by the conquistador himself. After a short wait in the reception room, the President of Peru entered. General Faupel and the presidential secretary retired discreetly after I had been presented, leaving me alone with the dictator.

I found myself talking to a tiny man of fragile stature who looked like a European intellectual. His thick white hair was brushed back and neatly parted on the right side. His eyes were light blue. There was no trace of Indian blood in his clean features. He was very carefully dressed. His demeanor was suave.

President Leguía first addressed me in fluent English until I surprised him by saying it was easier for me to converse in Spanish. He said he had spent many years abroad, some of them involuntarily because he had been a political exile. After a while he turned to his own country. It was very difficult, he said, to get anything done because of the indolence of the Peruvian people, the majority of whom had Indian blood.

"We have a great social problem in our country," he said, "a fact which applies to most of the South American republics. There is a numerically small upper class, mostly of Spanish origin, which represents most of the wealth and the education of the country. Then, there is that vast majority of the populace, mostly Indians, which hardly speak any Spanish. These people are terribly poor and uneducated. Under these conditions it is very difficult to do any constructive work.

"Our country is endowed with the most precious natural treasures. But they have hardly been touched. Transport facilities are practically nil. The Andes form a tremendous barrier. In many instances the airplane is the only means of communication. To get to Leticia in the tropical region of our country ordinarily takes three months. Formerly one had to go to New York by boat, then down to Brazil, and all the way up the Amazon River. Now the trip takes two hours by airplane. Road or railway construction is extremely difficult and horribly expensive. We have to jump, so to speak, from the mule to the airplane.

"In order to develop our natural resources we need a lot of foreign capital. I pride myself on having persuaded American capital to invest heavily here. I know I am severely criticized by my adversaries for doing that. But what else can I do? Nobody likes the Americans any too well here. But at least they are full of energy and get things done, whereas my own countrymen prefer to discuss things and make speeches. We do not like to admit this, though at heart we envy the Americans their pep. Your countrymen also have done a very good job here. We have many old German commercial houses in Peru.

"I know that many people call me a tyrant and a dictator. But if I did not kick them in the pants once in a while nothing would be accomplished in this part of the world."

At this moment the secretary announced that a delegation was waiting. Leguía wished me a pleasant journey and a nice stay in the Argentine. I wished him success for the future of his country.

Though I thoroughly enjoyed the cocktail party at the Faupel residence in the afternoon, I began after two hours to get restless, wondering if my good ship *Tenu* was still at her anchorage. I told Faupel about my misgivings.

"You don't have to be worried in the least," he replied with a grin. "As

I told you before, I would not let the *Tenu* leave without you. But we don't even have to take any special steps. I doubt that she can leave on schedule. Don Emiliano Figueróa, Chile's special Ambassador, is giving a farewell party aboard your ship. You can at least give us another hour of your time."

Finally, around eight o'clock, I was driven to the pier by my host and Mr. Schröder, both of whom I thanked enthusiastically. Faupel's job lasted only fifteen more months. The Leguía dictatorship was overthrown and the dictator lost his life. That ended Faupel's career in Peru.

The *Tenu* by no means looked as if it were about to sail. A gay throng of civilians and officers in uniform crowded the deck and social halls. The band was playing dance music somewhat out of tune. The ship's crew seemed to have its full share of the frolic. I finally worked my way through to the smoking cabin. There the ship's master was leaning heavily against the bar in a desperate effort to keep "afloat." He waved to me with a limp arm and muttered:

"Please, Prince, will you take my place. Don Emiliano has succeeded in drinking me under the table. The boat was to have sailed a few hours ago but in this condition I can't navigate. I must first sober up."

He forgot to introduce me to the stately gentleman with a long gray beard who was standing next to him.

"Have a drink with me, Prince," this gentleman said in a deep voice after the captain had left. This was my introduction to Don Emiliano Figueróa Larrain, a former President of Chile and one of South America's ablest statesmen. He had just concluded the famous Treaty of Lima which settled the century-old Tacna-Arica border dispute. Don Emiliano, who seemed immune to alcoholization, kept on ordering drinks. The next morning I awoke with a terrible headache. The ship was at sea.

I got to know Don Emiliano well during the seven days which it took the *Tenu* to go from Callao to Valparaiso. He believed in "live and let live."

After calling at the ports of Arica, Iquique, Antofagasta, and El Chañaral, with highly informative stopovers for me, we entered the beautiful Bay of Valparaiso, the "valley of paradise." Another sea voyage had come to an end. During the sojourns at different ports, the Hollywood affair had not been mentioned. But at all of them some local Ford representative had contacted me and placed a car at my disposal.

At Valparaiso, I was met not only by the manager of the Ford branch in Santiago, but also by German Consul General Poensgen. At the German Club, where we went first, I was asked to enter my name in the guest book. In the column marked "profession" I wrote *Fordarbeiter* (Ford worker). This caused considerable consternation in the German colony, which was very conservative and somewhat high-brow.

For the journey to Santiago, Don Emiliano graciously invited me to board his special car. Aware that I knew nobody in the capital, he offered me his help and advice. He had already telephoned to the Club de la Unión to reserve a room for me. He remained my mentor throughout my visit in the Chilean metropolis.

The Santiago railway station was filled with an enormous crowd who welcomed their emissary of peaceful negotiations as though he were a conqueror. The Chilean cabinet, led by the Foreign Minister, offered him its congratulations. The German chargé d'affaires was there to greet me and drive me to the Club de la Unión.

From the newspapers I became aware that Count Porto Seguro had carefully prepared my visit. The front pages of *La Nación* and *El Mercurio* were dedicated to Don Emiliano Figueróa Larraín and to the *Príncipe de Prusia*.

A hectic period of social engagements, semiofficial visits, and private invitations began. I found Chilean hospitality to be overwhelmingly spontaneous but definitely ruinous to the digestive organs of the body. It took me weeks afterwards to recover from this "Chilean cure."

I called on the German minister, Dr. Ohlshausen. We immediately "clicked," to use that expression; I am very glad that we did under the special circumstances, which were odd.

I thanked His Excellency for having sent the consul general at Valparaiso and his chargé d'affaires here at Santiago to meet me, adding that though I was on no official mission whatsoever, it was the first time that the German diplomatic representatives had bothered about me.

"I know that," he answered. "And you perhaps know, too, that I am not exactly what one calls a rightist. I never have been. Nevertheless, I shall introduce you to President Ibáñez and we shall make other official calls. But I want to ask your co-operation in one matter. The German colony of Santiago and Valparaiso is very conservative and in its majority monarchical. I have a very difficult time with these compatriots. They may use your presence to embarrass me. I know that your situation is quite delicate, but I should be very glad if we could stick together. I want by all means to avoid giving the spectacle of national discord to the outside world. I have the duty to represent my country here and nothing else. Will you please help me to do that?"

"I have already heard about the strained situation, Your Excellency," I answered. "Under no circumstances do I want to be used as a tool to endanger your position and that of Germany in the eyes of the Chileans."

"Thank you, Prince!" Ohlshausen said and stretched out his hand, which I grasped to give it a warm shake.

Well, the "battle" began soon after this first meeting. The German clubs of both Valparaiso and Santiago invited me for evening receptions. This was a very thoughtful and apparently innocent gesture. The German Minister was invited also. That, too, was all right and according to diplomatic custom. But now came the hitch.

Both clubs let it be known that in my honor they would decorate their clubrooms with the old Imperial German flag. For me as a private citizen this would not have been embarrassing. I thought it most unfortunate that Germany had done away with its old flag, which apart from all other considerations I preferred to the new one from an aesthetic viewpoint. I believe that the combination of black, white, and red is more beautiful than black, red, and gold. But for Ohlshausen, as the official representative of the Weimar Republic, it would have meant, among other things, immediate removal from his post had he accepted the invitation under these circumstances.

It was obvious that the two clubs wanted to snub the German envoy, thus forcing him to abstain from accompanying me to the receptions. Now the moment had come for me to stick to my guns. I had a long telephone conversation with the president of the German Club at Valparaiso. I explained that under no condition would I attend if it were made impossible for the German Minister to come. I tried to persuade him that this flag business was not worth the while to start a social scandal. But he claimed it was impossible for his club to change their attitude. I did not yield, and the Valparaiso evening fell flat.

After this demonstration of firmness, the German Club in Santiago was more open to reason. It decided not to show any flag at all. The bust of my grandfather was merely to be decorated with flowers and evergreen. This solution was acceptable to Ohlshausen. So we both went and had a jolly time.

From letters I later received from home I learned that conservative circles had branded my attitude as highly unpatriotic and disloyal to the old traditions. My family did not seem to be very pleased either, having been informed only of one side of the picture. After my return, though, when I had a chance to tell my own story, they agreed that I could not have acted any other way.

Another well-meant gesture caused momentary embarrassment to the unfortunate Ohlshausen and myself. The minister and his wife gave a luncheon party at their private home in my honor to which they invited several diplomats of other nations, among them the Spanish Ambassador, who was the senior-ranking diplomat at Santiago. When lunch was announced, Mrs. Ohlshausen asked the representative of Spain to sit at her right and me at her left. From the viewpoint of a diplomat of the Weimar Republic this was correct. But the Spanish Ambassador demanded categorically that I should have the seat of honor.

"But you are so much older," pleaded the hostess. "I am sure the prince does not mind at all." There she was absolutely right.

"Age does not count in this case," retorted the envoy. "I am a monarchist, and the prince is my King's godchild. I am sorry indeed, but I cannot accept the seat of honor. It is not due me."

Fortunately the other guests did not hear that little "word duel." The old diplomat remained adamant, and we swapped seats.

A few days later we called on Chile's dictator-President, Carlos del Campo Ibáñez. He had a huge study at the Palacio de la Moneda which dated back to the Spanish conquistador Don Pedro de Valdivia.

Ibáñez wore the gray uniform of a Chilean Army colonel. He was a tall man in the forties. His thick black hair was cut short. He sported a mustache. His voice was deep and musical. Our conversation was rather short and did not leave the safe ground of generalities. From what Ohlshausen and others told me later, I gathered that Ibáñez was the figurehead of a political group mostly representing the army. He did not last long.

I saw Don Emiliano frequently. He spent several evenings a week at the Club de la Unión, during which I briefly reported my experiences.

Though the Chileans I met possessed great charm, they lacked the broad outlook which distinguished Don Emiliano in such a high degree. Theirs was a happy-go-lucky attitude towards life. They evinced none of the melancholy which I found later to be a characteristic of the Argentine people. One thing which became somewhat tiresome was the exaggerated patriotism of the Chileans. There is a plausible explanation for this. The Chileans are deeply connected with their country, which affords some of the most beautiful scenery on the globe. But they are practically cut off from the rest of the world by the Pacific Ocean on one side and the Andes Mountains on the other. This gigantic mountain range acts like a supernatural "stop sign" of Nature herself.

With me, the urge to look beyond this colossal wall grew constantly. The Chileans, however, are affected by its constant presence in the opposite way: they feel protected by their Andes and have no urge to look beyond; on the contrary, they distrust everything that lies on the other side of the *muralla*.

One of Don Emiliano's many nephews who ran a Ford agency was a reserve officer in the Chilean Air Corps. One day at the airport he suggested that I fly with him to Buenos Aires. I accepted enthusiastically. Little did I realize that his single-engined plane with a 150 h.p. motor could never have climbed the 22,000 feet over the Andes. The whole thing was a reckless plan, but the captain had his flying commander's permission. Fortunately, the approval of the Argentine Government for the flight was required. That's how the whole undertaking was frustrated. Dr. Ohlshausen and the Spanish Ambassador went to work behind my back on the Argentine Ambassador, who in a diplomatic note to the Chilean Foreign Minister, who also had been taken into their confidence, expressed Argentina's profound regret that under the circumstances such a permit could not be granted.

Much of my time in the Chilean capital was given to Ford activities. I visited the Ford branch at Santiago and most of the Ford agents. One evening I was invited to a dealers' meeting. In most Latin countries business is combined with pleasure. After the dinner the Ford manager made a welcoming speech and announced that the Príncipe would say a few words.

With deep conviction in my voice I gave an enthusiastic description of *Don Enrique* (Mr. Henry). I asked all the dealers to swear allegiance to the prophet of motorization and the creator of the most popular vehicle. A few days later *El Mercurio* published an article full of sarcastic witticisms about Mr. Ford's self-appointed promoter. It insinuated that the shrewd American capitalist had taken advantage of my lack of experience in practical life to add a few more dollars to his fabulous wealth!

I could easily have spent another month or two in hospitable Chile. But my money ran out. I even had to obtain a loan from the Banco Alemán Transatlantico to pay for my railway ticket to Buenos Aires. My departure was delayed for more than a week because of snow in the Andes. The train finally left in a thick morning fog which also clouded my senses, strongly affected as they were by the farewell night spent in the company of Don Emiliano and his friends.

It took about three hours to reach the terminal of the Transandine Railway at Los Andes. The ticket from there to Mendoza, the terminal on the Argentine side, cost about four hundred dollars, although the two towns are only one hundred miles distant as the crow flies. It took the narrow-gauge train ten hours to cover that distance, for it had to climb to a height of thirteen thousand feet in grandiose serpentines. Some years later it was completely supplanted by the airplane.

The panorama which unfolded before my eyes has hardly been equaled by anything I have seen since. Only the thinness of the air somewhat spoiled the pleasure of enjoying the breathtaking scenery. Some of the passengers became airsick. There was no provision for oxygen.

At the highest spot of the mountain pass we reached Puente del Inca, the border station between Chile and Argentina. The famed Christ of the Andes, a tremendous crucifix, marked the border. From Puente del Inca on the descent was much less steep than on the Chilean side. At about ten o'clock that night we arrived in Mendoza.

Chapter Twenty-one

Cooling Off in Argentina

(1929–30)

I N MENDOZA we had two hours until the departure of the Buenos Aires Express. Two representatives of the governor and the military commander of the city took me on a midnight drive. My hosts said they were bored to tears in this provincial town and longed to get back to the capital. No wonder! Perhaps more than in any other country, Buenos Aires is the center of the country. It offers every kind of amusement for even the most spoiled globetrotter. Life on a big *estancia* (cattle ranch) is a thousand times preferable to the small Argentine country town.

During the night trip to Buenos Aires a melancholy mood befell me. My plans for the stay in Argentina had suddenly lost their attraction. In the quietude of my compartment I realized that my heart had remained in California.

In the dining car the next day it was almost impossible to eat, for although all the windows were closed and the shutters drawn, sand and dust penetrated in heaps all over the car. The passengers tried to fight the dust clouds with Mendoza wine but did not succeed.

My friends Enrique Susini, Ricardo Frers, and Luis Romero, as well as the music critic of *La Razón,* welcomed me at the Buenos Aires Railway station that July evening in 1929. Fortunately no reporters or news photographers! We went directly to Susini's house.

"We know all about your adventures in Hollywood, *amigo Luís,*" Susini said. "But you know our national character. We as your sincere friends do not want you to become the hero of a comic opera. What do you intend to do, now that you finally got here? The press will want to know."

"I'm going to be a workingman and not a banker," I replied a little sharply.

"But weren't you going to join the bank of Tornquist?" Susini asked in amazement.

"I was, but not any more," was my firm reply.

"If that's what you really want to do, that's perfectly all right with us. Carlos Alfredo will be a bit sad, and Heaven only knows what your family will say about your change of program. You'll have to do the explaining to them; I won't accept any responsibility. By the way, where in the world do you want to work?"

"At the Ford branch, of course," I answered, rather offended.

"I didn't know such a thing existed in our town," the music critic remarked contemptuously.

"A music critic isn't expected to know such things," I snapped, my Fordman's pride deeply hurt. "The Ford factory is situated in the Calle Villafañe."

"That's a very aristocratic neighborhood," Romero remarked drily. It was, as I soon learned, one of the slums in Buenos Aires.

"Well, Luís," Susini resumed, "for the time being I hope you'll stay with me as my guest until you find yourself an apartment. Let's have a bite to eat and then go to the Teatro Colón. Erich Kleiber is conducting a symphony concert tonight." This was good news, for I knew Kleiber well from Berlin.

The next morning I took a taxi to the Calle Villafañe. Everything in this factory district looked very poor and dirty. At the Ford establishment, which was built like most Ford assembly plants all over the world, I asked for the manager.

A tall man in shirt sleeves, with blue eyes, a bull neck, and a bald head, extended a large hand for a cordial handshake.

"So you want to work with us down here," my new boss, Griffith by name, said. "I'll put you through the whole works. I think we'll get along all right. Our men down here are not very different from those you've worked with up north. But they are perhaps more radical. They all know of your coming down here. You don't have to worry about them. We haven't had a single strike as yet in our factory, although there's labor trouble everywhere else. They printed this little pamphlet welcoming you. Do you want to read it?"

To my great surprise it was not at all antagonistic. Quite the contrary. It expressed their satisfaction at having a member of a former ruling house among them and their intention to receive me with open arms. It ended with the recommendation that their *niños bien* (contemptuous word for rich young boys) should emulate the young prince from Germany. Then Griffith called in his managerial staff to introduce me.

"Until Monday, then," he said as I took leave. "Next week we'll have a car ready for you. Dearborn instructed me to give you one for your use."

I drove on to the Banco Tornquist.

"Welcome, Luís Fernando," Don Carlos Alfredo exclaimed, embracing me in the Spanish way. "Did you finally get here? We already thought you got lost on the way."

"I came to tell you that I am not going to work for you," I said, slightly embarrassed. "I want to continue my work with the Ford Motor Company which I started up in the States. I have just called on the manager of the Buenos Aires branch. Monday next I shall start in."

Tornquist gave me a quizzical look and remarked: "There is a slight difference between a banker and a motor-car manufacturer. But if that's what you want to do, I am the last one to interfere with your plans. I am very sorry, however, that you won't work with us. Whenever I can be of any help to you, please tell me. Well, Luís, lots of success."

My life during the next few months was strictly regulated. My Argentine friends teased me a lot about the voluntary slavery I had chosen. For the first four weeks I stayed at Susini's house. Meanwhile, through my friend Ricardo Frers, I had found a new, unfurnished, two-room apartment in a quiet neighborhood. I needed only a few pieces of furniture to make the place look cozy. Frers lent me an old Indian servant, Vicenta, to look after the place. She was very faithful, trustworthy, and an excellent cook. But she did not appear before noon, because she also had some work to do at the Frers home. My work at the Ford plant started at 8:00 A.M. I therefore tried at first to prepare my own breakfast. But it was a complete flop, as I lack all qualities of a cook, patience being one of them. So I decided to fill my stomach in some near-by restaurant. But the Argentine capital evidently did not have eating places that were open so early.

Driving down to the Ford branch, however, I had often noticed all kinds of lunch wagons at the docks. They looked none too appetizing, but I had to choose between overcoming my hygienical inhibitions or working on an empty stomach. I chose the former. My courage was amply rewarded. The owner of one of these "ritzy" emporiums, a born Spaniard, prepared an excellent breakfast. He loved to talk and discuss the events of the previous day. Like all Latins he was interested in politics. The day the Spanish dictator resigned he remarked: "I believe Don Alfonso (meaning the King of Spain) has made a great mistake in letting Primo de Rivera go. I am afraid that he will have to follow him eventually."

This political diagnosis of a simple, almost illiterate, Spanish emigrant was only too accurate. Less than a year later King Alfonso also left the country. As a result of these conversations and others, I wrote a letter to my godfather, in which I tried to give him an objective view based on the opinion of his former subjects, who still felt very friendly towards their old country and kept worrying about its future.

In 1936, I met my godfather in London where he was living in exile. He agreed that my *gallego* in Buenos Aires had not been so wrong after all.

The keen political interest of my breakfast gallego was shared by my fellow workers in the Ford factory. A feeling of general political restlessness and discontent was noticeable among them. It was not based on ideological convictions, socialist or communist, but manifested itself in widespread criticism of the aging President Ipólito Irigoyen and his whole administration, which was degenerating into a corrupt dictatorship.

The fact that he had kept his country out of World War I in spite of strong pressure, especially by the United States, had won Irigoyen the hearts of the majority of his countrymen. His re-election had been a unique triumph. But soon it became clear that he had lost his one-time vigor. The septuagenarian chief of state now seemed to have but one concern: women.

The economic depression which began with the "Black Friday" on the

New York stock exchange soon made itself felt in Argentina. A high tariff for meat and grain imposed by the United States did the rest. Fourteen months after my arrival in Buenos Aires, Irigoyen and his party were removed from power by an almost bloodless revolution.

I met the President only once. Shortly after my arrival, there was a gala performance at the Teatro Colón. I was introduced to him by Susini, who belonged to the same party as Irigoyen. He was a tall, heavy-set man, with a cone-shaped head and penetrating blue eyes. Some people said Irigoyen was a Basque; others, mainly his enemies, claimed he was a Turk and not even a Christian. I was never able to find out who was right.

Standing at a buffet loaded with exquisite dishes and with a champagne glass in one hand, Irigoyen very amiably thanked me for the congratulations I had sent him from Berlin on the occasion of his re-election. I assured him that my countrymen never could forget his attitude during the war. That was about all we had time to say to each other; the next act of the opera was about to begin. I thus added another number to my list of dictators.

My work at the factory was unattractive. Griffith evidently was aware of this, for in a report he sent to Dearborn he wrote, "I cannot call Dr. Ferdinand one of my best workers."

Unlike their American colleagues, my fellow workers during the lunch hour all went to little restaurants in the neighborhood. I soon joined them and consumed my lunch in a dirty little place opposite the factory. The food was anything but delicious.

The general outlook on life of the native Argentine, I found, was far from optimistic. He did not believe in unlimited opportunities. A deep resignation often led him to be morbid and even sarcastic.

On the whole, my first months in Buenos Aires were rather monotonous. At times I felt very lonely. I could have had invitations every day. But social life in Argentina at night never started before ten o'clock, and luncheons generally lasted for two or three hours. Such a life was out of the question if I was to stick to my Ford job.

Following the old Spanish or Moorish custom, young girls in Argentina were not allowed to go out alone with a gentleman. An old aunt or member of the family had to accompany her. Dancing in public places or night clubs was just not done.

I knew several families which treated me as one of their own and in which there were charming and pretty young girls. Whenever I suggested that we go out alone, the girls explained that they would gladly accept my invitation if they could but that they would never find a husband if seen alone with a young man before they were married. My masculine pride was deeply hurt, and I just gave up seeing Argentine girls at all.

One evening I was having a night cap with Ricardo Frers when Antonio and Jane X——, a couple who had been on the trans-Andean train with me, happened to drop in at the same cafe. I had almost forgotten them but was very pleased to meet them again. They invited me out to their home in Belgrano the following evening. From that day on we became very close friends. Antonio, who was highly intelligent and an excellent businessman, had to do a lot of traveling and was frequently absent from the capital. He was quite satisfied to leave his American wife Jane in my care. As a typical American she could not get used to the kind of life the Argentine women were expected to lead.

So we decided, with her husband's consent, to do things in the American fashion, regardless of possible criticism. We were all *gringos,* so what did we care! We went to the theater, the movies, restaurants. We bathed together in the muddy waters of the La Plata. We went dancing in the only night club of Buenos Aires.

Jane was an excellent companion, a real sport. She had read all about my Hollywood adventure. Her outlook on life was practical, her education solid, and her mind open. Besides, she had a sense of humor combined with sentimentality and tenderness.

As we kept very much to ourselves, nobody bothered about our friendship. Not even General Kretshmar, Faupel's successor, whom my family had asked to keep an eye on me, ever found out about it. I was definitely sad when the X——'s left Buenos Aires about five months ahead of me, Antonio having been transferred to Chicago. There we met again in 1932. In 1933, I was their guest in Mexico City.

By December 1929, I had worked myself from the top floor down to the ground floor of the Ford factory and reached the end of the assembly line. My mechanical Ford education was finished for the time being. At my request, I was transferred to the sales department in which I was really interested—much more so than in production. I had undergone the mechanical training only because the Ford system required anyone aspiring to an executive position to work from the bottom up.

If I was to play a responsible part in the huge Ford organization, it was of course essential to know how our product was manufactured. But from the viewpoint of my personal inclinations, which were mainly sociological, it was much more important to know the individuals who made the product. I believe it a most unfortunate habit of our age—perhaps one of the main reasons for certain of its grave problems—to think in terms of masses and not of individuals.

At the beginning of December, I asked Griffith for a few weeks' leave, which he readily granted. After months of strenuous physical work in the factory, I felt a great urge to retire to the loneliness of Misiones and to enjoy the company of Adolfo and Elena Schwelm. A letter to Don Adolfo, asking if he would give refuge to a workingman from Buenos Aires, was answered by a telegram extending a cordial invitation.

I spent much of my time on the journey in an attempt to learn the Russian alphabet. Just before leaving the capital I had bought a Russian grammar, not having the slightest inkling that I would subsequently marry a Romanov.

The minute I boarded the Paraná River steamboat at Posadas, the terminal of the North-Eastern Railway, a strange, almost uncanny, atmosphere engulfed me.

Up in these regions it was still the Guaraní who determined the atmosphere. This Indian tribe once had populated a large part of South America. Now it had receded to these regions. It still made up the majority of the population of Misiones and Paraguay. Its extremely melodic and poetic language had given names to many rivers, towns, and villages.

The fate of these people has been rather tragic. With the advance of modern civilization these Indians had been reduced to common laborers. They generally did not possess anything besides their machete, a long knife for cutting the trees in the jungles.

The system adopted by most of the big lumber and plantation companies was to pay a month's salary or even more in advance. Instigated by the hiring agents, the Indians spent most of that money in a few days or even in one night on *caña,* a very potent sugar rum. Like their cousins in North America, they could not withstand the temptations of liquor. They got more and more into debt. They had to buy all their daily needs in stores owned by their employers, where they practically never got out of debt, thus forming a type of modern slave.

As individuals, these natives were excellent workers and faithful servants. They combined physical courage with great national pride. When intoxicated, however, they were untamable and ready to commit almost any crime, running completely amuck in many cases. One had to be very careful not to hurt their pride because they are vindictive.

I noticed a certain uneasiness and restlessness on the boat, without being able to put my finger on it. A few months later the captain of the boat was found murdered in his cabin with his throat cut.

Our steamer, sailing under the Argentine flag, served the ports on both Argentinian and Paraguayan territory. From time to time it approached one of the shores. These ports consisted of nothing but a little free space in the jungle. Sometimes there was a small beach. The steamer had to drop its anchor. A small rowing boat was lowered, and passengers and goods were taken ashore.

Especially after nightfall this landing procedure struck me as very strange. The sound of the flowing waters of the river, the low, melancholy voices of the boatmen, and a few torches ashore suggested mystery and loneliness. By the time the rowboat had returned, the lights had disappeared and the port was gulped up by the night.

I later discovered that one could not judge the settlements by their landing facilities. The homes of the settlers in many cases were built at a considerable distance from the river in order to avoid the *mguaribís,* a small mosquito which is a real plague, especially near and on the river. The natives are more or less immune to their bites, but the newcomer is almost eaten up if he does not constantly use *citronela,* a liquid with a sweetish smell.

When I reached my destination, Don Adolfo was again standing on the beach, as he had on the occasion of my first visit in 1926.

"Willkommen, Herr Fordarbeiter," he greeted me with an undertone of irony in his deep baritone voice. He was an excellent amateur singer. "Has the noise and dirt of the factory gotten on your nerves? At any rate, we'll do our best to straighten them out again up in the loneliness of our virgin woods. Now let's walk up to the house. Elena is waiting for us.

"For the moment I have to put you in the same room you occupied three years ago. But next week I shall move you over to the guest house, which you see over there," Don Adolfo said proudly, pointing at a nearby little frame house in something of a Bavarian style. "The governor of Misiones was supposed to inaugurate the new building, but now this honor will come to you."

When I emerged from my room, Don Adolfo was, as usual, sitting on the veranda with his drinks. Without asking whether or not I cared for a libation, he filled half a glass with a brown liquid. It was a concoction made up chiefly of Black and White whiskey mixed with a water containing much iron.

"For Heaven's sake," I protested.

"Now don't be a baby," my host insisted. "This can't do you any harm. Well, here's to your health, Prince. I hope you won't be too bored up here with an old man like myself." He drank his glass in one gulp and refilled it.

A few minutes later our hostess appeared on the porch. With a shy glance at her husband, she exclaimed: "Is Adolfo also making you take that terrible stuff, Príncipe? Do you really like it?" I mumbled that I was not used to anything so strong.

Adolfo, who seemed to be slightly irritated by his wife's remark, grunted: "Now, Elena, don't worry about our guest. He'll get used to it in due time, I am quite sure."

Before the conversation could take another turn, dinner was announced. The conversation during the excellent meal was very animated. Schwelm asked me many questions about my doctor's thesis. I teased him by calling him the mental father of my scientific brain child. My plans for the future were also discussed.

Schwelm did not wholeheartedly approve of my present job. He thought I should have stuck to my first plan. I gained the impression that he did not like the idea of my working for an American firm.

Apparently he looked at North America through British spectacles.

"Please sleep as long as you wish and do not bother about the rest of us," Elena remarked as we all retired.

I certainly made use of her offer. The early hours in Buenos Aires had meant quite an effort. Now I could look forward to several weeks during which I could sleep to my heart's delight. Usually I did not turn up before noon.

I had brought a German edition of several of Dostoyevsky's books to Misiones. For several years now this great Russian writer had been my favorite author. During the quiet nights of Eldorado, I plunged into the immense ocean of the human soul, which Dostoyevsky reveals to the reader with almost unequaled profoundness and mastery.

As regards the Eldorado settlement, which had seemed so thriving in 1926, it appeared that the colony had reached a stage of stagnation, at least in the sense of expansion. Most of the settlers had left Germany in the early twenties during the bad years following the collapse in 1918. The majority of them belonged to the intellectual classes, which had lost their savings as the result of inflation. There were only very few real farmers among them. As conditions in the fatherland had meanwhile gradually improved, the flow of immigrants had ceased almost completely.

My host viewed this situation with anxiety. The saturation point was far from being reached, yet it had to be attained to carry out the great project which he had conceived. About 130 miles inland he had discovered a forest which extended over many square miles and contained most valuable trees. In order to exploit this fabulous wood, colonization had to be carried right into that region. If the immigrants ceased to arrive, his grandiose plan would be frustrated.

Soon after my return to Buenos Aires, I was arrested because I didn't know the customs of the country. I had made it a habit to drive from the factory in my overalls, thus avoiding the trouble of changing clothes twice. One afternoon I was leisurely driving home when I suddenly was stopped by a policeman. He claimed I had overlooked his stop sign at the street crossing. I reached for my driver's license. After considerable fumbling I discovered that I had forgotten my wallet and did not have a single paper to prove my identity. I told the policeman who I was and asked him to accompany me to my home, which was only a few blocks distant. He gave me a short look, then said contemptuously: "If you were the Príncipe Luís Fernando, you would not be driving around town in this outfit. I have an impression that you are just a hoodlum and a common thief. Come along to the police station, where you can tell your tale to the *comisario*. If he believes it, it's all right with me."

After an hour's waiting, I was finally led before the comisario. At first he was even less amenable than his subordinate. But after a long palaver he finally let me drive home accompanied by a policeman to fetch my driver's license and identity papers. When I produced my credentials, insinuating that I felt rather hurt at this kind of treatment, he answered with a smile: "If you choose to wear this kind of disguise, you had better always keep your papers handy. We are not used to princes driving around in dirty overalls. I am very sorry, but I have to ask you to pay a twenty peso fine; it is the regulation, you know."

When I looked in the mirror at my apartment that same evening, I had to admit to myself that the policeman was fully entitled to his diagnosis. I somehow always managed to get much dirtier than any of my fellow workers.

The next morning I told the whole story to my friends in the Ford factory. Instead of earning sympathy I was the laughingstock of the whole place. It was, however, good-natured ribbing and showed me once again that my fellow workers had accepted me as one of them. I was told that the thing to do when stopped by a policeman was to insert two pesos into one's driver's license booklet. I had occasion later to convince myself that such a procedure was both cheap and involved no delay.

On the whole, I was on excellent terms with the Buenos Aires police force, especially after I had made the acquaintance of Teniente Salgado, a police lieutenant whose duty it was to supervise the Ford factory and everything connected with it. After my transfer to the sales department, we visited every precinct station, the police force being one of our substantial customers.

Shortly before the arrival of my mother, who was to come from Germany in the spring of 1930 to look after her "prodigal son," I called on Señor Santiago, the chief of police of Buenos Aires, in the company of

Salgado. Santiago was perhaps the most powerful man in the capital, and people were rather scared of him.

I announced my mother's visit and asked for his help and, if necessary, protection. He was most gracious, promising everything within the reach of his "small" power, as he chose to term it. He kept his word.

For years my mother had wished to travel to South America, and a visit had long been envisaged. The immediate occasion for her journey, however, was not only her *Wanderlust* but also worry over the emotional condition of her son. My family actually feared that Lily Damita might be with me in Buenos Aires!

As this did not prove to be the case and as I was able to create the impression of one who had cooled off measurably, a quite relaxed atmosphere prevailed, and my mother could enjoy her first contact with the New World as much as I did. She, too, was received with great cordiality, and her hosts were enchanted.

Fortunately, her stay did not fall within the period of the revolution which occurred a few months later. By a curious coincidence, however, she found herself for a whole day sitting between the two main actors of the impending drama during an outing. As guest of honor, she was seated between General Toranzo, inspector-general of the Argentine Army, and General José de Uriburu, head of the plotters.

The revolution, when finally it materialized, came off almost without bloodshed, in fact, almost gemütlich. Revolution had been in the air for weeks, and everybody knew what was bound to happen. Hence, when on the morning of September 6, 1930, airplanes appeared over the city and dropped leaflets announcing the approach of the revolutionaries, everybody waited passively to see what would happen.

My friend Susini and I had some difficulty even to find the revolution as we drove around town. Presently, several hundred military cadets led by Uriburu arrived from the May Field. They seemed like a peaceful band of merrymakers and were greeted with storms of applause by the population, of whom more and more joined these marchers.

Everything might have proceeded on schedule except for the fact that several members of Congress, loyal to the government, in a brief show of heroism fired a few shots from Parliament Building. But that did not dampen the enthusiasm of the revolutionaries. A delegation was sent into Parliament House, which brought the recalcitrants quickly to reason. Irigoyen had fled anyway! He now reappeared only as a symbol, in that a stuffed armadillo labeled "Irigoyen" was suspended from a rope hanging from the balcony of the Government Palace amidst the howls of delight of the mob.

By evening the revolution was completed, and all was again quiet on the La Plata.

Towards the end of my Buenos Aires stay, aviation became my main diversion. It will be remembered that I had had to interrupt my activity in this form of sport suddenly in Hollywood. Here an opportunity presented itself to resume it. Several fellow workers in the Ford factory told me about an aviators' club to which they belonged, which bore the ambitious name of *Centro de Aviación civil*. The interesting thing about aviation in Argentina then was that the wealthier classes looked with disdain upon sports flying, partly because they considered it as not "classy" enough, and possibly also because they deemed it too dangerous. As a result the members of the aviation club were almost exclusively workers—chauffeurs, mechanics, and so forth. They saved their hard-earned pennies to take flying lessons.

My teacher, Don Marcelino Biscarret, a former taxi chauffeur, was extremely strict. He was determined that his pupils must never attempt to show off. To him I owe my sense of responsibility as an aviator, which was destined to save me from many an accident later. Many pupils yield to the temptation to put on a show and do daredevil stunts. This was an unforgivable sin in the eyes of my teacher. If anyone committed it, he would break out in violent oaths.

Back on earth, he was charm personified. He loved his pupils. His eyes beamed with delight when he was able to hand me my *carnet de aviación* after I had successfully passed the pilot's examination.

Chapter Twenty-two

Return to Germany

(1930–31)

I N OCTOBER 1930, I finished the additional work on my thesis. I had assembled enough facts to support my theory of immigration. The only thing to do now was to go back to Berlin, have the thesis printed, and thereby formally obtain the Ph.D. degree for which I had already qualified by passing the required examinations.

It was not easy to explain to my Argentine friends that I was about to leave. They had treated me with extreme hospitality regardless of their profession or social status. I was considered one of them, and it was assumed I would stay there permanently.

As for myself, I considered my stay in Argentina as a transitory "exile." I planned to return to the United States on the assumption that the Lily Damita incident had meanwhile been forgotten. To tell the truth, once back in the States, I believed I could renew my romantic ties. During my mother's visit I had evaded any assurances of giving up my marriage plans, though she had made it quite plain that I would have to choose between Lily and the family.

My decision to leave the Argentine was not entirely based on sentimental reasons, however. I had come to the conclusion that I would fit better into the United States, especially because I thought there would be more for me to do there.

My most difficult problem ahead was that of convincing my family, mainly my grandfather, that I ought to return to the United States after a few months in Europe to continue my work with Ford. I had already told my mother of this firm decision.

I asked my grandfather's permission to go back to Germany via Detroit, because I wished to report to my old boss on my work in Argentina. To my great relief I received a very kind affirmative reply. The whole tone of the letter indicated my Hollywood escapade had been forgiven.

My friends of the Civil Aviation Center, who had afforded me the opportunity to obtain a private flying license, gave me a very touching farewell party. I took leave of my pals in the Ford factory, made numerous other farewell calls, and paid my respects to General Uriburu, head of the provisional Argentine Government which succeeded Irigoyen.

On my arrival in New York late in November 1930 after a twenty-one day voyage, I traveled to Detroit immediately.

"We are building a factory in Germany. Would you like to run it, Louis?" Henry Ford asked after I had made my report on Argentina. I replied that I felt extremely flattered but that I needed some more experience in the field.

"There is no hurry at all," he said. "Come back here and we shall make you fit for the job." It was agreed that I return to Detroit as soon as possible.

"But I don't want you to do anything your grandfather disapproves of," Mr. Ford added with a little twinkle.

"I am certain that I shall get his approval," I answered with my tongue in my cheek.

Before leaving Dearborn, I had a long telephone conversation with Lily in Hollywood. I told her about my plans for the future and promised to get in touch with her after my return from Germany. She congratulated me on my decision to stick to the Ford flag. There was no mention of any matrimonial plans.

Next I spent two days with Poultney Bigelow, who took me to Albany for a short courtesy call to the governor's mansion. "By the way," he said as I narrated my experiences, "I had a very nice tête à tête with your Lily Damita. I don't blame you for falling in love with her. But she is not the marrying type. She does not want to have any children. It is your duty to produce a lot of young Hohenzollerns once you are married." Noticing my surprised look he added, apologetically:

"It is not my practice to stick my nose into other people's personal affairs, especially not their love affairs—I had too many myself—but I am only carrying out orders from your grandfather. While you were sweating it out down in Buenos Aires, I went to Doorn. I apologized to the Kaiser for all the nasty things I said about him during the war. He forgave me most graciously. We are again the best of friends. I promised to visit him every year from now on."

On the passenger list of the North German Lloyd liner *Columbus,* I found the names of General Werner von Blomberg and Dr. and Mrs. Hjalmar Schacht. Blomberg had made a study tour at the invitation of the United States Army. I saw quite a lot of the Schachts. Frau Schacht was rather shocked at my Americanized ideas. The *Reichsbankpräsident* made it rather clear that he was playing with the idea of running for President of Germany in 1932, when Hindenburg's term expired.

At Bremerhaven, I was greeted by my parents and my younger brothers Hubertus and Friedrich, as well as by the local Ford dealer, who on orders from Detroit presented me with a new car. My family was visibly impressed by this evidence of my good standing with the Ford organization.

After a short sojourn at Potsdam, I took off for Doorn. I was prepared for a rather stiff welcome. The contrary happened.

"I thought you would at least become President of Argentina," the Kaiser joked, "and all you achieved to be is a Ford mechanic. But then, this saves me giving you a new car every year. I am sure Mr. Ford is in a much better position to do so than I am. Now come in and tell me all about your experiences in America. Poultney Bigelow has already given me some advance stories."

That, then, was the reception I had been dreading ever since I left Hollywood! My grandfather never even hinted at the Lily incident. I told him about my future plans, which he viewed with sympathy.

"Now go back to Berlin and get your thesis published," he concluded. "That will give me time to think what to do with you afterwards."

In Berlin, I handed Professor Bernhard the enlarged manuscript of my dissertation.

I hope I am not presumptuous in giving a thumbnail outline of this effort of mine. Its concept of immigration is based on the assumption that every country to which immigrants flock has particular characteristics which motivate the potential immigrant to choose it as his new

homeland. I call this "specific attractivity." It is compounded of certain
factors that can be divided into two categories: first, the "natural heritage" of the prospective country—its physical resources, climate, scenery,
peculiarities of the native people; second, the country's "cultural heritage," that is, its civilization, language, political mores, and culture in the
more specific sense. The first part of the thesis deals with this theory.

I then applied it to Argentina as it could be to any other country open
to immigration. I reached the conclusion that Argentina does not enjoy
conditions as favorable as the United States, which from the viewpoint
of the theory represents the "ideal case" in respect to both its natural and
cultural heritage. If Argentina possessed advantages similar to those of
the U.S.A., at least forty to fifty million inhabitants would live there instead of the eleven million with which it was populated in the days
when I wrote the dissertation.

Soon we left my thesis and discussed my trip to the two Americas.
Bernhard told me about the repercussions my American adventures had
produced in Berlin and wholeheartedly approved of my plan to continue
working for Ford.

Having tasted the advantages of independence I felt no urge to go
back to Count Platen's apartment. I leased two comfortable rooms from
a tailor near the *Reichskanzlerplatz*. My new landlord, Herr Henseler,
was the first person to tell me about a certain Adolf Hitler and his new
party. Many a time he accompanied me to a middle-class beer garden
where I usually took my meals.

"Germany is in the throes of a terrible economic crisis," he would say.
"There are almost seven million unemployed. The Communist Party is
growing almost hourly. *Reichskanzler* Brüning is trying desperately to
cut down the government expenses, but nobody seems to be able to put
the people back to work. The only man who can save Germany from
bankruptcy and bolshevism is Adolf Hitler."

The next time I visited Professor Bernhard, I asked him what he
thought of a man named Hitler.

"He is more or less of a political clown," he answered. "Nobody in responsible circles takes him very seriously."

He then thrilled me with the information that my doctor's dissertation in its final enlarged form met with his approval and could go to the printer. Grosspapa had guaranteed the expense of publication!

Reading proof took only an hour or two a day, after which came a longer interval of waiting for the printed product. During this time I secretly slipped off to Paris and London for my first visits to these two capitals. I succeeded in eluding the press, thanks to Dr. Paul Schwarz, the German consul in New York, who had issued a second passport to me under the name of Count Ravensberg, the incognito formerly used by my parents. On my return I proudly told my parents that I was the first Hohenzollern to visit France and England after World War I.

During the spring, this time with grandfather's consent, I motored to Prague, Vienna, Budapest, and Belgrade with Juan Terrasa, who had meanwhile been appointed secretary of the Spanish legation in Belgrade. We returned via Venice and Switzerland and finally separated in Munich.

One day my landlord told me excitedly that *Der Führer* was to speak in the *Sportpalast*. Dr. Roberto A. Ramm Doman, a friend who had just arrived from Buenos Aires, and I decided to go to the meeting. The pattern of these meetings is so well known that I can forego a description. Suffice it to say that Doman and I agreed the whole performance had been cleverly acted. Doman remarked: "I guess we shall hear a lot more about that strange man who looks like Charlie Chaplin and talks like an Austrian janitor."

While in Germany, I was eager to obtain a German private pilot's license in addition to the Argentine. The German aviation authorities were ready to recognize my Argentine license, as my Buenos Aires club belonged to the *Fédération internationale aeronautique*. But the *Luftpolizei* (civil air police) insisted upon the three prescribed *Ziellandungen* (aimed landings). When I taxied back to the hangar after the third landing, the loudspeaker on the roof of the airport restaurant played the old imperial national hymn. I reproached the owner of the plane for this well-meant but politically unwise gesture.

"I had nothing to do with it," he replied, dryly. "The man who runs the restaurant claims nobody can stop him from playing 'God Save the King.' British planes, you know, land and take off here several times a day." The tunes of the British and the former German anthems, it will be recalled, are identical with "My Country, 'Tis of Thee."

My European home leave was drawing to a close. My book was ready. A few luxury copies were in leather binding, the rest were in pasteboard covers. A hundred copies were delivered to the University of Berlin for distribution to other German universities and libraries, according to a prescribed procedure. With about twenty other candidates I was handed a big diploma written in Latin, stating that I had passed my examination *cum laude* and acquired the degree of a *doctor philosophiae*.

The same night I left for Doorn. Armed with the diploma and a leather-bound copy of my thesis, I reported to my grandfather. He took the book, looked at the diploma, and disappeared into his study. After a few moments he emerged again and returned my diploma. He had written on the bottom: *"Gratulor*. Wilhelm I. R."

"I must study your book, Lulu," he said jokingly. "You have certainly put a lot of statistics together. That's always very helpful, even if one wants to prove the greatest nonsense."

At luncheon, contrary to custom, champagne glasses were in evidence. Presently Grosspapa said:

"Now that you have your doctor's diploma I don't see any reason why you should not go back to Detroit and get yourself a Ford diploma. I doubt, though, that it will be written in Latin. *Bon voyage,* dear boy. I raise my glass to Dr. Louis Ferdinand," he added, smiling broadly, his eyes sparkling with joy.

He thus gave me the green light for my American career. A few days later I was on the *Europa* steaming westward.

Chapter Twenty-three

America in the Throes of the Depression

(1931–32)

I WAS BACK in Detroit. But the Ford plant was shut down. America had been hit by the Great Depression. Nevertheless, I was told to go to work. Almost everybody in authority from Henry Ford downward was out of town, vacationing, I was told. Was it because of the hot season or because of the depression? I never knew.

Anyhow, I reported for work in the motor building department. The huge structure was as dead as a cemetery. After searching for quite a while I ran across a blond giant.

"Who the hell are you looking for in this d——d place?" he growled.

"I am looking for Mr. Berglund," I answered, slightly scared. "I was told to report to him for work."

"I'm the guy. So you are the Kaiser's grandson. Why did these so-and-so's send you down here? There isn't a d——d thing going on here right now. But in the meantime I'll teach you how to build a motor. We have a hell of a lot of time to do that."

"Besides building motors I'm sure you'll teach me a completely new vocabulary, Mr. Berglund," I remarked, regaining my self-assurance slowly.

"If that's what you want to learn it's all right with me," he grinned. "From now on I want you to call me Swede. I don't go in for that fancy stuff of Mister."

"My name is Louis," I replied. My hand was swallowed up by a gigantic paw. It took my fingers at least a week to recover from that hand-shake.

For several weeks the big Swede and I were about the only occupants of a building in which in normal times at least ten thousand men were at work. My new teacher had been a sailor in the Swedish Merchant Marine, later a policeman in Java, and now, after ten years with Ford, had become a section foreman.

One morning Charlie Sorensen showed up, accompanied by several assistants. Berglund did not seem impressed by the visit of the almighty production chief.

"Now, Louis, show Sorensen what you know about building motors," he grunted. The longer my demonstration lasted, the redder Sorensen's face and the wider Berglund's grin. For almost every part of the motor I applied another of the Swede's abusive words. Sorensen, who seldom smiled, suddenly broke into roaring laughter, and so did everybody else.

"Congratulations, Prince Louis," he said, "not only for the technical knowledge which you seem to have acquired, but mainly for the way you have absorbed all the technical terms used by our factory help. Since I started as a mechanic thirty years ago they seem to have created a lot of new swear words which would make even the toughest hooligan blush."

In the early autumn, business seemed to improve slightly. Orders for several thousand cars had come in. The assembly lines began moving again, and the place began to look normal again, at least for a few weeks.

With the exception of the big Swede, my new companions knew nothing about me. They noticed very soon that I did not "belong," that I was not a mechanic, and that the work was unfamiliar to me. From the very beginning they were very helpful and friendly. If I made some terrible mistake and spoiled a precious part of the motor, they only smiled indulgently and never tired showing me over and over again what I could not grasp readily. "Let me show you," was their formula. In Europe, I found people are likely to hold back their knowledge, whereas an American is inclined to give it away and share it with others.

At the plant everybody used only his first name. So everybody called me Louis. It was touching to notice what sincere interest my companions were taking in my life. "Well, how is Louis getting along today?" or, "Hello, kid, how is everything?" I heard dozens of times.

I found it quite entertaining to watch how my companions gradually discovered my identity. "Are you the Kaiser's grandson? Are you really a prince? How in the world did you get into this factory? Don't you live only in palaces? Where were you during the war? Did you have to leave Germany after the revolution?" I was asked hundreds of questions of this kind. One of the most frequent was: "How is the Kaiser, have you seen him lately?"

I never shall forget those weeks of anxiety when my grandfather was reported in serious condition. Every day my friends in the factory brought me newspaper clippings discussing the Kaiser's health. These good, friendly people did everything to dispel my worries.

"Well, granddad seems to be getting along much better today; everything will be all right in a short time," they would say. I only wished I might transmit these sincere feelings to the lonely man in Doorn.

During my first few months in Detroit, I found little time for anything but work. I had to get up shortly after five o'clock every morning, because I had to use the streetcar. After Mr. Ford's return to his empire, however, the situation changed. I was handed a new Ford coupé.

With the help of Ben Donaldson, I found a comfortable one-room apartment which cost me fifty "bucks" a month. After half a year I graduated to a two-room apartment with a little kitchen at a monthly rent of seventy-five dollars. At that time I was getting five dollars a day at the Ford plant. In addition my family sent me a monthly allowance of two hundred fifty dollars. With roughly four hundred dollars a month I could manage comfortably without trying to buy the town. Soon, though, it became more and more difficult to transfer money from Germany into foreign countries. During the last year I worked for Ford, I had to live completely on my salary.

Because of the early hours, I took my breakfast in a restaurant on Woodward Avenue, which was run by a highly intelligent Greek. Sitting beside taxicab drivers and other early morning workers I learned to order "a bowl" and a "stack of wheats." It was a thrilling experience to have breakfast in the company of all these early risers.

The first editions of the papers always lay before us. I got quite a new angle on world politics by discussing the happenings of the day with these toilers. The opinions I heard sometimes were not very flattering for the persons concerned, but they were certainly sincere.

I decided not to accept social invitations because of my early rising hours and was determined that nothing must interfere with my work. My offishness in social matters was frowned upon by the society hostesses of the "gasoline aristocracy," as my fellow workers maliciously called Detroit's Upper Ten. The only exceptions from the rule were Mr. Ford's old-fashioned dance lessons, which I attended regularly during the winter season. My boss once told me that nothing had disposed him more favorably towards me than my social preference for his factory workers.

Besides the big Swede, my special friends were Otto Olbrich, Roy Frank, and Billy Duncan. Otto and Roy were considerably older than I. Otto was a bachelor with a baldish head, sentimental brown eyes, and a bit of belly. His parents had immigrated from Germany.

Roy Frank was a sort of popular philosopher with a rather melancholy sense of humor and a golden heart. He really did not fit at all into that world of noisy motors and gas fumes. Once, while we were driving in a funeral procession of a foreman, he remarked dryly: "Louis, my boy, never forget this. If you keep your 'ass' flat on the ground you cannot fall very high." Roy Frank's pride and hope was his son Charlie, who was studying to be a concert pianist. Roy himself knew a lot about music and other cultural things.

Billy Duncan for the moment was the only member of his family with a job. His father, a Scotch blacksmith, and two of his brothers were also Ford workers but out of jobs because of the depression. There was a younger brother and an older daughter. After Billy had taken me to meet his family, the little frame house of the Duncans became my second home. It is impossible to describe the kindheartedness and hospitality of that family, which in many ways typified the American industrial population.

Though these people all were hard-working, they were quite comfortably off compared to European standards—that is, in normal times when they all had jobs. Right now they were pretty hard up. The old man and his sons felt deeply humiliated to be out of work.

In spite of that situation their views were the opposite from radical.

They considered themselves free and independent citizens. All they wanted was to make a decent living. They were intelligent and broad-minded enough to recognize that old Henry, their employer, in spite of all his millions would go broke in a short time if he kept them all on his payroll. They knew that Ford alone as a single individual was not able to change the depression into prosperity. They were not easily discouraged. The atmosphere in their home was a gay one. The children deeply respected and loved their parents, who did not try to lord it over their offspring. Hardly a Sunday passed without some kind of excursion. The Duncan boys would bring their friends along, which included not only every European nationality but also Syrians and other representatives of the Near East. Horseback riding, swimming, golfing—this without me—visits to the movies and theaters and frequent dances were included regularly in the program. When I returned to Europe nobody wanted to believe me that everyday Americans led such a luxurious life. To my great satisfaction these activities were all on an individual basis and not a collective one, as was the case especially in my country during the Hitler days, but also before that era. My contacts with the Duncan family perhaps constitute the strongest and most positive impression of my whole American experience. America, to my mind, is made up of millions of Duncan families. And these Duncans never will lose their individual independence and adopt some kind of collective ideology or system provided they are allowed to keep up a high standard of living, which they believe is due them. This standard of living, though, they do not expect as a gift from the community or the state. They want to create it with their own hands and on their own initiative. That is the whole secret of American democracy as I experienced it during the days I lived as a Ford worker in Detroit.

My two main pastimes were music and flying. Through Ben Donaldson and Fred Black, I found a tutor under whom to study music and an aviation school to prepare me for an American private flying license.

Dr. Francis L. York, director of the Detroit Institute for Musical Art, became my music teacher. I had met him in 1929. Though I was booked for only two hours a week, these piano lessons generally lasted a whole afternoon, sometimes extending into the evening. They were the high lights of my week. Love and veneration are the words to describe my feelings for this wonderful old gentleman three times my age, whose culture was deep and real. Many a time after the lesson Dr. York took me to his cozy home, where he, his wife, and their daughter Dorothea did their best to spoil me.

"We want you to feel that Detroit does not consist only of mechanics and Ford cars," my music teacher said time and again.

Once, I recall, he canceled my lesson as in deep anxiety he told me about a plot that was "being hatched to assassinate you." It appeared that I was suspected of being some sort of a German spy, and, according to Dr. York, my enemies were planning to get rid of me by dropping on my head a casting or something like it from an overhead conveyor, making it appear as an accident. He had heard about this alleged plot through one of his girl pupils.

At the time I thought someone had been "spoofing" my teacher and laughed it off, but later I learned that a plot against me had really existed. The true version, however, seems to have been that I was to be gotten drunk, taken for a ride, killed, stripped, and my naked body left somewhere along the roadside. Unbeknown to me a bodyguard was ordered to shadow me until it was believed that the threat no longer existed.

Having obtained an Argentine and a German flying license I could not remain content without an American one. The American civil aviation authorities did not recognize foreign flying licenses as valid. That meant I had to start all over again. Leonard Flo, a friend of Black, ran a small private aviation school on Haggerty Field. Flo, a nice young chap about my age, son of Norwegian parents, was carrying on a plucky fight to make a living as a flying teacher. He lived rather miserably with his old mother, who spoke very broken English, and his sister, who was studying music at the University of Michigan. His air fleet consisted of an old-fashioned wooden Curtiss biplane.

Flying was by no means popular with my boss. None of the leading Ford officials was allowed to use an airplane while traveling in the Ford service.

Leonard did not have much trouble with my practical flying. The theoretical part was a much bigger hurdle to take. My Ford vocabulary did not suffice for the written examination, which I passed only as satisfactory. The flying test made up for my lack of theoretical knowledge.

When we landed at Haggerty Field after I passed the test we were received by the Flo family, Fred Black, and a press photographer. Fred had dug out some bathtub gin to celebrate. I warned Leonard that Fred and I would probably be excommunicated from the Ford organization once Old Henry had read the morning paper. "We need not be afraid in the least," Fred remarked. "Mr. Ford surely won't mind, knowing that Louis is crazy about flying."

The picture appeared the next morning with some flattering remarks which the examining officer was said to have made about the candidate's ability. This was the first time my name again got into the Detroit press.

At the next Ford dance party Mr. Ford surprised me by congratulating me on my achievement. I told him my greatest joy would be to fly around a bit on Sundays and have a look at his empire from above.

"Don't be too reckless, though," the old gentleman said. "I still want you to run that plant at Cologne for me."

One afternoon shortly afterwards the telephone operator called me: "A Miss Damita just telephoned from New York. She wanted to talk to you. Do you want me to call her back?"

Trying to look as calm as possible I asked her to put the call through at once.

"I am on my way out to Hollywood," Lily said. "I got in from Paris this morning. Could you meet me at Chicago next Monday at the Drake Hotel? I am only spending a few hours there before taking the Santa Fe train for Los Angeles."

It was a Friday. Previously I had been invited to fly to Cleveland the following Sunday for the annual air races for the famous Johnson trophy. From there I had only to take the night train to Chicago and one day extra leave.

I spent a very interesting day at Cleveland, where I met Eddie Rickenbacker for the first time. I felt very elated as a German to witness the cordial reception given to Ernst Udet, the former German war ace, by the American public. Udet, whom I already knew from Germany, carried out the most nerve-racking stunts. For instance, he picked up a handkerchief from the ground with the wing tip of his plane.

On Monday morning in Chicago, I went straight to the Drake Hotel and ordered a suite for our rendezvous. I was in a happy mood, sure that this time I had gotten the better of the news hawks. My mood changed immediately when I discovered my picture on the second page of the *Chicago Tribune* with a short article giving away my "secret."

I did not have much time to ponder, because I had to rush to the station to meet my girl. Lily did not arrive as scheduled. Finally, hours later, she turned up. There was no time for the planned stopover of several hours. We decided that I should accompany her on the train as far as Chilli-cothe and then take the next train back to Chicago. But my whole pleas-ure had been spoiled. Lily did not succeed in cheering me up during the three-hour trip. In Chillicothe a dejected young Ford mechanic emerged from the "Sunshine Limited" feeling that he had been a fool all over again. This feeling became even more acute when I bought the morning papers. There it was splashed all over the front page of the *Daily Mirror* —the story of my Chicago escapade. Worst of all was the assertion of the paper that Lily Damita was traveling in the company of some wealthy California sportsman whom she allegedly was about to marry. So I had been made a double fool.

This was the finale to my romance.

The body-and-car assembly on which I was working at this time was nothing new to me. I had gone through that chapter already in Los An-geles and Buenos Aires. But in spite of my mild protests, I had to go through with that part of my training program. I felt I was wasting time. I had been fastening enough nuts and bolts to satisfy me for the rest of my life. I used to complain to Ben and Fred about it. They persuaded me to be patient, to stick it out a little longer. They did everything to re-lieve my boredom. Whenever some distinguished foreign visitor was to be shown around the Rouge Plant a call came from the head office for Dr. Ferdinand. In this way I met many a well-known industrialist or banker from Holland, France, and other countries of Europe.

Besides the boredom, it was my health which was affected by the con-tinuous stay in the factory air. I began to develop a nasty cough. The head surgeon of the Henry Ford Hospital found that I was suffering from anemia and that my lungs were slightly affected. He advised that I stop my factory activities. But for the time being I could not find the courage to tell my boss that I wanted a change. Finally, I did resort to the direct approach, certain events having been helpful in that direction.

Next to the Duncans it was the Cushings whom I saw most of. George

Washington Cushing was the representative of *The Cosmopolitan* magazine in Detroit. We were practically neighbors. During the hot summer months he, his wife, and his two teen-age sons always rented a small cottage on Lake Huron on the Canadian side. I was their frequent week-end guest.

One evening George turned up at my apartment with another gentleman who was most elegantly dressed.

"Louis, I want you to meet my boss Dick Berlin," he said. "Mr. Berlin is on an inspection tour of the Middle West. I thought it would be nice for you to get acquainted."

After some general conversation Mr. Berlin let the cat out of the bag:

"My call is not merely a social one, Prince Louis. I came here mainly to ask you to write an article for *Cosmopolitan* about your life in America."

Noticing an expression of alarm in my face, he went on:

"You needn't be afraid that your personal life will be exposed as some papers have done lately. We are mainly interested in your experiences as a Ford worker. I am sure our readers would like to hear something about them."

We finally settled on a three-thousand-word article, to be entitled "My Discovery of America," for which the pay would be $750. My only condition was that Mr. Ford must know the contents of the article before publication.

The deal fitted perfectly into my schemes. I was contemplating a little Christmas trip to Europe and a rest for my shaken health. The fee for the article would easily pay for a return trip. The factory was shut down half of the time anyhow. So I had lots of time on my hands. Besides, a month later I was to drive my brother Friedrich, whose visit to America I have already described in the chapter on F.D.R., to New York for his return trip.

Meanwhile I settled down to my first venture into journalism.

I made my "literary" headquarters in George Cushing's office. I had never tried to write an article in English before. I composed a lengthy document which was returned once from New York because Dick Berlin wanted more personal background about my early childhood. I showed the finished product to Bill Cameron. He gave his full approval. "I don't even have to show it to the boss," he said.

An invitation followed from Dick Berlin for my brother and me to stay at the Ritz Towers in New York as Mr. Hearst's guests. With the $750 check I booked passage tentatively on the SS *Berlin* for the beginning of December 1932, and for safety's sake paid the return trip in advance so that nothing might prevent my return to the United States.

I was back in Detroit by the middle of November and went to the Rouge Plant almost reluctantly. My success as a "writer" had swelled my chest. I even toyed with the idea of leaving the Ford organization altogether to devote myself to writing.

A few days later I woke up with a high fever and a hoarse throat. I was hardly able to ring up the personnel department to say that I was in bed with the flu. That afternoon the telephone rang. Dazed by the fever, I stumbled to the old-fashioned phone.

"Who is it?" I grunted, rather ill-tempered, because I had given strict orders not to accept any phone calls.

"This is Henry Ford," a soft voice came over the phone, almost in a whisper. I thought I had some fever illusion. My boss had never once rung me up.

"Yes, Louis, that's me, all right. Mrs. Ford wants to talk to you. Here she is."

"Hello, Prince Louis, this is Mrs. Ford," a forceful voice came through. "A friend of your grandmother is here with me. She has just arrived from Germany. She says that they call her Moni. She wants to see you. She is here with me, and I am now handing the phone to her, good-by."

I did not have time to explain that I was quite sick. Moni turned out to be some Silesian countess, vaguely known to me.

"I have promised your step-grandmother to look you up," she said. I explained my situation. "Oh, that does not matter in the least," she answered in a gay voice. "I shall come to visit you tomorrow with Mr. Buchmann and the other friends."

Before I was able to attempt some kind of an answer she had hung up. In the evening papers I discovered a long article on Mr. Buchmann and his "Oxford Group," later known as "Moral Rearmament."

"Next Sunday the members of Mr. Buchmann's party, which consists of ten of his most active apostles, are going to preach from several Detroit pulpits," the article read.

At eleven o'clock the following day the telephone girl announced that Countess Moni and a Mr. Buchmann were waiting in the lobby.

"Are they alone?" I asked hopefully.

"Oh no, Dr. Ferdinand, there are at least nine or ten in the company. How many shall I send up?"

"Send them up all at once," I gasped. "And don't forget to notify a funeral parlor if you don't hear from me any more."

The "Oxfordians" entered with a loud chatter. Mr. Buchmann and Moni, whose real name was Countess Monika von Crammon, settled on my bed. The others were introduced and then told to wait in the next room. They all seemed to feel perfectly at home. Moni told me about my step-grandmother. Then Mr. Buchmann took over and initiated me into the secrets of his Oxford movement.

"I am in direct contact with God all the time," he said cheerfully. "That you are ill right now does not amount to anything. I shall send Him a message immediately, and you will be well in no time. My brethren out there in the next room will do the same thing. Our movement comprises all social classes and political parties."

The Oxfordians stayed for several hours. They all had lunch and tea, which was ordered from the dining room. After sundown they finally left in high spirits. I nearly passed out.

A few days later the fever subsided, and I was able to get up. Not relying entirely on his "wireless messages to Heaven," Mr. Buchmann had sent one of his Detroit followers, who was a physician at the Henry Ford Hospital, to look after me. The doctor found that I was in a rather run-down condition. I told him about my worries as far as my work in the factory was concerned and that I did not know how to broach the subject to my boss.

"If you'll let me, I shall play Fate for you," the kindly physician said. "Your boss at the moment happens to be a patient in our hospital. He has been operated on for appendicitis. I see him almost daily. I'll tell him about your physical condition. I, too, think it's high time that you get out of that plant."

"I have good news for you, Prince Louis," he greeted me the next evening. "Mr. Ford hasn't the slightest objection to your trip to Europe for Christmas. But he would like to see you before you leave. He'll have to stay at the hospital for at least another week."

The day before I left Detroit, Mr. Ford gave me his farewell audience. He received me sitting on the edge of his bed in the bare hospital room.

I asked him about his condition. There had been rumors that an attempt had been made on his life in connection with a demonstration of unemployed workers near the cashier's office of the Rouge Plant. Harry Bennett had been gravely wounded. As it happened, almost simultaneously it had been announced that Mr. Ford had to undergo an operation for appendicitis.

"Oh, that little operation, that's nothing," Henry said. "Won't you sit down, Louis," he added in his whispering voice, pointing to the only chair in the room.

"Mr. Ford," I began my carefully prepared statement.

"Oh, yes, Louis," he almost timidly interrupted me. "Why shouldn't you go back to see your folks for Christmas? I am all for it."

"Yes, but what about my transfer to the sales department?" I interjected.

"We'll see about that after you have talked to your grandfather."

Was there some underground communication between Doorn and Dearborn? I wondered as I closed the door on this lonely patient of the Henry Ford Hospital.

Chapter Twenty-four

Advent of Hitler's Third Reich

(1933)

WHEN I ARRIVED in Bremen in December 1932, Christmas was only a few days off. I therefore decided first to go home to Potsdam; I would visit my grandfather on his birthday on January 27.

Shortly after my arrival I had an impromptu audience with President Paul von Hindenburg. Ernie Liebold, Henry Ford's secretary general, had asked me to take a letter to Dr. Otto Meissner, in charge of the presidential chancellery. Meissner had met Liebold on a visit to Detroit. When I was ready to leave Meissner after a short visit, he asked me: "Would you like to see the Reichspräsident? He is right next door."

I protested that I was neither dressed nor prepared for such an occasion.

"That does not make the slightest difference. The old gentleman will scold me for not bringing you in if he finds out that you were here with me."

After a few moments Meissner returned to say that the Reichspräsident would be glad to receive me at once.

Hindenburg was sitting at his desk. The room was medium-sized and rather dark. The only window opened out on a garden. In this room and at this desk the Iron Chancellor, Prince Bismarck, during many years had molded the fate of Germany and Europe.

The old gentleman rose slowly, grasped my hand, and held it for quite a while in both of his hands. Meissner meanwhile had retired discreetly. The President wore a long black Prince Albert coat which added to the dignity of the old man.

"To my great distress I am accused by many people in Germany of being disloyal to your grandfather and your family," he began in his deep voice. "I am a monarchist and shall always be loyal to your house. At the same time I must do my duty towards the German people, who have twice shown me their confidence." That Hindenburg was not merely trying to be amiable was later revealed in his political will, in which he recommended the restoration of the Hohenzollern monarchy. This part of the will was suppressed by Hitler after Hindenburg's death and became known only years later.

On the basis of my personal experience I was able to tell the venerable Chief of State that he not only was held in high esteem by the Germans living on the American continent but also enjoyed the respect and confidence of many Americans who had no trace of German blood. This apparently pleased him very much.

It was the only time I ever talked to Hindenburg during the time of his office as Reichspräsident. It was also the last time I saw him.

That the situation in Berlin and the country at large was anything but settled was evident. The police were in a permanent state of alarm.

My former teacher, Professor Bernhard, told me that General Kurt von Schleicher, who had succeeded Franz von Papen as chancellor, was on good terms with the moderate labor unions which held a large majority in the organized labor movement. The National Socialists and the Communists had joined hands to oust the general.

As our train pulled out of the Friedrichstrasse station on January 26, 1933, bound for Holland, I was standing next to my father. At sight of the huge Reichstag building I asked him:

"Do you think that Schleicher will hold out for any length of time?"

"I wonder," he replied gloomily. Five days later Hitler had taken his place.

When I arrived at Doorn that evening I was in high spirits. My grandfather, following his old habit, was sitting in the library where he read aloud from a book after dinner. The other members of the family as they arrived had greeted him with great reverence. To the utter consternation of everybody present, I slapped the venerated head of our family on the shoulder in true American fashion, exclaiming cheerfully: "Hello, old boy." Then I settled on his lap and gave him an enthusiastic hug.

The only one who did not seem to mind this new kind of court etiquette imported fresh from the Ford works was the victim of my demonstration.

"Ach, da ist ja mein kleiner Amerikaner" ("Well, there's my little American"), he responded just as cheerfully. Ever after that scene he usually referred to me in these words and thoroughly enjoyed the bewildered looks of some old stiff-necked former general or other exalted figure.

On January 30, 1933, I was guest at the wedding of Princess Marianne of Prussia to Prince Wilhelm of Hesse. Representing my grandfather as head of our family I had to attend numerous family functions of that sort, including funerals. Old General Wilhelm von Dommes, our so-called *Hausminister,* always had quite a time finding victims for that kind of an assignment. Every member of my family looked around for an excuse to get out of these engagements which were considered an awful bore. After a while a system was worked out by which I was to "do" the former ruling families of southern Germany whenever representation by our family was required. After my workshop life I did not mind rubbing shoulders with royalty for a change. My foreign experience also produced a neutralizing effect on our southern relatives, many of whom, ridiculous as it may sound, still nursed a deep grudge against my family for having been remarkably successful in former centuries. The fact that we all had left the political scene at exactly the same time and in exactly the same involuntary way had not appeased these jealousies. Personally, I got along famously with these "southerners."

Marianne was a distant cousin of mine, daughter of Prince Friedrich Wilhelm of Prussia, who had died several years previously. He had been an excellent violinist in his day and pupil of the great Hungarian violinist Joseph Joachim. During the wedding luncheon two bands were taking turns. One was provided by the local Steel Helmet organization with which my Prussian relatives were on friendly terms. The second band was formed by Nazi Storm Troopers, to whom the bridegroom belonged.

We had all just drunk the health of my grandfather, following an old family custom, when the news came that Hitler had been asked by Hindenburg to become chancellor. The general reaction of the guests was one of consternation, for nobody had expected this sudden development. The Brown Shirts, of course, cheered wildly. That same evening Hitler made his famous speech in which he asked the German people: "Give me four years' time and you won't recognize Germany again." The tone of the speech was moderate and dealt mostly with the economic crisis and the general unrest of the country. He promised the German people the restoration of order, work for the unemployed, protection of the workingman against exploitation, and support to the artisans and small businessmen. His program had something for every class. One point which appealed to me, I am quite ready to admit, was the substitution of class co-operation and amalgamation for class conflict and strife, for I had seen how well this amalgamation worked in the United States.

I believe it neither just nor reasonable to condemn as criminals all the millions who voted for Hitler or joined his party after his first pronouncements. Though I am far from comparing Hitler to Roosevelt, many people voted for Hitler in Germany for exactly the same reasons which prompted people in the United States to vote for Roosevelt. The tragedy lies in the fact that Hitler was not a Roosevelt. The German people, in a fit of desperation, fell for a frenzied corporal who began his career in the disguise of a savior but turned out to be a megalomaniac and satanical tyrant. To my mind it was a gigantic tragedy that this man appeared on the German political horizon at a moment when an aging former war hero, who was highly venerated but unable to restrain Hitler and his cliques, was at the helm. This is not meant as an apology for all the dreadful things which have been carried out under Hitler in the name of the German people. I only wish to make it quite clear that I reject the theory as totally unfounded that the Germans are the only people capable of producing political miscarriages like Hitler. What about Stalin and Tito? Countries which have never felt the horrible yoke of ruthless and lawless tyranny will never understand what physical and mental torture it means for those who live under such a regime.

After the Hesse wedding, I underwent a period of observation at the Stubenrauch Hospital in Berlin, where our family doctor, Friedrich Wilhelm Schulze, was chief surgeon. My friend Schulze in substance gave the same verdict as the doctors of the Henry Ford Hospital in Detroit! I must take a long rest with a healthy diet and regular hours. He added that it would not do me any harm if my consumption of alcoholic liquids was reduced considerably. Dry America had converted me into something resembling an alcoholic.

Schulze suggested that Doorn would be an ideal place for the cure and sent a detailed report about his observations to my grandfather.

A few days later he received a telegram: "Shall gladly take care of your patient. Have him leave immediately. Shall apply special treatment."

During the two weeks of my "internment" at the hospital, I was a frequent guest at the Ribbentrops. Their villa was within easy walking distance. Ribbentrop tried hard to enlist me in the new Nazi "cause." He even played up to my personal vanity and potential political ambitions. We spent long evenings talking about foreign affairs and the internal events in Germany. He professed a sincere love for England and great admiration for America. He advocated close co-operation with the Western powers, France and Britain. We agreed wholeheartedly as far as our Western sympathies went. One day he said: "With your experience in America and other trans-Atlantic countries you could be of great value to Germany. The only thing you lack is direct contact with the German people. If you were ready to march with us, as your Uncle Auwi (Prince August Wilhelm) does, I could envision a great future for you."

At this time Ribbentrop was still his normal self. He changed completely in later years. I frankly admit that Ribbentrop's overtures seemed to me quite alluring at the time.

Knowing much less about German than about American politics, I could easily have fallen into Ribbentrop's trap, I am not ashamed to say. Had I not been under my grandfather's "treatment" and protection during those fateful months, I would probably later have shared my Uncle Auwi's miserable life in an internment camp for prominent Nazis.

During these months after my return from the States, I made the acquaintance of another important Nazi, Dr. Ernst F. S. Hanfstaengl, nicknamed "Putzi" by his friends. He belonged to a very distinguished Bavarian family, whose publishing house had world renown especially among art lovers. Putzi was half American, his mother having been born Sedgwick of Boston. He was a graduate of Harvard University and had spent half his life in the United States.

Hanfstaengl, it seemed to me, looked at the whole Nazi business more or less from a theatrical viewpoint. He was the very opposite of a fanatic and soon realized that something was wrong. Each year he gave a luncheon in his two-room apartment at the Pariser Platz on George Washing-

ton's birthday, to which he invited about fifteen "big shots" of both nationalities, such as the American Ambassador, Dr. Schacht, Dr. Eckener,
Louis Lochner, and others. The pastor of the American church in Berlin
was invited, too, to say grace. It was hard for me to contain myself from
bursting out into laughter when I noted the host's pious demeanor during that ceremony, for in ordinary life he had never shown much religious fervor.

Chapter Twenty-five

Three Cherished Months with Grandfather

(1933)

EVER ON THE watch, a very friendly one in my case, American news-papers sometimes referred to me as the "Kaiser's favorite grand-son." Though I felt flattered by this characterization I don't believe that my grandfather really had any favorites among his children or grandchildren. For instance, he sincerely loved my older brother Wilhelm, in whom he placed all his hopes for the future of our family and Germany. What perhaps earned me my grandfather's affection more than anything else was a romantic and even adventurous streak in my character which paralleled a similar one in him.

I am aware that many people have pictured my grandfather as a despot and war lord. History, always fair in the end, I trust, will judge whether this picture was right or distorted. I do know that it underwent a con-siderable change between my high-school days and the beginning of World War II.

I had visited my grandfather many times before but had never lived with him for any length of time. During the three months I now spent with him, I had him all to myself. Not even my step-grandmother was present. These unforgettable twelve weeks brought me very close to my host.

My grandfather led a methodical life following a strict daily routine, which was altered only on rare occasions. I am told that he followed a similar rigid routine during his thirty years on the German throne. This was also the secret of his excellent physical condition almost until the day of his death.

My grandfather regarded me as his patient, for whose recovery he was personally responsible. From his viewpoint my health had been undermined by my submission to the fatigues and strains of a workingman's existence in a motor-car factory. He had also to cure me of a light case of alcoholism acquired in the country of prohibition.

As I was a patient, my tolerant grandfather left it up to me to follow his own daily routine or do whatever I felt like doing. He by no means required me to rise as early as he did.

The Kaiser regularly got up at seven for half an hour's stroll in his parklike garden. Next he fed the wild ducks from the bridge leading up to House Doorn, which was surrounded by water like many other old castles and manor houses in Holland. He cherished these little animals and visited them in the morning, at the noon hour, and shortly before dinner, regardless of weather. At one end of the bridge several meteorological instruments were installed. Before crossing the bridge the Kaiser invariably glanced at these instruments. Meteorology was one of his favorite interests, and several foreign and German weather bureaus regularly sent him their charts and reports.

Shortly after eight-thirty the whole household, including members of the family and the house staff, assembled in the entrance hall of House Doorn. At eight forty-five the Kaiser came down the stairs from his private quarters. After greeting the "congregation" he would step up to a lectern near the staircase. On weekdays he read some psalm or other verses from the Bible, followed by the Lord's Prayer. The short ceremony was ended by his invoking the Lord's blessing upon everyone present. On Sundays, if a clergyman was not available, my grandfather frequently read a sermon that had been delivered by his friend, former Court Preacher Doehring, in the Berlin Protestant cathedral a week before. (It was Doehring who married Kira and me in the very hall in which my grandfather started his day by praising the Creator and asking for His help and blessing.) Once in a while Grosspapa discoursed on a theme chosen by himself. I believe no professional preacher could have done better.

The simple, unaffected way these religious ceremonies were conducted by the Kaiser deeply impressed those who witnessed them. Visitors from Germany from all walks of life, mostly complete strangers who just wanted to say hello, were invited to attend.

My grandfather's religiosity was deep and sincere. He was a convinced Protestant but by no means intolerant. He loved to discuss religious problems. The famous German theologian, Professor Adolf von Harnack, who was considered a religious liberal and violently attacked by many of his more orthodox colleagues, was held in high esteem by the Kaiser, who never imposed his own religious convictions on anybody, not even on members of his family.

After the morning devotions my grandfather went up to his rooms for breakfast. The "patient" was ordered to miss the devotions for the present and have breakfast in his apartment, located in the *Orangerie,* a former hothouse converted into a comfortable guest house. At nine-thirty I would meet my grandfather before the house for a twenty-minute car drive to the woods of a friend, Count Goddard Bentinck, near Amerongen.

Our main work consisted of clearing the underbrush. My grandfather worked with his right arm, which was quite strong, using a small hatchet or a handsaw. He was assisted by two skilled Dutch lumberjacks who were in his employ as gardeners.

In the woods we were joined by two other gentlemen, Herr von Ilsemann and Colonel van Houten. Ilsemann had been a young captain in the imperial general staff and one of my grandfather's A.D.C.'s. He had accompanied his emperor into exile and later married Count Bentinck's daughter. The Kaiser had a deep affection for this faithful officer.

Houten was a retired colonel of the Dutch equivalent of New York State Troopers. During the first years after 1918 it had been Houten's task to be both guard and watchdog, since the Dutch Government had guaranteed the Allied Powers that the Kaiser would not leave Holland without permission. Houten was also in charge of a small body of men, both in uniform and in plain clothes, who were stationed at the gate house at the entrance to the Doorn estate. This building contained administrative offices of the household and several guest rooms.

Van Houten played his delicate part with tact and skill. Gradually the restrictions were lifted, making it unnecessary for Houten to accompany the Kaiser wherever he went. Being a man of settled habits and principles, my grandfather nevertheless always invited his friend Houten to accompany him whenever he visited people at any greater distance.

Another permanent member of our small wood-chopping party was the court physician, a position voluntarily filled by a group of German doctors who took turns spending about three months each at Doorn. Besides watching over the Kaiser's health they also looked after the members of the household and their families. This little circle, organized by Dr. Schulze, included even Dr. Huebner, now from Cincinnati, but formerly a German Air Force officer who regularly spent his vacation in Doorn.

During the outings in the Amerongen forest it was my grandfather assisted by his two gardeners who did the real job. The others mostly kept at a safe distance, pretending to be working. One day I innocently offered to take one end of a big saw while grandfather took hold of the other. I soon gave up exhausted, whereas grandfather's muscular arm showed no sign of fatigue.

After an hour of hard work, the imperial woodman sat down for a fifteen-minute rest, during which hot tea and sandwiches were passed around. The gardeners received two cigars each from my grandfather. In case of rain or snow a tent was put up. During the pause, Grosspapa loved to give ratings to the participants. Those he thought particularly lazy had to tell some joke or funny episode in their lives to make up for their indolence. In reality he did not care whether anybody worked or just stood by. He had a hearty laugh when some of his potbellied guests, former generals or court officials, perspired all over and panted like old steam rollers. But whether one worked or not, he was grateful if one kept him company during his daily exercise which he needed as he did his daily bread.

After the pause the work went on for another hour. Then the party would return to House Doorn. During those months I, as his only guest belonging to the family, always had to sit on his left side in the back seat. After getting out of the car he always thanked me for my co-operation and efficient help—nothing worth mentioning had been done by me— with his usual mischievous twinkle in the eye. Then we separated, bowing formally. It was just a little game between us.

Depending upon the season of the year the wood-chopping expeditions were superseded by work in the garden. My grandfather was very proud to have created an outstandingly beautiful rose garden in the country of tulips. It was separated from the rest of his estate and open to the public. He also had planted a little forest of rare pine trees for which friends had sent him the seedlings from all over the world.

Until lunch time, following his daily workout, my grandfather studied the daily press. Ilsemann gave him a general survey culled from Dutch, German, American, French, and English dailies. All important news events were pasted on sheets. If my grandfather thought them momentous he read them to his after-dinner listeners in the library. Many papers, especially the foreign ones, were studied from the first page to the last. My grandfather also received more than half a dozen European weeklies and monthlies, and innumerable friends in all parts of the world sent him newspapers, magazines, and clippings, every one of which he read avidly.

A cruel moment came for Grosspapa shortly before the outbreak of World War II, when he was advised by the administrator of our family budget that there wasn't foreign exchange enough to continue certain subscriptions, principally American and British.

"It's a shame to cut me off that way from the rest of the world," my grandfather said. "But if we have to economize in the interest of the family, I guess it has to be done." The administrator in his exaggerated zeal to keep the family fortune together overlooked the fact that he was thus robbing the old gentleman, who was a cosmopolitan at heart, of one of his greatest pleasures, one of the few which Fate had left him in his monotonous existence.

While grandfather was absorbed in his perusal of the press, I usually returned to my rooms. Invariably I would find a little pre-luncheon snack waiting for me, consisting of a few sandwiches and a small decanter of port wine, enough to fill two glasses. This had been approved by my host. A stomach specialist from Bad Kissingen happened to be on duty during that particular period. He had advised my grandfather that his patient should get something to eat every few hours. He also averred that the port wine would have a good effect on the digestive functions of the stomach.

At 12:45 noon, a gong was sounded for the first time. That was the signal to wash up and walk leisurely over to the house in time for the second and final luncheon gong. If there were any luncheon guests, especially ladies, the Kaiser received them outside at the bottom of the steps leading up to the entrance hall.

At exactly one o'clock the *Hofmarschall* (court chamberlain) announced that luncheon was served. The doors of the main dining room were inconspicuously opened from inside, and everybody walked in, the ladies always first. This dining room was situated opposite the entrance to the hall and had three large windows facing the garden. The Kaiser invariably occupied the same seat with his back to the door, to enjoy the view of the garden. My step-grandmother, if not visiting in Germany, sat opposite him.

The luncheon party ordinarily consisted of my grandfather, the court physician, the court chamberlain, and the A.D.C. These functionaries were all elderly men who during their voluntary tour of duty were the Kaiser's guests and had their traveling expenses paid. Their "work" did not constitute a sacrifice. In fact, they virtually enjoyed a prolonged holiday.

In contrast to most of his guests my grandfather was an extremely moderate eater and drinker. The luncheon and dinner menus frequently consisted of only one or two dishes, but these were deliciously prepared. In his younger years the Kaiser had been a very fast eater. During his ruling days luncheons did not last more than twenty minutes. Slow eaters would have their plates removed before having had a chance to eat a bite.

Though my grandfather during his exile had calmed down considerably in this respect, his eating speed was far too "American" for his Americanized grandson. In this respect I was a hopeless case. But as he considered me his patient, even after my health was completely restored, I was given the privilege of setting my own eating pace. My imperial host would not only wait patiently but would encourage me to have a second and third helping.

"You must get strong again if you want to go back to that horrible Ford factory," he used to say. Visiting relatives who did not know of my special arrangement looked at me with bewilderment and disapproval when they noticed that I kept the Kaiser waiting at the dinner table.

During this period I was always placed between my grandfather and the doctor, "for reasons of supervision," as he expressed himself. It was the doctor's duty to see to it that the patient drank only the quantity of red wine—two glasses—allotted to him. The only luxury the Kaiser indulged in was half a glass of sparkling Burgundy. Almost invariably the doctor would be "bawled out" for not making the patient stick to his alcoholic diet. Faking irritation and desperation, the Kaiser would exclaim: "Lulu drank at least half a bottle today. You scoundrels are all in a plot with my grandson. I seem to be the only reliable person in this room. From now on I shall watch him myself."

The conversation at table was always very animated. Though my grandfather loved to talk, he was also an excellent listener. With foreign guests of Latin countries he spoke French almost as fluently as he did English, which he mastered perfectly.

After the meals the ladies left the room first. Following an old German habit my grandfather shook hands with the gentlemen, saying, *"Mahlzeit"* ("good meal") to everyone. If Spanish or Latin American guests were present, he would surprise them by wishing them *"buen provecho"* ("good digestion").

After lunch my grandfather's favorite "post" was on a window sill of the library, from where he could look out on clusters of rhododendrons in the midst of which was a small statue of my grandmother. Half sitting, half leaning on this window sill, he smoked one of his favorite Russian-style cigarettes with a long paper mouthpiece. The other guests were offered cigarettes, cigars, coffee, and a glass of brandy.

It had become a custom for the main guest to be asked to converse with my grandfather during that luncheon postlude of about a quarter of an hour. Then my grandfather, with a bow to everybody present, retired to his rooms on the second floor. He strongly believed—as I see Winston Churchill does—in a long, wholesome siesta of about two hours for which he undressed and got into bed. To people who scoffed at this habit he would remark:

"If you had a nap as I do, you would not snore in the evening when I am trying to read something to you."

The period between luncheon and dinner was reserved by my grandfather to himself or to the members of his family. Tea was served at five o'clock. During my step-grandmother's absence he always had his tea served in his study.

During those three months I was his only tea guest. I usually found him sitting on his saddle chair, leaning over his high writing desk, reading or writing. Sometimes he was so concentrated on the object of his interest that he did not notice my presence. I especially enjoyed these moments when I could observe his fine profile from a corner of the room. Only the noise of the tea table as it was carried in would cause him to look up over the rims of his spectacles which he used only for reading and writing.

In this room, filled with objects and souvenirs which reminded him of his earlier life, my grandfather was perhaps in his most intimate mood. During these tea hours we discussed everything under the sun. I often tried to get him to talk about his past, hoping to hear some criticism, for example, of his puritanical educator Hinzpeter, or of Bismarck. But he always somehow sensed my intentions and changed the subject. In this old-fashioned and cozy environment my grandfather had given me his blessing for my various ventures into the great world, and I there witnessed his reading an enthusiastic telegram from one of his sons who had been present at the so-called *Tag von Potsdam*. On that day in March 1933, Hitler, using the historic Garrison church of Potsdam as a stage and facing the vault of Frederick the Great and Friedrich Wilhelm I, had tricked old President von Hindenburg into enabling him virtually to become the sole ruler of Germany. In amazement and disgust my grandfather exclaimed, as he stamped angrily with his foot:

"These idiots believe they can jump from the Rococo age into the age of motor cars and airplanes."

During the summer months the Kaiser frequently took a stroll into the village after tea. He always left his estate by a side gate which he opened with his own key. Then he passed through the rose garden and reached the main road which connected Doorn with Utrecht and Arnhem. Practically everybody, on foot or bicycle, greeted my grandfather.

He always answered in a chivalrous way, taking off his straw hat with a grand gesture. Many a time motor cars with German or other foreign license plates would stop, and their occupants would cheer the lonely walker. At a discreet distance, my grandfather was followed by one of Houten's plain-clothes men.

During the winter months the Kaiser remained indoors, concentrating chiefly on his studies of archaeology and other scientific topics. He also devoted much time to the affairs of his family estate. Though he generally did not interfere, he insisted on being kept up to date about everything concerning the family, on which he exerted an inestimable moral influence. On one point he would not stand for any nonsense. I mean marriage.

He firmly believed in the family laws of our house, which were based on the principle of *Ebenbürtigkeit* (eligibility due to equality of birth). This principle was upheld by almost every European royal family on or off the throne. My grandfather used to express his adherence to it with a drastic comparison taken from horse breeding: "A good horse breeder does not mix Thoroughbreds with Percherons." This application to human relations has ever met with severe criticism and ridicule, especially in our day. During my "revolutionary" days I had no use for these old-fashioned regulations, which I then believed were meant only to make people unhappy. I have since revised my views.

Marriage is a gamble anyway. But if one chooses somebody of one's own stratum of life there seems to be a better chance that the two partners will swing into step eventually after the first passions of love have given way to a more placid temperature. I have found—I may of course be wrong—that in marriage the unspoken things, the little everyday details, count most. They are apt to create a paradise if harmonized, or outright hell if in dissonance.

It was in connection with this firm belief in Ebenbürtigkeit that my grandfather received perhaps his greatest disappointment during the years of his exile. I believe he never quite recovered from it. I refer to the announcement of my brother Wilhelm's engagement to a commoner. Ever since his student days in Bonn my older brother had intended to marry the young lady he had met in that city. He had announced his intention loyally to my parents and my grandfather. He had been to Doorn to discuss the matter with the chief of the family. In a very fatherly way my grandfather had finally succeeded in dissuading my brother from his marriage scheme. He had even suggested to Wilhelm that he take a trip around the world for a change of atmosphere.

One morning after our return from wood chopping, the village barber welcomed me with a grave face. He was a typical Figaro who otherwise always laughed and joked.

"Poor Kaiser," he said, handing me the local newspaper. The front page carried a picture of my brother and a young lady and under it a long story announcing the engagement.

When I saw my grandfather at luncheon he looked gray and dejected. He spoke hardly a word during the meal but sat brooding gloomily. Ilsemann had shown him the Dutch paper. I have never seen him as distressed and heartbroken.

During tea he looked at me with sad eyes and said:

"Lulu, I am sorry, but I cannot let you go back to America any more. You'll have to take your brother's place and settle down in Germany. I know that this is upsetting all your plans for the future. But you cannot blame me for your brother's deciding to marry that girl. I did everything I could to dissuade him." That, for the moment, was his only reference to the event. It came as an awful blow to me.

My grandfather, as I have said before, deeply loved my elder brother. He deeply regretted the fact that his oldest grandson for unknown reasons had hardly ever visited him. I am convinced that had my brother known how he was loved by his grandfather, he would have refrained from taking the step he finally did.

The evening meal at Doorn was as modest as was the luncheon and generally consisted of only one course. After dinner my grandfather read aloud to his guests and the members of his family in the library. The sessions usually began with a talk on some interesting event of the day. From time to time my grandfather also read editorials or articles from some English, American, or French magazine. Both his English and French pronunciation were excellent. But he knew only too well that in many instances his effort was more or less wasted, because the old-guard gentlemen forming his miniature court were seldom able to grasp the meaning of the articles. He therefore took the trouble to translate whole passages into German.

After that he would turn to the main item of the evening program. It included scientific books, memoirs, novels, plays, and detective stories. These readings were fascinating. My grandfather almost acted every part in these books. Nevertheless, many a time someone in the audience fell asleep, and a loud snore could be heard from some corner of the room. My grandfather ignored these sounds, knowing that they were not signs of disrespect but mostly of progressing old age. But once in a while he took his little vengeance by examining the snorer on what he had read and enjoying his hopeless victim's frantic efforts to reconstruct some of the contents.

Generally around ten or ten-thirty, after a short conversation, the Kaiser rose and with another bow to those present left the room. Thus ended another day of a life strictly regulated in every detail and almost by the minute.

To my grandfather, who was often called the *Reisekaiser* (traveling Kaiser) by his subjects, the monotony of his postwar existence must frequently have been almost unbearable. But his alert mind and his firm religious faith enabled him to bear his fate with a simple dignity, slowly rising to heights of wisdom and serenity.

After my grandfather had recovered from the first shock caused by his oldest grandson's engagement, I discussed the new situation that had been created for me by this event. It goes without saying that I accepted his decision that I must step into Wilhelm's shoes and assume the rights of the first-born.

"But," I argued, "I would feel like a deserter if I did not go back and tell Mr. Ford personally that I must quit working for him on your orders."

"I certainly don't want your boss to believe that one of my grandsons does not keep his word," Grosspapa replied, "and I don't want to spoil your fun traveling about the country as a salesman. I shall give you another seven months, but promise to be back on my next birthday. If we don't fix a date, as I know you, you'll never come back at all."

On May 1, 1933, I was "discharged" from my Doorn sanatorium with the verdict of "completely healed." I had gained about forty pounds. I have never been in a better physical condition than after those three months spent as my grandfather's patient.

"Before you go back to America, I want you to make a short survey of the German motor-car industry for me personally," he said a few days before my departure. "You can do that in two or three weeks. Possibly you can come back here with a few suggestions on your way to Detroit. But I think that now you had better join your parents, because they will want to talk to you about Wilhelm's engagement. I am sure your mother needs your company more than I do, though I'd like to keep you here as long as you care to stay."

The Greek Orthodox wedding ceremony.

Above: At the Lutheran wedding ceremony in Doorn, with Ex-Kaiser Wilhelm II. *Below:* Official signatures at civil rites.

Chapter Twenty-six

Two More Dictators – and London

(1933)

From Doorn, I motored down to Florence, Italy, where my parents were staying at the time. We all went to Rome to attend an international horse-jumping meet, the *Copa Mussolini,* which was won by the German team on May 6—my father's birthday. Knowing that he visited Mussolini every time he was in Rome, I asked him to take my Brother Hubertus and me along for his next call. I was eager to add another to my list of dictators. Mussolini would bring the number up to five.

My father consented after some hesitation, because he did not quite know how *Il Duce* would regard the influx of so many Hohenzollern at one time. It was agreed that father would see Mussolini first and then call us in. Meanwhile, Hubertus and I waited in the anteroom of the Palazzo Venezia which was adorned with precious pictures, old armors, and other art objects. After about half an hour the door was opened and my father called us. Mussolini stood next to him and not at the famous desk at the other end of the huge room.

The Italian dictator did not seem impressive to us. Hubertus remarked afterwards: "Well, he looked exactly like one of those restaurant keepers whose inns we have visited in small Italian towns." He was shorter than I had expected.

I politely told him in broken Italian that I felt honored to make his acquaintance.

"So am I," he shot back in a musical mezzo-soprano voice, with a slight undertone of mockery. To his question as to where I had learned to speak Italian, I replied that the fishermen of Rapallo had been my teachers. I did not tell him, though, that they were all fanatical anti-Fascists!

Then he switched over into German, talking to my father and my brother Hubertus. This audience lasted about ten minutes. I felt that Benito was play-acting all the time, trying to impress his guests with glances and gestures. No doubt he was bright and quick-minded. Unlike Hitler whom I met a few weeks later, he listened attentively. His German was fluent, his French equally good. He even threw in a few words of English.

I met Hitler a few weeks later. I therefore had a good chance to compare the two personalities. A few days after my return to Berlin, Putzi Hanfstaengl telephoned that he had arranged for a meeting with the *Braunauer* (man from Braunau), as he liked to denominate his boss not too reverently. After waiting about fifteen minutes in the Führer's outer office, Putzi emerged from his chief's sanctum with two American businessmen who seemed extremely elated by their interview. When the two gentlemen had left, Putzi opened the door to Hitler's office.

The chancellor was standing behind a mahogany writing table not half as big as Mussolini's. He let us both walk about half the length of the spacious room before he gave up his position behind the table and came forward towards us. Like his Italian colleague, Hitler, too, was in mufti. But his attire was far less sloppy than that of Mussolini. He could be almost called well groomed. His demeanor was courteous, of Austrian ease, and definitely less theatrical than that of Mussolini. His light blue eyes had a rather forlorn romantic expression directed more into space than at the person he was talking to. I must admit that I sensed a certain magnetic force emanating from him.

At the beginning of the audience he was very modest, almost shy. He called me merely Prince. To test his vanity I addressed him as "Your Excellency." From that moment on he called me "Your Royal Highness." Only the very first moments of our talk deserve to be called a conversation. After I had told him that I was going back to Detroit and asked whether I could take any message to my American boss, he embarked on a monologue which lasted the whole length of our forty-minute meeting.

"You can tell Herr Ford that I am a great admirer of his," he said in part. "I shall do my best to put his theories into practice in Germany, which is still very backward as far as motorization goes. I formerly hated everybody who drove by in a large, luxurious car, while I had to walk the highway. But I have come to the conclusion that the motor car, instead of being a class-dividing element, can be an instrument for uniting the different classes, just as it has done in America, thanks to Mr. Ford's genius."

At first he spoke in a normal manner, but gradually his voice worked up to a high pitch. He was finally shouting as if he were addressing a great crowd in the Sportpalast.

Just the same, I was amazed how thoroughly he had studied the whole problem. He claimed that besides the high prices of automobiles their maintenance was far too costly for the little man. In a rage he denounced the silly regulations which hampered motorization, such as the ban on parking cars on streets at night.

As far as automobiles were concerned, Hitler's views seemed sound. Had this been the case with respect to other matters, everything would be quite different today. It proved to be the first and only conversation I had with Hitler, even though it was rather a monologue.

It must be added, though, that at that time he was only an embryonic dictator. Hindenburg was still the German nation's Chief Executive. Hitler was still playing the second fiddle, if not in fact, at least *de jure*.

A few days later, complying with my grandfather's "order," I set out to study the German motor-car industry. I visited the Horch works at Chemnitz, the Bayerische Motorenwerke at Munich, the Mercedes works near Stuttgart, the Adler factory at Frankfurt, and finally the Opel establishment at Ruesselsheim.

I was received with great hospitality everywhere, but the managers could not quite conceal a certain suspicion which underlay their rather patronizing manner. This Prussian Prince in the service of Henry Ford was slightly mystifying to them. They let me feel that they did not take me, or the concern I represented, any too seriously. I parried their veiled attacks by intimating that I thought their establishments and production methods quite out of date with the sole exception of Opel, which had been taken over by General Motors.

A week's work in the Institute of Statistics in Berlin enabled me to accumulate the necessary figures, whereupon I wrote a short report which I proudly handed to my grandfather.

At that time British General Waters was my grandfather's house guest. He suggested that I spend a few days in London in order to find out that America was not the only country in which English was spoken. The retired general, a delightful old gentleman, said he would gladly volunteer to show the sights of the town if only he were a few years younger. Instead of himself he recommended his friend Bruce Lockhart.

"He will take excellent care of your grandson," he remarked to my grandfather. "Bruce knows everybody worth knowing in town from the Prince of Wales downward," he added with a twinkle. "I shall write him today. When the prince gets to London a week from now, all he has to do is to ring up Lockhart. He will take care of the rest."

The plan was immediately approved by the Kaiser, who was unaware of the fact that I had visited the shores of "perfidious Albion" once before.

The two weeks spent in London were interesting in every sense of the word. Through Bruce's kind offices I met my cousin Edward, with whom I had a long conversation in Spanish. I was entertained by Lord Beaverbrook, both at Leatherhead, his country estate, and in his town house. I paid H. G. Wells' taxi when he was short of change and was rewarded by a complete collection of his works with a personal dedication. I had lunch with Winston Churchill, who in those days was considered to be "definitely" out of politics by many of the people I met. I visited Lloyd George and had a touching Wiedersehen with Miss Brimble, my old English governess, as already described. The hectic London days found a harmonious conclusion in General Waters's cozy country house near Southampton, where I boarded the *Bremen* for New York.

I left Britain deeply grateful to old Waters and Bruce Lockhart, whom I still consider one of my dearest friends.

Chapter Twenty-seven

The Beer Trip

(1933)

WHEN I REPORTED to Henry Ford at Dearborn, I told him about the events which had radically changed my personal situation. I nursed a faint hope that my boss would suggest a way to talk my grandfather out of his decision. He did not.

"Having spent most of my time in the Rouge Plant, I have seen hardly anything but assembly lines and motors," I argued in desperation. "I don't want to go back to Germany without having seen a lot more of America."

"We have laid out a nice program for you," Henry replied gently. "Now you have only six months left; so we'll make you a free-lance roadman. You can go wherever you like, and let us know from time to time how you're getting along. But don't miss your boat to be back on time for your grandfather's birthday." I believe Mr. Ford created this job only in that moment.

Chicago was to be the first stop, with St. Louis, Santa Fe, Los Angeles, and San Francisco to follow. "If you should like to visit any other place we didn't think of, it won't make a bit of difference to us," said Jack Davis, the assistant general sales manager, to whom I was to report.

Though my duties as a roadman did not include actual selling, I could not resist the temptation to try a hand at it in my own fashion. Neither Mr. Ford nor anybody of his organization even suggested that I do so.

The idea of a "beer trip" was conceived in Otto Eitel's Bavarian *Bierstube* in the Bismarck Hotel, Chicago.

"Why don't you visit Milwaukee?" Eitel said one day.

"I should love to," I answered, "but won't the brewers run me out of town if I show up there representing the man they hate most?"

"Judging from your activities in our Bierstube you are the very man to show those people that even a Ford man is a normal being. And beer is not the only thing the brewers drink," Eitel added with an ominous smile. "All you have to do is to go to Milwaukee; meanwhile I'll ring up some of my brewery friends. The rest will take care of itself."

My entrance into Milwaukee was not very triumphant. I got there in the evening and went to the Pfister Hotel. There I was told that because of a Shriners' convention all rooms were filled to capacity. I therefore spent the night in a rather dismal third-rate place.

The next morning I called on Bill Brumder, a tall, healthy-looking fellow with an open face.

"Where in the world have you been?" he asked. "We were expecting you last night." I told him about my mishap.

"That's going to burn up my uncle who owns the hotel. He had reserved the whole top floor for you. But that serves him right. Now you'll stay at our house as our private guest. I suppose the desk clerks expected a sort of Indian Maharaja instead of a Ford mechanic." I was not exactly overdressed!

Bill took me to his lovely home, thus landing me in the very midst of Milwaukee's brewing dynasty, the Brumder-Uehlein-Pabst clan. I spent much of my time meeting more and more members of these three huge families, trying in vain to keep their names and family relations straight. Their hospitality and friendliness were overwhelming. With almost every meal my hosts offered me the choicest samples of their wine cellars, of which they were rightly proud.

I never heard them utter any criticism of my boss but soon noticed that anything connected with the name of Ford was taboo. The manager of the local Ford branch, who was personally on excellent terms with all these families, warned me. "As far as selling a Ford car to them, you might as well talk to a stone wall."

After one of our brewery inspections my hosts suggested to visit a place called Maxl. It was a small beer emporium run by a giant weighing three hundred pounds. A staff writer on the *Milwaukee Journal* who was with us suggested that a picture be taken of Maxl and myself both holding up a battery of steins.

"Won't you lose your job if Henry Ford gets to see that picture?" my friends asked.

"On the contrary," I retorted. "We'll send him a copy. He would despise me as a hypocrite if I as a German did not like your beer."

The picture appeared on the front page of the paper. I did not lose my job, and the Milwaukee brewing dynasties ended their long feud with my "dry" employer by ordering a few Ford cars.

My next stop was St. Louis, Missouri, another citadel of the American beer-brewing industry, ruled by the Busch family. Adolphus Busch, Jr., then the head of the Busch clan, lived in a stately mansion surrounded by a large park which contained mementos of General Grant. The Busches had for years maintained cordial relations with my grandfather and his children. They regularly visited Germany, where they owned much property.

In spite of these multiple ties linking our two families, they were of very little use to me in my capacity as a Ford representative.

"As a grandson of dear Kaiser Wilhelm you are welcome to me and my family," old Adolphus told me when we first met. "But please don't mention the name of Ford in my presence."

After having spent at least two weeks almost daily or nightly with the Busches, the old gentleman told me on the day of my departure: "We shall forgive your boss and even buy his cars, if you can get him to make a public statement reversing his attitude on drinking."

"You cannot expect Henry Ford to make such a statement, which would make him the laughingstock of the whole world," I retorted. I left St. Louis feeling rather low, convinced that I had lost that battle for my Dearborn boss. When I arrived in Los Angeles a few weeks later, however, a wire from the local Ford branch manager in St. Louis advised me that Adolphus Busch had ordered Ford cars!

Between St. Louis and Kansas City, I stopped at various smaller towns and villages to look up the local Ford dealers. My hosts received me like an old acquaintance. When I expressed surprise they answered: "It's very simple. Look at that number of *The Ford Dealer*." It carried my picture with a story of my life and an explanation of my new job.

Together with the local dealers I visited many farmers. They were badly hit by the depression and the drought. Their homes looked shabby, with holes in the roofs and machinery rotting in the back yards. I called on Henry J. Haskell of the *Kansas City Star* and at Emporia, Kansas, met William Allen White, Jr.

At Santa Fe, New Mexico, I spent about two weeks. The atmosphere of this city with its Spanish-Mexican background was a unique experience. I became acquainted with Senator Bronson Cutting, who invited me frequently to his beautiful home situated on a hill outside the city. The view from the terrace of his house was almost breath-taking. The senator was one of the most cultured persons I have ever met. His untimely death in an air accident was a shock to me.

From the Grand Canyon with its gruesome magnificence I drove in one stretch to Los Angeles. By mere chance I came out on Franklin Avenue, Hollywood, where I passed the Chateau Elysée and the Villa Carlotta. This time no romance detained me!

In San Francisco, I established myself in the swanky Mark Hopkins Hotel with its superb view of San Francisco Bay. I did not have to worry about expenses. At the beginning of my trip I had regularly sent in my "swindle sheet." But somewhere en route I had found a letter from Jack Davis suggesting that I stop sending in expense accounts. The local Ford dealers would take care of that detail thereafter, because it would save him the trouble to correct the mistakes I regularly made in adding.

During my six happy weeks in the City of the Golden Gate, I experienced the end of prohibition in America. Together with Bob Lowe of the *San Francisco Examiner* and a colleague of his, I visited as many bars as possible to study the reactions of the people to repeal of the law.

Around five o'clock in the morning I accompanied Lowe to his office and, feeling rather high, composed a long wire to President Roosevelt, congratulating him on having liberated his country from the tyranny of prohibition. When I met Lowe later in the day he confessed he had edited the telegram somewhat, because it smelled a bit too much of liquor!

In order to renew my flying license I put in several hours of flying in a small private plane, which I rented at a private airfield from a young German.

My days were filled with visits to Ford dealers and dealers' meetings, the evenings with social functions. Rather reluctantly I resumed my tour. Time was getting short.

I was next headed for San Simeon, William Randolph Hearst's fairy castle. Dick Berlin had recommended me to his boss. I enjoyed Mr. Hearst's overwhelming hospitality for ten days. The strangest experience, for me though, was the fact that some of the editors and managers of Hearst papers were almost at the brink of desperation because they had to wait for weeks to talk business with their host. Mr. Hearst, who had no regular office hours, argued that it would do these officials good to relax and forget about their business problems and worries. The only time in the day he was ready to be "interviewed" was shortly after lunch, when the rest of the guests had their nap. It was tragicomical to see these people, little kings themselves in the newspaper world, lying in ambush in the great hall next to the churchlike dining room. They lingered about in order not to miss their chance, because that might mean another week or two for them before they could get back on their jobs. Dick Berlin advised me to follow the same procedure if I wanted to have an undisturbed talk with Mr. Hearst before I left.

I eventually succeeded, and the newspaper king talked for over an hour. He felt very friendly towards my country and also towards my family and prewar Germany.

One of the highlights of my California stay was a visit with Will Rogers, who asked me to spend a week end with his family. When I arrived, he was riding on a beautiful horse, lasso in hand, which he aimed at another horseman who turned out to be Elliott Roosevelt. Rogers hit his target every time. "This was the way I started making a living," he remarked as we went inside.

The house was furnished with delightful simplicity but included all comforts of a modern house. Every piece of furniture revealed that it belonged to a lover of horses.

"I hope that you won't be bored, but I have to play a match at our polo club before dinner," he said presently. "Would you like to come along and watch us play?" I told him my father was an enthusiastic polo player and I had been brought up on horseback from childhood.

When we returned from the polo club I asked: "When do you do your writing? You are a terribly busy man."

"Oh, that's very simple. At breakfast I read the local morning papers, and then I choose the subject which seems to me of the greatest human interest. I always try to bring out the humorous side of life without hurting people's feelings. I don't believe in cynicism, you know," he added with a wonderful smile.

A few days after my visit I found an article in the *Examiner* concerning a certain "outlaw who happened to drop in on me over the week end. We had a pretty good time together. He did not even try to cut my throat and to my great surprise did not ask to eat a baby for breakfast." It was signed Will Rogers.

As time was getting short, I decided to use air transport for the second part of my roving sales trip. Someone suggested I ought to visit Mexico before going back to Europe. I agreed, chiefly because Antonio and Jane X—— were now living in Mexico City.

The X——'s, as well as Mr. La Joux, the manager of the local Ford plant, were very popular with the diplomatic corps, hence I met more foreign envoys than native Mexicans. Mr. La Joux introduced me to Ambassador and Mrs. Josephus Daniels, who invited me several times to their home.

The diplomats seemed to form a big family. I witnessed the arrival of the new German minister, Rueth von Kollenberg. During the reception given in his honor at the German Club, a strange, gloomy-looking individual was pointed out to me:

"That's the representative of the Nazi Party. He is an obscure office clerk, but he is the real representative of our country. It's a great shame." Later during our trip around the world Kira and I found the same situation wherever we went. The German diplomats, well trained for their jobs, were powerless vis-à-vis these obscure *Landesgruppenleiter* who spied upon and terrorized their compatriots.

The Mexicans are very patriotic. Each day when I passed the Independence Monument in Mexico City, I noticed that a new wreath had been deposited and that one or two persons, mostly civilians, were standing at attention. Antonio X—— explained that at least once a day some Mexican citizen, or even a foreigner, would dedicate a wreath and would act as voluntary guard for the national shrine.

I gladly followed his suggestion to *hacer la guardia,* as the Mexicans call it. He informed the city authorities about my wish to have the honor of guarding the monument of liberty. Armed with a large wreath draped in the colors of the old Imperial German flag we arrived at the monument at nine o'clock in the morning, where we were received by an official of the city who mounted guard with us.

Through the mediation of Ambassador Daniels and the direct intervention of President Roosevelt, I was able to spend Christmas 1933 as the guest of General Charles H. Danforth at Randolph Field. This invitation came as a surprise. I had merely mentioned to the ambassador that I was a great aviation fan and had read Arthur Brisbane's articles about Randolph Field. Stepping out of the Mexican passenger plane at Brownsville, Texas, I was met by two American officers. The older one, a very kind and jolly-looking gentleman, approached: "Are you perhaps the German Prince I am supposed to fetch at the President's orders?"

Slightly embarrassed, I answered yes.

"My name is General Danforth, and this is my aide, Captain Douglas. I did not expect such a youthful guest, though," he added with a slight undertone of irony. "You certainly seem to stand in well with our President. But now let's drop your luggage at the hotel. I'll give you an hour for rest, and then we'll run over to Matamoros. Texas is still dry, and Mexico is not, as you perhaps don't know."

Because of the sudden change of climate caused by the great difference of altitude, I felt rotten and knew that I was running some temperature. But an hour later Captain Douglas entered my room.

"Aren't you ready yet? The general is very anxious to get going."

I explained to him how I felt.

"Well, that's nothing unusual. Many people flying down from Mexico City get that kind of fever. We'll both see to it that you will be cured in due time."

The general, who had changed into civilian clothes, was waiting in the lobby. We passed the Mexican border without even stopping. The general seemed to be well known to the border officials. At a typical Mexican *fonda* (village inn) we sat down at a simple wooden table without a tablecloth. Supper was already waiting for us. When I woke up the next morning I had somewhat of a hang-over. But the fever was gone.

The following day we took off for San Antonio. The general asked me to climb into his open two-seater plane which he was piloting. That was the only time I flew in a plane piloted by a general. Mrs. Danforth welcomed me most heartily.

"This is our only child," she said, pointing to a big German police dog.

"That's the famous Pilot," I exclaimed.

"How in the world do you know his name?" the general asked. I explained that I had studied Arthur Brisbane's articles on Randolph Field in the Hearst papers.

The following day the general took me through the whole establishment. He also flew me over to the bomber school at Kelly Field. We drove to San Antonio and visited various villages in the neighborhood, which were mostly settled by Germans.

A few days before New Year's Eve, I took off for New Orleans, my last station on my "beer trip." When I was ready to get into the plane I was approached by a gentleman.

"Would you mind giving up your seat for a little baby who is seriously ill?" he asked. "We are trying to get him up to Philadelphia to a famous specialist. It is a question of life and death for my child." When I arrived at New Orleans on a later plane I was received by Mr. Cooper, the local Ford manager, and a whole army of newspaper reporters and photographers.

"The child is already en route to Philadelphia; the plane is being flown by one of our ablest commercial pilots," they told me. It was a headline story.

To my greatest embarrassment, the story was played up to such a degree that by the time it reached Germany, I became the pilot who had flown the baby to the North through snowstorms and gales! I even received enthusiastic telegrams from my parents, congratulating me on my "heroic exploits." For a whole year afterwards I was asked in Germany about this flight. All I could do was to excuse myself, explaining that the American press apparently had gone too far in giving one of its victims a break.

In New Orleans, I felt more like being in Europe than in any other American city. New Year's Eve turned out to be one of the gayest I ever spent in my life. Two days later I landed in New York in deep winter.

When I said good-by to my boss in Dearborn, Henry Ford told me: "If you ever feel like working for us again, just let me know."

Chapter Twenty-eight

Pre-Marriage Interlude

(1934–38)

ABOARD THE *Bremen* that cold night in late January 1934 to return to the land of my fathers, I was by no means in good spirits. I knew that this meant farewell to cherished plans and hopes and to a career that would have given me real satisfaction. It meant farewell to an independent life in the world's most independent country.

I am frequently asked by Americans: "Why didn't you stay in the United States?" If my brother Wilhelm had not married a commoner I most probably would have remained there. My choice to return to Germany and Europe for good was not voluntary. Had I put up a stiffer resistance, my grandfather might have extended my leave, but he would never have agreed that I stay abroad permanently. True, in being obedient I did not live up to being a "rebel." But I should have despised myself for letting down a grandfather who had taken my side during all these years. I did not deem it right to add to his grief. I would have felt like a deserter had I not fulfilled his wish to take my brother's place.

But I also firmly believed that God nullified what seemed the "chance of my life" because He had another one in store—I mean Kira and the seven lovely children with which our union has been blessed. That we had to live through the darkest hours in the history of our country does not alter my feeling of immense gratitude to God.

I returned to the Old World to settle down. But this Old World was anything but settled. I felt like a stranger in my own house in more than one respect. I felt indifferent to the point of disgust about the political hysterics which held Europe, and especially Germany, in their grip. I had adopted the American viewpoint that politics is a sort of game in which one side emerges as the winner and the other side as the loser, after which the opponents get into a friendly huddle.

I had arrived at Doorn just in time to congratulate my grandfather on his seventy-fifth birthday. "I almost thought that you were not coming back," he greeted me. I explained that the *Bremen* was two days late in getting into Cherbourg harbor. At Cherbourg the French customs director, who received me at the quai to extend the courtesy of the port to me, had conducted me to a waiting Ford car, saying: "Please give my best regards to *l'Empereur*. I always was an admirer of his." This surprising treatment by the French authorities in connection with my grandfather's birthday was touching. The gift of the Ford car showed me that I was still considered as "belonging" to the Ford organization, even if only in an honorary capacity.

I remained behind in Doorn after numerous other members of our families had left, and I had several long talks with my grandfather. He said he would like to see me get acquainted with the administration of the family estate, which I was to inherit eventually.

"I do not want to press you," he said. "Have a look around first and then tell me when you are ready. I know it will take you some time to adjust yourself to this sort of thing after having roamed over half the world."

I made up my mind to keep away from the family administration as long as possible. I wanted by all means to keep up my connections with the great outside world. The prospect of becoming a country squire was utterly disconcerting to me. This was a prejudice which experience corrected. Today, if given the choice, I should prefer the country to the city.

For the first few months after my repatriation I just loafed in Berlin, taking in the atmosphere which had changed considerably during the intervening seven months. Already, in Doorn, I understood that my position was definitely awkward. In fact, the only one who fully accepted me in my unchosen capacity of "heir apparent" was again my grandfather. The rest of the family had a difficult time getting used to the thought that such an eccentric person with Americanized ideas would eventually become the head of the Hohenzollern House.

My brother Wilhelm was now living on one of my grandfather's estates as an administrator. Shortly after his wedding the family had announced that he had forfeited all his rights of succession. My brother, however, maintained that he had renounced only his rights to the inheritance of the family fortune but considered himself the legal pretender to the nonexistent German throne.

Quite a number of people in Germany shared his view, many of them claiming that family laws and marriage restrictions based on class prejudice were antiquated and invalid in our modern day. Certain members of my family still hoped for some solution which would restore my brother to his old place. Even the possibility of a later divorce was mentioned more than once. It was an uneasy situation for everybody concerned. For the time being, the touchy problem was never mentioned in the family circle, at least not in my presence. There was of course no immediate need to present a "candidate." But the monarchical issue still lurked in the background.

It was the American Ambassador, Professor William E. Dodd, and his family who helped me to adjust myself by offering me their home and their friendship. The Dodds' private residence, a cozy house in the Tiergartenstrasse, became my second home. I could drop in there at any time of the day or night. Another home where I felt like a member of the family was that of Hilde and Louis Lochner.

At the Dodds, I met many leading Nazis during the first two or three years, when they thought it expedient to be on friendly terms with America. Later, the Dodds became more and more ostracized because of the ambassador's liberal views and sharp utterances even in public. The longer Mr. Dodd stayed on his job, the less he could reconcile his Jeffersonian liberalism with the totalitarianism of the new German regime.

Many an evening I was the only guest at the Dodd table. When the servants were out of sight we opened our hearts.

"If you don't try to be more careful with your talk, Prince Louis," the professor used to warn me, "they will hang you one of these days. I'll come to your funeral all right, but that won't do you much good, I am afraid," he added with a sad smile.

Having lots of time on my hands, I decided to specialize in flying and to work for a transport pilot's license to add to my Argentine, German, and American private licenses. I entered the German Air Traffic School, where I acquired the license early in 1935. I had made it quite clear at the beginning of the course that I wanted to fly for the sake of flying and not for becoming an active pilot in the future *Luftwaffe*. My arguments were accepted grudgingly. Most of my copupils had to sign a statement obliging them to enter the German Air Force once it had been created. In March 1935 the Luftwaffe became a fact.

Next, I took up blind flying under the auspices of the *Lufthansa,* the German civilian air transport organization. I came into close personal contact with the seasoned Lufthansa pilots, who ranked among the best aviators in Europe. During this course I decided to work for the Lufthansa, not as a professional pilot, but in the general administration of the company. At a diplomatic reception, I had made the acquaintance of Hans Karl von Winterfeld, head of the foreign department of the company. When I told him that I was deeply interested in international air traffic, he intimated that I could find a vast field in which to apply my knowledge of other countries, especially of the Americas, in his department, and he promised to talk the matter over with the management of the Lufthansa.

Three months elapsed before I finally entered this organization. After the creation of the Luftwaffe, I felt that the most convenient solution would be to obtain a reserve officer's commission in the German Air Force. That would enable me to continue my flying without giving up my liberty as a private citizen.

I told the personnel department of the Luftwaffe that I held the rank of a second lieutenant in the Imperial Army, bestowed by the Kaiser on my tenth birthday. But the air force authorities argued it would be the best for me to rise up from the ranks, as this was the new system for reserve officers. In spite of a certain reluctance at the beginning, I am very glad for having had the experience of starting from the bottom. It gave me the chance to correct certain prejudices I held concerning "Prussian militarism."

I started as an ordinary private and went through all the noncommissioned ranks with the exception of that of a corporal. Though the Luftwaffe was a creation of the Nazi Government, it had adopted most of the rules and regulations of the old Prussian Army. One of the main criticisms of Prussian military education is its aptness to break the individual. As far as I was concerned it had the opposite effect on me. Being rather sensitive, I was quite bashful at the beginning. At the end of the three-months' course I shouted and cursed more than even the professional subofficers.

Thanks to my doctor's degree or to some mistake of the personnel department, I was assigned to a course for physicians of the Luftwaffe reserve. They were about sixty men, mostly around thirty years of age, some considerably older. The courses for ground drill were held at a place near the small city of Neubrandenburg. A tiny, single-motored sports plane was the entire flying equipment. To my great advantage I was the only pilot in the outfit. Many a time when the others had to sweat during ground drills, I was called upon to act as "air" taxi driver to take our superiors, mostly noncommissioned officers, for a joy ride.

Admitting that ground drill was emphasized less in the Luftwaffe than, for instance, in the infantry, the fact remains that the treatment was the same in all branches of the armed forces. I had no difficulty submitting to the general discipline without feeling humiliated or suppressed. The common soldier was well protected against abuse by his superiors. His physical condition was constantly watched. He was even reprimanded severely if he did not report illness. I never had the feeling of being a helpless victim of injustice. Later as a company commander I learned that the officers were bound by many rules with regard to their subordinates. These rules and traditions, handed down through the centuries and worked out by several generations of my ancestors, were regarded as a sort of sanctuary which even the Nazis for a long time did not dare touch. This sanctuary was destroyed only towards the end of the war, when the armed forces were virtually run by political commissars.

Up until World War II, and even during the first years of that war, the armed forces were looked upon by countless Germans as a veritable heaven, because there the dignity of the individual was still respected. Many people who had to fear for their lives asked to be taken over by the armed forces, in which, as members, they were fairly protected against the persecution and revenge of the Gestapo and other party institutions. Hitler was well aware of this situation and for that reason never quite trusted his regular army. It is greatly to be regretted that only very few military leaders realized the strength of their position and did so little to safeguard and defend that sanctuary. All the greater is the credit due the heroic few who risked their lives in connection with the events of July 20, 1944, which I shall touch upon later.

During the summer of that year I made an unsuccessful attempt to find myself a wife. But I think Kira should tell her version of the story:

KIRA'S STORY

I was in Paris in the summer of 1935 when I was invited by a friend of my family, Mme Olga de Mumm, Russian-born wife of the champagne producer, to spend a week end with her at Johannisberg on the Rhine. Mme Mumm knew and liked Louis Ferdinand and for some time had cherished the idea of a possible match between him and me. She knew that my parents were in favor of such a union. Louis's mother was first cousin to my father, second cousin to my mother. In the good old days before World War I they had of course often met in Russia, France, and Germany, but since then no meeting had taken place.

Once when I was about sixteen I had visited Berlin with my Coburg cousin Sibylla. Our parents told us to be sure and pay respectful visits to our Aunt Cecilie at Potsdam and to the other numerous uncles and aunts there. So we drove out to Cecilienhof and had tea with the Crown Princess. That was the first time I met my future mother-in-law. I liked her immensely. We spoke Russian together, and she asked about my family, was interested to hear how and where we lived, and to learn details of our flight from Russia in 1917 and of our three hard years of refugee life in Finland.

I thought Cecilienhof the loveliest place in the world. We had to take our leave much too soon for my taste. However, we were still to make the acquaintance of our cousins, Wilhelm and Lulu, who appeared from somewhere and were told by their mother to show us around the garden.

We were all rather shy of each other and not very sure as to who was who. Anyway, I am certain that we flappers did not make much impression upon our nineteen- and eighteen-year old cousins. Nor were Sibylla and I overly struck by them. We both were having much more interesting flirtations at the time in Berlin!

Some years later, though, a match was contemplated by their respective parents between Wilhelm and Ingrid of Sweden, a meeting to take place at Sibylla's wedding in Coburg. Wilhelm put in a very belated appearance at the wedding-eve dinner.

I don't know whether this breach of etiquette had anything to do with it, but Wilhelm failed to attract Ingrid and nothing came of the meeting. It is interesting to reflect that had Wilhelm married Ingrid and not a commoner, perhaps Louis Ferdinand would never have wedded me as he would then have remained in America.

But to return to the invitation to Johannisberg. With my parents' permission, I accepted. Mme de Mumm, or Olala as we called her, had managed with some maneuvering to get Louis as guest for the same week end. Our meeting was to be a casual, informal affair, just fellow guests at a house party.

Frankly, I was quite excited. I had heard a lot about Louis, his unusual linguistic abilities, his extensive travels and the time spent in America. I was particularly interested in his South American experiences, as I had always longed to visit Argentina and Brazil myself.

Olala had described Louis as a most attractive young man, tall and good looking, very charming, gay, and, best of all, intelligent. Also, and this appealed to me particularly, I knew Louis to have affection for everything Russian. So all in all my curiosity was aroused. As far as Louis was concerned, according to what he told me much later, he did not care much one way or the other but thought he might as well have a look at me.

We met at breakfast in Olala's garden. I had one peep at Louis from a window and rather liked his looks. Ten years had passed since our meeting in Cecilienhof, so we were really strangers to each other. Louis's first impression of me, he tells me, was not so favorable. He found me too conventional. Perhaps I should have left some of my good manners at home! But Olala had not told me that Louis disliked convention and reserve, and at the time, of course, I was not aware of this disapproval.

After a very merry breakfast (Olala was a wonderful hostess and one of the wittiest people I knew), we were dispatched for a walk. It was a very hot day, and we did not go far. We found a shady bench and sat ourselves down to get better acquainted. I think Louis did most of the talking (he still does). Of flirtation there was none. If I had let go a bit and made a few cousinly advances I might have had success. But

I was so determined to seem casual that I continued to give an impression of offhandedness and superiority, which irked my future spouse. On the surface of things, however, we got along very pleasantly. I even imagined that Louis liked me.

In the afternoon we went swimming in the Rhine, accompanied by Olala's elder son. Louis's swimming prowess did not impress me; I could do better myself and thought to impress Louis by it. But I did not. Louis has never cared much about sports and was indifferent to Olympic achievement. After the bath, I thought to present a pretty picture by letting down my hair to dry. An old and very feminine trick and one which in my experience had never failed to create a sensation. My hair in those days reached below my waist and was of rather a nice quality. However, even my golden tresses did not cause a tremor in the region of Louis's heart. He preferred short hair!

In the evening we played a hilarious game of poker. This is about the only card game anybody has ever been able to induce Louis to play. He hates cards and thinks them a waste of time. I am a bridge fiend and love a good game of poker, too. But the poker we played that night was a riot. Louis was much more interested in the golden Rhine wine liberally poured by my hostess. In the intervals of sampling it Louis staked wildly and, when he won, gave half his chips away. He rejoiced when finally he was broke and could stop playing to devote his undivided attention to the delights of the grape.

Next day we all drove to pay a visit to my sister, Princess Maria of Leiningen, called Mashka, at the beautiful little town of Amorbach. Louis and Mashka were friends at once; kindred spirits in their lack of and dislike for conventionalities, their use of strong words (to put it mildly), and very Slavic temperaments.

By the end of the second day together I was not sure that Lulu and I would make a go of it and confided as much to Mashka. She told us to go and hug in the hall while the rest of the party retired for a nap. We did not hug, but a spark of affection was kindled that evening while driving to Frankfurt to catch our respective trains home. We discussed quite dispassionately whether or not we were suited to each other and decided that we could not be certain after so short a meeting. We would be glad to meet again at some indefinite future date, agreed not to write in the meantime, and would consider ourselves in no way bound.

Having settled these embarrassing questions we felt much more at ease and even quite chummy. Perhaps the dark helped; soon we were holding hands, and before parting I gave Louis a quite un-cousinly kiss. It seems that this was the first moment in those two days that Lulu really liked me! "She can't be so bad after all," he apparently thought.

We went our different ways, and three years passed before we were to meet again.

Chapter Twenty-nine

The Rickenbacker Air Tour

(1935–36)

Hans Karl von Winterfeld visited me a month before I finished my basic training at Neubrandenburg. He told me that the management and the board of directors of the Lufthansa approved of my going to work for them. I was to begin on November 10, 1935, a day after my birthday. I had already written my grandfather that I had changed my plans as far as my activities for the immediate future were concerned.

"You have double-crossed me as usual," he replied. "I hope your new work will be interesting and more satisfactory than what I had in store for you. Come and see me as soon as you can get away."

As regards the management, I was soon to find out that the Lufthansa did not live up to what I expected such an internationally known air traffic organization to be.

My immediate boss, Winterfeld, was a very likable but extremely erratic fellow, not easy to work for. He had been an officer in the Imperial Army.

A typical bachelor, he spent most of his nights in restaurants and night clubs. I had nicknamed him *Höllenhund* or *Chien d'enfer,* because frequently in the middle of the night he would ring me up from one of his favorite haunts, asking me to join him for a nightcap. He could get very sore if I refused. Even without such extravaganzas, my professional activities did not allow for much sleep. The members of Winterfeld's department, a sort of public relations outfit, had to take care of visiting foreigners. Though we were envied by the other Lufthansa employees, we sometimes were thoroughly sick of our job. However, our department was the least bureaucratic, and we enjoyed more independence than the rest. This was mainly due to Winterfeld's independent attitude. He did his work for the fun of it and not because he had to earn a living. He had a comfortable private income.

With all his eccentricities Hans Karl was a gentleman, and we became the best of friends. He was about the only person who would not take any shouting from the technical director, Baron von Gablenz, but would shout back at him at the top of his voice in the best military fashion and make dramatic exits, slamming the door behind him. The two would not speak to each other for days. The Lufthansa management was greatly handicapped because every decision had to be O.K.'d by the civil aeronautics branch of the government. We had constantly to fight bureaucratic stinginess in authorizing expenses for the entertainment of some famous foreign guest.

Eddie Rickenbacker was one of the distinguished visitors from the United States. I was assigned to make the arrangements for his stay. I thus had a fine opportunity to become closely acquainted with him.

Eddie, who was making a study of European civil aviation, suggested that I come over to the States to study American civil air transport.

"We can all learn from each other," he remarked.

"Nothing could tempt me more than to follow your suggestion," I answered. "But alas, even if you were to extend an official invitation, the 'big shots' would take advantage of such a wonderful opportunity."

"Perhaps you are right," Eddie continued. "I feel sorry for you. They let you do the dirty work and then take the credit for themselves. Anyhow, I'll see what I can do for you once I get back to the States. Let's keep our plan secret for the moment."

Our little plot materialized sooner than any of us had expected.

In the spring of 1936, Dr. Heinrich Albert, the German legal adviser of the Ford interests in Germany and a member of the board of directors of the German Ford Motor Company, invited me to accompany him to Detroit. Official quarters were exerting considerable pressure on the Ford organization to have some of its production moved from Cologne to Berlin. Albert had tried to stall these plans. But matters had reached a point where he could no longer ignore these "suggestions." He thought that my presence as an old friend of the Fords would make it easier for him to conduct his negotiations at Dearborn.

I obtained a four weeks' leave from the Lufthansa, happy to get away, be it even for a week. A few days before my scheduled return Eddie Rickenbacker asked me out for lunch in New York.

"I want you to be my guest at the Indianapolis auto races a month from now," he said.

"I should love to accept," I answered. "But what am I going to do in the meanwhile, and what am I to live on? I have marks but no dollars. Besides, the Lufthansa will hardly extend my leave."

"You don't have to worry about anything," Eddie smiled. "This is the moment to put our little scheme into operation. I have already telephoned Gablenz, suggesting that you fly the different American airlines and make a thorough survey of our civil aviation. He told me it was O.K. with him and that your leave will be extended another six weeks, until after the races. He could not very well refuse my little request, could he?" Eddie grinned.

We both went to Eddie's office.

"I have already mapped out a whole schedule for you," Eddie said. "You'll go out on Transcontinental to Los Angeles, stopping over at Kansas City. You will fly back from San Francisco by United Airlines with stopovers at Cheyenne and Chicago. The schedule will bring you back to New York just in time for the arrival of the new dirigible, the *Hindenburg*. Then you will still have ten days left to fly Eastern Airways down to Miami and Pan American to Havana. I have booked you on the plane leaving Newark Airport at midnight. I suppose you want to get on the road as soon as possible."

This was certainly a "Blitztour." My professional curiosity was more than satisfied, and on the trip itself I was given every bit of information and explanation I desired.

In Kansas City, I spent a day looking over the repair shops and the ground organization. The manager of the Kansas City Airport, a fine young man, was Herbert Hoover's son. In Los Angeles, Tom Hamilton, inventor of the propeller that bears his name, took care of me. Will Hays, "movie tsar," whom I had met through Walter Trumbull, also happened to be in town. I told him that Lily Damita, who had become Mrs. Errol Flynn, had invited me out to her home for dinner. He strongly advised me not to accept the invitation "after all the trouble you had a couple of years ago." I felt like a coward but followed his advice. "You can tell her that I told you so. She'll understand," he smiled.

Spending two nights at San Francisco, I had an opportunity to visit Pan American's Pacific base at Oakland and to witness the take-off of a China Clipper. On the return trip a day was spent at Cheyenne, the operation center of United Airlines. One thing to which I could not become accustomed was the fact that the flying personnel were armed with pistols. I was told that in several instances the pilots had been attacked.

The arrival of the *Hindenburg* on its maiden voyage turned out to be a great sensation and a personal triumph for Dr. Hugo Eckener. It was known that Eckener was in disgrace with the *Führer* for refusing to christen the airship "Adolf Hitler" and preferring the name of Germany's late and last president to that of the dictator whom he detested. He was hailed as the "Columbus of the Air" by the American press.

I had gone down to Lakehurst mainly to meet my friend Louis Lochner who was making the round trip representing The Associated Press and was on close terms with Eckener. I spent the night waiting for the dirigible to land in the company of numerous news photographers and reporters. I also made the acquaintance of the congenial Commander Rosendahl, the American Eckener.

When the *Hindenburg* arrived a few hours late, I did a little interpreting to help the German passengers get through the customs. Some of them apparently had never been outside their own country. I could hardly keep a straight face when I translated the question of one of the customs inspectors—"Have you any pornographic pictures on your person?"—and saw the helpless, bewildered expression of the person questioned.

I spent most of the time with Louis Lochner during his two-day stay in New York. Together with his daughter Betty, now Mrs. William J. Sailer, I went down to Lakehurst to see him off. We had a big laugh when the fat mayor of Frankfurt, Krebs, was heaved into the airship, as he could not climb the ladder. For some seconds only his enormous "fanny" could be seen from underneath bathed in the radiant light which some mischievous person had beamed on that "target."

The day after the *Hindenburg's* departure I boarded a plane for Miami. Disregarding well-meant warnings, I caught a tremendous sunburn at Key West. I also flew to Havana and there met Mr. and Mrs. Ernest Hemingway, who had come over from Key West in their fishing cruiser. Their engaging naturalness won my heart immediately.

Eddie Rickenbacker had chartered a plane for himself and his guests to attend the Indianapolis races. At the airport, Eddie was greeted by the racing committee and several newsmen, who took pictures of the "American War Ace and the Prussian Prince."

At the invitation of the Reverend Mr. Daries, I attended two services in a Lutheran church of Indianapolis, one conducted in English and the second in German. After the second service the pastor introduced me to his audience and made me shake hands with everybody.

The races were very exciting to me. But some people were disappointed because nobody was killed. We all had a grand time of it. At one of the receptions I was introduced to Governor Paul V. McNutt, who was to be Kira's and my host in Manila a few years later.

We all flew back to New York in a cheerful mood. I boarded the *Europa,* extremely grateful to Eddie Rickenbacker for this opportunity.

I stopped off at London for a few days. Bruce Lockhart was again my friendly guide. I called on Queen Mary, who received me very graciously. She remembered the wedding of my Aunt Victoria Luise, when my brother Wilhelm and I had walked in front of her in the Berlin Schloss. She asked me to sign my name in a book but first asked the date of my birthday—November 9. Opening the page under that date she remarked with a sweet smile: "You will find yourself in very good company." The only name written across the page was Edward VII.

"He was my godfather," I remarked proudly.

An appointment with my cousin David, who had become Edward VIII since I last saw him, did not materialize though a date had already been set. He was in the midst of the Simpson drama and "very hard to see, even for the Prime Minister," Bruce sighed.

I finally gave up waiting, especially because my Lufthansa superiors were getting restive. The day I left for Berlin, I listened to a speech by Anthony Eden on the Abyssinian situation. I was not aware that I had been on an important mission in the House of Commons, but according to a story in one of the London papers I had been sent on Hitler's special orders to report on that historic session!

Chapter Thirty

End of Bachelorhood

(1936–38)

IN MY report to the Lufthansa, I made it very clear that American civil aviation seemed far ahead of the German, especially as far as the comfort and the treatment of the passengers were concerned. I also pointed out that the different air lines were managed by a type of high-class, aggressive young men who were not hampered by too much outside interference.

During the summer of 1936 we were busy taking care of innumerable air guests who had come for the Olympic games. Berlin for a few weeks became Cosmopolis. The Nazis did everything to put their best foot forward. Hitler relished playing the host to distinguished foreign guests. The great influx of foreigners from all over the world and the universal applause for the magnificent organization of the Olympic games were amply exploited by the Nazis to fortify their position in the eyes of the German people.

During a short training period with the Hindenburg Squadron at Neubrandenburg following the Olympic games, I was given a special assignment. I was attached to two Argentine air officers who had been sent to study the Luftwaffe and to receive additional air training. Having been a flying pupil in the Argentine, I was now very pleased to act as instructor for these two young men.

I loved to patronize a canteen for privates and "non-coms" and, when I returned as a reserve lieutenant the following year, kept on visiting this place regularly, the food at the officers' mess being rather poor. Besides, I preferred the company of my old pals the non-coms to that of my new comrades, many of whom were "stuffed shirts." One day I was told to report to my group commander, Major Schoeneich.

"You are accused of a terrible crime, Leutnant Prinz von Preussen," he said. "Our squadron commodore has instructed me to inform you that you are undermining the discipline of the air base." He spoke in a grave voice, trying to look fierce. "It has been brought to the colonel's attention that you patronize the canteen and associate with privates and noncommissioned officers. This attitude, the colonel has ordered me to tell you, is incompatible with the dignity of an officer of the Luftwaffe and altogether too democratic."

Then he added with a smile: "I quite understand that you don't want to give up those friendships of last year. But in order to save both of us further trouble I advise you to use a special room for such purposes."

Later I was ordered to address the officers and soldiers in our camp on the subject of the United States. I tried to impress upon my listeners that freedom and strength, both physical and moral, can be very successfully combined. I sounded a warning that the strength of the United States must not be underestimated. My listeners showed a keen interest and fired pointed questions at me. After the lecture, Schoeneich whispered into my ear: "I hope they won't shoot both of us at dawn. Anyhow, it was something different for once."

In December 1937, I accompanied Winterfeld to Greece to inaugurate the new Berlin-Athens Air Line. Winterfeld had spent much time and effort in Budapest, Sofia, Belgrade, and especially Athens to obtain the necessary concessions, and I had supported him in Berlin by conducting such negotiations as needed a follow-up there. After the return of King George to the Greek throne I had given Winterfeld a letter of introduction to my cousin Paul, the present King of Greece.

Prince Paul was keenly interested in aviation. As the government did not approve of his going in for such a "dangerous" sport, he had secretly learned to fly. Winterfeld gave him a frank picture of the methods which had to be used to "induce" the Greek Government officials to render a favorable decision. My cousin was rather discouraged to learn about all the "squeezing" which had to be done.

During Winterfeld's and my stay in Athens we were beautifully entertained by the Greek civil aviation authorities and by the aviation company, Air Héllénique. I was privately invited to my two royal cousins. Both wanted a meticulous description of Athens night clubs and taverns, which they in their exposed positions could not visit.

Quite some time after our return from Athens, Winterfeld, roaring with laughter, informed me:

"You are the unwitting cause of a great international complication. The gentlemen of the air ministry and our directors are dying to get some Greek decoration. Now, the Greek legation remains adamant on the point that according to Greek court etiquette you are entitled to the highest decoration, since you are a first cousin of the King. This would, however, be a terrible humiliation for our 'big shots.' What can we do about it?"

I rang up my friend, the Greek minister, Rizo Rangabé. The best solution we could find for this diplomatic entanglement was to strike my name off altogether.

I was always glad in the evening to get back to my bachelor apartment at the *Mathaeikirchplatz*. It consisted of three rooms in a so-called *Gartenhaus* which one reaches by passing through a small courtyard. It was a very quiet little corner. I enjoyed inviting my closest friends for intimate dinner parties. Once in a while some well-known pianist, German or foreign, would come after his public concert and play by the hour for a few friends. My piano teacher, Rudi Hauschild, whose wife was a Pole, had close contacts with Polish musicians who always willingly played Chopin, my favorite.

Louis Lochner, music lover that he has always been, was a regular guest. Through the years I had become deeply attached to this friend, who combined brilliancy of the mind with the heart of a saint. In many respects Louis had taken over the part which his namesake Luis de Valdivia had played in my life. He had become a sort of confessor in whom I confided absolutely and whose opinions I valued highly. Louis is the living proof that one can be a good practicing Christian. He lived in perfect harmony with his charming wife Hilde, his three children, Betty, Rosemarie, and Bobby, and his parents-in-law, old Herr und Frau Geheimrat Steinberger.

Louis knew everybody worth knowing in the Weimar Republic and at the same time had managed to watch the rise of the Nazi leaders from their modest if not obscure beginnings. He had friends among the old aristocracy, the industrialists, the military, the intelligentsia, and the socialists. He was liked by the great majority, respected and even feared by a minority. Louis's integrity was above criticism. Invariably his reports were objective and accurate. During the Nazi regime he had many secret and underground informants because his discretion was absolute. I believe that he was the only foreign correspondent who was taken into their confidence by the members of the so-called "July plot" with which I shall deal later.

Louis was as proud of his German origin as he was of being an American who first saw the light of day in Lincoln's home town of Springfield, Illinois, on Washington's birthday. His love for my fatherland was sincere but critical. A liberal of the best cosmopolitan type, he nevertheless had a full appreciation of prewar Imperial Germany and its old traditions. He deeply admired the efforts and the marvelous comeback of Weimar Germany and held in great esteem Stresemann and Brüning, the latter of whom I had to meet secretly at Louis's home, for Brüning's life was in danger ever after his resignation in 1932. He finally escaped to America in 1934.

After my return from the states, Louis and I made it a habit to have lunch together at least once or twice a week. We took turns "picking up the tab." Louis's favorite place was the Restaurant Kempinski and mine was Pschorrbräuhaus. At these meetings Louis would brief me on the international and domestic situation, as he was in constant touch both with the Nazi authorities and with his underground informants. Again and again he warned: "The longer this Nazi business lasts, the less difference will people abroad make between the Nazis and the German people." Louis later elaborated this point in his book *What About Germany?* His despair grew each time we met. Sooner than almost anybody else he saw clearly that Germany had been tricked into accepting the leadership of a regime which turned out to be as cruel as it was rotten and unscrupulous. My friendship with Louis outlasted all the horror of the war.

To get away from my office I had asked Gablenz's permission to fly as second pilot on some of the Lufthansa's foreign lines. I was thus able to make a few flights to Paris, London, and Stockholm.

During the fall of 1937, I spent another few weeks with the Hindenburg Squadron, this time serving as a second lieutenant. During the air maneuvers in honor of Mussolini's visit to Germany, I was flying at the head of a unit which was to "attack" Hamburg. One of the twin engines quit abruptly, and I had to make a forced landing in "enemy" territory, which happened to be the Hamburg Airport. This little incident came to be talked about because a large party of high-ranking Luftwaffe officers and foreign air attachés had been watching the operations from the airport observation tower. Immediately after my landing a car drove up from which descended General Stumpff, the head of the air force personnel department. He was quite surprised to discover that I was the pilot of the "enemy" plane. After questioning me about the reasons for my mishap, he said with a smile:

"From now on you and your crew are my prisoners. Come along and have a drink at the restaurant. I am glad that nothing worse happened to you and your plane." I found that this was a charming way of saving an awkward situation.

My last year of bachelorhood was not eventful with the exception of its last days, when I became engaged out of a clear sky. Kira will describe how this came about:

Kira's Story

During the three years before we met again after our visit to Olala Mumm, both of us went through bad and some very good times. In 1936 my mother died. With her death the bottom of the world dropped out for all of us. My father was a sick man and the blow of this bereavement crushed him utterly.

I tried to take my mother's place, to be a companion to my father and a mother to my young brother. I learned to think of others more than of myself. The new tasks softened some sharp corners of my character, even changed my outlook on life. As my sister Mashka put it, at last I became human. Mashka's remark made me reflect what an extremely selfish and self-centered person I must have been before.

In the winter of 1937 my father, brother, and I were invited to London to stay with my aunt, the Infanta Beatrice of Spain. Aunty Bee thought it would be a splendid thing if Louis's brother Hubertus and I could meet and come to like each other. Hubertus was expected in London soon. So now I became interested in Hubertus and thought no more of Louis.

Hubertus did not turn up. Instead, I met his youngest brother Fritzi, who was working in the City at the time. Apparently Fritzi approved of me and thought his brothers should, too. So he got busy in the unselfish role of Cupid and wrote to his mother, suggesting that she invite Vladimir and myself for Christmas. I understand there was a family conference upon the subject, to which Louis contributed a careless, "Oh! let them come."

On December 20, Vladimir and I set out on our journey in high spirits. The thought of spending a real German Christmas again in a big family and in such beautiful surroundings made us jump for joy.

Cecilienhof looked even lovelier than I remembered it. Aunt Cecilie met us in the hall, and a moment later Uncle Wilhelm joined us. That was the first time I met my future father-in-law. Neither Lulu nor Hubertus was at home; only Fritzi had arrived. My two future sisters-in-law were also there to greet us.

Two evenings later Louis returned from a celebration at the Neubrandenburg Airport given in honor of his old commander. We met just before dinner. A slight embarrassment hovered between us as we eyed each other anew. Louis was very courteous. I fancied even that I detected something new in his attitude towards me. But I was not going to "kid" myself. For my part I felt at once and rather perturbingly attracted to Louis. Had we both changed?

The following day we were joined by Hubertus, on Christmas leave from his flying school. I had been put to some pains to stifle my fledgling love for Louis until I should meet Hubertus. Louis had given no signs of his intentions towards me; besides, it seemed only fair to give Hubertus a chance, for he was the one whom the well-meaning matchmakers had this time elected for me.

We took stock of each other across the luncheon table. I don't know precisely what Hubertus thought of me. I liked him a lot, but I knew that if Fate was to give me the choice between him and his brother, Louis would win.

After dinner that night—this was December 23—came the traditional

The Prince and Princess as Hyde Park guests of the Roosevelts. *Left to right:* Poultney Bigelow, biographer of Kaiser Wilhelm of Germany; Mrs. Sarah Delano Roosevelt; Prince Louis Ferdinand and his bride; President Roosevelt; James Roosevelt and wife; and Mrs. Eleanor Roosevelt.

"For Louis Ferdinand with the warm regards of his friend Franklin D. Roosevelt."

decorating of the Christmas tree. All were supposed to help. The men of the party, after a few mild efforts, retired to easy chairs from which they watched and criticized us. Their withdrawal, by the way, coincided with the entrance of a steaming bowl of punch.

In my zest for decorating I had climbed the ladder and was somewhere in the region of the top branches. Chancing to look down at the group of lazy men, I caught Louis's eye upon me. No, I did not fall off the ladder to be caught in his arms, but I did clutch the rung above me a little tighter. This time I felt sure that I had interpreted his expression correctly.

When the party broke up for the night, Lulu offered to escort Vladimir and me to our rooms. My brother tactfully took himself off to bed.

"Well, how about it? Is it a deal?" Louis suddenly said after we had chatted for an hour or more. I knew it was but thought a little hesitation would be proper and asked if I might sleep upon it first. But Louis would have none of that. He held out his hand, and I clapped mine into it. Then we sealed the pact in approved style.

We got Vladimir out of bed. Louis decided that his parents, too, must be told at once. It was now around one o'clock in the morning. So the three of us marched off to find Papa, who was having a few nightcaps with his chief adviser. Louis seized me firmly by the hand, saying, "Papa, may I present my bride to you!"

Papa rose, opened his arms wide, and bade me welcome as his future daughter-in-law. Then he turned to his son and, slapping him on the back, said: "A bit sudden, but well done this time, my boy!"

Aunt Cecilie had retired by now, but Lulu insisted upon our going, all of us, to break the news to her. Sitting up in bed, between tears and laughter she embraced us and gave us her blessing.

After a while we got coherent enough to sketch our plan of behavior for the next day or two. Our engagement could not be announced before Grosspapa in Doorn had given his permission as head of the family. It was early morning of Christmas Eve when we finally separated. Despite the unusual hour Lulu insisted, however, on rousing his friend Louis Lochner from sleep and telephoning him the exciting news.

Louis's drowsy initial comment was: "Lulu, you must be tight or crazy. Go to bed." But when he realized that his friend had at last chosen a life's mate, a luncheon date in Berlin was immediately arranged for me to meet him and his wife Hilde.

I need hardly add that this Christmas Eve was the loveliest and happiest I ever enjoyed. I always hoped later to annex the sofa upon which Lulu proposed. I had visions of myself showing it to my children and grandchildren with a sentimental story about how mother and daddy became engaged on Christmas Eve. Fate has since written another story. Cecilienhof was to become the scene, eight years later, of a worldshaking conference and was lost to us as a home.

I still possess, though, the gown I wore that night, saved incredibly out of wrecked homes and hurried flights. It came from a famous Paris house and bore the name *un conte*—a fairy tale!

Chapter Thirty-one

Around-the-World Wedding Trip

(1938)

SHORTLY BEFORE our marriage I asked Baron von Gablenz about my chances for promotion in the Lufthansa. He answered bluntly that they were extremely limited, mostly because I was a Hohenzollern, a family regarded by Nazi officialdom with great distrust if not outright dislike.

I had had that same impression for quite a while. In fact, I had made up my mind to quit working for the Lufthansa and told Gablenz so. In order not to make my exit look abrupt, I suggested he give me a year's leave, for in any case I was going to ask my grandfather for a trip around the world as a wedding gift.

Gablenz said he could see no objection to such an elegant solution and proved very co-operative. I wrote to my grandfather. The old gentleman was rather hesitant about approving my request, mainly because he thought my bride would be exposed to Soviet intrigues in the Far East. Gablenz was a great help in overcoming my grandfather's reluctance by instructing the representative of the Lufthansa in Tokyo, Dr. Gottfried Kaumann, to cable him that our visit could be useful to foster the friendly relations between German and Japanese civil aviation. Kaumann's cable was forwarded to Doorn, and the Kaiser gave his consent.

But another obstacle arose from an unexpected quarter: my father suddenly showed great concern about the possible dangers which such a long journey might have for our matrimonial relations. His arguments were not devoid of practical reasoning. Indeed, I was told later by officials of various travel bureaus with which I came in contact during our trip that prolonged honeymoon journeys often proved fatal to the newlyweds. My father wished I would settle down after a relatively short honeymoon, start building our nest as soon as possible, and go about my daily business.

This time it was Louis Lochner who did the pleading during a prolonged evening at Cecilienhof when the two of us were my father's only guests. Louis, who was held in very high esteem by both my parents and whose knowledge of my character was in no way contested, finally dispelled my father's doubts. He won out with the statement: "Lulu being your son, I am quite inclined to believe that the trip will be shortened by the natural trend of events."

"Poor Kira," my father sighed, replying with a knowing twinkle. "My dear Mr. Lochner, if you have such confidence in my son's ability to build a family, I believe I shall have to give my paternal blessing to the plan."

Louis's prediction came true. We were back home after exactly six months. His godson Friedrich, our first-born, was the "natural trend of events" which shortened our honeymoon, although it could have lasted another six months as far as Kira and I were concerned.

For a description of our wedding, or weddings, I quote from the notes of my new boss, Kira:

KIRA'S STORY

We never tire of boasting that we were married three times. It came about this way:

The Kaiser's wish was to have the wedding in Doorn. To this we of course agreed joyfully. But Huize Doorn was not large enough to accommodate the many guests that were to be invited. Some part of the wedding festivities would have to be held in Potsdam at Cecilienhof.

Now, naturally my hope was to be married both according to the German Evangelical Church rites and those of my own church, the Russian Orthodox. We agreed to have the Russian wedding ceremony on May 2, 1938, with full pomp at Cecilienhof, the Evangelical marriage two days later in Doorn. For Louis and me this arrangement implied two full-dress weddings and something of a strain!

A Russian marriage is a very elaborate, deeply moving ceremony. The service in the great hall of Cecilienhof was conducted by Father Adamantov, Russian priest for many years in Wiesbaden, who was closely associated with my family. He was assisted by several priests from the Russian church in Berlin. The fine choir of the Russian church in Berlin sang the beautiful wedding liturgy.

I was married in a magnificent gown dating back to my grandmother, Grand Duchess Marie of Russia, Duchess of Edinburgh. It was a court dress of heavy, encrusted silver brocade. With it I wore a small diadem and a very old, fine lace veil, both of which my mother-in-law lent me for the occasion. Louis appeared in the full-dress uniform of the German Air Force.

That same night we all entrained for Doorn. A sleeper was chartered to transport us. Louis and I were severely separated; we were not yet fully wed!

Our second wedding, exquisitely organized by our grandfather who attended to every detail personally, occurred on May 4. *Hof und Domprediger* Bruno Doehring married us. His is a remarkable personality to which one cannot do justice in a few words. But I want to mention at least that his sermon re-echoes in our hearts even today. This time our rings were placed on our fingers to stay.

The Kaiser was a wonderful host. Doorn was in the full beauty of flowering lilacs and rhododendrons and fruit blossoms those May days. The gracious charm of the whole place enveloped us in a sense of utmost harmony.

And the third wedding? It was really the first. We were married in a civil ceremony by the *Bürgermeister* of Potsdam just before the Russian service in Cecilienhof. This good man, though a Nazi official, went as far as he could to lend dignity to the occasion. He was a trifle nervous all through, especially at the conclusion of the celebration when in accordance with the Hitler regulation he presented us with a copy of *Mein Kampf!*

So that is the story of our three weddings. Well and truly married, one might say.

LOUIS'S STORY RESUMED

We started out from Doorn in May 1938 and returned there in November after having circled the globe following the course of the sun. I had declined the invitation of the North German Lloyd to take a cruise around the world on one of their boats. This would of course have been the easiest solution in the face of the currency restrictions. As long as we were aboard a German boat we would have unlimited credit. But we wanted also to try other lines.

In order for us to have some foreign exchange for running expenses, I had asked my bride to suggest to her friends in France that she would prefer a few dollars instead of other wedding gifts. On the whole, however, we trusted to our good luck for managing somehow. We had no other choice if we wanted to make the trip at all.

We considered it a foregone conclusion that the United States ought to be visited first. We had received a very cordial invitation from President Roosevelt. Also, I naturally wanted to show Detroit to my bride and introduce her to my old boss, Henry Ford. Charlie Sorensen had been in Germany shortly before our marriage and indicated that the Ford people would gladly keep an eye on us. Besides Hyde Park and Dearborn we had no fixed itinerary, except in a very broad sense. After four weeks on the American Continent we planned to spend a month at Honolulu. For Japan, Manchuria, and China we had reserved two months. The rest of the time was to be spent on the Philippine Islands and in southern India.

I shall not bore the reader with a detailed description of the countries visited but shall merely give a few high lights and mention some of the many people we got to know, whose hospitality we enjoyed, and with whom we became friends. One conviction both Kira and I already held was confirmed and deepened during this trip: The human individual is worth while meeting in any country and in any region of the world. But there was another thing we felt quite strongly: Everyone we came in contact with seemed to share our happiness and tried to add to it.

This honeymoon keynote was struck by the ship reporters on our arrival at New York aboard the SS *Bremen* and was kept up until we landed at Rotterdam six months later. We were thus spared answering many delicate questions with reference to Germany and the world situation. The newsmen to whom we talked quite freely off the record just did not want to spoil our fun. I wish here to express my gratitude for their kindness.

The high spot of our stay in New York was naturally our visit to Hyde Park, which has been described in detail previously.

In New York City we were entertained by both Kira's and my friends, Kira having been there in 1929. We spent much time with the Walter Trumbulls and with Ellen and Frank Mason. Roy Howard and his family entertained us. Roy gave us a whole bag of letters of introduction which were very helpful in Honolulu, Japan, and the Philippines. Poultney Bigelow, with whom we spent several days, did not make us get up at 5:00 A.M. to have a swim in the Hudson River!

"This is a great exception and concession I am making only to you, lovely Kira," he remarked.

On our way from Washington to Detroit in a beautiful limousine placed at our service by the Ford organization, we decided to break our journey when we reached a little town, Cadiz, which looked attractive. After registering as Mr. and Mrs. Ferdinand we went to a near-by restaurant. A few minutes later an important-looking man followed by eight husky fellows walked in and came straight to our table.

"Say, are you the guy you are supposed to be?"

"Who am I supposed to be?" I asked.

"Well, are you that Prince Louis who just got married?"

"I'm your man, and this is my wife," I answered.

"Well, that's fine. I'm the sheriff and these are my men. We'll just stick around and sort of guard you."

After dinner we all went to the movies. Afterward the sheriff introduced us to the crowd gathered outside the theater.

"Folks, meet the prince and his wife." We were told that Cadiz was the home town of Clark Gable.

When we walked into a small restaurant at Monterey about two weeks later for a hamburger the owner after one glance at us remarked with a smile: "How does it feel to be married?" That's American publicity for you!

At the River Rouge Plant, I introduced Kira to my old pals. Frank Watza, the superintendent of the assembly line, was delighted at Kira's keen interest in technical matters. As a special honor he asked her to drive a car off the line and try it out on the testing grounds.

I was extremely proud that she hit it off so well with my old friends, who of course did not spare me a lot of teasing. One of them said:

"So you went and fell in the same trap I did, and that after all you said at the time. I says to you, I says phooey!"

We had lunch with Harry Bennett in his private dining room. When I told him we were planning to go by train from Chicago to the Coast to catch the boat for Honolulu, he protested:

"That's no way to show our country to your bride. I say, you are not going across the continent by train. Let me take care of that."

In the evening we were Mr. Ford's guests at one of his dance parties. My former boss spent most of the evening dancing with Kira, who had known these old-fashioned steps ever since she was a child. There was an embarrassing moment when Mr. Ford, to conclude the evening with the usual polonaise, invited Kira to be his partner. She had suddenly disappeared. I finally discovered her in the pantry, where she was smoking a cigarette. "I just had to have a puff," she said.

The following day we had lunch at Henry Ford's residence. When we talked about our traveling route, Mr. Ford mentioned in a casual way that Kira would not see much of the country if we went all the way by train. So Friend Harry had already told him!

"When you get to Chicago, we'll have a car for you there. You can drive it out to the Coast, I think," the old gentleman said to Kira. "Your husband knows how to drive a Ford car by now. But now let's go over to Greenfield Village." For almost two hours Mr. Ford showed Kira all over the place. We almost had to tear ourselves away to catch the train for Chicago.

"Bon voyage," our host said with a warm light in his eyes. "Be very happy and let us know when you get home safely." That was to be the last time I saw that great man who had meant so much in my life.

A few hectic but enjoyable days divided between Chicago and Milwaukee followed, with the Eitels and the Brumders as our hosts, and with many of my other friends entertaining us. The Ford people offered to drive our car to Denver to break it in while we would travel to Colorado by train. On the streamliner to Denver we suddenly noticed that a bag containing most of our clothes was missing. We had not even locked it! But it joined us five weeks later in Honolulu. Not an item was missing.

We visited Buffalo Bill's birthplace in the Colorado Mountains, made stopovers in Santa Fe, the Grand Canyon, and Los Angeles, and arrived in San Francisco June 22, where we motored across the Golden Gate Bridge, visited the World's Fair grounds on Treasure Island, and somewhat sadly abandoned the car which had given us such a wonderful trip to board the Matson Line's luxury steamer *Lurline*. On the ship we turned in for the next twenty-four hours to rest up from all the exciting experiences on the American Continent.

To summarize the high lights of our four weeks in Hawaii: As the guests of Governor Poindexter, whose private residence was the former royal palace, we were shown the bedroom of Queen Liliuokalani, the composer of the famous song "Aloha Oe." To Bill Cross, our friend and guide throughout our stay, we owe an interesting fishing trip in a smart yacht owned by Jimmy Cromwell and his then wife, Doris Duke, besides many other sightseeing excursions, one of them to the seldom visited Island of Kauai. Army and navy people frequently invited us out to Schofield Barracks and Pearl Harbor. The Dillinghams entertained us on their Crow Bar Ranch estate and afforded us an opportunity to ride on horseback to our hearts' content, besides watching Mr. Dillingham and his four sons play polo against the army team.

I am sorry that we met only a few native Hawaiians. But it did not take us long to sense the tragedy surrounding the downfall of the dynasty with its consequences for the local population. The commercial note which tourism had inflicted upon the natives made the picture even more tragic.

Upon our arrival in Yokohama we were surrounded by two dozen newspapermen and press photographers, who tried to extract statements on their war with China which we dodged politely.

Some co-passenger divulged that a Honolulu doctor had assured us that a little Hohenzollern was on the way. The Japanese press enthusiastically played up the item. Wherever we went in Japan thereafter we were always asked about the "baby," as if it were about to be born right then and there. For the Japanese it was a foregone conclusion that our first-born would be a boy. When the baby finally arrived we received many touching congratulations from our new Japanese friends.

We were the house guests of the German Ambassador, General Eugen

Ott. On his way out to Japan he had stopped off at Washington. After consulting his colleague Dieckhoff, he decided to treat us as "distinguished private citizens." This attitude was also taken by the Japanese Government, which apparently had been briefed by the German Foreign Office. Ambassador Count Mushakoyi, whom we knew well from Berlin and who now held an important position with the imperial household, called on us shortly after our arrival.

We asked him frankly whether we ought to call on the imperial family, my wife having known Prince Chichibu. He intimated that we had better not make such a gesture. Any exception to the rule of receiving official personages only, especially in our case, could be misinterpreted in Berlin. With an ironical smile he remarked: "The distance from Berlin nowadays seems to be considerably shorter than that to Washington."

Count Mushakoyi's disapproval of Japan's pro-Axis policy was shared by many colleagues and a large part of the Japanese press. In the English language *Japan Times,* a newspaper close to the Japanese Foreign Office, I read a derogatory article about Goering and other leading Nazis. I asked Ambassador Ott if he had read that article. He said: "Yes, but I don't dare send it to Berlin."

Roy Howard had given us a letter of introduction to Shingoro Takaishi, publisher of the Tokyo *Nichi Nichi* and the Osaka *Mainichi.* He expressed grave anxiety about the trend of world affairs and was definitely out of sympathy with the aggressive adventures in which "this jingo gang of crazy majors" had involved his country. One day he gave a cocktail party for us in one of Tokyo's most fashionable clubs, to which he invited Japanese notables in all walks of life. The government was represented by General Araki, minister of education.

Takaishi did us the greatest honor a Japanese can offer a foreigner: he invited us to his house in Osaka over the week end, asking us to live with his family in Japanese style. It was an experience we shall never forget. We were even admitted to the family bathing room, where hot water is poured over the men by girls of the house. Our German hosts in Tokyo were almost speechless when we told them about our Osaka experiences.

"You can spend a lifetime in Japan without ever being invited to the private home of a Japanese, even if he is your best friend," one of the old-timers of the embassy said.

Because of the unusual character of this visit and a less extensive and intimate one which preceded it, I shall now yield the floor to Kira and quote from her diary notes:

KIRA ON JAPAN

During our stay in Japan we twice enjoyed the rare privilege of visiting in a Japanese home. The first to extend this courtesy to us were the celebrated artist Mr. Araki and his wife in Tokyo.

Our hostess received us in the gracious, almost humble, Japanese manner, helped relieve us of our shoes, and bowed us into her house. She as well as her husband wore the national dress. Both spoke a little English. We were offered refreshments and tea as we sat more or less comfortably on the spotless floor of the living room. This and the adjoining rooms were furnished entirely in the exquisite, sparse Japanese style.

Mr. Araki showed us many of his paintings, delicate drawings of birds and flowers. To demonstrate his technique for us our host made a quick sketch in black and white of the famous heron and bamboo variety. We watched with fascination, amazed at the precision of each swift stroke of the brush. We learned that all such pictures are painted entirely from memory, i.e., without models and not from nature. The basis of this art, of course, is a profound knowledge of the native flora, fauna, and landscape as well as an intensive study of drawing with the paint brush.

As a parting gift Mr. Araki offered us one of his flower paintings, a lovely reproduction of a deep red, feathery poppy.

Our second visit to a private home was in Osaka where we lived with Mr. Shingoro Takaichi and his family at the seaside. First we were invited to witness a boys' school display of physical exercises on the beach and to take a swim ourselves. Afterwards Mr. Takaichi asked us up to his house for drinks and a bath.

The house was decorated partly in Japanese and the rest in European style. To our eyes the Japanese furnishings were infinitely the more attractive ones. The bath now was wholly native and as such worth describing. The ladies of the house led me first, however, to the bath apartment to initiate me in the proper use of its facilities. There are two tubs; in the first you wash, in the second, larger one, you just sit and cook in clean, hot water. An extremely pleasant, hygienic arrangement! The tubs are of wood, round or oval shaped, and deep, much cosier than our slippery, cold porcelain bath tubs.

Emerging from these ablutions we gathered in the garden, where we sat around on the lawn in comfortable deck chairs sipping cold drinks; quite European again, what pity! The only national notes were the pretty, flowered kimono of our hostess and the straw slippers which we were offered in place of our stuffy shoes. The young daughters of the house wore modern frocks, thereby losing all claim to grace.

At the many dinner parties to which we were invited in the geisha houses we invariably sat on the floor with, at best, a thin cushion beneath us. This position became torture after an hour or so.

Manfully, with grim determination we ate our way through the identical succession of weird dishes which we came to dread. We found only the soups, the rice, and occasionally the fried fish really palatable. Mostly we did not know what we were eating.

These meals were accompanied by tiny bowls of hot *sake,* beer, whiskey, and brandy. I, personally, never managed to down even a thimbleful of *sake*. The same cannot be said of the gentlemen who were our hosts or fellow guests. I suspect that *sake* alone would have done the trick, but anyhow the combination of this potent national drink with beer and whiskey usually proved too much for the imbibers. As there were no tables to fall under or chairs to fall off, the little gentlemen just toppled over backwards.

We found the opening ceremonies of each dinner party charming. We admired the little serving geishas in their colorful, rich kimonos, with their painted, masklike, little doll faces; their graceful kneeling as they offered one tiny lacquer dish after another. Their high-pitched, unintelligible chatter sounded like the twittering of birds.

I learned the use of chopsticks from these little ladies well enough to convey odd bits of food into my mouth. But we marveled at the dexterity with which these nimble people dismembered a fish or propelled a whole bowlful of rice into their mouths with nothing better than these knitting needles.

At one big cocktail party we were entertained with music and dances. Strange sounds and strange movements if judged by our standards of both. But if one listened to and watched without prejudice and with a little knowledge of what these arts are supposed to convey, one found them full of melody and grace. In the dances each gliding movement, every twist of the head, the swaying of the body, the contortions of hands and feet all have a meaning, represent something which of course one cannot hope to comprehend at first sight.

In Tokyo we visited the famous kimono market. Here one found every conceivable variety, from the most gorgeous embroidered silk to the plainest cotton kimono. Here one could buy material by the yard or ready-made garments. Not all of these were new. In fact, some of the most beautiful costumes were wedding kimonos, worn once and sold to the market. The prices were very high for the best of these.

We were shown a collection of rare old pieces. They were of an astonishing beauty but way beyond our means. Finally we found something that we could afford among the more modern ones. It was of emerald green silk with a magnificent design in gold embroidery of curly waves, fantastic fish and turtles. I have it still, but it is so beautiful that I never wear it!

Ordinarily when we speak of kimonos we think of a loose garment with flowing sleeves which one throws on carelessly as dressing gown or bath robe. This is not at all the proper conception of a kimono. In reality it is a very complete and even formal dress, with much more to it than one imagines.

In the first place, not the kimono but the obi, the broad sash, is the chief thing. These obis are yards long, of stiff silk or satin, elaborately embroidered with splendid woven design. They are wound around the waist, almost up to the arm pits, in an intricate manner, tied at the back in a huge, flat bow. The obi often costs more than the kimono itself. Beneath the kimono a white underdress is worn that folds over high at the neck and shows above the gown. Formerly this gown was topped by the tremendous hair-do which the modern Nippon lady has discarded in favor of short or plainly dressed hair, or which she wears only in the form of a wig, as I discovered among the geishas upon one occasion when they dressed me up for fun at an evening party in a complete outfit, wig and all.

We visited many temples, mysteriously beautiful, ornate buildings. Most of them were so dimly lighted inside that one could only guess at much of their beauty. Besides, one felt shy about peering too closely into dark corners or examining the countless objects of worship with as much curiosity as one felt.

Many of these temples were in bad disrepair and none too clean. But we were much struck by the natural piety of the Japanese people. Often we observed men, women, and children, sometimes whole families together, at their devotions. Oblivious of onlookers they bowed, knelt, and prayed in deep concentration. Usually a small offering was left at the feet of one of the holy images.

Once of an evening, when the temple was already closed, we watched a woman mount the steps and kneel before the gates to the interior. As she rose to leave she threw a penny or two through the bars of the gates as an offering to the gods (or to the priests, who would collect the pennies the next day).

LOUIS'S STORY RESUMED

Judged by Western standards, the life of a Japanese housewife is that of a slave and is regarded as humiliating to the extreme. People who ought to know, however, assured us that this is true only on the surface. In reality the Japanese wife runs everything even to the extent of paying her husband's geisha bills. At least so these "experts" claimed.

I may insert parenthetically that somewhat later, on our trip from Kyoto to Mukden, we met a Japanese general who was traveling with his wife, a boy, and three girls. He and the boy were traveling first class; the feminine part of the family had to put up with third-class accommodations, even on the boat between Shimonoseki and Fushang.

Most of the time in Tokyo we spent with Eveline and Gottfried Kaumann. We called them *Kaumann San* and *Kaumann Oksan,* the Japanese equivalent for Mister and Mistress. Kaumann, whose cable to Gablenz had clinched the trip around the world for us, was a delightful guide and companion. He knew the Japanese as well as any European is able to know them, yet even he complained: "The longer I live here, the less I understand them."

We picked up a few words of Japanese like *saionara* (good-by) or *arigato* (thank you). The Japanese language sounded very pretty to our ears because of the many vowels resembling Spanish or Italian to a certain extent. The greatest difficulty for everybody, the Japanese included, was their script, which they took over from the Chinese. I was told that the ordinary Japanese spends most of his life trying to learn how to read and write.

The religious attitude of the Japanese was baffling to us as Occidentals. My friends told me that a Japanese can be a Buddhist, a Shintoist, and a Christian all at once.

Kaumann and other friends told us that many Japanese wished that the *Teno* (Emperor) would make more use of his powers to curb the militaristic extremists who were engaging the country in the Chinese adventure and were misusing his name. Mushakoyi and other Japanese intimated that Hiröhito and the imperial court were by no means elated about the Axis friendship and that their sympathies were decidedly pro-English.

In their homeland the attitude of the average Japanese was courteous, even humble. This changed abruptly when we came to Manchuria and Japanese-occupied China. Here the Japanese acted and felt as the masters. From what we were able to observe and learn from informal sources, the personnel of the occupation authorities represented second- and third-rate types of Japanese.

Before we left Sinking we were assured by the Japanese authorities that it would be safe to travel from Mukden to Peking in spite of Chinese guerrilla activities along that line. We arrived at Mukden in the evening just in time to catch our night train to Peking. We had left instructions at our Mukden hotel to have the rest of our luggage brought to the sleeper. When we boarded the train, there was no luggage. It was too late to go to the hotel and fetch it. So the train left without us. When we reached Peking on the following evening by day train we heard that the night train we had missed never arrived. The Japanese headquarters at Sinking must have had some premonition that it would not be safe to travel at night, but it would have been a loss of face to admit it. Instead, our luggage had purposely not been put on our train!

The Japanese occupation of northern China had produced a rather awkward situation for the foreign diplomats accredited to Chiang Kai-shek's government. The heads of the diplomatic missions were supposed to move to Chunking in the distant Szechwan Province, whereas their staffs remained at Peking. But some of these dignitaries preferred

Peking to Chunking and took their time before making the long voyage. They continued to lead a gay social life in their own little community.

Because of the war situation it took us more than a week to get from Peking to Shanghai. The railway was cut. We had to take a boat from Tientsin to Dairen and another one from Dairen to Shanghai.

As the Japanese were in control of only a very narrow stretch of land around Peking, we were able only to visit the summer palace and could not go as far as the famous Ming graves.

As a whole, Peking, especially the Forbidden City and even more so the Altar of Heaven, presented one of the strongest impressions we received in the Far East.

We had time to visit Port Arthur, where my father-in-law had served with the Russian Navy in the Russo-Japanese War. Standing on the once blood-drenched Telegraph Hill we had a beautiful view of the whole town and the coast. In those waters the *Petropavlovsk* had struck a mine. Kira's father was swept off the sinking boat and spent hours in icy water until he was rescued.

Crossing the China Sea we received a wireless invitation from the High Commissioner of the Philippines, Paul V. McNutt, and another from President Manuel Quezon to be their guests at parties arranged for us the following week.

Our boat made a twelve-hour stop at Tsingtao. After some negotiating with the port authorities I was permitted to go ashore. Accompanied by another German, who knew his way about town, we hired a taxi for a tour of the city and the old German fortifications. All in all, the place looked rather run down. The Chinese taxi driver spoke German fluently. He had been an orderly to several German officers before World War I. He raved about "those good old days" and abused the present masters with a perfect vocabulary of cuss words such as one hears on any German parade ground.

Not far from our boat a large Japanese steamer was being loaded with wounded soldiers. Apparently the Japanese did not want the passengers on our boat to see this grim sight and had permitted no foreigner except myself to go ashore. Kira had remained aboard ship, not feeling well. Nevertheless the White Russian colony of Tsingtao assembled on the quay to catch a glimpse of "their" Grand Duchess. Ever since our arrival at Yokohama the White Russians living in Japan or on the Asiatic Continent had demonstrated their adherence to Kira and her family in the most fervent manner, inviting us to parties and presenting us with gifts. Usually the Japanese authorities had not interfered with these demonstrations. We even had the feeling that they sponsored them to a certain extent. But this time nobody was allowed aboard ship. So the priest, who was always present on these occasions, gave his blessing as our boat was pulling out for Shanghai.

At Shanghai the White Russian colony turned out in large crowds to welcome Kira. They had already been to the pier several times, since they expected us earlier. A big reception had been prepared at the Cathay Hotel, but we had to disappoint them because Kira, not feeling well, was confined to her room. Scores of Russians, nevertheless, simply walked into the apartment, and Kira had to receive them lying on a couch. The enthusiasm and loyalty of these émigrés was very touching. I spent most of the night and the early hours of the day studying Shanghai night life. Russian and German émigrés seemed to outnumber all other nationalities.

On the way to the dock the next morning we saw the appalling destruction caused by the Japanese in the Chinese part of the town.

The *Victoria,* which took us from Shanghai to Manila, was an up-to-date, beautiful Italian vessel. We had our meals with the captain, a husky and very jovial man, and the ship's chaplain, who was teasingly nicknamed "Don Giovanni" by the dining room *maître d'hôtel.* Our table partners soon revealed that they were staunch anti-Fascists and had no sympathy for Hitler either. We thoroughly enjoyed the Italian food and their great choice of excellent wines, served in beautiful Venetian glasses. The four-day trip to Manila was interrupted at Hong Kong, which I found to rank third after Rio de Janeiro and San Francisco as far as scenery is concerned.

After a stopover at beautiful Hong Kong, our boat docked at Manila harbor at six o'clock in the morning. In spite of the early hour we were met by the aides of the American High Commissioner and the President of the Philippines. We were also met by the German consul, Sakowsky, and his wife and by Mr. and Mrs. Arsenio Luz. The Luz's, a Filipino couple, were intimate friends of the Roy Howards. Arsenio was nick-named "Arsenic" by his friends. At the request of Roy Howard he was one of the main organizers for our entertainment during our stay on the Philippines. The Sakowskys asked us to be their house guests. With Consul Sakowsky, I first called on McNutt and immediately afterwards on Quezon. This was the prescribed etiquette. McNutt received me very amiably in his office, and we renewed our acquaintanceship of Indianapolis. Quezon, who lived in the Malacanan Palace, seemed pleased that I addressed him in Spanish. He welcomed me in typical Latin style with a glass of French champagne. The McNutt and Quezon receptions in our honor came off beautifully. Innumerable cocktail parties, luncheons, and dinners followed. The Sakowskys gave an official luncheon at which, besides the Quezons, the McNutts, and many others, General and Mrs. MacArthur were present. We met the general on several other occasions and were fascinated by his keen outlook on world affairs, revealing the mind of a true statesman far beyond the scope of a mere soldier.

We also were guests of the Spanish colony of Manila, important because of its number, wealth, and great tradition. Many of them disagreed with Quezon's demand for early Philippine independence.

"The Japanese are only itching for a chance to gobble us up," they argued.

Quezon, a delightful conversationalist, did not share their worries about the Japanese, who were evidently trying to play up to him. He showed a strong interest in Germany, remarking that he planned to visit my country. He undoubtedly was one of the most important political leaders in that part of the world. We were rather surprised to learn that the Filipinos considered themselves emphatically as belonging to the Occident. Both the century-old Spanish colonization and the influence of modern American civilization seemed to have produced this phenomenon, quite unique, I believe, among the peoples of the Far East.

The day we sailed from Manila the papers wrote about the possibility of imminent war. The Sudeten crisis had culminated in the Munich Conference. When we arrived at Singapore three days later it looked as if war might break out any minute. The British passengers of the *Scharnhorst* all left the boat and canceled their tickets. We had dinner at the house of the newly appointed German consul, General Windecker. He was in a frenzy: "Is that madman in Berlin going to start a war?" he kept on saying.

The next morning we drove out to Johore, where the Crown Prince received us and showed us his father's palace. Windecker dropped us at our ship and went to the British governor to find out about the situation. He returned after an hour with the governor's assurance that Kira and I would be allowed to cross over to Sumatra if war were declared during the next few hours.

Our boat sailed in the afternoon, and we entered Belawan Harbor the next morning. This port was filled with German boats, whose captains had all received secret orders to reach a neutral port.

By the time we reached Ceylon, our next stop, most people advised us to hurry home. But the German consul, our friend Baron von Plessen, urged us to stay. We had no cause to be sorry for having followed his advice. We spent about six wonderful weeks in Ceylon and southern India.

The atmosphere encountered in Singapore hardly a week ago, which was one of panic and desperation, had suddenly changed into enthusiastic optimism in view of the outcome of the Munich Conferences. We convinced ourselves that nobody out there, excepting only a small clique of Japanese, wanted war. The general reaction was one of hope for a peaceful future.

Living at Plessen's house we went on many interesting sightseeing excursions and met a great number of British Government officials and their wives.

This last leg of our honeymoon trip was overshadowed by the death of Kira's father. He had been taken to the American Hospital at Paris, which we rang up from Colombo. The doctor told us that my father-in-law's condition was hopeless. If Kira wished to see her father alive she would have to board an airplane immediately.

Considering Kira's condition such an air trip was a big risk. Torn between her duties of a daughter and a future mother she decided not to take it. The news of her father's death reached us on the boat between Colombo and Cochin. Kira's calmness and self-restraint when she received the sad news was remarkable.

Three Maharajas, of Cochin, Mysore, and Travancore, were our hosts in India. An old German gentleman played an important part at the Mysore court. He had come from Dresden or Leipzig as a boy and through the years had risen to the position of director of the royal gardens and palaces. The Maharaja used this kindhearted man as a sort of private adviser on almost anything. Under his supervision the great dam, the prize of Mysore, had been built. After our return to Europe we both read Louis Bromfield's *The Rains Came*. This fascinating book reminded us of the local atmosphere we had met in Mysore.

From what we were able to judge the most progressive of the three states was Travancore, thanks to its young Maharaja, not forgetting the Maharani and the able Prime Minister Sir Ramaswami Ayer. This Maharaja had visited my father at Potsdam during the Olympic games and now invited us to his birthday festivities, which lasted a whole week. We were quartered in a palatial guest house.

The climax of the festivities was a religious procession. The young Maharaja rode on a huge elephant. In front of the elephant walked the notables of the state led by Sir Ramaswami, who was barefooted and in native costume like the rest. As a Brahman he even outranked the Maharaja, who belonged to the second highest class of warriors.

The Gandhiists, who had mostly come from outside the state, staged a demonstration against the Maharaja by lining the streets as he drove in an open carriage. They cried *"Gandhi Jee,"* something like "Hail, Gandhi," in Indian.

At the Maharaja's suggestion we motored to the northern part of the state into a region known for its wild elephants. From a small motor launch we could see the elephants pasturing along the shores of the lake only a short distance away from us.

We spent the last night on the Indian Continent at Cape Comorin, the southern tip of India. We crossed over from Tuticorin to Colombo in the company of about two thousand goats and several hundred natives.

At Travancore a wire from my grandfather had reached us, urging us to come home. The Kaiser was right. A doctor at Colombo strongly supported Grosspapa's anxiety. "By the end of January next year your heir will be born," he said. Several days later at Colombo we boarded the *Potsdam* from which we disembarked at Rotterdam three weeks later.

On November 9, which happened to be my birthday, we were between Port Said and Genoa. Captain Prehn called me aside to tell me about a new atrocity perpetrated by the Nazis the night before—the burning of synagogues, the looting of Jewish stores, and the arrest of thousands of Jews, allegedly to avenge the murder of a young attaché in the German Embassy at Paris by a young Hebrew.

Prehn was furious. "I have kept this horrible news out of the daily bulletin," he said. "On top of all this I must deliver a speech tonight to commemorate the Munich *Bierputsch* of 1923." Somehow he succeeded in delivering a very diplomatic address from which one could easily detect his political attitude which was one of cordial hatred of Nazism. Prehn told me he was on a continuous war footing with the *Ortsgruppenleiter* of the boat, a tearoom steward who as the political boss of the ship had practically more power than the captain. The Nazi Party usually picked types like that for such a job. There was no difference between them and the dreaded commissars of the Communist Party. On ships like the *Potsdam* their power generally went to their heads to such a degree that they not only lorded it over the rest of the crew but also tried to interfere with the running of the boat. Navy skippers complained that the safety of the boats was impaired. They had frequently to appear before Sailors' Courts at Bremen or Hamburg to defend themselves against ridiculous accusations and denunciations invented by these abominable creatures who undermined the foundations of navigation and safety which the German Merchant Marine was proud to possess to a high degree.

When we arrived at Doorn my grandfather stood before the *Torgebäude* (Gate House) with a large bouquet of roses.

"I was afraid your globe-trotting husband would kill you if I let him go on honeymooning any longer," he said, giving Kira a hearty hug.

"Now be a good girl and lie down right away," he added with a very proud look as he led her into the house.

Chapter Thirty-two

The Months Before the Storm

(1938–39)

THE FIRST two dinner guests at our new home in the Berlin suburb of Grunewald were my father and Louis Lochner. We had arrived from Doorn in the morning. The blue Ford cabriolet, Henry Ford's wedding present, was waiting for us at the station.

Reminded by Louis, my father gladly admitted that his apprehensions had been unfounded and that the prognosis of "natural events" had come true.

Our next-door neighbor was Mrs. Hugh Wilson, wife of the last American Ambassador to Germany. Her husband had been recalled by President Roosevelt after the burning of synagogues in November 1938. Mrs. Wilson, too, soon left.

The house was taken over by the American naval attaché, Commander Albert Schrader, and his family consisting of his charming Cuban-born wife, nicknamed Tina, and their eighteen-year-old son Al, Jr. In order to escape observation by spies and snoopers—the Americans ever since Roosevelt's "quarantine" speech were looked upon with distrust by the Nazis—we had made a hole in the fence separating our two gardens. We called it the "peace door." Usually in the evenings, after the commander's return from his work, we dropped in on each other. After disconnecting or covering up the telephones we always settled down for long political discussions. We agreed on everything with the exception of American domestic politics, the Schraders being staunch Republicans. They had many German friends who were more or less openly opposed to the Hitler regime. The commander was a descendant of an American branch of an old German noble family. Schrader held much the same views as Louis Lochner on the German situation. He loved the German people and, as a navy man, held the old Imperial German Navy in high regard. He saw quite clearly, though he always hoped for the best, that a war was inevitable into which his country would also be drawn eventually.

Perhaps the most prominent of Schrader's anti-Nazi friends was General Kurt von Hammerstein, whom I shall mention in greater detail in the connection with the July 20 plot against Hitler. The Schraders, together with the Lochners, were our dearest friends, whom we trusted blindly.

Especially after the war had started and Kira had to remain at Berlin alone for long intervals, the Schraders did everything to console her and help her get over bad spells of loneliness. Neither Kira nor I shall ever be able to forget their friendship which outlasted the war. The couple visited us at our Kissingen refuge in 1946. They thus kept the promise given us before they left Germany that neither wars nor revolutions would change their affection.

After our return from the honeymoon we decided to enjoy our new nest as much as possible in spite of the clouds on the political horizon. Our house was very cozy, and Kira applied all her art of interior decorating to make it even more gemütlich. We were both fanatical believers in the Russian-American style of hospitality of having our friends drop in on us at their own convenience. Occasionally we gave small dinner parties for not more than two or four guests at a time. My piano teacher Rudi Hauschild was a frequent guest. Kira, who loves music no less than I do, thoroughly approved of my bachelor habit of inviting musicians.

We were two very happy people in harmony with the globe we just had encircled and in happy anticipation of our little "baby-san."

The Roosevelt cable incident has already been mentioned. It naturally caused a certain amount of annoyance and anxiety to both of us. But we soon forgot all about it.

I had to attend grandfather's eightieth birthday without Kira. It was his last big family reunion. His health and spirit were still unbroken, although I noticed that he had aged considerably. He was as concerned about Kira's condition as I was and awaited the blessed event with impatience.

On February 9, 1939, shortly before midnight, our first child was born. It was a boy. I went almost out of my wits with joy. Kira's room the next day looked like a hothouse. Our friends, many of them foreign diplomats, sent in whole truckloads of flowers. Though the Goebbels-controlled German press was forbidden even to mention the name of our family, we pulled a trick by inserting a paid birth notice in several newspapers, including even the *Völkische Beobachter*. Louis Lochner saw to publicity in the world beyond Nazi Germany. We received congratulations from all over.

Kira and I had decided to call our boy Louis Ferdinand. But my grandfather, whom I visited especially for that purpose, felt that the family tradition should be kept up, by which the oldest son was called Friedrich Wilhelm. Though we both were quite disappointed, we would not dream of disregarding his wishes. His happiness and pride about the new bud on the Hohenzollern family tree were deep and sincere.

After the christening, which was celebrated in my parents' home, Cecilienhof—Louis Lochner was godfather—Kira and I traveled to Doorn, taking our baby with us in a basket. Kira spent two months at Doorn while I was doing air service with the Bölke Squadron near Hannover. I visited her several times over week ends. My grandfather took excellent care of her. It was touching to witness his interest in his first great-grand-son.

While Kira was at Doorn, President Roosevelt made his peace offer to Hitler and Mussolini, asking them to guarantee the borders of the neighbors of Italy and Germany. In a two-hour Reichstag speech a short time later Hitler ridiculed and rejected the whole plan. His direct answer was the cancellation of the naval accord with Britain. It was now obvious that Hitler wanted no peaceful settlement. The political atmosphere grew tenser every day.

My year's leave with the Lufthansa was ended. Gablenz and I agreed that this would be the best moment for me to quit entirely. From now on I wished to concentrate on our family's affairs. We decided to spend a few months at Schildberg, one of our family estates about one hundred miles northeast of Berlin, in order to study farming. Late in August 1939 we moved our little household there. Our hopes that I would have much time for this new plan proved disappointing. Approaching Schildberg we met with long convoys of trucks heading East towards the Polish border.

We had just unpacked our trunks and established ourselves when I was called back to Berlin to attend the funeral of some old general of the Imperial Army at my parents' request. In the evening I was to meet my old friend Valdivia, who had come to Germany to attend some memorial exercise at the Tannenberg monument in East Prussia, where Hindenburg was buried. As I was getting ready for my dinner with Valdivia the telephone rang and a cryptic voice said: *"Der A-Fall ist eingetreten"* ("Case A has happened"). It was Major Goebel of the district command. He was responsible for the air reserve officers of my section of Berlin. He had promised to notify me immediately. His communication was, of course, secret. He told me I could return to Schildberg to await further orders.

I spent a very uneasy evening with Valdivia, who was completely in the dark about events. He was convinced that he was going to East Prussia the next day. We were sitting on the roof garden of the Eden Hotel. Almost next to our table I saw the Polish Ambassador, Josef Lipsky, who was dining with several members of his staff, all with sad faces.

When I passed his table he whispered: *"Es ist alles vorbei, leben Sie wohl"* ("Everything is lost, farewell").

This amiable diplomat had tried to create a better atmosphere between our two countries. Now his life's work was shattered. I never saw him again. We heard over the radio that he had entered the French Army as an ordinary private.

I went straight back to Schildberg. A few anxious days followed. Then Hitler announced before the Reichstag on September 3 that he had given orders to the German Army to march into Poland in the early morning hours.

"This gray tunic I shall take off only when I have won this war. Should Fate decide against me, I shall not survive my defeat," were his melodramatic words. Kira's and my mood was a mixture of fury and despair.

Chapter Thirty-three

War Service and Retirement

(1939–44)

A FEW DAYS later I was ordered to report to my flying unit the following day. This unit was a transport group, mainly made up of Lufthansa men. Its commander was Baron von Gablenz, who was soon promoted to the rank of colonel. My rank was that of a second lieutenant and my war assignment that of a second pilot. The group was stationed at Tempelhof Airport, Berlin.

I happened to be at Cecilienhof the day England and France declared war on Germany. My parents were in despair. My mother tearfully said to me as we walked out in the garden: "When you were children during the other war I always prayed that my own children would never have to go to war. Now you are all grown up, and again there is a war."

This world holocaust came as a surprise to the majority of the German people. Thanks to the appeasement policy of the Western powers and because of Hitler's methodical assurance that he would "accomplish everything without going to war," most Germans were convinced that Hitler would get away with his bluff this time also. The conclusion of the Russo-German nonaggression pact was generally interpreted as the best guarantee for peace. Few people stopped to think that this pact was the green light for Hitler's invasion of Poland.

Consequently, there was practically no enthusiasm anywhere when the blow fell. Some of Hitler's opponents began to hope the war might take a bad turn for Hitler and his henchmen.

The Polish campaign was over so quickly that our unit hardly got into action. We moved a few troops from West Prussia to Slovakia and made a few flights into Poland from an East Prussian airport near Königsberg to provide necessary fuel for a Panzer division which had run out of gas.

Our last task was to move as much material as we could out of the airport of Brest Litovsk before it was taken over by the Soviets, who "very gallantly" marched into Poland after its army had been completely crushed by the Germans.

Our unit was retransferred to Berlin to await further orders. I took a short leave to bring my little family back to Berlin. I was thus able to spend half of the lull between the Polish and the French campaigns living with my family in our Grunewald house.

Life in Berlin in spite of the war restrictions—our car had been requisitioned in October—was still relatively comfortable. The circle of our foreign friends had been largely reduced, but our American friends were still there. The Schraders and the Lochners drove us around in their cars, which they as foreigners had been allowed to keep. During these months I was contacted by the resistance group which was hatching new plans for the overthrow of the Hitler regime.

We celebrated Christmas and New Year trying to make it as cozy and cheerful as possible. Towards the end of January 1940 my unit was transferred to Salzwedel, an airport halfway between Berlin and Bremen. We all sensed that some action in the West was in the offing. Hitler's so-called peace offer to England had been turned down. In March, I received orders to report to Gablenz at Berlin. He had been relieved of his command of the transport unit and was now appointed inspector general for blind-flying instruction.

"There is every likelihood that your transport unit will be used for the invasion of the Netherlands," he said. "I imagine you would not be keen to invade Holland, which has behaved so gallantly towards your grandfather all these years. Your new assignment will be at the blind-flying school at Rahmel near Danzig. Take a week's leave before you go there. I trust neither you nor your wife will be angry with me now," he added with an engaging smile.

My new assignment was that of company commander of the so-called *Wirtschaftskompanie,* or businessmen's unit. My men were mostly elderly shopkeepers, artisans, handicraftsmen, and other sedate citizens. On Gablenz's orders I took a course in advanced blind-flying, because he wanted to use me as a blind-flying instructor. He knew that commanding a ground crew would not be after my taste.

On March 22 that year—1940—on Good Friday, our second child was born. I had just been to the small village church when I was called from Berlin. Our housekeeper phoned me that the baby would be there almost any minute. I was able to catch a train for Berlin. I got there in the late evening hours and rushed upstairs into Kira's bedroom. "It's another boy," she said with a happy voice.

We wanted to call him Michael. But again Grosspapa intervened. Our second son was born on Emperor Wilhelm I's birthday. My grandfather, who greatly admired his own grandfather, insisted that we call the child Wilhelm Heinrich. We compromised on calling him all three names. For us, however, he was "Mikie," the nickname of Kira's nephew, the young King of Roumania.

We christened our second-born on May 9, Kira's birthday. This time the baptism took place in our Grunewald home. Pastor Doehring performed the ceremony. He had married us at Doorn and had christened our first-born. He was later to christen the next three children.

Our little house almost burst at the seams, so crowded was it. We had invited all the members of the family living at Potsdam and most of our Berlin friends. Hilde and Louis Lochner and Tina and Al Schrader were among the guests, as was the Spanish military attaché Count Rocamora and the Danish minister Hjerulf Zahle, who represented the King and Queen of Denmark, who were to be godfather and godmother to the child. I had been able to scrape together sufficient food, which in the Danzig region was still more easily obtainable than in the rest of Germany. It was a warm spring night, and everybody felt relaxed amidst the tensions of war. The guests did not leave until long after midnight.

It was to be the last party in our Grunewald house. When we woke up the next morning we heard that the invasion of Holland and Belgium had begun that night.

A few weeks later my brother Wilhelm was mortally wounded on the battlefield as the German troops marched into France. Although his body was brought to Potsdam quietly, word of the hour of burial spread like wildfire and some fifty thousand persons filed by his coffin. This fact was observed with consternation by Nazi officialdom. It was obviously a spontaneous pro-Hohenzollern demonstration.

I returned to Rahmel after Mikie's baptism and had Kira follow me with the children after the first British raid on Hannover. We found a very comfortable apartment at the Kasino Hotel at Zoppot. I was permitted to spend the nights with my family, commuting between Rahmel and Zoppot daily. We thus spent almost three very happy months together. Kira, who loves the sea, thoroughly enjoyed living on the Baltic coast. Our little Friedrich screamed with joy splashing in the water. Little Mikie slept in his baby carriage, which stood alone on the lawn in front of the hotel.

When a year later, in June 1941, the Kaiser's health gave cause for alarm the whole family hastened to Doorn. Every one of us was permitted to visit him briefly. I, too, had a last talk with him.

Grosspapa was lying in bed as I entered. His face was appallingly pale, but his eyes flashed as always and his voice was still strong. He inquired in detail about Cadinen and asked affectionately about my wife and our two boys. The photos of my little family which I had sent him only a little while previously were standing near his bed on a dresser, and he pointed to them with pride.

He referred neither to his condition nor to the reason for my sudden visit; nevertheless, he was obviously aware of his approaching end, for as he kissed me good-by and gently squeezed my hand he said: "I'm comforted in the thought that you two (meaning Kira and me) are bringing up your boys as good Christians. God bless you."

For some days hopes revived. The Kaiser rallied once more. The physician even counseled that immediate danger had passed and urged that the members of the family leave as soon as possible so as not to disquiet the patient. I remained nevertheless. The Kaiser's condition improved even to the extent that he could take normal nourishment in small doses.

All the greater was the shock when on the evening of June 3, I was urgently summoned to his room. To the left of his bed sat Kaiserin Hermine; to the right his only daughter, the Duchess of Brunswick, my Aunt Cissy. My step-grandmother whispered to me: "He is dying."

We remained at his bedside all night. His last struggle lasted well into the following forenoon.

Hitler was in a dilemma when the news reached him. He was in the midst of a war in which he needed the support especially of his professional soldiers. These men knew that tradition demanded a burial with military honors for the Kaiser. Hitler speculated, we now know, that he could even capitalize on the situation by bringing the mortal remains of the late emperor back to Germany and staging a pompous show. This hope was dashed to the ground by the codicil to my grandfather's will which read:

Doorn, December 25, 1933

To THE MINISTER OF THE ROYAL HOUSE.
Codicil to My Last Will.

Should God decide to call me from this world at a time when the *Kaisertum* has not yet been reinstated, i.e., when a non-monarchial form of government still exists, it is my *firm will* to be buried provisionally in Doorn, inasmuch as I am entering upon eternal rest in *exile* in Doorn.

At the spot opposite the house at which a bust of me now stands before the rhododendrons, the coffin is to repose before it in the sarcophagus designed by the sculptor Betzner and approved by me, and is to be protected against the weather by a canopy to be designed by Betzner. Beds of flowers with bright-colored cineraria and salvia are to surround it. The obsequies are to be simple, unpretentious, quiet, dignified. *No* delegations from home. *No* swastika flags. *No wreaths.* The same thing applies to Her Majesty in case of her death in Doorn. If I should die in Potsdam, my remains are to be interred in the above-named sarcophagus in the mausoleum near the New Palace in such a manner that it will stand *between* the *two* empresses. *Military* burial, *no swastika flags. No funeral address.* Songs. Prayer.

(signed) WILHELM
I. R.

Thereupon Hitler decided upon a two-fold course of action: First, the German press was given the facts about the Kaiser's death but with instructions to "play down" the story—the shorter, the better; second, an honor battalion of army, navy, and Luftwaffe soldiers was dispatched to Doorn, and the Nazi administrator for occupied Holland, Artur von Seyss-Inquart, was delegated to represent Hitler and deposit a huge wreath with the inscription "Der Führer" on the bier.

My grandfather was laid to rest in the tiny chapel on his Doorn estate according to simple rites which he had prescribed minutely forty years previously. The Reverend Bruno Doehring after a brief service sprinkled the coffin with earth taken from before the Antique Temple of Sans Souci Park, Potsdam, where my grandmother, Empress Auguste Victoria, lies buried. He pronounced no eulogy. The Kaiser had specifically ruled this out.

From the flagstaff of ivy-clad Huize Doorn fluttered solely the black and white standard of the House of Hohenzollern—no Nazi flag was displayed. Attendance at the funeral was limited to the immediate family, Seyss-Inquart, and his entourage, deputations from the Hungarian and Bulgarian armies, and nonagenarian Field Marshal August von Mackensen.

Soon after the funeral I was called into my colonel's office: "I want you to read the characterization I am sending to headquarters." These reports on each subordinate office had to be sent in by the superiors from time to time. The colonel continued:

"It is my duty to show it to you, because it is not altogether favorable and may be detrimental to your future career in the air force." The colonel had made a careful study of my character; he considered himself a great psychologist. The two negative points were my unmilitary attitude, which was rated as much too jovial and informal, especially towards superiors, and my political *Weltanschauung*.

"You do not seem to be a very enthusiastic supporter of the Third Reich," the colonel said, looking at me gravely.

"How could I be, Herr *Oberst*," was my answer.

"I quite understand, and I did not expect you to feel otherwise. I guess that's all. *Hasta pronto* (see you later,)" he concluded cheerfully. He had lived in Venezuela for many years, and we always spoke Spanish when we met privately.

In July the school was transferred to Klützow, an airport near the little Pomeranian town of Stargard. This was the end of our Zoppot interlude. I transferred my family to Cadinen, my grandfather's estate near Elbing in East Prussia. As air raids on Berlin were to be expected, Kira had agreed with me not to return to Berlin. This was quite a sacrifice for her, because she had grown very fond of our little nest in the Menzelstrasse.

The Schloss at Cadinen had not been lived in since the first years of the last war. It had been shown to the public as a sort of museum. The furniture was ghastly from our modern viewpoint of comfort. We first fixed up the second floor while people still were led through the rooms of the first floor. Finally we took possession of the whole house.

Meanwhile I had received my instructor's license. I spent most of my time in the air. This job also gave me a chance to visit my family almost every week end, weather permitting. This was a little concession to the flying personnel of the school to keep up their spirits. It did not make any difference where we flew to as long as we put in the hours required for each pupil. My pupils were glad to get away from their barracks and fly to Elbing Airport with me.

I liked my new job. In the long run it became a rather nerve-racking business. Though it was against the rules, I never used the black curtain which was to prevent the pupil from cheating when flying in good weather. But because of that curtain there were many head-on collisions in mid-air with the sun shining, because the teacher had no way of watching what was happening on his left side. Several of my colleagues lost their lives because of the curtain and because of physical exhaustion. My pupils got used to my methods. They usually had a general idea of instrument flying before they started their course with us. We were to teach them mainly practical blind-flying navigation.

The courses usually lasted from four to six weeks. Many of the pupils had already had front experience, especially after the battle of England had started. As time went on, though, the percentage of active air-force pilots became smaller and smaller. The pupils in many cases were drafted from civilian professions and did not show the slightest enthusiasm for their war job.

After my brother Wilhelm's funeral, Hitler had issued a secret order that the members of the former ruling families of Germany must be gradually eliminated from the armed forces. Front assignments were strictly forbidden, not to save our lives, but to prevent us from distinguishing ourselves or even to gain fame by dying in battle. Hitler and his henchmen feared that popular discontent with the regime might lead to a counterrevolution in favor of restoring the monarchy. This order somehow had leaked through. I again had a talk with Gablenz. I asked him about my chances of promotion in the Luftwaffe.

"They are practically nil," he answered, as he had done when he was

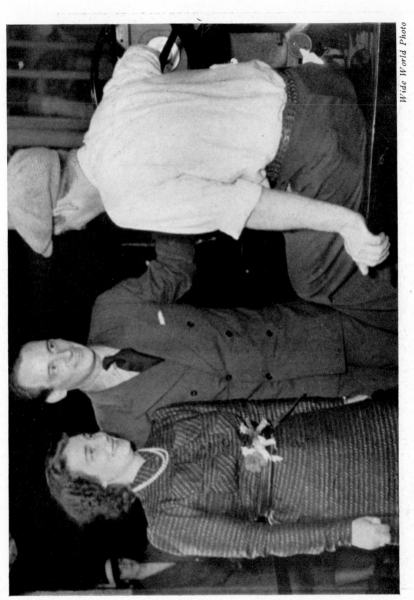

The Prince and his bride during honeymoon visit to the Ford assembly line.

The baptism of the Prince's first child, Prince Friedrich Wilhelm Louis Ferdinand Hubertus Michael Kyrill of Prussia. *Left to right: Seated:* Crown Princess Cecilie, Princess Kira, Princess Cecilie (now Mrs. Harris of Texas). *Standing:* Prince Hubertus, Crown Prince Friedrich Wilhelm and Prince Louis Ferdinand.

manager of the Lufthansa. "You are flying only because I am taking that on my own chin. You are supposed to be kept on the ground."

I asked him what he would do in my place.

"Ask for a discharge before you are thrown out altogether."

I talked it over with my father. He decided to put in a discharge request, giving as a reason that he had lost his oldest son and now needed his second one to look after the family estate. On December 30, 1941, I received my honorable discharge from the Luftwaffe. At first it had to be renewed every three months. Later on nobody bothered any more.

I was a civilian again and "retired" to Cadinen, where I joined my family. Kira was happy. So was I.

My father entrusted me with the administration of Cadinen. This was a natural solution, because my wife and children were settled there for the rest of the war and would stay there for many years after, we hoped. For three years I became a landowner, or Junker. I was very happy living in the country, much happier in fact than living in the city. Cadinen was a small paradise on earth. Woods, hills, fields, the *Frische Haff* (inland sea), and the Baltic formed a unique combination. The Schloss was nothing but a medium-sized farmhouse with enough rooms for all of us. After my air-force discharge we dissolved our Berlin household. Most of the furniture we moved to Cadinen. Kira added her own furniture—heirlooms which she took with her after selling the parental house at Coburg. It included a grand piano, so that we had two of them in our music room. The house became cozy and livable. We made it a point to leave Cadinen as little as possible. Traveling in Germany during the war was no pleasure anyhow.

We never were bored, nor did we feel lonely. Somebody dropped in almost every day. We made a lot of friends among the citizens of near-by Elbing and among the Catholic clergy of Frauenburg, the seat of the bishop. My Elbing friends, mostly businessmen and intellectuals, had been Freemasons and were hence anathema to the Nazis. One of them was Bruno Reuter, who ran the restaurant in the Elbing railway station. He and his wife became our best East Prussian friends.

Another great friend was Father Schröter, the Catholic priest of the little town of Tolkemit, a lively and cheerful man who liked, and also possessed, a good glass of wine. He loyally kept me informed of what was going on and what people said about us. He hated the Nazis and tipped me off on their intentions on several occasions.

Another dear friend was my music teacher, Gerhard Wagner. He had been head of the conservatory at Elbing until the Nazis closed it because he was a Mason. He had, however, kept his job as organist of the *Marienkirche,* the main Protestant church in Elbing. I took up organ playing with him. Dr. Doehring, who was a traditional summer guest at Cadinen, had suggested that I play the organ in our Cadinen church, which had been completed during the second year of World War I and belonged to our family. Kira and I called it our "pocket cathedral." During the summer months Herr Wagner came out to Cadinen and gave me lessons in our church.

During those years our first two daughters were born. Both were christened by Doehring in our church.

In the summer we used to spend several weeks at Kahlberg, a small bathing resort on the *Frische Nehrung,* where we had rented a bungalow. This arrangement was ideal, because we could bring the food over from our estate on the mainland. It took the *Tolkemit,* a small steamboat, about thirty minutes for the five-mile voyage from the town of Tolkemit to Kahlberg. The ship's captain, Herr Voss, a native of Kahlberg, his wife, and his two children also became excellent friends of ours.

With the big landowners of East and West Prussia we had practically no contact. None of them was an immediate neighbor of ours, and without a motor car it was difficult to reach them.

The harmony of our country life was disturbed only by my two administrators, who were ardent Nazis. Not being a farmer myself, I had to rely heavily on them. Both were quite able from a professional viewpoint. But both held important jobs in the Nazi Party. I tried hard to get rid of them but failed. They terrorized our farm laborers, who had been working for us ever since my grandfather bought the estate in 1899, and forced them to say "Heil, Hitler," which, however, they never did when I met them alone.

The only employee I could trust politically was Wilhelm Dietrich, the manager of our pottery and brick works. My grandfather had hired him in 1909 as an apprentice. His friends were also mine.

Although our relations with the Nazi authorities were outwardly correct, they were more than superficial, to say the least. From what I was told by my friends, they considered us a sort of a happy-go-lucky family, indifferent not only to Nazism but to politics generally. A fellow who played the organ during the Sunday service in his church was something of a crackpot in the eyes of these hard-boiled roughnecks. This opinion of us and of our retired way of living to a large extent saved our skins. Though we were constantly being spied upon by our own employees, nobody suspected that the *Gutsherr* of Cadinen was up to his neck in a conspiracy against Hitler and his regime.

Kira and I had become truly attached to Cadinen. We considered it our real home in Germany. We did not wish to live anywhere else. We had learned to love the country and the people. Everyone, even the poorest, led a prosperous life compared to other German regions. The Cadinen area could have been situated in some part of old Russia, hence it made Kira feel at home so much more. The whole attitude on life was much broader and of a wider scope than in western and southern Germany. Therein consisted the great charm of Germany's eastern provinces, especially that of East Prussia.

Chapter Thirty-four

The Ill-Fated July Twentieth
(1944)

JULY 20, 1944, deserves an important place in the modern history of the German people. A number of courageous Germans, representing almost every group of the population, risked and lost their lives in a supreme attempt to overthrow the Hitler tyranny by force. The failure of this plan does not diminish its merit and redeeming evidence against the accusation that nobody tried to get rid of Hitler and his clique. Many of those involved in the plot since 1939, and even earlier, dedicated their whole intelligence and activity to finding a means of abolishing the Hitler regime, thereby paving the way for a new and peaceful Germany.

Since many of my closest friends and acquaintances were involved and sacrificed their lives for their convictions, I feel it my duty to devote a chapter to their activities and to describe my personal connection with this date.

Since the beginning of July 1944 the military situation on the East front had become critical. The Bolshevik forces had made their great break-through at Minsk, and nobody seemed able to stop them during their thrust towards East Prussia and the Vistula.

My wife was expecting a baby during the second half of August. Though in our little corner we still lived in complete peace, the atmosphere of nervous tension created by the bad news from the theater of war grew constantly. Kira and I seriously considered moving her and the children westward before it was too late.

After many long discussions we decided it would mean suicide to stay at Cadinen in the event of a Soviet invasion of East Prussia. Though we had not the slightest ill feeling against the Russian people and tried to be objective about the Soviet system, we had no assurance that the Soviets would feel the same way about us.

To be quite sure before deciding finally, I wanted to get an expert opinion on the military situation and planned to visit Field Marshal Georg von Küchler, who was now living in retirement at Königsberg. He had been a frequent hunting guest of ours at Cadinen. His highly intellectual wife was often the despair of her quiet and reserved husband because of her habit of making the most drastic remarks about Hitler and the Nazis. The field marshal and I agreed in a telephone call that July 20 would best suit both of us for my call.

The railway station of Königsberg presented an alarming picture. The platforms were crowded with civilians, apparently members of the newly formed *Volkssturm,* who were armed with pitch forks, shovels, and other tools. Among them were many foreigners.

Most of these people looked rather gloomy, awaiting their departure to the front to build the nonexistent *Ostwall.* They were shouted at by Nazi officials in brown uniforms who were heavily armed but unable to hide their nervousness. It was not an encouraging picture.

The Küchlers received me with their usual cordial hospitality. I asked the field marshal pointblank what he thought of the military situation on the Eastern front. He thought it was grave. The Red forces had reached the German border and were beginning to invade East Prussia. The entire army group north, formerly commanded by Küchler, was practically cut off in the Baltic states. Küchler time and again had warned Hitler that this was bound to happen, if the front were not shortened. But the great "genius" did not relish such advice and sent Küchler home. Now there were practically no troops left to defend East Prussia. The formation of the *Volkssturm* was a desperate last-minute attempt to stop a tidal wave with ridiculously inadequate means.

Should I move my family West? Küchler knew as well as I did that this meant farewell forever to Cadinen. I could see by his expression that his answer cost him great effort, his military pride being involved.

"Take your family away as soon as possible," he finally replied. I had hoped against hope for another answer. Frau von Küchler strongly supported her husband's view. Throughout the years we had known her she had always been pessimistic about the outcome of the war.

I felt a great urge to return to Cadinen by the next train, but the Küchlers persuaded me to remain overnight, as this would give us time to discuss the situation in detail.

Before lunch we visited the royal palace, which I had never seen. I was shown the court chapel in which my ancestor, Friedrich I, was crowned King of Prussia, also the Muscovite Hall in which another ancestor, Friedrich Wilhelm I, had to go through a whole week of feasting and drinking in honor of his Russian guest, Peter the Great. A few months later this historic building was destroyed totally during an air raid.

Küchler advised finding a place for my family west of the Vistula, if possible even west of the Oder River. I immediately thought of Golzow, a family estate in the Neumark. The administrator, Herr Durnio, and his attractive wife were good friends of ours. I had visited them a while ago and discussed the possibility of temporarily quartering my family with them. Though they had only a small house they assured me we would be welcome at any time. These good people later unfortunately failed to escape the Soviet advance. Durnio was shot by the Bolsheviks merely because with his portly figure he looked like a "capitalist" to them. Frau Durnio after horrible experiences fled into the British zone where she did hard work but remained unbroken in mind and body. My third son, Louis Ferdinand, our fifth child, was born and christened in the Durnio house. During the saddest and most crucial period of our lives this couple proved to be real friends.

In the afternoon I accompanied Frau von Küchler to the university for a lecture on Greek tragedy while her husband went to the hospital to visit his sick son. When we returned to the Küchler home at six o'clock Sybilla, the fourteen-year-old daughter of my hosts, told us in a voice trembling with excitement that according to a radio announcement an attempt had been made on the life of the Führer but that he had been miraculously preserved.

I called Cadinen. My wife had also heard the radio announcement but said everything was quite normal. She gave me the alarming information, however, that our second son, Michael, suddenly had a strange attack at noon and had to be put to bed. It turned out to be meningitis, and it is almost a miracle that we did not lose our little boy.

At ten o'clock the telephone rang. After a conversation of several minutes, during which he took notes and quietly said "yes" and "no," the field marshal rejoined us with a grave face.

"General Woodrich, the commander of Königsberg," he said, "just told me that he had received strange orders from Berlin to the effect that Hitler was dead, that a new government had been formed, and that he was to arrest Erich Koch, the *Gauleiter* for East Prussia, and his whole staff. He had then called the Führer's G.H.Q. and had been able to get through to Field Marshal Keitel. Hitler was alive and practically unhurt, Keitel had assured him. In Berlin a small group of officers had tried to overthrow the government by force, but the situation was well in hand. Under no circumstances should he follow any orders from Berlin. Keitel had asked all field marshals and commanding generals to send messages of loyalty to Hitler. Woodrich will ring up again when he has more news. I certainly shall not send any message of loyalty."

We were thunderstruck. Küchler finally broke the silence by saying: "How could they do such a thing and not be successful?" Frau von Küchler and I tried to contradict him. We doubted that Keitel spoke the truth.

A few minutes later the German radio announced that Hitler would address his people. The usual martial music began, but it took almost an hour before Hitler's voice came over the air, promising dire punishment to the plotters and asserting that the Almighty had visibly protected him to bring the war to a victorious end.

That night I could not sleep. I tried to assess my situation and that of my family by cold reasoning. Here I was, visiting a field marshal whom Hitler had discharged in disgrace, on the very day an attempt was made to kill Hitler and a plot put into action to overthrow the Nazi regime! This fact alone could have most serious consequences. I did not know what Küchler's position was. Apparently he was not directly connected with the plotters, but a few remarks uttered previously suggested that he knew "something" about some organization opposed to the government. His feelings, I knew, were anything but friendly for Hitler. He detested the operatic showmanship of the Führer and viewed with dismay how the virtues and the very roots of centuries-old military traditions were being destroyed.

He was staunchly supported by his temperamental wife. When her husband was made a field marshal she had dryly remarked to people congratulating her on this great event in her husband's life: "After the war is lost, I shall be glad to get a job as a toilet caretaker in London." The story was known all over East Prussia.

I tried to figure out what to say in the event of a Gestapo inquiry: that my visit to the Küchlers was a courtesy call in return for their recent visit to Cadinen; that the date of my trip to Königsberg was a coincidence and in no way connected with the events of the day. That was the simple truth—but would it convince my interrogators? Amazingly enough, it later did!

My mind now turned to a more general question. Was I connected with the events of the twentieth of July? Not directly. But indirectly? For the moment I did not know for certain. No names of the plotters had been mentioned as yet over the radio. Were my friends involved? Several movements, I knew, for the overthrow of Nazism were afoot.

I let the last seven years pass in review before my mental eye. One thought recurred again and again: where was my friend Dr. Otto John? I had last seen him in January. He had planned to go to Spain and stay there. Had he escaped or was he caught?

I visualized the scene when we first met seven years ago. Otto John had introduced himself as the new second legal adviser of the Lufthansa. After a few introductory remarks he had begun to sound out my position towards the Nazi regime and indicated he was a political sympathizer with my family. My answers had been noncommittal, almost curt. He later told me this first meeting had been a bitter disappointment to him. But I had already learned not to trust anybody at first sight, especially not in matters of a political nature. This attractive young man, I had feared, might be a stool pigeon of the Gestapo.

It was my piano teacher, Rudolf Hauschild, who weeks later asked me whether I knew a man named Otto John. He added that John was a friend of one of his best friends, Hans von Dohnanyi, and was absolutely trustworthy; it would be worth while to get better acquainted with him. As I trusted Hauschild and his good sense, I heeded his advice. I really hated myself for having distrusted a person who called on me in good faith. But during those years, distrust was a matter of self-preservation. I hope my children will never know the humiliating experience of look-

ing upon every person whom one does not know as a potential de-
nouncer and traitor.

A few weeks later I met John again. This time we had a heart-to-heart
talk. I explained why I had been so offish. We got deep into politics and
found ourselves in agreement. The Hitler regime, John argued, was
leading Germany into chaos. He said many others thought as he did and
that they had all concluded that the only way to save Germany was to get
rid of Hitler and his clique, by force if necessary.

To my question whether any organization existed to realize that purpose, he replied a movement was in an embryonic state. I told him I
would be glad to co-operate, provided his organization had a sound platform and proceeded in complete secrecy. He promised to keep me
posted.

Meanwhile my engagement to Kira, our marriage, and our honeymoon trip had pushed all other thoughts into the background. I did not
see much of my office or of my new friend. After our return from our
world trip, however, I resumed my contact with John. I confided the
impressions of our trip to him which culminated in the realization that
Hitler's Germany had no friends in the whole world, including the Japanese and the Italians.

Otto informed me that the opposition group had made little headway
because it was almost impossible to secure the co-operation of the army,
the only body which could eliminate Hitler by force. It seemed to him
that war was imminent and unavoidable, as nobody would stop Hitler
from starting it. It did start soon thereafter, and I was called up as a reserve officer!

One afternoon in November 1939, John called on me with his colleague, Dr. Klaus Bonhöffer, and proposed a walk in the near-by Grunewald woods. Both there told me that General Franz Halder, chief of staff
of the general staff, had been won over to their side. Halder was convinced that Hitler would attack France and England and was willing to
help put an end to the whole madness of war by getting rid of the
Führer.

John and Bonhöffer urged me to meet more of their collaborators, to
which I agreed, John to act as liaison man. Subsequently, I became acquainted with Hans von Dohnanyi; Dr. Justus Delbrueck of the secret

service; Jacob Kaiser, leader of the Christian Trade Unions; Ernst von Harnack, *Regierungspräsident* at Merseburg and a prominent member of the Social Democratic Party; Bonhöffer's brother Dietrich, active in the international Protestant church movement; Dr. Joseph Wirmer, closely connected with the Catholic Centrist Party; and others. These people would come to my house on some pretext or other or would meet me in the near-by home of Dr. Bonhöffer. These meetings were always camouflaged as musical or cultural. In Harnack's case this was easy. He was the son of the famous professor of theology who had been a close friend of my grandfather. So there was a certain family connection. Besides, he was a good flutist. As an introduction to every session he played some of Frederick the Great's compositions or standard classical music to the accompaniment of Kira, our confidant in all our deliberations.

Of all these men, only two survived July 20. All of them knew they were gambling with their lives; all but Otto John and Jacob Kaiser paid with theirs.

I asked this group bluntly why they were so eager to include me in their schemes. They replied they needed some stabilizing and unifying figure on whom they could build before the execution of their plot and especially during the period following its successful outcome. I expressed surprise that I should be their choice. They argued that I would be acceptable to both the army, with its conservative attitude, and to the labor organizations, with their progressive tendencies. My employment in a Ford factory and my friendship with President Roosevelt weighed heavily with them, especially with Kaiser and his labor friends. The army people, on the other hand, stressed the point that I was the legitimate Crown Pretender.

I replied I would like to help them, but there were grave family complications. My grandfather, father, and older brother were still in the picture. Although Wilhelm had renounced his status of the first-born as far as the family was concerned, I knew that he still considered himself politically as the rightful pretender. His main passion being soldiering, he was extremely popular in army circles, especially the younger ones, whereas these same people distrusted me because of my internationalistic outlook. I told my new friends that it was up to them to clarify this involved situation. As a private person I certainly would help them in every possible way.

In March, 1940, I wrote a letter to General Ludwig Beck, former chief of staff, which John took to him, asking for an interview in an urgent family matter and intimating the concern I felt about the future. He replied that, although he shared my concern, he deemed it unwise for us to meet as he was being watched closely by the Gestapo. For the moment, he let me know, he was in no position to do anything, because Hitler had already given the order to invade Holland, Belgium, and France. But he was following events closely and would keep in touch with me through John. He urged me to keep in the background so as not to excite the curiosity of Hitler's men.

In those days I wrote a lengthy memorandum in which I made clear my views in that decisive situation. It was meant principally for my children, as I had to reckon with injury or death as a pilot of the Luftwaffe. Otto John and I each kept a copy of it but decided two years later to burn them when one after another of the plotters was arrested.

Hitler's smashing victory over France definitely seemed to destroy all hopes of John and his friends for an indefinite period. The generals now felt less inclined to do anything, having a good argument to calm their consciences in their assertion it would be foolish to interrupt the course of German victory.

When Hitler attacked Soviet Russia in June 1941 the spirits of my friends began to rise again. The re-election of Roosevelt had already given them the certainty that the United States would soon enter the war. In May, I had brought Kira and the children to our family estate at Schildberg near the city of Soldin in the Neumark. In July, Louis Lochner and Otto John visited us there. I had seen Louis only a few weeks previously at my grandfather's funeral which he attended as the only American correspondent. He had known my grandfather and had repeatedly interviewed him.

John had suggested the Schildberg trip because he thought it useful if a detailed interview, written by Louis on my relations with President Roosevelt, could be circulated among the commanding generals of the army. We sat down together, and I gave Louis an exact picture of my relation to the American President, most of which was already known to him as my intimate friend. The report was written, and Otto and Louis returned to Berlin. I saw the Lochners only once more—on the day Hitler declared war on the United States.

When the first setbacks on the Eastern front came during the winter of 1941-42, Otto John urged me to come to Berlin for a secret meeting with General von Hammerstein, chief of staff of the Reichswehr under Chancellor Brüning. Hammerstein had resigned in 1934 for religious reasons. He and General Beck, his successor and close friend, were considered the most brilliant military brains in Germany then. I already knew Hammerstein.

We went to the general's villa after dark for obvious reasons. He received us cordially but gave the impression of a sick and disillusioned man. He was suffering from a cancer of the cheek which proved fatal. I told him I thought it was high time that the army acted against Hitler and that I was ready to issue an order, because of my right to the throne, in case that were necessary to compensate for the lack of civil courage prevailing in the German military caste. I spoke, prompted by John, with great emphasis, expressing the anxiety my friends and I felt.

Hammerstein replied that he understood our feelings and that Hitler and his whole system had to be eradicated, a job only the army could do. "But," he finished his long and clear exposition, "they will never do it; they don't have *Zivilcourage* (civil courage—a term coined by Bismarck, who regretted that the Germans had so little of it). I don't see the slightest chance for such action. The German Army will be defeated utterly, and only then will Hitler fall also. I appreciate your readiness to co-operate, but neither Beck nor I are able to do anything, certainly not at the present moment. The only advice I can give you, also in the name of Beck, is to go back into hiding at your country place and keep alive. I shall of course be glad to keep in touch with you through John."

Hammerstein's pessimism came as an awful blow, yet we knew that he was right. Through the centuries my ancestors had educated their officers' corps to be brave in the field and to take orders. This attitude had not changed after the Hohenzollerns had ceased to give orders and a president of the republic had stepped into power, nor after a former corporal had become the supreme war lord. The philosophy of the Prussian

Army was expressed in the words: "The army is the sword which can be used by whoever runs the country, but not by the army itself."

We agreed that our interview with Hammerstein had been negative throughout, but we also thought or wished to think the general's pessimism was caused by his illness. We took some comfort in the knowledge that he would tell Beck about our visit. We agreed it would be wisest for me to stay put in Cadinen, where I could live more or less unnoticed. We also decided that the next person for me to meet was Dr. Goerdeler, who had expressed the wish to see me. Dr. Goerdeler had resigned as mayor of Leipzig in 1933 because the Nazi Party had removed the bust of the composer Felix Mendelssohn-Bartholdy before the *Gewandhaus* concert hall which Mendelssohn had founded together with a magnificent orchestra. The Nazis had explained their action by pointing out the composer's Jewish ancestry. Under Hitler his music could not be played in Germany.

Since his retirement, Goerdeler had worked for the overthrow of Hitler under the disguise of some business affiliation. Countless men and women from all layers of the German populace opposed to Hitler placed their hopes in him. He acted as their liaison with the military. He was a friend of General Beck. John was to bring Goerdeler to Cadinen. The Goerdeler family had a summer home near Königsberg, and a visit by him would seem natural.

In July 1942, Otto arrived in Cadinen one day ahead of Goerdeler, unnoticed—as was Goerdeler, also—by the Gestapo. On Goerdeler's arrival I asked him whether he would mind walking the mile from the railway station to our estate rather than taking a horse carriage which might arouse the curiosity of our village people, among whom there were Nazi spies. Goerdeler laughed at my precautions. He was known to be rather reckless and absolutely fearless.

Even on our estate we fooled the Gestapo. We addressed Goerdeler by an assumed name whenever a servant was around. He arrived at three thirty in the afternoon and left at eight o'clock. We shall never forget his visit. He seemed to have contacts and friends in many foreign countries, especially in England, which he had visited many times. In the autumn of 1937 he had been to the United States, and he spoke English fluently. He had just lost his second son on the Eastern front. Kira never saw him again. I met him only once more, about nine months later, in Otto's home.

Dr. Goerdeler asked me whether I had any connection with the army or any army leader. I told him that I had been discharged by the Luftwaffe only a few months ago and that General von Küchler was the only commander known to me still in active service (this was before his dismissal by Hitler). John mentioned my memorandum and the fact that I had tried to get in touch with General Beck and had seen General von Hammerstein.

Goerdeler said it was high time to stop the war. Only by removing Hitler could reasonable peace terms be obtained. The army, he was convinced, had the power to force Hitler out; to resort to assassination was against his Christian principles. He said he would now try to visit some of the army leaders at the front and talk them into action.

As to myself, he advised me to stay in Cadinen and keep as quiet as possible. He promised to keep me posted. He still hoped some general could be found to lead a revolt before it was too late and that then all the other generals would follow suit.

The year 1942 passed, and nothing happened along the lines we had been hoping for. Early in March 1943, Otto John summoned me to Berlin, where he told me Goerdeler had succeeded in contacting at least one army group leader, apparently Field Marshal von Kluge, but without any immediate success. The situation of the plotters, he said, was getting more and more difficult. Hitler and Himmler were becoming more suspicious every day. Swift action was needed.

Our group met at the home of Professor Bonhöffer, father of Klaus and Dietrich, who was absent. With the exception of Ewald von Kleist, the others present were already known to me—Klaus and Dietrich Bonhöffer, Jacob Kaiser, and Attorney Joseph Wirmer. Kleist was especially insistent that it was high time that action was taken. The front generals did not seem to have the courage to start; now it would be up to the home forces to do the job. He and the others appealed to my patriotism and sense of duty as the rightful Crown Pretender to give the order for the overthrow, an order which would probably be obeyed by the generals.

I told my friends that I was ready to take such a step if the situation demanded it but that I did not think it right to leave my father (my brother Wilhelm had fallen on the Western front meanwhile) out of the picture both because he was the legitimate heir and because General Beck was very devoted to him. I retired to another room with Jacob Kaiser for a man-to-man talk in which I again explained the difficulties of my position in connection with my father. Kaiser had a deep and warm understanding for a Crown Pretender whose conscience was torn between the duty towards his country and loyalty towards his father. We agreed that I should see my father that very evening.

Herr von Kleist was to see General Olbricht, the second in command of the home forces, to get his views on the action to be taken.

I proceeded at once to Cecilienhof, where my father and I had dinner all by ourselves. Father inquired what I had on my chest. I asked him cautiously whether he would be ready to use his authority and undoubted popularity among the high-ranking German officers, many of whom had served under his command as young lieutenants or captains, to move them to action if the fatherland could be saved by such an act.

Since the war started we had not met frequently. Both my parents resented the lack of enthusiasm and confidence in final victory which I had shown from the beginning of the war.

Though Hitler had promised to put the Hohenzollern dynasty back on the throne, he had done everything possible to humiliate and terrorize my father once he became master of Germany. At the beginning of the war my father had been practically isolated. No high-ranking officer in active service had been allowed to visit him. General von Stülpnagel, who at the outbreak of hostilities had been appointed head of the war council, had been deposed a few days later only because my father had congratulated him over the phone on his promotion. My father's offer to take command of an army or a smaller unit at the front had been flatly refused by Hitler.

In spite of all this my father had maintained a chivalrous attitude towards the former corporal. My parents to a large degree adhered to the principle, "Right or wrong, my country," shared by a large majority of their generation. This viewpoint, which deserves respect if properly understood, was inapplicable in the eyes of the younger generation to a new ruling class made up largely of ruthless criminals.

After listening patiently to me, my father replied he had kept completely aloof from all subversive movements and would do so in future. He strongly advised me to do the same. Other people, he said, had lately approached him with similar suggestions, but none of the schemes proposed seemed to him sufficiently sound to warrant even a chance of success.

Thus my mission ended. Did he know that his son was deeply involved? Perhaps he had an inkling, because his warning to me was so emphatic.

The next afternoon Goerdeler turned up at John's home. He was rather dejected. He had seen General Olbricht who had declared categorically that for the moment he could not act. Any "order" from my father or myself would be a useless risk, Goerdeler believed. During his trip to the Eastern front, he reported, he had been able only to get through to Field Marshal von Kluge, commander of the army group center in Russia, but had not been able to get a definite promise from him to take the initiative.

Goerdeler this time was much more pessimistic than during his visit to Cadinen. The invasion of France by the Allies was imminent. The difficulty of keeping the plot from being discovered by Himmler was becoming insurmountable. Still, he had not lost his energy nor his faith in the final outcome. As for me, he did not see that there was much I could do except to rejoin my family and stay in the background. This was my last talk with this German patriot.

A few months later—it was the middle of July 1943—John asked me again to come to Berlin. I had just settled in my temporary lodgings when a great surprise was sprung on me. The door opened and in came my Spanish friend Juan Terrasa whom I had not seen for eight years. Juan told me he was now working for the Spanish Foreign Office in the department which dealt with the interests of countries at war with each other. As such, he had greeted the American diplomats and journalists from Germany at the Franco-Spanish border on their way home to the States via Lisbon. To my great joy he had there met Hilde and Louis Lochner and their daughter Rosemarie and found them in good health and spirits after their five-month internment at Bad Nauheim.

The next day, deeply moved, I said adios to Juan. Would I ever see him again? Thank God, we had a joyous reunion in Switzerland quite recently. As to Otto John and his brother Dr. Hans John, who joined Otto and me when the time for parting came, all three of us had the feeling that this might be farewell forever. In Hans John's case it was; he was executed after July 20. In the case of Otto and myself it might easily have been.

These were some of my meditations during that restless night in Field Marshal von Küchler's home. The outlook was not bright. The Nazi prosecutor could pin a charge of high treason on me for every one of these secret meetings and conversations and for the fact that I did not report them to the authorities as was my duty as a reserve officer of the Luftwaffe.

As I boarded my train I waved farewell to the city which was the cradle of my family's royal throne. I knew I would never see it again. Königsberg now lies in Soviet Russia, not Prussia. Its new name is Kaliningrad. Prussia is no more. There is no Cadinen or Schildberg or Potsdam, at least not for us, the members of the royal house of Prussia.

When I arrived at Cadinen that evening Kira, who met me at the station with the carriage, in her quiet and marvelously self-possessed way answered my question about Mikie by saying he was none too well. But when we reached our bedroom she could no longer restrain her tears. The doctor, she said, had left only an hour ago and had indicated the possibility of cerebral meningitis which had apparently been caused by whooping cough which all the children had had during the summer.

Dr. Joost, our family physician, had said he could not make an exact diagnosis until forty-eight hours later but could be reached by telephone at any time. He was a native of Cologne and had been ordered by the Nazis, whom he hated, to practice in Elbing. We trusted him blindly, especially after he had treated Kira for a bad case of pneumonia.

Little Mikie lay in his bed unconscious, his eyes strangely contorted. In the face of the imminent Soviet invasion and the consequences of July 20, this was the last straw. But we had to keep our senses together. Kira listened calmly to my report. She and the children would have to leave Cadinen as soon as possible. Besides, a visit from the Gestapo was to be expected. Never have I adored my wife as deeply as at that moment. For the third time she was about to lose her home and everything material that was dear to her, including the last of her personal belongings and art objects. The only question now was to save her and her children's lives. As a Romanov and Grand Duchess of Russia, she knew the probable score better than anybody else. And then on top of everything, Mikie's serious, almost hopeless, illness and the threat to her husband's life! But she lived up to the occasion—every inch a mother, a wife, a princess.

We discussed the steps to be taken. I would wait until we knew for certain what was wrong with our second son. Then I would go to Golzow to tell the Durnios about the transfer of the family and try to be back within three days. Meanwhile, Kira would prepare the luggage, for we sensed that later there would be no chance to send anything by train transport.

We shall never forget that night, the worst in our lives. Kira, the governess, and the Protestant visiting nurse of our village took turns at Mikie's bed. Our regular children's nurse had had a collapse, because she could not stand seeing Mikie tossing around with terrible convulsions.

We rang up Dr. Joost twice, but he asked us not to worry unduly as these convulsions were nothing out of the ordinary. Next the visiting nurse, also nervous by now, declared categorically that something must be done and that it was my duty as a father to call a brain specialist from Königsberg. But how to do that in the middle of the night? I again called Dr. Joost. He insisted there was no immediate danger for Mikie and advised us to wait. The next day the convulsions were less violent, and in the afternoon our boy began to recognize us. The following day he was much better. Dr. Joost told us that the danger had passed. Our joy and gratitude to God can hardly be described.

I left for Golzow. The Durnios immediately offered to fix up two rooms on the first floor and two on the second. I hurried back to Cadinen, happy to be able to assure Kira that everything would be ready at Golzow. The obstetrician who had delivered both our daughters urged us to travel the following week, as the new baby would be born within a month; if we waited longer he could not take responsibility for anything. The trains, he pointed out, were still running westward, even though terribly crowded. For safety's sake he also asked the midwife who usually assisted him to accompany my wife. The departure was set for August 4.

On August 2, I went to Elbing to buy tickets and get the heavy luggage checked. This was a difficult job, because thousands of other people were doing the same thing. But my Elbing friends were of great help, especially Bruno Reuter of the railway station restaurant, who knew all the people concerned with this transaction.

When I returned to Cadinen that evening it was raining buckets. I rang up our office to have the carriage sent to the station. My secretary told me two gentlemen of the Gestapo had been waiting since noon to see me. I told the coachman to drive straight to the office. There I shook hands with the two visitors and asked whether they could wait a few minutes while I put on dry clothes; I would invite them to our house as soon as I was ready. They told me courteously to take my time; they were in no hurry. Before leaving the room I asked whether their business would take very long. One of them answered dryly: "That depends." This sounded somewhat mysterious.

I ran over to the house and found Kira preparing our handbags for the departure. I told her about the uninvited guests. We knew this was IT. The only precaution we took was to place President Roosevelt's picture with its personal dedication to me into a pocketbook, all folded up. As we had never conducted any political correspondence, we could be quite calm in that respect. I changed my clothes, had a bite to eat, and then went down to my study, which had been Grosspapa's study. One of its walls was adorned with a painting of the Kaiser in the uniform of a Prussian field marshal. I always seated my callers, especially if they were Nazi officials, in such a way that they had to face my grandfather. I placed a few glasses and a bottle of wine, as well as some cigars, on the table. Kira said she would join the party if needed.

After these preparations I telephoned the office that I was ready to receive the gentleman of the Gestapo. I could watch them coming up the driveway. They were followed by a lady carrying a typewriter. That looked rather serious! As I ushered them in, one of them said:

"My name's Hohenberg. I am from Elbing. And this is my Comrade Stieberitz from Danzig." The lady was also introduced. I seated the two men at a low table on big leather armchairs facing my grandfather's painting and started the conversation with the ironical question as to what gave me the honor of their visit.

Hohenberg, head of the Elbing Gestapo, started off. His real name was Goralski; government employees under the Nazis had to change their Polish or Slav names into German-sounding ones. He had been with a military unit in the German colony of South-West Africa for some years before World War I. An Elbing shoemaker had told me that Hohenberg was a decent fellow who on the whole had a good opinion of me, especially because he had learned that I liked conviviality. Giving me my full title, a thing Nazis generally tried to avoid, he said:

"Your Royal Highness, my Comrade Stieberitz and I have come to ask you a few questions in connection with the events of the twentieth of July. We brought the lady along because we have to draft a protocol which you must sign."

Well, I thought, here we go! But the effect of two hours of conviviality at Bruno Reuter's in the Elbing station restaurant had not yet worn off. So I answered laughingly:

"Gentlemen, did you come to find out whether I hid the bomb that was used?" They accepted the joke with a grin, and then Stieberitz asked:

"Could you tell us where you have been lately, and did you do any traveling these last weeks?" I told them that I had just returned from Golzow, where I had arranged for quarters for my wife and children, who all needed a change of climate badly.

"Was that your only trip?" was the next question. For a few seconds I meditated, but believing that truth is always the best lie, I said:

"I visited Field Marshal von Küchler, and it happened to be on the twentieth of July." Then I described to them what I had done during the day. Hohenberg asked me whether I had any connection with army circles and academic people. I denied both, telling them only about the lecture at the University of Königsberg, which I attended with Frau von Küchler. Then I asked them as innocently as I could:

"Do you think Field Marshal von Küchler is connected with the

July 20 plot?" Both smiled and answered: "Not he; as far as we know he is all right."

Next they wanted to know what guests I had had lately. I told them about Küchler's visit which I had returned by my trip to Königsberg. Turning to Hohenberg—I called him Hohenthal several times, a carelessness which could easily have betrayed me, for that was the name of the last American military attaché in Berlin!—I said:

"My life in Cadinen lies before you like an open book," I said to him. "Most of my friends, all Elbingers, are personally known to you. They come here to shoot my game and drink, if there is something in my cellar; otherwise they bring something along. We usually have a good time."

"I know that," Hohenberg answered.

"Is that all?"

"That's all."

Comrade Stieberitz, whom I called Herr *Kommissar* all the time, after a while began to dictate the protocol. He apparently had some difficulty. So I sat down at my desk, grabbed my typewriter, and was all set to take the dictation by either Gestapo agent. But the protocol caused considerable difficulty.

After the inquisition I had filled the glasses with Marsalla wine and proposed the health of my guests, not once but several times. Hohenberg had willingly followed my example, whereas Stieberitz was a bit slow. But after a while he, too, joined us. My cigars and cigarettes were also accepted. Pretty soon the four of us were in a convivial mood. Hohenberg and I composed the completely harmless protocol. It reported only the questions which had been asked and my replies.

Meanwhile Kira had joined us and had discussed our family and the value of a change of climate with Stieberitz. She had a terrible cough, and my inquisitor showed great sympathy, stating he had been susceptible to colds all his life. Hohenberg, whom I continued to call Hohenthal, told us about his days in the Imperial Colonial Army, and we almost ended by calling each other by our first names. At 2:00 A.M. the Gestapo representatives left us in high spirits, evidently thoroughly satisfied with their seven-hour session.

Hohenberg had told me that every step of ours was being watched and that he and his colleague were glad that I had told them the full truth. Finally, he asserted that the main reason for the inquiry had been their desire to protect me and clear me of any possible suspicion. Even if, as I suppose, he was lying, the protocol must have produced the desired effect in higher quarters, or else my plotting friends of July 20, in spite of being tortured before dying, had not given me away.

Chapter Thirty-five

The Debacle

(1944–45)

W HEN I RETURNED to Cadinen after having established my family in Golzow, everybody was surprised to see me turn up alive. According to rumor, I had been arrested and probably executed in connection with the July plot. On my desk I found a short communication from the Berlin air-force district command, stating that I had been excluded from the reserve officer corps of the Luftwaffe in accordance with a secret order dated July 21, 1944. My first thought was that the date had something to do with the events of July 20. It turned out to be a mere coincidence.

My senior officer, whom I looked up in Berlin around Christmas, told me he had written me a long private letter along with the official communication, explaining the order. I never received his letter and never learned its contents.

In those weeks and months I felt like a man running about with a rope around his neck. The names of most of my plotting friends in Berlin were published in the papers among the arrested and the accused. I heard nothing from my friend Otto John.

For a long time we hoped that Goerdeler had escaped to some neutral country. But his discovery and arrest shattered that hope also. On August 25, I received a wire from Kira: "Lulu born today, everything O.K." This was a wonderful piece of news. The next day I was again on my way to Golzow. In spite of all the preceding excitements and present worries everything had gone quite normally. The baby was a healthy little seven-pound boy, our third son. This time nobody could stop us from calling him Louis Ferdinand. He was christened on October 23 by Pastor Doehring. My mother and a few other members of the family attended. We had transformed the dining room of the Durnios into a chapel. In spite of the impending catastrophe, which we all knew by then was only a matter of time, we tried to forget the anxieties of the moment for a few hours as we celebrated with our relatives and local friends.

After the christening Kira accompanied me back to Cadinen. The quiet before the storm on the Eastern front was still continuing. Trains were running normally as far as Königsberg. Kira wished to fetch several things she had left behind in August which she would need badly in the winter, especially warm clothes. It may sound strange, but in the midst of general pandemonium we were able to spend three peaceful weeks in Cadinen. Yet the quietness of the house without all the gay noises of our children was rather oppressing.

We went once more to the *Kirchblick* (Church View), a little hunting hut in the heart of the woods. From that point one looked down on Cadinen, the church, the Haff, and the Baltic.

When we finally drove to the station of our little local railroad, Kira knew that this was probably her last visit to this beloved place. It took a supreme effort on her part to tear herself away from this paradise. Only her love and sense of duty towards her children kept her up in that moment.

I spent Christmas and New Year's Eve with my family at Golzow. Then I returned to Cadinen. This was to be my last sojourn there. We both knew that "staying on the job" was of very little practical value. But as the representative of the owner, I had to keep up appearances to the last moment and avoid any impression that I was running away. It was dangerous even to hint at the possibility of an evacuation to my administrators, who still professed to believe in the final victory. Under threats of severe, even capital, punishment nobody was allowed to leave his village or estate. The Gauleiter of West Prussia, Forster, had announced that he would give the evacuation orders if and when necessary.

My last fourteen days were almost grotesquely normal. It was the calm before the storm. Anybody with any brains knew that a catastrophe was in the offing, but everybody acted as though nothing untoward was likely to happen. As in other years, I invited our friends and neighbors for the annual hunt, a battue, on our estate. Among my guests was the chief forester for the province, Erich Nicolai, accompanied by his wife and the commander of a submarine, Lieutenant Maetner.

I showed our pocket cathedral to Mrs. Nicolai and the naval officer. I lighted all the candles on the altar but left the rest of the little church in semidarkness. My guests insisted that I play the organ. It turned out to be an hour of touching farewell from Cadinen. No candles have burned on the altar since, nor has the sound of the organ again been heard. The Red Army destroyed the instrument completely, although they left the altar intact, I have been told.

On my arrival in Cadinen our administrator, Darge, an ardent Nazi, had told me that he had been made evacuation commissar for Cadinen and the neighborhood and that he alone was responsible for, and authorized to organize, the evacuation.

"If worst should come to worst," he bragged, "nobody will be left behind. The confusion which occurred elsewhere can't happen to us. We have organized everything down to the smallest detail. But of course I am firmly convinced that there won't be any need for these measures." All I could do at the time was to think: What a fool!

The Nicolais and my other guests had no sooner left than Darge visited me: "I have just come from the *Kreisleiter* in Elbing, who instructed me to prepare everything for the evacuation of the Cadinen population. But he doesn't believe the evacuation will actually prove necessary."

That same evening the first German columns arrived from the East in a state of military dissolution. An endless stream of automobiles, horses, and human beings inundated the otherwise so quiet village of Cadinen. Everybody was animated by but one desire: to reach the Nehrung, a long and narrow tongue of land separating the Haff from the sea, from where one could proceed to safety. The confused reports of these people indicated a completely hopeless situation. Telephone connections with Elbing had been cut off. The little railway to Elbing had ceased to run. Soviet tanks had entered Elbing and had blocked all main roads, including the one on which our evacuation was to have taken place. Our only chance of safety lay in our crossing the Haff, but even this was not certain, for grotesquely enough German icebreakers were cruising to and fro to keep one lane open! Fortunately, it was so bitterly cold that the lane froze almost immediately once the icebreakers had opened it. We could therefore hope to cross it with our horse-drawn sleighs.

Nobody any longer spoke about an organized evacuation. Our commissar's strategy was completely shattered. The order of evacuation had been given much too late here, as everywhere. The cowardly Nazi bosses fled, leaving in the lurch a population forbidden to move without their permission, yet now compelled to shift for themselves as best they could.

All we could do was to get on a sleigh and run for our lives. Most Cadiners refused to leave the place where they and their ancestors had been born and lived all their lives. They just could not abandon the lovely little homes my grandfather had built for them. They argued: "What difference does it make whether we stay here and get killed by the Soviets or die of hunger or cold during the flight? Where shall we go, anyhow?"

Only a few decided to come along. Most of the men who remained in Cadinen were deported by the Soviets; many of them died during the transport. I had only one thought—to join my family. I imagined the agonies my poor wife must be going through without knowledge of my fate.

When I drove over the Haff on January 25, 1945—it was bitter cold, but there was radiant sunshine—I could not but make a sad comparison with my ancestor, the Great Elector, who had crossed the Kurische Haff several centuries earlier, also in wintertime, but not as a fugitive. I was one of the last to depart. The Bolsheviks reached the Haff half an hour later.

In Danzig the trek of sleighs disbanded. Everyone had now to shift for himself, doing what he thought best for escaping. I was able to board one of the last trains leaving for the West. I was accompanied by the seventy-five-year-old baker, Fritz Ligowski, from Elbing. He was a dyed-in-the-wool, uncompromising monarchist, even though he was the laughingstock of the Nazis. He insisted that he would flee, if at all, only with the grandson of his Kaiser.

We were packed like sardines in a compartment in which there were also some SS men, and the venerable old monarchist could not refrain from telling everybody who I was. As it happened to be January 27, this proved the most unusual way I ever celebrated the Kaiser's birthday!

In Stargard, I climbed out through a car window at 4:00 A.M. in the hope of making connections for Golzow. I got as far as Pyritz. While I was waiting there for transportation to Golzow, I met a friend of mine from Soldin, a town only a few miles from Golzow. He told me my family had left Golzow in a truck bound for Potsdam on the same day on which I fled from Cadinen. The Reds, he said, were already approaching Küstrin and might reach Pyritz almost any hour.

Fortunately, I was able to find a train leaving for Berlin the same afternoon. It arrived in the capital late in the evening. The last suburban train for Potsdam had already left. I therefore decided to walk on foot through nocturnal, war-ravaged Berlin and make my way to the Netherlands Palace, the center of the Hohenzollern administration, in the hope of telephoning to Potsdam and advising my loved ones that I would take the first train in the morning for Potsdam.

Sure enough—there was the old night watchman, on duty as though normal conditions prevailed and as though this were merely another night in his forty years of service. I thought it an interesting illustration of the paradoxical things that happened during the last days of the war.

I cannot better express the scene that ensued when at last I could join my family in Cecilienhof than to quote from Kira's diary:

We must thank God for great mercies. The first was Lulu's arrival in Potsdam early on the morning of January 29 . . . Suffice it to say that he arrived safely, tired out, grimy, without luggage, but well. Still under the impression of all the woe, anxiety, danger of the past few days. At first we could hardly speak for relief and happiness at being together again.

Meanwhile, Kira had gone through hell, not knowing what had happened to me or whether we would ever meet again. As though this uncertainty were not enough, some foreign radio station had reported that I had fallen into the hands of the Red Army. But she and the children had also been in deadly danger, with the Soviet troops advancing steadily and swiftly. Had my mother not been able to send a truck placed at her disposal by friends, in addition to one passenger car, I would probably never have seen my family again.

Kira kept a diary during the anxious days after my departure from Golzow for Cadinen. This story would not be complete were I not to quote, albeit in very greatly abridged form because of lack of space, from her revealing entries:

Golzow, January 23, 1945

The next few days and the coming weeks, perhaps months, will be the most fateful in our lives. I want to keep a record of them, not only to ease the anxiety that weighs on my heart, but also as a document that may serve as illustration of the horror of these times.

The worst has not yet happened to us. My children are still safe, in perfect health, comfortable, and happy. And the children's welfare is the only really important factor just now. But the fate of countless others, children and their parents, is so awful that no words can describe it. Only God's mercy has so far preserved us from a like fate.

Lulu is in Cadinen. I know nothing of what is going on there. Now the Soviet advance is stretching toward Königsberg. If not held up by some miracle it will engulf Cadinen within the next week.

Will Lulu remain in Cadinen at his post till the last as planned? Will he be able to give me news? My last letter sent today may not reach him. It is useless to try and put into words the torment of being separated from Lulu at such a time. Every thought of mine is with him; I long to be at his side, to be of use there at home, to share his burden of responsibility and worry.

I dare not think of our beloved home, of all that we may lose. Others, too, have lost their all and still must face life. We shall build another home, wherever it may be, and still be happy. If only God grants us to remain together and to keep our children safe!

Here we are forging plans for the dreaded possibility of evacuation. It is terrible to think of but must be contemplated and planned for. The worst of the prospect is that when and if the time comes hardly an able-bodied man will be left here.

Wednesday, January 24

My brother-in-law Hubertus and his wife Mädy came today. Such a relief to discuss everything with them. A new situation has arisen. Mama has organized a truck to fetch the children and myself to Potsdam. The car is expected tomorrow. Friday we should start if all goes smoothly.

We have told the children nothing yet of the plan. When the moment comes I shall try and make it seem like a delightful surprise, an exciting journey in the big lorry to visit granny. We will try and make ourselves as comfortable and warm as possible, of course, but I dread the cold for the little ones and the adventures we may have on the road.

But all this would not be so awful if only I were in touch with Lulu. To leave here so suddenly without being able to inform him, without knowing where he is, or how and when we shall meet again, is dreadful.

Thursday Morning, January 25

The truck has arrived! Letters and messages from Mama. A private car from an embassy in Berlin will perhaps be coming tomorrow to take me and the babies, Mama writes, as she fears it will be too cold in the big motor car. I have decided to travel with the boys in the truck and pack Ella (our nurse), the three babies, little Anastasia (Hubertus's child), and Erika (Anastasia's nurse) in the second car if it really comes.

This afternoon to my joy came a letter from Lulu. He writes that they are waiting for marching orders and are busy preparing the trek. He intends to accompany it as far as Neustadt (near Danzig) and then come on here as quickly as possible.

The thought of leaving tomorrow when Lulu may be arriving here any day is torturing. Now I must pack the last things. Am tired and so nervous that I shiver and feel cold all day.

And so good-by to Golzow for the present! It has been a happy time in spite of everything, and I feel deeply grateful for all the goodness of our kind hosts. A bit of my heart will always remain here as the birthplace of our beloved little Lulu.

Potsdam, January 27

We arrived safely about ten-thirty last night. Hubertus and Mädy with baby and "following" had arrived (in Golzow) from Wildenbruch. The "suite" consisted of the baby's nurse, Erika, the crippled Countess Elisabeth Dönhoff, and her Russian maid, who were obliged to flee from East Prussia and were taken in by Hubertus and Mädy. They were to travel with us.

Poor Hubertus and Mädy were desperate at parting with their baby. They remained in Wildenbruch to organize the inevitable trek. Mädy and I were in tears most of the time. The children excited and restless. Our luggage took no end. It seemed to grow in quantity by the hour. Finally there was only just enough space left for the three baby carriages and the four passengers. Elisabeth Dönhoff was lifted in first and placed in her wheelchair, the prams wedged closely together, and poor Ella and Erika had just enough room to stand. I sat in front with Friedrich and Mikie, and we at least were well off.

The last good-bys found everybody in tears. It was horrible. Before reaching the highway we met a stream of refugees turning in to Golzow. Heaven knows where they were put up. These were only the first of the endless number we passed on the road, one cart after another with shapeless forms muffled up in blankets; tired, plodding horses. Snow fell the whole day, and an icy wind swept against us.

My nervousness came on again as we neared Berlin. I dreaded an air alert. Thank God none came. We crossed Berlin quickly and easily. Ruins and trams were to be the first, and probably last, impression of our boys of Berlin.

Here our welcome was lovely after the trying days. It seemed incredible that all should be as usual here. The contrast was so sharp that it left one almost speechless. Mama was so happy to have us under her roof.
Later
Oh joy! News of Lulu! A call from Schildberg. I feel hysterical at the mere thought of seeing Lulu again.

Because of the uncertainty of my whereabouts, Kira had had to make her decisions without me at Potsdam. It was senseless to stay in Cecilienhof, because the Soviets were bound to get there, too, eventually. Herr von Müldner, my father's former A.D.C., suggested Bad Kissingen in northern Bavaria. He telephoned his old friend Dr. Paul Sotier, who had regularly gone to Doorn to look after my grandfather's health. The Sotiers answered that their house was full, but that they would somehow find room for us.

The journey to Bad Kissingen, on which we had to start the same day, January 29, was anything but a joy ride. Again I quote sentences here and there from Kira's notes:

Kissingen, February 1945
Our journey was a nightmare. But again we had something to be thankful for and owed it all to Frl. Sauer (of the travel bureau) who organized our transport with wonderful resourcefulness. Compared with the tortures other people with their children have to endure on train journeys these days, ours were mild.

We got to the station all right, and through byways to the platform and into our reserved compartment, avoiding the horrible stampede which preluded the departure of all trains. These facilities were a great favor accorded us by the railway authorities.

We numbered seven grownups and six children, a Red Cross nurse having been added to look after Countess Dönhoff. Lulu and I, with Ella and our five babies, occupied one compartment and the others one next door. But for the entire journey of nearly twenty-four hours there was no communication possible between us, as the corridor was jammed full of people. No one could move in either direction.

At first our car was unheated and the cold intense. The planned hauling in of our countless pieces of hand baggage through the windows was not possible as the windows were frozen and would not open. Fortunately, we had come so early that the corridors were not yet jammed, and the baggage could be brought in normally.

Light there was none, and if a full moon had not been mercifully shining we should have sat the whole night in darkness. Awful with the children and their hundred-and-one needs keeping us in constant cramped motion.

A few hours after the train started the heating came on. At first welcome, it soon became a torture. We were so tightly packed that moving much or stretching was almost impossible. The poor children tried to sleep in every position. One after the other was either hungry or thirsty or had to disappear. But where? Once or twice I felt near fainting and only saved myself by pressing my face against the icy window pane. Lulu slept peacefully in utter exhaustion.

Some time in the night a soldier added himself to our company. He had backed into our compartment to allow someone to struggle past in the corridor, and as he had been standing for hours we offered him a seat on our provision bag. It made things tighter still, but he picked up the children and held them by turns and generally made himself useful.

Nearing Ebenhausen where we were to get out, a feeling of panic overcame us. How to get ourselves and our luggage out? Lulu and our soldier friend worked on the window. They scraped away the ice with a penknife, tugged and pulled and rattled, but at last the window moved. We roared in triumph. It meant not only the solution of getting out but also a sorely needed means for relieving ourselves.

Six hours later we arrived in Ebenhausen. I wriggled out first and received child after child through the window. Poor Elisabeth Dönhoff must have suffered more than any of us, but she was still cheerful and brave. We hoisted her onto a baggage cart and trundled her with all her bags to the waiting room. Her wheelchair was lost on the journey.

From there we made our way to a little tavern where we breakfasted and waited for our next train. We found kind helpers all along and got ourselves into the train with no loss of luggage. A short trip brought us at last to Kissingen on the evening of the day following our departure from Potsdam. We were most kindly welcomed by our hosts. They apologized for having nothing better to offer us, and we apologized for thrusting ourselves upon them!

We crowded into two attic rooms, which were to be our new home for the next twelve months.

"Some come-down," I remarked when we had settled.

"Let's be thankful we are all united and alive; so many people aren't," Kira answered calmly.

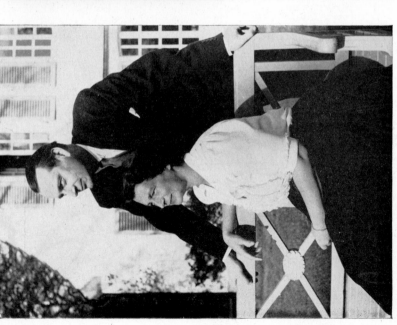

Left: With his wife, Princess Kira. *Right:* With his son, Prince Louis Ferdinand.

With his family at their Bremen home.

Chapter Thirty-six

Attic Life in Kissingen

(1945-46)

IT WAS no easy matter to settle into our cramped quarters. At first chaos reigned. Our initial dinner with the other occupants of the large Sotier house was most depressing. All were homeless like ourselves! Each had his or her own story of woe.

There followed the wearisome process of filling out endless questionnaires, going from one government office to another until a permit to reside, ration coupons, identity cards, and other documents were obtained. New problems arose when Mama, with Hubertus and Mädy and two maids, also fled to Kissingen from Potsdam and space had to be provided for them. We had each other, our children, and our hopes for the future. But Mama was very alone, her feelings torn in many ways. Yet she bore her lot bravely. Papa, we knew, was safe in Mittelberg, Bavaria.

An entry from Kira's diary tells of unusual devotion on the part of our housekeeper, Miss Emma Heck, who had been with us virtually since our return from our honeymoon trip:

Hubertus and Mädy have left us with their baby and their nurse Erika to stay with the Isenburgs in Büdingen. The departure of Erika would have been a catastrophe for us, as Ella could not manage the care of our five children alone. But by the grace of God, who should turn up two days before the departure but Fräulein Heck! Half dead, an awful series of adventures behind her, but faithfully dragging an impossibly heavy trunk with Lulu's belongings and the few last salvaged treasures from

Cadinen. She had gone on with the trek after Lulu had left it. Her experiences would fill a book.

It is indicative of the general confusion in Germany at this time that the following item dated February 2, 1945, in other words after we had already established ourselves in Bad Kissingen, appeared in *Nachrichten für die Truppe (News for the Armed Forces)*, a paper printed by the Allies in the German language.

Efforts through diplomatic sources to determine the fate of Prince Louis Ferdinand of Prussia and his wife, Grand Duchess Kira, concerning whom there has been no news whatsoever since the occupation of Elbing by the Soviets, have proven in vain.

Prince Louis Ferdinand, the oldest living son of the Crown Prince, was residing with his family on the former imperial model estate of Cadinen near Elbing, now occupied by the Russians. It is not known whether Prince Louis Ferdinand got away in time or whether he is now in the hands of the Soviets. His wife, Princess Kira, a Russian Grand Duchess, would be the first member of the former Tsar's family to fall into the hands of the Soviets since 1917.

A tragedy struck our family when the Gestapo arrested and murdered Baron von Plettenberg, chief administrator at this time of the Hohenzollern properties and affairs. The Berlin Gestapo claimed he had flung himself out of a window on March 10.

Throughout the last stages of the collapse one single wish underlay all our emotions: an early end of the war. But despite a feeling of resignation which often befell us, of absolute powerlessness vis-à-vis an overwhelming, catastrophical historic process, Kira and I never abandoned hope. We knew that the end of the Hitler regime entailed the loss also of much that we cherished, but we were buoyed up by one hope of regaining our personal freedom.

As in many other cities, an SS general tried to bring disaster to the city and its inhabitants by ordering that it be defended to the last. Fortunately, the occupation suddenly was an accomplished fact, devoid of any drama. One beautiful spring morning the Americans were simply there—that was all!

My first encounter with an American was a humorous one. The Sotiers possessed an exceptionally choice wine cellar. One of their chief worries was to protect this liquid treasure from the thirsty throats of the trans-Atlantic conquerors and to bring it to a place of safety. All of us helped, including four Catholic nuns. Two of them, Kira, and I were pushing one carefully covered cartload up a steep street when a GI, considerably the worse for wear, met us. The sight of two nuns and two harmless-looking German civilians panting and pushing seemed to call for chivalry. He therefore came to our aid, and in the sweat of his brow helped us to bring into safety a treasure which, had he known its nature, would quite likely have been annexed by him as war booty.

My second encounter with the occupation was much more decisive. One afternoon in May 1945, I went to the Military Government offices in the beautiful old town hall of Kissingen to obtain a pass for driving to a near-by village for food. The chief interpreter surprised me by saying: "The American captain wishes to meet you." He ushered me into the mayor's private office, now taken over by the military governor for our town.

The moment had come to which I had been looking forward with anxiety and hope ever since I had said good-bys to my American friends in Berlin. Opposite me, I noted with emotion, sat a representative of the country which had almost become my second fatherland. During the month intervening since American troops had occupied Bad Kissingen, neither I nor any member of my family had been approached or even talked to by an American. Obedient to their instructions the conquerors, without being provocative or overbearing, had been extremely reserved, almost offish, so different from the natural, human type that I had so admired during my various sojourns in America. But only a few days previously the nonfraternization orders had been somewhat mollified, and I knew now everything would be all right.

Captain Merle Potter—this was his name, as I gleaned from a little sign on his desk—was anything but a "conqueror" in his demeanor. He arose, seized my hand, shook it cordially, and said, quite naturally: "I'm certainly glad to meet you, Louis, please sit down and have a cigarette."

It seemed almost like the good old days in Detroit to have the captain call me Louis immediately. I put the cigarette in my pocket, explaining bashfully that I was not much of a smoker but that I knew my wife would enjoy it much more.

"Captain, are you an active officer?" I asked, after we had exchanged a few pleasantries.

"Heavens, by no means," he said. "In normal life I am a newspaperman." What luck, I thought to myself!

"Perhaps you can tell me something of the whereabouts of Louis Lochner, my oldest friend?" I inquired.

"I don't know him personally, but I shall be only too glad to find out and let you know."

This finished our conversation, as another caller was announced. The captain said:

"Why don't you come tomorrow evening after dinner? I should like to talk some more with you. There are so many things I'd like to discuss with you. Auf Wiedersehen."

Two packages of cigarettes had somehow made their appearance at the edge of the table nearest me. The captain mumbled: "Didn't you say your wife's favorite cigarettes were Chesterfields?"

The next evening our conversation lasted almost until the birds began to sing. It was followed by several others. I brought my wife and Mama down to the *Rathaus* to meet "my American captain." We discussed the problems of Germany, of the United States, of the world. One night the captain said:

"Why don't you sit down and write everything we talked about and a lot more?"

"It might fill a whole book to do that," I answered.

"Well, what of it?"

And that is how I came to write this story of my life. Had it not been for Merle Potter's insistent prodding I doubt whether I should ever have made the effort. I shall speak of a second "assignment" of his a little later.

It wasn't long before Louis Lochner turned up. Somehow word had reached him at SHAEF headquarters in Paris concerning our whereabouts. Fortunately he had a roving commission from the Associated Press to go wherever he sensed a story. He lost no time getting himself a press car and spending several unforgettable days in Bad Kissingen.

His godson Friedrich, as well as Mikie, had the time of their lives play-ing chauffeur on the intriguing jeep.

Because of my friendly relationship with the American military gov-ernor, I found myself unexpectedly much in demand by my fellow countrymen, who came with all sorts of problems and requests which they believed might be solved or fulfilled through my intervention.

During this period of waiting in Bad Kissingen, I turned more and more to music. A Hungarian composer of light operas, who had fled before the Russians to Kissingen, initiated me into the principles of musical composition. I composed several lieder, three of which were produced soon thereafter in a public concert and encouraged me to continue.

Our stay in the Villa Fürstenhof of Dr. Sotier lasted eleven months. There were periods when we hungered and froze. In January 1946 we obtained permission to move into the home of the former Nazi Kreis-leiter. Originally requisitioned by the occupation forces, it had been released. Potter tipped this fact off to us so we could apply to the Wohn-ungsamt (housing administration) before anybody else. What happi-ness to have a home of our own again! It was even furnished. In March our fourth boy Christian was born, for whom Merle Potter became a godfather.

Our good fortune was not to last long. In August the house was again requisitioned by the occupation forces, despite Potter's efforts to prevent it. We were assigned a much smaller dwelling near by. We were lucky at that. But this abode was without furniture and looked like a pigsty. We did the best to make it livable and spent a tolerable autumn. Then, how-ever, came the excessively cold winter of 1946–47. Again I quote from Kira's notes:

We suffered severely from the cold. We were able to heat only the tiniest room with small stoves. There, we were usually huddled together throughout the day. At dusk the electric current was cut off, and we had no candles. We often sat in complete darkness with the children, singing songs with them or telling them fairy tales. One day the water mains burst and water ran down the walls of the unheated rooms and froze in icicles. When we went to bed we only half undressed and took our chil-dren with us into our beds to keep them warm. It was a difficult time:

our nerves, our health, our patience shattered. Surprisingly enough our children remained in good health. The boys had fun sleigh riding. Only, that meant that their shoe soles wore off quickly, and new soles were not to be had. Friedrich finally wore my shoes stuffed with paper.

During this hapless time the first food packages arrived from America. They were gifts from Heaven. Our gratitude and joy cannot be described in words.

Spring had just come when this home, too, was requisitioned. The original orders were to vacate within three days, but since Kira was only just getting over a severe attack of the flu, our doctor's certificate gained us a few days' respite.

The housing authorities did not know this time what to do with us. Finally they insisted that a doctor who owned a sanatorium make four rooms there available to us. He refused. The season for the cures had just begun, and he could obtain much better revenue from patients renting these rooms.

We were the painful witnesses of a forced evacuation by German police and an American MP. But what could we do? All living accommodations were subject to assignment by the housing authorities.

The eight months which we had to spend in this unhappy sanatorium were months of privations, difficulties, and chicanery but also of wonderful instances of kindness by compassionate men and women.

In December 1947 an end to our troubles came when the possibility opened up of moving to Bremen.

As to Merle Potter, the dramatic high point of his era as Kissingen governor was the founding of a Cosmopolitan Club and the subsequent events which led to his fall upstairs. One day he sent his cook over to ask my wife and me to lunch. It developed that this was the opening ceremony for the founding of the club. He was in excellent spirits.

"It is high time that better relations develop between Americans and Germans," he said. "I have therefore decided to organize a German-American friendship club. Will you help me?"

The club did not get far. The correspondent of the *New York Times* sent a detailed report to New York. Potter received strict orders to liquidate the venture as quickly as possible, as its existence did not accord with policies. He was relieved of his post.

But Merle would not take his defeat lying down. He demanded a court-martial. He wrote to congressmen and other influential Americans. The matter came to the ears of General Lucius D. Clay. Far from joining in the clamor against Potter, he added him to his personal staff with orders to found similar clubs throughout the American zone! Even though he had to leave Germany when Clay's regime ended, Merle did succeed in playing a historic role in the development of relations between postwar Germany and the United States. He drove an opening wedge into the wall of hatred and enabled the forces of reconciliation to enter.

I spoke above of a second "assignment" besides that of writing this book. Some time after we had first met, Potter requested me to express my ideas on the future of Germany in a written report. We had meanwhile had many a bull session discussing this question, and Merle considered it my duty to formulate my ideas in writing and—which rather astonished me—make them public.

"How am I to do that?" I asked.

"Leave that to me. I haven't been a journalist all my life for nothing."

Well, "orders is orders," especially from a military governor of an occupation force, and I wrote the desired paper, in which I argued that the Four Freedoms must be made a factor in the re-creation of Germany if my fatherland is to have a future as a member of the family of nations. Potter took it, but for some time shrouded himself in mysterious silence concerning it. Then, on Christmas Eve, 1945, he called on us in our attic rooms. First depositing a number of voluminous packages on our table, he spread out before us the Christmas edition of *The Bavarian,* official organ of the American occupation forces in Bavaria. There it was—a three-column headline: "Teach Germans Meaning of Four Freedoms, Prince Urges," and the subhead: "Louis Ferdinand Expresses Views on Policies Necessary to Prevent Psychological Chaos in Germany."

Only much later did I realize what an unusual procedure it was for the official army organ to publish the free and independent opinion of a German subject only seven months after unconditional surrender and what courage it had taken on Merle Potter's part to commit this form of "fraternization."

Since writing the paper it has become clear that the Four Freedoms must not only be re-established in Germany. They must be defended in Europe and all over the world if our civilization is to survive. It has fallen to the United States to carry the main weight of that task, but millions of people in Europe and other continents will be ready to help them achieve it.

All I ask from life for Kira, my seven children, and myself is that we may be permitted to do our part, small as it may be, to help attain that goal.

Chapter Thirty-seven

A New Lease on Life

(1947–52)

THE FOUR years in Bremen since we virtually fled from Kissingen have been a breathing spell after everything that happened before. We have finally settled down to a normal life again. True, after three years here we had again to move. But this time we have signed a ten-year lease with an option to buy our present abode, the Wümmehof, in the Bremen suburb of Borgfeld. We are very happy here. We enjoy its village atmosphere. Our two neighbors are real *Bauern* (farmers).

The house is located on a little stream, the Wümme, a tributary of the Weser River. Across it we look out on a wide pasture where the farmers keep their cows and horses during the summer. Across that plain we look towards the East—nostalgia has never left us. But we share it with fifteen million other Germans who also lost their homeland. We by no means lack gratitude towards our new surroundings. But our yearning for East Prussia will probably never leave us until the end of our days or the day we return with God's help.

There is nothing exciting about our Bremen life. From a professional viewpoint it has proven a disappointment. My activities in the Ford agency, in which my father had invested some money and which I headed until his death, did not turn out the way I had hoped. But I was able to make a three-month trip to the United States in November 1948, and there I discovered that all my old friends whom I had not seen for ten years had not changed in their attitude towards me and my family as well as towards my country.

I have also been able to continue my composition efforts which started in Bad Kissingen. At a lecture of my old friend Carl Lange of Danzig on his experiences in the Soviet zone prisons, and after reading several of his poems, I met *Kapellmeister* Curt Koschnick. He accompanied a friend of Lange's, Fedor Gardemin, who sang two of my songs to words by Carl Lange. Koschnick told me he was connected with our Bremen opera and frequently worked with Bremen's two best opera stars, Frau Liselotte Thomamueller and Herr Caspar Broecheler. He asked me whether I had written some more songs; he would be glad to show them to his vocalist friends. I gave him everything I had produced.

After a few days Koschnick rang me up and asked me to come to the old opera house, where he introduced me to the two singers. They said they had gone over the songs with Koschnick and liked them, especially because they were melodious. It was agreed that the two would study my songs to sing them in public.

The date of my birthday was approaching, and we had invited our friends to our house for a little evening party. Kira behind my back had met the three artists. They formed a conspiracy.

On the evening of November 9, 1950, after all our guests had assembled, Kira said a little surprise was waiting for me in the dining room. She had secretly converted it into a miniature recital hall with several rows of chairs. She asked us all to sit down. Then another door opened and in strode the three artists. Koschnick announced the guests would hear lieder written by an unknown living composer. He asked them kindly to pass judgment on these highly "modern" compositions. Frau Thomamueller started, and after four songs it was Broecheler's turn. So they alternated through the whole program, she with her lovely soprano and he with his warm baritone voice. The rendition was perfect. Most of my songs I had never heard sung.

At the end of the concert the guests demanded to know the composer's name. Our guests agreed that the lieder were romantic and by no means modern in the sense of atonal music. Koschnick then with a big grin revealed that the composer was the birthday child. This recital was naturally one of the loveliest birthday presents I have ever received.

It was agreed that we ought to go before the public. The next concert was to be held in the house of Dr. Otto Leist before a much larger audience and with the press invited. It took place a few weeks later and was favorably received by the public and also partly by the music critics of

Bremen. Others, however, called my songs *Gefuehlsmusik fuer den Hausgebrauch* (sentimental music for home consumption). They represented that part of critical music opinion which claims that art has nothing to do with one's feelings. For them it is a grave heresy to dare write from the heart. But the public in its great majority thoroughly disagrees with them.

Since that birthday concert my "artistic clover leaf" has given *Liederabende* in more than half a dozen German cities, exclusively with my songs. Kira and I always traveled along with them. We heard time and again from people in the audience that they had expected to hear cacophonies instead of melodies and harmonies but were relieved to hear the latter. We also experienced that the simplest songs please the public most. These concerts, which will continue during the next season, are given for the benefit of the local refugee and expellee organization, thanks to the kindness of my artist friends who only have their expenses paid.

Last year some of my lieder were also sung in Spain. In May 1951, Kira and I went to Spain to visit Kira's brother Vladimir and his wife Leonida in Madrid, where Vladimir has been living for the last four years. We traveled on board a small German freighter from Hamburg to Barcelona on this first journey outside Germany we made together since World War II started. We traveled like any other citizen.

In Barcelona we were watching our entry into the port from the bridge. The captain noticed that the pilot was directing our boat to the official pier. "I have my orders," the pilot said. Approaching the dock, we discovered a crowd of people, mostly in brilliant uniforms.

"This must have something to do with you," our captain smiled. "On this pier I certainly cannot get rid of my cargo."

We rushed to our stateroom to get tidied up. Hardly had the gangplank been lowered when a whole stream of uniformed people and a lady with a big bouquet of flowers invaded our little salon. A dignified gentleman with the stripes of an admiral addressed us in fluent English:

"I have the honor and the pleasure to welcome you in Spain in the name of the Spanish Government and in my own name. I am Admiral Cervera, the naval commander of Barcelona. This is my wife and here are two of my daughters." After that he introduced the rest of his party, at least sixty. The admiral, it turned out, had known my wife when she had been in Spain as a girl. When we bragged about our seven children he said modestly that he had fourteen.

In Madrid the next morning we were met by Vladimir, Leonida, and my old friend Valdivia, who had become physically rather frail. But his spirit was as enterprising as ever. For curiosity's sake I had brought photostats of my songs along and one day showed them to him. After a short glance at them he said:

"A niece of mine, Consuelo Rubio, is one of our best concert singers. She is going to sing your songs in Madrid." As this was said about a week before our return to Germany, I expressed a doubt.

"You leave that to me," Valdivia retorted. A few minutes later we burst into Consuelo Rubio's apartment. Valdivia's niece, a beautiful young lady, is married to a Roumanian gentleman named Uscatescu. Hardly taking the time to introduce me, Valdivia shoved the music into his niece's hands.

"Now, Consuelo, you learn this stuff as fast as possible. Next Friday you must sing it in public."

The concert was held in a beautiful old hall. Miss Rubio sang six of my lieder in the course of an international program of French, Italian, English, German, and Spanish songs. Though she did not speak a word of German she gave a perfect rendition of my compositions. She drew an enthusiastic response from a public which represented eight hundred of the music lovers of Spain's capital. It was a very happy day in my life and also in Valdivia's.

While still in Madrid we received news from home that my father had suffered a heart attack but that the doctors were not particularly worried about it. The day we returned to Bremen early in July, I rang him up at his home in Hechingen, Württemberg. He told me he was still rather tired but feeling much better. We naturally did not want to bother him with too many questions, but Mama told us that the heart attack had been rather frightening.

At six o'clock on the morning of July 20 our telephone rang. A rather unusual hour for a phone call, I thought to myself as I ran down the stairs to answer it.

"This is Hardenberg speaking," a gloomy voice said. Count Carl Hans Hardenberg was my father's plenipotentiary. "It is my very sad duty to inform you that the *Kronprinz* died of a heart attack this night at 3:00 A.M." In a daze I left for Hechingen that rainy morning.

I believe my father died of a broken heart. Besides losing the throne he had been born to occupy, he had seen his country collapse twice during his lifetime. He had lost two sons and his home town, Potsdam, and was stranded at Hechingen in a shabby little house with a few pieces of furniture saved from the general chaos. From there he could look up to the Hohenzollern Castle near Sigmaringen from where his ancestors set out seven hundred years ago.

Deep sadness and resignation began to cast a shadow on my father's life long before the war came to a disastrous end for Germany. The wedding of my sister Cecilie with Clyde Kenneth Harris of Texas at our ancestral castle was his last truly happy day. Hardly a year later, in May 1950, he had placed the urn with the ashes of my brother Hubertus, who had died in faraway Windhoek, South Africa, on the same altar before which Cecilie and Clyde had been married.

Now, another year later, his coffin covered with the imperial standard reposed in state at the foot of the altar in Burg Hohenzollern. When my father's remains were laid to rest at the spot which he had selected in the little garden overlooking the wide plain of Württemberg from the Alps to the Black Forest, innumerable mourners paid their last respects.

On that July 20, 1951, through the vicissitudes of life, my turn came to take up the thread where my father left it. May God help me to hand it over to my children in a day brighter with sunshine and happiness for our Old World.

THE END

INDEX OF NAMES